THE KO.....

This book tells the full story of the first, and critical, test by the Communist bloc of Western military resolve. Instead of concentrating wholly on the American involvement which was of course dominant, Michael Hickey also sets in context the contributions – many of them quite out of proportion to the size of their contingents – of the other nations that answered the UN call and sent troops in response to the North Koreans' surprise attack. Altogether some 100,000 British troops served, together with proportionate numbers from Australia, Canada, India, New Zealand, South Africa, Turkey and elsewhere. Despite problems of culture and logistics, these troops' participation was often crucially important. The Republic of Korea's own army also became steadily more formidable under tough American training.

Set in the midst of international power politics and fears of a general conflagration, the Korean War at its height involved rapid, large-scale troop movements over long distances as each side experienced both outstanding success and disaster. It included masterstrokes like MacArthur's landing behind the enemy lines at Inchon, drama such as the 'glorious Glosters' episode, and both collaboration and mutiny in the prisoner-of-war camps of either side.

Michael Hickey draws on a number of hitherto unused sources from several countries, including recently declassified documents, regimental archives, diaries and interviews. His book adds extensively to our knowledge of one of the most significant conflicts of modern times.

Colonel Michael Hickey FRUSI MRAes himself took part in the Korean War. He is a graduate of the Staff College, Camberley, the Joint Services Staff College and the Royal Military College of Science, was a Defence Fellow of King's College, London, and was later Director of the Museum of Army Flying. He is the author of the critically acclaimed *The Unforgettable Army*, on Slim and his 14th Army in Burma, and of *Gallipoli*.

THE KOREAN WAR

The West Confronts Communism

1950–1953

MICHAEL HICKEY

JOHN MURRAY
Albemarle Street, London

© Michael Hickey 1999

First published in 1999
by John Murray (Publishers) Ltd,
50 Albemarle Street, London W1X 4BD

Paperback edition 2000

A catalogue record for this book is available from the British Library

ISBN 0–7195–6150 7

Typeset in Ehrhardt by
Servis Filmsetting Ltd, Manchester
Printed and bound in Great Britain by
The University Press, Cambridge

Contents

Illustrations

The author and publishers wish to thank the following for permission to reproduce illustrations: Plates 1, 2, 3, 4, 6, 7, 19 and 56, © Hulton Getty; 5, US Air Force; 8, 9, 27, 40, 43 and 46, US Army Military History Institute; 10 and 38, the late Revd Lorentz Pedersen; 11, 13, 18, 24 and 26, Australian War Memorial (Accession Nos. PO1813.576, PO1813.659, PO1813.865, PO1813.745, PO2201.125); 12, 45, 52 and 54, Museum of Army Flying, Middle Wallop; 14, 20, 21, 29, 30, 32, 34, 41, 42, 48, 50, 53 and 55, Imperial War Museum; 15, 22, 23, 25, 35 and 39, Lieutenant-Colonel Alf Argent; 16 and 17, Mr A.E. Hales; 28, US Army; 36, Lieutenant-Colonel Barney Henderson; 47, Colonel M. Farmer; 51, US Signal Corps. Plates 31, 33, 37, 44 (crown copyright) and 49 are from the author's collection.

Preface

Commanding an RASC transport platoon as a newly commissioned Second Lieutenant I was an insignificant packhorse in the Korean War. Like my contemporaries I was ignorant of the higher strategy and politics that had brought us there. Our main preoccupation was survival through that first terrible winter of the war; great events such as the sacking of General MacArthur, our commander-in-chief, passed almost unnoticed, whilst few of us spared a charitable thought for that God-forsaken country and its unfortunate people. For young men who had never left the shores of the United Kingdom, Korea in 1950 came as a dreadful shock: a nation assaulted and raped, deprived of its very identity by forty years of Japanese occupation, now shattered by invasion from the north. Filthy, malodorous, its population reduced to beggary and totally demoralized, it presented an unlovely picture.

All those of us sent from Britain to Korea in 1950 were painfully aware of the parlous state of the British economy, and particularly of the armed forces; looking back over half a century it is astonishing that, from an army of several hundred thousand officers and men, it proved so difficult to assemble and equip a brigade to go to the other side of the world without resort to a call-up of reservists. Much of the force's equipment was of 1939–45 vintage, a lot of it much older. During that first winter we had to live mostly in the open in appalling weather conditions with inadequate winter clothing and tentage. Despite this, the performance of British and Commonwealth troops, sailors and airmen was in the highest traditions of their services. The youngest national servicemen who served there so admirably are now old age pensioners and it is hard to realize that all this happened nearly fifty years ago – the same gap as separated us in 1950 from the Boer War. This account aims to show something of the British and Commonwealth contribution to that campaign, in relation to the far greater undertaking of the Americans and South Koreans. Its aim will have been achieved if the reader emerges at the end with a sense of what it was like to serve in MacArthur's curious Tokyo headquarters, shiver in a frozen slit trench, swelter in the baleful humidity of a Korean summer, endure captivity, fly combat missions in bombers and jet fighters against formidable opposition, fight the treacherous tides of Korean coastal waters under the fire of hostile batteries, or march over the northern mountains in the depth of winter with the Marines.

My intention had been to write an account of what turned out to be the last military adventure of the 'old' Commonwealth: Britain, Canada, Australia, New Zealand, South Africa and India. I soon became aware of the sheer size of the American involvement and the sacrifice it entailed. Our share was indeed small, though easily the largest from the rest of the United Nations. It was the first occasion on which the United States, which by 1943 had supplanted Britain as the leading western power, assumed its responsibilities as champion of the free world. It was also the first war to be fought in the shadow of the emergent nuclear threat. At the same time it was the baptism of fire for the young United Nations Organization and the pattern, however flawed, for its subsequent coalition wars and peacekeeping operations.

I have reverted throughout to the geographical names in use at the time of the war, when Mao Zedong, Jiang Jieshei, Guomindang, Beijing and Taiwan would have been unrecognized. A glossary, annotated bibliography and list of sources will be found at the end. As the nomenclature of British regiments can be confusing (especially now that most of those mentioned in this narrative, sadly, have ceased to exist) I have adopted the simple names by which they were commonly known at the time, hence 'Glosters', 'Borderers', 'Ulsters' etc.

I have received much help in the writing of this book and due acknowledgement follows hereafter; as an author I place on record the immeasurable debt I owe to all at 50 Albemarle Street whose patience and courtesy have never failed – in particular Grant McIntyre, Gail Pirkis, Howard Davies and Stephanie Allen, and to Roger Hudson whose professionalism as an editor turned my sow's ear into something nearer a silken purse. And as I would never have fallen into the hands of this venerable publishing house without her introduction I owe a considerable debt of thanks to my agent Mandy Little.

Finally, and because it was he who, over twenty years ago, prodded me into writing my first book, I dedicate this one with affection to the memory of Brigadier Shelford (Ginger) Bidwell; historian, critic, mentor and friend.

Acknowledgements

I sought and received the generous assistance of many in writing this book. They include the staffs of museums and libraries as well as veterans of the campaign – some of whom I have known since we served together in Korea nearly half a century ago, and who allowed me to interview them. I list them in approximate alphabetical order:

Lieutenant-Colonel (retd) Alf Argent, Melbourne; the staff of the Australian War Memorial, Canberra – particularly Douglas Alexander, Bill Fogarty, Peter Hawker, Ian Smith and Margaret Thompson; Lieutenant-Colonel (retd) John Avery; Colonel Jonathan Bailey, Staff College; Lieutenant-Colonel (retd) Paddy Baxter; Major-General (retd) V.H.J. Carpenter; Major (retd) Pip Chambers; John Crawford and Ian McGibbon, Historical Branch, New Zealand Defence Department; Major-General Peter Downward; Colonel (retd) Micky Farmer; General Sir Anthony Farrar-Hockley, British Official Historian; Colonel Vincent Fauvell-Champion (late French battalion in Korea); Diana Feilden (formerly Angier) for permission to quote at length from her late husband's letters; Richard Gorell and Major Bob Leitzel, US Forces Korea History Office, Seoul; Olwyn Green; A.E. Hales (late 41 RM Commando); Colonel (retd) Ross Harding, Canberra; Lieutenant-Colonel (retd) D.L.J. Harrap; Major Bob Heron and Lieutenant-Colonel Walter Robins, for their invaluable assistance at the Duke of Wellington's Regimental Museum, Halifax; Lieutenant-Colonel (retd) Barney Henderson; Major (retd) Donald Hobbs; Major Chris Hodgkinson, Director, Elizabeth Cotterell, Executive Officer, and Ewan Hyde, Chief Librarian, New Zealand Army Museum, Waiouru; Reuben Holroyd, Editor, *Morning Calm*; Mrs Carpenter of the Intelligence Corps Museum and Archive, Ashford, Kent; Professor Dr Claus Jessen, formerly of the hospital ship *Jutlandia*; Brigadier-General Jock Lello, Pretoria; Matthew Little, Archivist, Royal Marines Museum; Brigadier (retd) Mervyn McCord; Brigadier Peter McGuinness, late Defence Attaché, Australian High Commission, London; Ian Mackley, President, New Zealand

Korean Veterans' Association; Colonel (retd) Andrew Man; Major (retd) Ross Mason; Patricia Methven and Kate O'Brien of the Liddell Hart Centre for Military Archives, King's College, London; Professor Allan Millett, Ohio State University; John Montgomery, Librarian, Royal United Services Institute, London; Major Mike Murphy, Royal Ulster Rifles Muniments, Belfast; Michael Muschamp; the Museum of Army Flying, Middle Wallop; the staff of the Department of Printed Books and Documents, National Army Museum, London; Professor Robert O'Neill, Australian Official Historian; Major C.G. Owen and Major Tim Timmons, HQ Queen's Royal Hussars (8th Hussars Archive), London; the late Colonel George Papangelakis, Athens; Brigadier Colin Parr, HM Embassy, Seoul; the late Revd Lorentz Pedersen; Michael Pollock, Librarian, Royal Asiatic Society, London; the librarians and staff of the Prince Consort Library, Aldershot; Major (retd) Claud Rebbeck, Lieutenant-Colonel Henry Radice, Major Sam Weller and Colonel Denys Whatmore, all veterans of the Glosters who kindly answered so many of my questions at their regimental museum; the late Lord Shinwell; the Revd Dom Alberic Stacpoole OSB; Nigel Steel, Documents Department, Imperial War Museum; Major Sadik Tekele and Serket Teskin of the Turkish Military Museum, Istanbul; Kate Thaxton, Royal Norfolk Regimental Museum, Norwich; Major (retd) John Yeoward. In Seoul: Chae Han-kook, Director, War History Department, Defence Institute for Military History; Hwang Chang-peong, Minister (1996) of Patriots' and Veterans' Affairs; Major-General (retd) Kim Dong-ho; Vice-Admiral Ko Chung-tok; Major (retd) Lee Sang-bok, Public Affairs Officer, War Memorial Service; Major (retd) Lee Yong-sup; General (retd) Paik Sun-yup; Suh Yong-sun, Senior Researcher, Defence Institute for Military History.

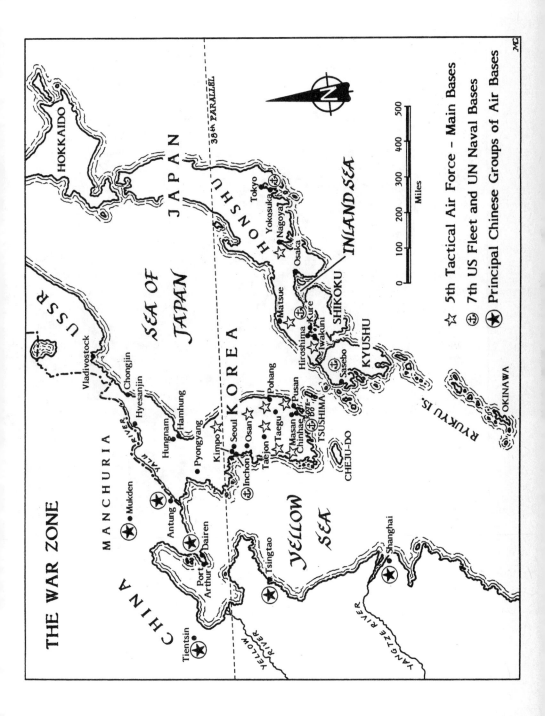

THE WAR ZONE

USSR

HOKKAIDO

CHINA

MANCHURIA

Mukden

Tientsin

Antung

Port Arthur

Dairen

Tsingtao

Vladivostock

Chongjin

Hyesanjin

Hamhung

Hungnam

Pyongyang

Inchon

Kimpo

Seoul

Osan

Taejon

Masan

Chinhae

Pohang

Taegu

Pusan

TSUSHIMA

CHEJU-DO

KOREA

SEA OF JAPAN

YELLOW SEA

YELLOW RIVER

Shanghai

YANGTZE RIVER

JAPAN

HONSHU

Matsue

Tokyo

Yokosuka

Nagoya

Osaka

Kure

Hiroshima

Iwakuni

Sasebo

SHIKOKU

INLAND SEA

KYUSHU

RYUKYU IS.

OKINAWA

38th PARALLEL

N

0   100   200   300   400   500

Miles

☆ 5th Tactical Air Force - Main Bases

⊕ 7th US Fleet and UN Naval Bases

✪ Principal Chinese Groups of Air Bases

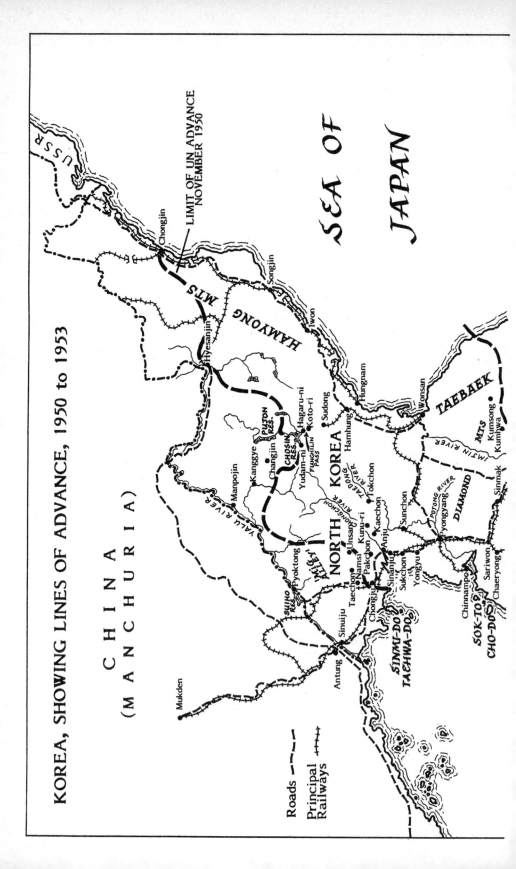

KOREA, SHOWING LINES OF ADVANCE, 1950 to 1953

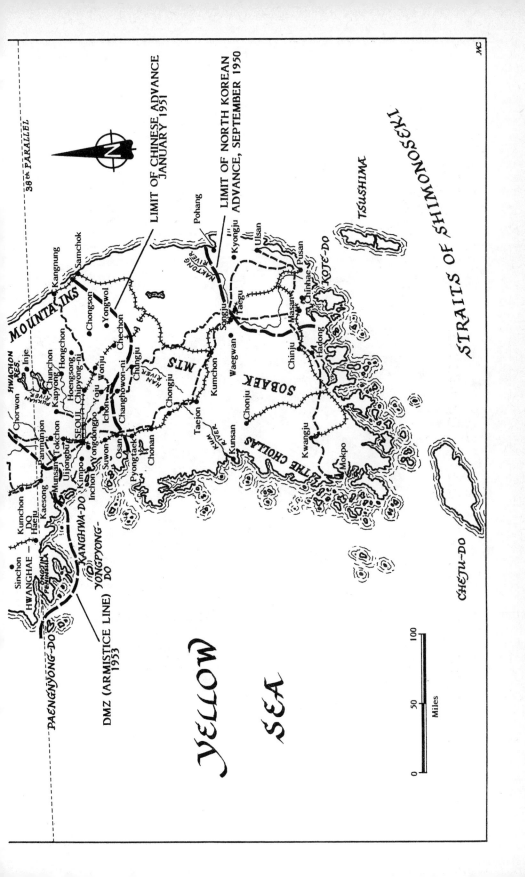

38th PARALLEL

LIMIT OF CHINESE ADVANCE
JANUARY 1951

LIMIT OF NORTH KOREAN
ADVANCE, SEPTEMBER 1950

N

STRAITS OF SHIMONOSEKI

TSUSHIMA

KOJE-DO

Pohang
Kyongju
Ulsan
Pusan
Chinhae
Masan
Chinju
Hadong
Taegu
Waegwan
Kumchon
Chonju
Kunsan
Kwangju
Mokpo
CHEJU-DO

THE CHOLLAS

SOBAEK MTS

KUM RIVER

Taejon
Chonan
Osan
Pyongtaek
Suwon
Inchon
Kimpo
Yongdongpo
SEOUL
Uijongbu
Munsan (Tokchon)
Panmunjon
Kaesong
Kumchon
Haeju
Sinchon
HWANGHAE

ONGIN
PENINSULA

PAENGNYONG-DO

KANGHWA-DO
YONGPYONG-DO

DMZ (ARMISTICE LINE)
1953

Ichon
Yoju
Changhowon-ni
Chipyong-ni
Wonju
Chungju
HAN RIVER
Chongju

Chongson
Yongwol
Chechon

Kangnung
Samchok

MOUNTAINS

Chunchon
Hongchon
Hoengsong
Kapyong
Chorwon
PUKHAN
IMJIN
Inje
HWACHON
RES.

NAKTONG RIVER

YELLOW

SEA

0   50   100
Miles

MC

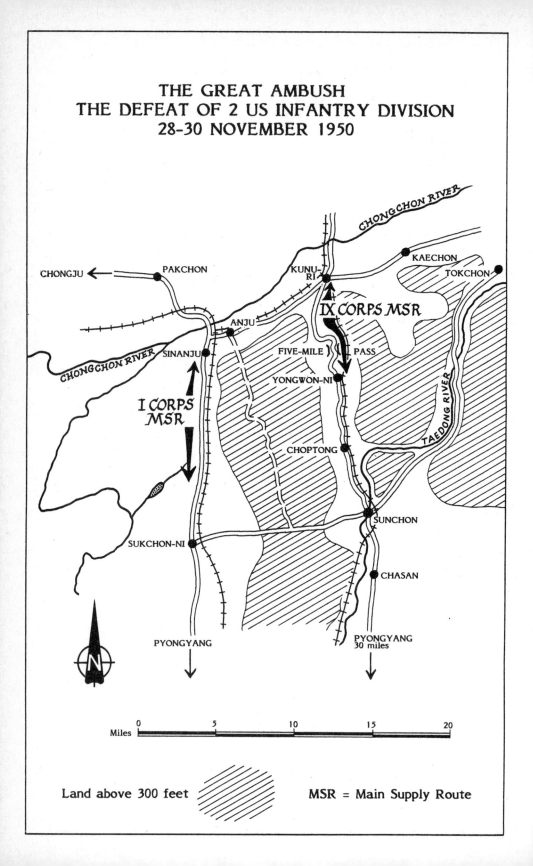

THE GREAT AMBUSH
THE DEFEAT OF 2 US INFANTRY DIVISION
28-30 NOVEMBER 1950

CHONGCHON RIVER

CHONGJU ←

PAKCHON

KUNU-RI

KAECHON

TOKCHON

IX CORPS MSR

ANJU

CHONGCHON RIVER

SINANJU

FIVE-MILE (PASS

YONGWON-NI

TAEDONG RIVER

I CORPS
MSR

CHOPTONG

SUNCHON

SUKCHON-NI

CHASAN

N

PYONGYANG

PYONGYANG
30 miles

0   5   10   15   20
Miles

Land above 300 feet

MSR = Main Supply Route

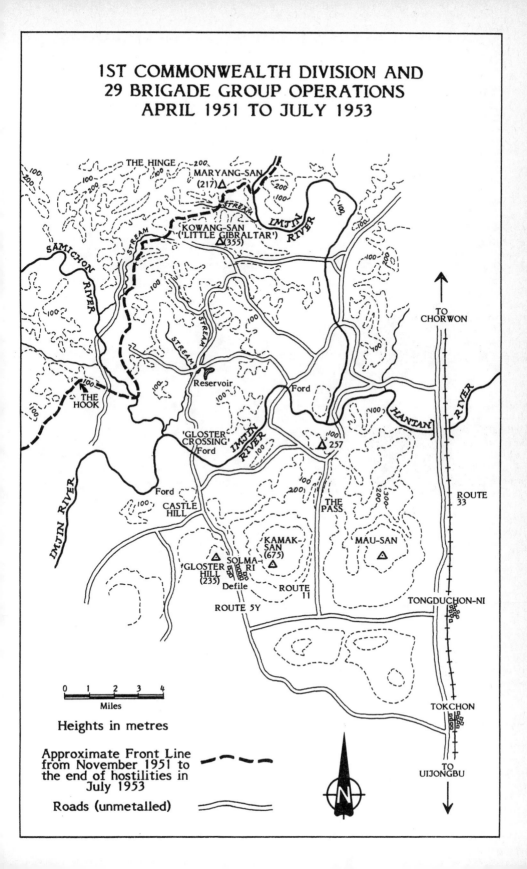

1ST COMMONWEALTH DIVISION AND 29 BRIGADE GROUP OPERATIONS APRIL 1951 TO JULY 1953

THE HINGE

MARYANG-SAN (217)

KOWANG-SAN ('LITTLE GIBRALTAR') (355)

IMJIN RIVER

SAMICHON RIVER

TO CHORWON

THE HOOK

Reservoir

Ford

HANTAN RIVER

'GLOSTER CROSSING' Ford

IMJIN RIVER

257

Ford

CASTLE HILL

THE PASS

ROUTE 33

KAMAK-SAN (675)

MAU-SAN

GLOSTER HILL (235)

SOLMA-RI

Defile

ROUTE 11

TONGDUCHON-NI

ROUTE 5Y

IMJIN RIVER

TOKCHON

0 1 2 3 4
Miles

Heights in metres

Approximate Front Line
from November 1951 to
the end of hostilities in
July 1953

Roads (unmetalled)

TO UIJONGBU

N

Prelude: November 1950

Shortly after daybreak the troopship passed between the high rocks marking the entrance to Pusan harbour and steamed slowly across the wide bay within, steering for a range of low sheds and cranes. As it drew near to the shore the passengers gazed silently at the land to which they had come.

The voyage from England, punctuated with brief stops at Port Said, Aden, Colombo and Singapore, had taken over a month. After the heat of the tropic seas the razor-like wind from the depths of Manchuria played on the hundreds of men lining the ship's rails, searing the lungs with every breath. Behind the grubby docks could be seen a large city, huddling at the foot of bleak hills; from its ramshackle buildings rose the smoke of thousands of wood fires as the inhabitants cooked their breakfasts. Borne by the wind came, stronger by the minute, a dreadful stench of decay, excrement, polluting smoke, and the noises of a dockland waterfront. Nameless debris floated past on the oily water as the ship steered past a group of anchored cargo ships waiting to unload. A goods train shunted fitfully behind the docks, its whistle sounding mournfully in the freezing air. Some sort of welcoming committee was being ranged on the dock-side: a line of bemused small children waving flags.

Then came a new sound, wild yet rhythmic, and a high-stepping black drum-major capered into sight around the corner of a warehouse, followed at a near trot by a strutting white-helmeted all-black military band on whose bass drum was the legend *56th US Army Port Band*. It was playing a Sousa march, but in a way unheard-of on any British army parade ground. The musicians writhed and side-stepped, the drum-major performed impossible feats with his mace. The soldiers, hitherto silenced by the sheer awfulness of the place of disembarkation, cheered up visibly and, as the bandsmen launched into a spectacular rendering of the 'St Louis Blues March', there was a great cheer from the ship.

PART ONE
Into the Fray

CHAPTER I

The Doomed Peninsula

The people of Korea have long dwelt between rival cultures, pulled this way and that between China, historically the 'Elder Brother', Japan, and increasingly in the nineteenth century, Imperial Russia. A Japanese invasion force was routed at sea in the sixteenth century by the great Korean admiral Yi, who used a revolutionary turtle-backed galley to sink the enemy's warships. As a result, Korea, under the enduring Yi dynasty, remained a Chinese tributary state, whilst retaining its own unique cultural identity, until further Japanese interference in 1895. Five centuries of the Yi dynasty's rule were finally ended as the result of Japan's decisive defeat of the Russians in the war of 1904–5.

From 1910 to 1945, when the country was no more than a Japanese colonial territory, Korea's national culture and language were all but erased. After 1910 all higher education, law, commerce and administration were conducted in Japanese. Old Korean place names were transliterated into Japanese and the national identity of an ancient people was deliberately suppressed.

As the Japanese tightened their grip on Korea they discovered that there were two strands of resistance to their rule. Christian evangelicals, converted by western missionaries in the latter part of the nineteenth century, counselled a policy of non-violence. Many of their leaders had attracted the attentions of the Japanese secret police, and they feared for the lives and safety of their supporters. On the other hand, the communist resistance, steadily gaining strength in the years between the two world wars, fomented industrial and terrorist action in order to discomfit the Japanese overlords. Both these resistance movements might have been working towards a self-governing Korea but their methods and ultimate objectives were far apart. The Christians, probably with tacit Japanese approval based on the principle of 'divide and rule', identified with the administrative, landowning and commercial élites. This marked them indelibly as collaborators with the hated Japanese and thus as targets for the communists.

During the Second World War Korea was used by Japan as a ricebowl and as provider of many essential minerals for the imperial war effort. Its economy, though stretched to the limit, prospered, and with it many individuals in the mercantile, landowning and industrial sectors. Thousands of Koreans were, however, forcibly recruited into Japan's armed forces or used as industrial slave labour. Many worked on the Pacific islands where the Japanese required airfields and fortifications. The 40,000 or so Koreans drafted into the imperial army seldom served in its front-line combat units, but were to be found as often brutal guards in the notorious Japanese prisoner-of-war camps in which thousands of British and Empire troops laboured and died. Thousands of Korean women were forcibly conscripted to be 'comfort girls' in Japanese military brothels. Many Koreans, in order to evade military service under the Japanese, fled to China where they enlisted with either Chiang Kai-shek's Kuomintang or Mao Tse-tung's 8th Route Army. Other Korean exiles migrated to the Soviet Union and served with Stalin's armies. Here, like their comrades in Mao's forces, they were thoroughly indoctrinated politically as they picked up a sound, if arduous, military education.

Although many of the Koreans exiled in the United States offered their good offices to help in the war against Japan, the American government rebuffed them. One of the leading lights was a certain Yi Sung-man. After several brushes with the Korean authorities at the start of the century, including spells of imprisonment and torture, he had gone into exile in the United States where he westernized his name to that of Syngman Rhee. Returning to Korea in 1910 he had been forced to flee back to America in 1919 after a failed rising against the Japanese. There he pursued a successful academic career, headed a self-styled Korean government-in-exile, married a formidably gifted Austrian lady, and bided his time until circumstances might permit his return to the country for which he had a fiercely patriotic love.

In a Washington preoccupied with the defeat of the Japanese in the Pacific and the formidable problems of invading their home islands, there were few with time to spare for Syngman Rhee and his band of supporters. American efforts, as far as mainland Asia was concerned, were concentrated on supporting the campaign of Chiang Kai-shek's nationalist Kuomintang forces, with their headquarters in Chungking, in their fight against the Japanese who had invaded China in 1937. As for the British, their policy since the turn of the century had been to accept Japanese hegemony over Korea, which in any. case lay far beyond the British sphere of interest.

The first inklings of Korea's destiny in the second half of the century surfaced at the Cairo summit conference of 1943 when the Allies started to ponder the shape of the post-war world, and began seriously to allot the possible spoils of a still uncertain victory. Even now, British interest in Korea remained marginal, although Anthony Eden, as Foreign Secretary in 1943, drew the attention of the US State Department, and of President Roosevelt, to the problem of dealing with the outlying fragments of the Japanese empire, including Korea and Indo-China, once the war was over. He vaguely suggested an international trusteeship for these territories but made no mention of the United Kingdom being one of the trustees, proposing instead that these should be the Soviet Union, the United States and China (where it was assumed that Chiang Kai-shek's Kuomintang would remain in power indefinitely). The Koreans in exile were unimpressed by the Cairo communiqué, as it seemed that the Allies were about to dispose of their country without consultation.

The Korean patriots were even less pleased with the outcome of the Teheran conference later in the same year when Stalin was formally invited by his American and British allies to join in the war against Japan three months after the defeat of Germany; in accepting, he demanded certain political compensations: Roosevelt hinted that Russia might be granted a Pacific warm-water port and also mentioned in passing to Stalin that Korea would need up to forty years' 'apprenticeship' before achieving full independence. At this time Roosevelt placed total trust in Stalin and entertained grand designs for post-war co-operation with the Soviet Union. He felt that since the Soviets had the military strength to obtain any of their territorial designs, whether overt or secret, there was no point in seeking confrontation when the immediate American aim was to wind down their war machine as quickly as possible and 'get the boys home' once Japan had been defeated.

By the beginning of 1944, with a clearer prospect of victory, Stalin's demands were more specific. He demanded the Kurile Island chain, the lower Sakhalin peninsula, long leases on the warm-water ports of Port Arthur and Dairen, control of the trunk railway systems in eastern China and south Manchuria, and international recognition of the independence from China of Outer Mongolia. There was as yet no mention of any intention by the Soviet Union to occupy any part of Korea. Stalin was in a strong moral position for hard bargaining with his allies; they had failed to invade northern Europe as promised in 1943. But by this time, the United States government was convinced of the need for a military occupation of Korea on the fall of Japan. Alarming signs of the surge of communism in China, combined with increasing disenchantment about Generalissimo Chiang Kai-shek's corrupt nationalist regime, were beginning to affect American Far Eastern policies. The insertion of an occupying force and the establishment of military government in Korea after the defeat of Japan appeared a suitable way of establishing a toe-hold on the Asiatic land mass even though little attention had hitherto been paid in Washington to the strategic significance of the Korean peninsula.

At the Yalta conference in February 1945, Stalin, sensing the drift of American policy towards Korea, proposed the setting up of a joint trusteeship for Korea by the United States, the USSR, China and the United Kingdom. Roosevelt was now paying little attention to the proceedings; he was tired and sick, but continued to delude himself that he had a special understanding with Stalin, putting it to him in private that any arrangement for Korea should exclude the United Kingdom. Instead, he proposed a Soviet–Chinese–American trusteeship which would prepare Korea for full self-government in anything up to twenty or thirty years. Stalin, on the other hand, favoured the inclusion of the United Kingdom, and a far shorter trusteeship. Nothing was committed to writing, and Churchill was certainly never informed of these discussions. The Foreign Office in London, not wishing to become embroiled in the politics of a remote country in which British interests were minimal, made no attempt to plumb these secrets. Nor was anyone in the State Department aware of what had transpired between the two men. Not even Vice-President Harry Truman, who succeeded to the presidency on Roosevelt's death in April 1945, was informed of the scheme. It was not an auspicious basis on which to lay the foundations of Korea's future.

In an effort to find out what Roosevelt had promised Stalin at Yalta Truman decided to despatch the experienced Harry Hopkins to Moscow to probe and confirm the private Yalta arrangements, and in particular to sound out the Russians on the trusteeship plan for Korea. Hopkins questioned Stalin on the date of Russia's proposed entry into the war against Japan and obtained the promise that it would be on 8 August. Stalin also told Hopkins that he endorsed the idea of a four-power trusteeship for Korea.

In July 1945 the Allied leaders met at Potsdam amid the ruins of Nazi Germany to discuss the way forward against Japan. Only Stalin remained of the old triumvirate. A Labour government had come to power in Britain, now represented by Prime Minister Clement Attlee. If Truman approached his first summit with trepidation he showed little sign of it. The Americans had successfully detonated a nuclear device and were well advanced with manufacture of the first atomic bombs, for use against Japan. Stalin showed curiously little interest when Truman, in strictest confidence, told him of this. He had almost certainly been briefed already by his own intelligence chiefs, informed by a highly placed Soviet agent in Washington, Alger Hiss.

With Stalin now aware of the atomic bomb, any idea of using it to destroy Japan's will to fight before the Russians could join in the war against them was stillborn. There was a real fear in the Pentagon and White House that an Allied invasion of the Japanese home islands would prove a bloodbath unless the bomb was dropped; and if such an invasion involved the use of Soviet troops, they would have to be accorded an occupation zone, as had been the case in Germany and Austria. Since this would effectively neutralize plans for the American occupation prior to the completion of a Japanese peace treaty favourable to Washington, it was not an acceptable option. Truman also knew that there were still intact Japanese combat formations in Manchuria and northern Korea and intended that the job of defeating and disarming these should fall to the Russians.

Truman therefore supported the idea of a Korean trusteeship. He had a brief before him, prepared by the State Department, for a three-stage plan: military occupation by the Allies, international administration under UN auspices, and finally full sovereignty. This was not put to the Potsdam meeting, however, for the Allies were already at odds over other issues such as plans for the dismemberment of the former Italian colonies in Africa. Later in the conference there was talk by the Russians of unspecified military operations across the Manchurian border and into northern Korea, in concert with American amphibious landings in the south of the peninsula; all this came to nothing. One thing, however, was becoming all too clear to the Americans: there was a distinct chance of a race against the Russians for possession of all Korea once Japan had been defeated. They began hurriedly, if belatedly, to plan the occupation of the southern half of the country.

On 6 August 1945, only four days after the end of the Potsdam conference, the first of two atomic bombs fell on Japan, at Hiroshima. A second followed days later at Nagasaki. Early on 9 August the Red Army struck at the Japanese army in Manchuria. Japan, with her fleet gone, cities wasted by American strategic bombers, her armies defeated in the field, scattered and out of supplies, was in no condition to fight on and surrendered at the Emperor's behest on 14 August; it is questionable whether the bombs actually accelerated the end, as secret overtures for a negotiated peace had been going on between Moscow and Tokyo for some time. All the old dreams of Far Eastern power which had eluded first the tsars, then the commissars of the early revolutionary period, Stalin now saw within his grasp.

In Washington, an emergency strategy had to be evolved rapidly by the State Department, where there was still a very strong 'China lobby' which believed that the USA had an important role to play in a post-war China ruled by Chiang Kai-shek. Here were huge untapped markets for America's industrial strength, galvanized by its stupendous war efforts since Pearl Harbor. State Department officials had felt themselves snubbed by Roosevelt in his last months, and they were now obsessed with the need to checkmate Soviet plans for outward expansion – above all, to avoid Soviet predominance in Korean affairs through the establishment of a pro–Moscow government in Seoul.

However, on 10 August the Russian 25th Army under Colonel-General Ivan Chistyakov entered Korea and quickly occupied the northern provinces down as far as Pyongyang. The Americans had been spectacularly wrong-footed; they had no significant body of troops closer than Okinawa, where a bloody campaign to exterminate the Japanese garrison had only just ended. It was now essential to agree the limits of the respective occupation zones as a prerequisite for the disarming of the large Japanese garrisons in Korea. Colonel Dean Rusk, a staff officer in the US Army's Strategy and Planning branch, later to make his mark as Kennedy's Secretary of State at the time of the Cuban missile crisis of 1962 – already present in Korea as part of a US military mission – came to an agreement with officers of the Red Army that the demarcation line should be the 38th parallel of latitude, which runs east–west across the Korean peninsula from the coast north of the Han river estuary. In the afterglow of victory it was not anticipated that there would ever be any need to control movement between the two zones, so it seemed irrelevant that the line was totally indefensible from a military point of view. A strong China, as one of the allies victorious over Japan, might have exercised its influence over the arbitrary partitioning of Korea; but China now lay ravaged by its eight-year struggle with Japan, by the civil wars that had preceded it, and by ominous signs that the uneasy wartime alliance between Chiang Kai-shek and Mao Tse-tung was coming apart.

As outriders of the US occupying forces the American XXIV Corps arrived by sea at Inchon, the port serving Korea's capital at Seoul, from Okinawa on 8 September 1945. Its commander, Lieutenant-General John R. Hodge, was immediately appointed commanding general, US Forces Korea by General Douglas MacArthur, Allied Commander-in-Chief in the Pacific theatre, now installed in Tokyo. Hodge, a competent fighting soldier who had worked his way up from the ranks, was a hard worker, tough and decisive but deficient in the political, intellectual and diplomatic skills needed for the thankless task ahead. He made his way directly to Seoul where he accepted the surrender of the Japanese garrison and established his military government as though taking over a defeated hostile territory.

From the outset, Hodge was adrift, openly branding the Koreans as 'the same breed of cats as the Japs'. He failed to sense or respect the extreme feelings of the people for their newly liberated country and their loathing for the Japanese. Matters got worse when Hodge proscribed as illegal the 'Korean People's Republic', formed more or less spontaneously on the Japanese surrender and before the arrival of the Americans. The KPR was a nationalist coalition of widely differing political factions which at least shared a common will to unite the country and included many of the former exiles who had returned to Korea from Russia, China, America and several countries of Europe. The KPR nursed hopes that it would be recognized by the new occupying power, and had already set up its own regional governments. Paradoxically, those in North Korea were dominated by the centrist parties, whilst those in the south came mainly from the extreme left. Within a month, all were declared illegal by Hodge (whose political leanings were far to the right). Immediately, strong opposition came from the communist party in the south. And when Washington sacked the Japanese governor-general without consulting Hodge, Hodge promptly lost face in the eyes of the Korean people. If one thing united the peoples of Korea at this time, it was frustration at the way in which the dream of unification had been snatched from their hands by their supposed liberators at the moment of Japan's defeat.

Within days of the Japanese surrender the American Chiefs of Staff asked their British counterparts for their views on Korea and received a very luke-warm response, drafted undoubtedly by the Far Eastern section of the Foreign Office which had little or no interest in Korean affairs. Indeed, one official saw fit to scrawl on the flyleaf of a file that 'Korea is not worth the bones of a single British grenadier'. There were no British commercial interests there and the presence of a Commonwealth occupation force – for which Whitehall felt the Americans were trawling – would serve no useful purpose. The British pres-ence in Korea, limited to a handful of commercial firms and the Anglican bish-opric, was served by a small consulate-general in Seoul. Even the provision of a token occupation force was distasteful to the Foreign Office.

It slowly dawned on Washington officials that the British were genuinely unaware of what had transpired between Roosevelt and Stalin, and they were obliged to spell it out as well as they could to Lord Halifax, the British ambas-sador in Washington, who broke the news to London that a four-power trus-teeship was intended. The British Cabinet now had to consider what to do. In the circumstances, with HM Forces already everywhere overstretched, it seemed a good idea to let the Australians represent the UK and the Commonwealth in the Korean arena. Plans were already in hand for Australian and New Zealand troops to assume occupation duties in Japan, together with a British–Indian division, and in view of increasing Australian interest in the Far East it seemed logical to extend their occupation duties to Korea.

In contrast to Hodge's XXIV Corps, the Russian 25th Army in the north had brought its own highly trained political staff, overseen by that of the next formation up, the 1st Far Eastern Front of the Red Army. The Russians also possessed a high-powered public relations and propaganda machine. They claimed to have entered North Korea to disarm the Japanese garrison and facilitate a 'democratic revolution', presenting the Russian army as liberators, not enforcers of an alien political system. After some initial looting and isolated atrocities, the Soviet troops were brought under control and held up as exem-plars of socialist behaviour and correctness. Apart from known Japanese col-laborationists, who rapidly 'disappeared', the Russians went out of their way to encourage political activity of all shades. This quickly identified likely dissi-dents; by mid-October, Chistyakov had made it clear that only those who toed his prescribed political line could hope to have a hand in government.

The Russians brought others in their wake; during the Japanese occupation many potential communists had been helped to escape to the Soviet Union for a thorough political education; those who displayed martial ability were received into Red Army training establishments and served with distinction in the armies of the USSR during the Great Patriotic War. The most promising of these were hand-picked by the Russians as their surrogates for the occupation of Korea north of the 38th parallel.

Among these was one Kim Sung-ju. Born in 1912 when Korea was already under Japanese rule, his family were ardent patriots and his father was imprisoned in 1919 for anti-Japanese activity. By 1930 the young Kim had joined the Chinese communist party in Manchuria, where he was trained as an anti-Japanese partisan for operations on the Korea–Manchuria border, after the Japanese seized power in Manchuria in 1931. He adopted, as a *nom de guerre*, that of Kim Il-sung, a legendary Korean hero in the Robin Hood mould, said to be a champion of the common people against the hated landlord class. Kim was sent to Moscow in 1941 for military and political training, returning to his fatherland in August 1945 as an officer in the Red Army. The Russians had carefully groomed him and he was appointed in February 1946 to chair the Interim People's Committee nominated by the occupying power as their instrument of civil government and administration.

Major-General Archibald Arnold, commanding the 7th US Division, was appointed by Hodge to be the executive officer of the American military government. Like Hodge, he lacked the experience that might have helped to avert some of the cardinal errors perpetrated, albeit in good faith, by the Americans in the following months. For two generations the Koreans had been denied advancement in a civil service run by several thousand imported Japanese officials, who conducted all business in Japanese. Koreans were permitted to serve in only the lowliest of posts. In order to retain at least a degree of order amidst the prevailing anarchy, Arnold decided to keep the Japanese civil and police officials in post whilst the Japanese Imperial Army in Korea was disarmed and until such time as the Koreans achieved a measure of political maturity.

There was an instant protest, but when qualified Koreans were appointed to middle-rank posts in the police and civil administration it was quickly found that they were tainted by association with the hated Japanese, and they had to be removed. By the time Hodge realized the degree of passion aroused by the retention of Japanese officials and had asked for the urgent posting in of experienced administrators from the USA, it was too late. The Japanese were replaced by hundreds of well-meaning American civil servants, few of whom managed to master even the basics of the Korean language; their presence did little to endear the American administration to the frustrated population. North of the 38th parallel the Russians, who had thoroughly trained a body of Korean administrators to run their zone as they wished, experienced none of the travails encountered by General Hodge in the south.

Arnold appointed the Provost Marshal of XXIV Corps, Brigadier-General Schick, to head the civil Police Bureau. As only a third of the national police force in 1945 were Korean nationals, an immediate manning crisis arose. Schick reopened the former Japanese Police Academy in Seoul in October 1945 for a series of crash courses for new recruits. In the following month the new Korean National Police Force, or KNP, was formed. From the start it faced an alarming internal security situation; political splinter groups were setting up paramilitary private armies, and there was a resurgence of banditry throughout the southern provinces, traditional home of bloody-minded opposition to whatever government was in power. A further force was clearly required and Schick recommended the setting up of a Korean national defence force of 45,000 men. There was no lack of manpower. At that time the population south of the 38th parallel was 15 million. Schick could afford to be highly selective; only recruits of the highest mental and physical quality were to be accepted and their equipment was to come from surplus American war stocks. Hodge approved this plan and referred it to General MacArthur in Tokyo, who in turn passed it to Washington for consideration.

Pending approval from on high, the energetic Schick set about the major problem besetting his command; few American personnel could speak Korean and very few of the Koreans could manage even the basic English required for their training. A language school was therefore established in Seoul, to instruct potential Korean officers.

Many paramilitary organizations – with the notable exception of two politically militant bodies, the Korean Volunteer Corps and the Manchurian communist guerrillas, who concentrated at Pyongyang – began to move on Seoul with the aim of enrolling in the national defence force. The officer cadre was formed round a body of English-speaking young officers who had been trained by the Japanese and were thus politically suspect to the older patriots. Many of the aspiring groups had to be disarmed and abolished at once. By now the bewildered American authorities were wallowing amidst the conflicting claims to legitimacy of a mass of leftist and rightist splinter groups, many with their own private armies, which were formally outlawed in January 1946.

On 1 May 1946, the language school closed down, to be replaced by the Korean Constabulary Training Centre. Graduates from this establishment were sent to serve in the military government as trainee administrators, filling the gap left by the departed Japanese. Washington was still shying at the idea of forming a full military organization, which it was feared might inhibit agreement with the USSR over the joint occupation of Korea. Further reason for delay was provided by the activities of Syngman Rhee, who had been permitted to return from exile in the hope that he would be able to impose a degree of order on the chaotic political scene in Seoul.

In the autumn of 1945 the only coherent political grouping had been the so-called People's Committees. As a counter to their evidently strong power base and popularity Hodge had invited the provisional government and Syngman Rhee (whom at first he greatly admired) back to Seoul in mid-October, where he presented the old man to the people at a huge rally in the national stadium. From the moment of his arrival Rhee began to rail against both the Americans and Russians, calling for immediate unification of Korea and the establishment of a national government; this was hardly in accordance with the vague principles agreed by the Allies at Teheran, Cairo, Yalta and Potsdam. As the American army worldwide began to run down, the 40th Division – part of Hodge's XXIV Corps in Korea – disbanded; many of its officers were seconded to the constabulary, which was recruiting beyond all expectation, and told to raise new units in the provinces. At the end of 1946, these officers formed the cadre of the Korean Military Advisory Group or KMAG, destined to play a key role in the evolution of the Republic of Korea's armed forces during the next four years.

Koreans on both sides of the 38th parallel realized that their hopes of unification were evaporating. At a meeting in Seoul in November 1945 at which all parties, including the communists, were represented, there had been calls for immediate reunification. Appeals were made to the Russians as well as to the Americans, whose officials on the ground were now inclined to reject the whole idea of a UN trusteeship. Hodge, desperate for a solution, proposed to the Russians that they agreed to the abolition of the 38th parallel as a frontier, obtained huge reparations from the Japanese for the reconstruction of Korea's infrastructure, and worked with the Americans towards early independence for a democratic Korea. The Russians spurned Hodge's proposals out of hand. In an attempt to free the log-jam the western allies pressed for a high-level meeting, which took place in Moscow on 16 December 1945. When the final communiqué was issued, it merely confirmed the old idea of an open-ended trusteeship for Korea. There was outrage in Seoul among all parties of the left and right. All had expected immediate national independence and the very idea of submitting to external political tutelage was nothing less than gross loss of face.

There was an unexpected development in January 1946, however, when the South Korean communist party, formerly vociferous in its condemnation of the Moscow agreement, changed tack and announced its satisfaction with the idea of trusteeship. It soon became apparent that they had done so on the Kremlin's command, in order to isolate the centre-right parties in South Korea when the Russians refused to deal with parties unsympathetic to trusteeship. The Soviets showed that they had no intention of proceeding other than on their own terms.

Despite the confabulations of a joint US/USSR commission, headed by Generals Hodge and Chistyakov, it was clear to the Americans by May 1946 that there was no alternative for them but to go ahead with their own programme for the establishment of a self-governing, sovereign Korea as soon as possible, even if only in the south of the peninsula. In the meantime, 435,000 Japanese civilians and nearly 180,000 military personnel had been repatriated; but as late as 1947, Japanese refugees were still pouring south across the 38th parallel. Another migration went on at the same time, as two million Koreans returned from abroad, many from Japan, others from north to south and vice-versa. The task of feeding and administering these was undertaken with remarkable efficiency by the American military government.

In December 1946 South Korea's interim legislative assembly was inaugurated in Seoul as a form of training mechanism for further democratic advance. It comprised 90 members, of whom 45 were elected, the others nominated by Hodge. The re-education of the nation posed enormous problems. By 1945 the national literacy rate had fallen to between 25 and 45 per cent. There was a chronic lack of trained teachers, adequate school buildings and teaching materials. Undeterred, Hodge's staff set up a scheme based on the Korean language, restoring the Hanggul literation in place of Japanese characters, and began to reintroduce the teaching of ancient Korean history and culture. Any adults showing signs of ability were encouraged to run their own show and accept increasing responsibility for local and regional education and administration.

The factories of South Korea had been used for years to support the Japanese war effort. Few Koreans had the technical and management expertise required to convert them to peacetime use. North and South were actually interdependent; hydro-electric and heavy industrial centres were nearly all in North Korea, thus making the Americans in the south dependent on the Russians for much of their power. The agricultural and textiles industries were, however, in the south. The former prosperity of rice farmers nationwide had vanished, for the Japanese had withheld fertilizers, needed to augment the malodorous use of human and animal excrement. The railroad network, laid out by the Japanese to serve their economy, was on the verge of collapse. Out of 474 locomotives in South Korea, only 182 were serviceable at the beginning of 1946. A complete rebuilding of the system – track, signalling, rolling stock, workshops – was needed, as well as the provision of skilled fitters. There were still fewer than 100 miles of metalled road in the south.

Attempts to get any movement from the Russians remained futile. At last, Washington re-entered the lists with a note to Molotov on 8 April 1947, drawing attention to the lack of progress and complaining that as the Soviet commander had now forbidden free movement and economic exchange between the two Koreas it was impossible to advance politically. Molotov declined to co-operate, stating that whilst the Americans were still talking with 17 groups opposed to Moscow, they were excluding such 'truly democratic' groups as the All-Korea Labour Confederation and the All-Korea Peasant and Youth Unions. As these were front organizations of the communist party, it is hardly surprising that they were under close scrutiny by Hodge and his staff. The 38th parallel was no longer a notional line on the map. By mid-1947 it had become a *de facto* frontier between two mutually hostile states.

CHAPTER 2

Confrontation, Frustration

In 1951, following the retreat of the North Korean People's Army after MacArthur's triumph at Inchon, a special US State Department team made a study of the North Korean industrial, agricultural and social scene. After two months spent travelling all over North Korea, interviewing hundreds of Koreans in all walks of life, and ploughing through thousands of documents in the Pyongyang archives, the American team had to admit that the Russians had managed to build up a strong indigenous regime on the Soviet model in the guise of a 'People's Democracy', run as a hierarchy of 'people's committees' – social and sporting organizations through which the masses were mobilized in support of government policies – and over these, an immensely powerful and pervasive communist party – the North Korean Labour Party – under a leadership totally beholden and responsive to Moscow.

At first, use was made of respected non-communist political leaders with identifiable followings, who were discarded once they had served their purpose. Then Kim Il-sung was quietly insinuated into the power structure, where he rapidly disposed of any possible rivals. Carefully vetted men from Korean communities in the USSR were installed in key positions, retaining their hard-won Soviet citizenship whilst remaining unseen in the background. One such was Ho Kai, First Secretary of the North Korean Labour Party, the shadowy figure who actually ran the North Korean People's Republic from his executive bureau in Pyongyang. Having inserted their nominees, the Russians thereafter ran North Korea with relatively few personnel. When their military occupation ended in 1948, following the setting up of the so-called democratic government, they left a Soviet mission, a well-staffed embassy, a host of representatives for special agencies, technical advisers, technicians, and managers for the Russian/North Korean joint stock companies involved in mining, electric power and heavy industry. Every precaution was taken to ensure that the lines back to Moscow worked well, whilst preserving the outward image of an efficient People's Republic run by and for Koreans.

Exports of strategic commodities to the USSR were steadily stepped up, but the manufacture of badly needed consumer goods was minimal. Increasing numbers of North Koreans found themselves compelled to study Russian and sent off on courses in Russian schools and universities. Gradually, all non-Russian influences were marginalized, and cadres trained by the Chinese communists in Yenan before 1945 were edged from positions of power. Relations with communist China, where the People's Republic was formally declared on 1 October 1949, actually cooled prior to 1950 as the Russian influence took hold. Mao's regime, exhausted by the long civil war, was too weak to protest at this stage. The North Korean People's Army (NKPA) was raised on the Soviet pattern, around Russian-trained cadres. Political reliability was assured by the presence of Soviet advisers, careful selection of Russian-trained Korean commanders, and reliance on Soviet equipment and training doctrines. As it grew, the NKPA came to be regarded as a strong back-up force for the state police as well as the potential spearhead for invasion of the south.

The performance of the Pyongyang regime in the years leading to the invasion of the south was impressive. The stagnant political and social system prevailing under Japanese rule was swept away by early reforms such as redistribution of land to the peasantry after its confiscation from landowners who had cast their lot with the Japanese. This revolution got under way in 1946, and was hugely popular with the rural population, especially the small farmers who little suspected that it would eventually bring them into the bondage of the state as collectivization took over. Land reforms were also designed to destroy the old hierarchies of landowners, whilst the Christian community, private manufacturers and the non-communist intelligentsia, already weakened by years of Japanese occupation, were now branded as 'traitors'. Whilst in Rhee's South Korea vast sums of foreign aid meant for the reconstruction of industry and infrastructure went into the pockets of corrupt politicians, the strategic industries of the north revived without foreign finance – even that of the USSR, whose internal post-war condition was such that it actually relied to a great extent on its newly acquired satellites for economic support. Lesser members of society were forced into innumerable committees and given the illusion that power rested with them. Coercive measures to improve productivity were applied, including conscription into the labour force. An army of informants kept their fellow citizens under close observation and the secret police were everywhere. Taxes were levied with rigour. Gradually, in terms of personal comfort, citizens of the north began to fare less well than those in the south. But the North Korean People's Army, the NKPA, did not go short. By 1950 it had reached a strength of 150,000. It had a strong sense of patriotic mission and high morale; its officers were among the élite of society; there was a total absence of the corruption and nepotism so rife in the south, and its soldiers were well fed.

The North Korean government relied not so much on public approbation as mass acquiescence; there were doubtless many who quickly realized that they were the dupes of an enormous confidence trick, but the dangers of dissidence were too clear for there to be any organized resistance except in certain regions where ancient feudal ways were still cherished.

In the south, Hodge and his subordinates worked with the best of wills to ensure that a democratic government evolved, but their lack of feel for the mood of the people enabled extremist political groupings to run riot. On his return to Seoul, Syngman Rhee had gathered around him the parties of the right to form the Korean Democratic Party or KDP. Opposition from the left was fragmented, based on various labour organizations, trades unions and people's committees; all had been active opponents of the Japanese and many of their members had played heroic roles in the resistance movement, unlike most of the prominent KDP members, many of whom had fled the country or collaborated with the Japanese. The opposition groups were quick to claim recognition from Washington, as granted to the KDP. It was given only grudgingly, for they were all branded as sympathetic to communism, a morbid fear of which had begun to stalk America's corridors of power. Winston Churchill's celebrated Fulton speech of 1946, when he warned of the Iron Curtain descending over eastern Europe, was at least partly to blame for this, but groupings of the extreme right in the Republican Party were to the forefront of the paranoia which henceforth tinged all American policy decisions as far as Korea was concerned.

The Central Intelligence Agency uneasily noted the preferment being granted to leading members of Rhee's KDP by Hodge and his staff, and whilst accepting that he was filling key posts in the Korean administration with 'safe pairs of hands' they privately regarded Rhee and his intimates as 'essentially demagogues bent on autocratic rule'. Some of the KDP leaders put forward by Rhee could be denied key posts in view of their overt former associations with the Japanese. Left-wing groups in the south, such as the South Korean Workers' Party, were brutally kept down by the Korean National Police (KNP), who were firmly in the hands of the KDP and whose higher echelons included many officers who had served in the Japanese secret police. The auguries for setting up a truly democratic state ruled from Seoul were no more favourable than in the north.

Denied the chance to rule both Koreas, Syngman Rhee set about building an interim parliament, the South Korean legislative assembly. On his direction it carried on business as though there were no 38th parallel and as if the assembly was the rightful government of a united Korea, despite the lack of representation from the north. With rising frustration in all quarters over continued division of the country, the communist party in the south began to amass support despite all efforts by the KNP to proscribe it. Very soon, alarming reports from neutral observers, missionaries and expatriate welfare workers confirmed the emergence of a brutal police state. A number of militant right-wing youth groups were allowed to flourish, many of whose members were refugees from the north. They were energetically resisted by equally extreme left-wing groups which, if caught on the streets by the KNP, were savagely dealt with. Prisons began to fill with political prisoners and there were increasing numbers of *disparus*.

By 1948, following several left-wing risings, guerrilla war was rife in many of the southern provinces. In North Korea a similar situation was evident in parts of the country where resistance still flickered against the Pyongyang regime. In the summer there were ominous signs that the South Korean police and constabulary were not only corrupt and inefficient, but thoroughly unreliable. There was a rebellion on the island of Cheju off the south coast, where the KNP and constabulary were particularly inept. Rebel leaders clearly intended it to be the start of a nationwide revolt and it duly spread to the south-western provinces of Yosu and Sunchon when the 14th Constabulary Regiment mutinied after being warned for duty on Cheju. The southern insurrection continued into the autumn before it was savagely put down; surviving dissidents joined the guerrillas in the mountains. There were further mutinies in the constabulary, including two by the 6th Regiment at Taegu in November and December. The internal security situation steadily descended towards anarchy; in mid-1949 Rhee was facing rebellion in five of his eight southern provinces. Apart from internal troubles, the rickety government was afflicted by increasing numbers of border clashes along the 38th parallel. By May 1949 the NKPA was testing its strength in a series of incursions across the line, although this was not entirely a one-way traffic, for there were frequent cross-border raids by the South Korean constabulary.

Rhee's government outlawed the communist party of South Korea in November 1948 with a series of draconian national security laws endowing his security forces with rights of detention without trial and summary judicial power. A Counter-Intelligence corps was set up to work closely with the Military Police commanded by Kim Chang-yong, a former officer in the Japanese Kempei-tai, and Won Yong-dok, a militant right-winger and prominent advocate of the 'March North' policy to which Rhee himself was dangerously addicted. Whilst it was clear that the NKPA was equipping with Russian T-34/85 tanks, artillery and ground attack aircraft and that these were obviously not intended for defensive use, the Americans shrank from the thought of a South Korean invasion of the north, as preached continually by Rhee with all the fervour of a crusade, and they turned down his repeated demands for tanks, artillery and combat aircraft.

At the end of 1948 the UN resolved to set up a Permanent Commission on Korea, or UNCOK, which would work for reunification. A UN motion was

then passed confirming the Seoul government as the only legitimate government for the whole of Korea and calling for the early removal of American and
Russian occupation forces. The USSR and its eastern European satellites voted
against the motion. A counter-proposal by the USSR to the effect that North
Korea was the only legitimate government was resoundingly defeated, its only
supporters being the bloc of Slav states. The next step was formal diplomatic
recognition by the United States of the Republic of (South) Korea. On New
Year's Day 1949 Washington announced that it would give every assistance to
the Korean people in their efforts to gain unification. The last Soviet troops had
already left North Korea and the Americans were obliged to follow suit as soon
as possible.

The mutinies in the South Korean constabulary in the autumn of 1948 had
alarmed the Americans. On their advice Rhee's government formed a Ministry
of National Defence at the end of the year and the constabulary became the
cadres of the Republic of Korea Army (ROKA). The American officers who
had previously been in command of constabulary units became advisers, with
the creation of the Korean Military Advisory Group, or KMAG. In North
Korea the NKPA had already been in existence for nine months, formed, as was
the ROK army, from an armed constabulary, but much more heavily equipped.
By March 1949 the infant ROK army was 65,000 strong. There were 4,000 men
in the navy and 45,000 in the police. As the United States had only authorized
the transfer from US reserves of infantry weapons for 50,000 troops, about half
the ROK armed forces had to be issued with ex-Japanese army weapons; many
were still in use in June 1950. The Americans also left some soft-skinned vehicles and a small amount of artillery, none of which was a match for the
modern Russian material pouring into the north.

Unmoved by the creation of the ROK army, the North Korean government
began to send out unmistakable signals of its intentions. On 14 October 1949
it minuted Trygve Lie, the UN Secretary-General, and General Carlos
Romulo, the Filipino President of the General Assembly: 'The government of
the Korean People's Democratic Republic deems it necessary to declare that
should the United Nations ignore in the future the will and strivings of the
Korean people, considering only the selfish interest of a small group of traitors
and betrayers of the Korean people it will not abandon the struggle and will
reserve for itself the right to continue by measures at its disposal the struggle
for removal of UNCOK and for final unification of the country by its own
forces into a united democratic state.'

The UN General Assembly voted on 21 October to continue with the tooth-
less UNCOK, charging its members to 'investigate any developments which
might indicate the North Koreans' intent of military invasion'. Pyongyang's
immediate response was the formation of the 'United Democratic Fatherland
Front of Korea' as a rallying point for dissidents in the south, to whom Pyong-

yang radio continually broadcast calls for rebellion in the winter of 1949/50.

If the North Koreans were looking for encouragement, they received it from Washington, where policy makers were inclined to pin their hopes more and more on the United Nations. On 12 January 1950 Secretary of State Dean Acheson, addressing the National Press Club in Washington, defined American Far Eastern policy in unmistakable terms. The United States' front lines, he said, now ran from the Aleutians to Japan, the Ryukyus, and down to the Philippines. If an attack was made anywhere else in the Far East, initial resistance must come from the people attacked, to be followed by 'the commitment of the entire civilized world under the charter of the United Nations'. Korea was thus seen by all to lie outside the American ring fence. Acheson's speech carried enormous weight. He had succeeded George Marshall as Secretary of State in January 1949 and as the holder of this key post was to all intents the Foreign Minister of the United States, responsible to the President for formulation and conduct of all relations with other nations.

There were other warnings. As early as September 1949 General MacArthur's Far East Command intelligence staff in Tokyo had noted the movements of large numbers of former Chinese communist troops 'of Korean descent' entering North Korea following the victorious outcome of Mao's war against Chiang Kai-shek and the withdrawal of the rump of the Kuomintang forces to Formosa (Taiwan). In March 1950, however, Far East Command concluded that there would be 'no civil war in Korea in 1950'. In May the ROK defence minister announced to the press that invasion was impending as units of the NKPA were on the move towards the 38th parallel. MacArthur dismissed these scares. At this time a number of American dignitaries visited South Korea. General Omar Bradley, chairman of the Joint Chiefs of Staff Committee (JCS) in Washington, Secretary of Defense Louis Johnson and John Foster Dulles, then special consultant to the Secretary of State, were in Tokyo to discuss the situation with MacArthur but there was no urgent review of the threat on the agenda. It was agreed in Tokyo that invasion was a possibility but the threat was not felt to be imminent.

Once Japan had been defeated in 1945 President Truman fulfilled his promise to 'get the boys home', and by 1949 the United States Army had been pared down from 85 to a mere ten divisions; with the exception of those now declared part of the NATO alliance, all were at greatly reduced strength. Those allotted to occupation duties in Japan were no exception. Recruitment for the regular army was so low that to flesh out even the divisions at 'hollow' establishment, recourse had to be made to the selective draft. This caught those who had failed to pass into university; almost indefinite deferment was granted to undergraduates, and few post-graduates were called upon to serve. Married men with young families and workers in key industries were also exempted. Thus, the burden fell on the blue-collar classes who had little expertise; on young men of little influence from the black ghettos, Hispanics, and the poorest whites. Most were of low educational standard; many were of poor physique.

The Allied occupation force in Japan in 1950 consisted of the 8th US Army, commanded by Lieutenant-General Walton H. Walker. It comprised four under-strength divisions: the 1st Cavalry (converted to the infantry role) and the 7th, 24th and 25th Infantry Divisions. There was also a token British Commonwealth Occupation Force, BCOF, under the command of an Australian, Lieutenant-General Sir Horace Robertson, consisting of an infantry battalion with an administrative headquarters based near Kure on the island of Honshu, and a detachment of the Royal Australian Air Force at Iwakuni air base, near Hiroshima. By the end of 1949 the Australian government was seriously considering the withdrawal of the infantry battalion. From time to time the port of Kure, a former Japanese imperial naval base, was visited by ships of the Royal Australian and New Zealand navies, and by those of the Royal Navy from their base at Singapore.

The American army in Japan was unfit for operations. Five years of easy occupation duties had eroded its combat efficiency. Units were widely scattered around the country and little serious training had been carried out; one notable deficiency, soon to be exposed, was that of practice in the difficult but essential skills of ground-to-air co-operation. All Walker's divisions were well below their authorized lower establishment of 12,500 men (as against their war establishment of over 18,000), each being short of at least 1,500 riflemen; none possessed any 90mm anti-tank guns. Instead of nine battalions, each division had to make do with six. There were two, instead of three, companies in each field artillery battalion, and the same applied to the tank battalions. There was no corps headquarters for operational command of the four divisions. The US 7th Fleet was a shadow of the great instrument that had won the Pacific war. The Far East Air Force, whose primary role was the air defence of the Japanese islands, was short of jet aircraft and had carried out little or no training in tactical deployment involving the setting up of tactical navigation and fighter control systems under field conditions.

The occupation of Japan had been entrusted to General of the Army Douglas MacArthur, formerly the Allied supreme commander in the victorious Pacific war. On the surrender of the Japanese he had moved into the Dai-Ichi bank building in the centre of Tokyo, one of the few structures still intact following the prolonged aerial bombardment which had destroyed virtually every major city in Japan. MacArthur remains one of the most fascinating of military commanders. His adored father, General Arthur MacArthur, holder of the Congressional Medal of Honor, collapsed and died at the podium whilst addressing fellow veterans of the American Civil War in 1912. The son graduated from West Point in 1903 into the US Corps of Engineers and continued with undiminished success through the First World War, where he was the youngest divisional commander in the US Army, to be Superintendent of West Point at the age of 39. Here, he introduced radically new training methods whilst adhering to the academy's hallowed traditions. From 1930 to 1935 he served in Washington as Army Chief of Staff, dealing robustly – many would have said heartlessly – with the Bonus Marchers demonstrating before the White House. He was sent next to the Philippines to organize the Filipino army, an appointment which gained him the rank of Philippine Field Marshal, before retiring in 1937. In July 1941 he was recalled to service. When the Japanese attacked in December 1941 he was at Manila in command of the American and Filipino army; after conducting the defence of Bataan and Corregidor he was ordered to escape to Australia by President Roosevelt, and became supreme Allied Land Forces commander in the Pacific theatre for the rest of the war. Haughty, vain, enormously competent in his profession, he lived a life coloured by melodrama; and in 1950, at the age of 70, he was coming to the end of a dazzling career.

MacArthur's technique for restoring Japan to democratic rule was that of a remote proconsul. He maintained a distance between himself and the Emperor Hirohito, on whose immunity from prosecution as a war criminal he insisted, choosing to retain the monarchy in a more constitutional form and using Hirohito as a revered figurehead, shorn of power but still a potent symbol of Japanese tradition and nationhood. MacArthur thus captured the hearts and minds of the Japanese people, who proved remarkably acquiescent as he steered them towards democracy and prosperity on lines which he firmly set out.

The senior staff of MacArthur's headquarters were a hand-picked band of trusted lieutenants who had served him in many cases since before Pearl Harbor. Others had been recruited during the Pacific campaign and owed their promotion to him. He presided over something like a princely court, which included a number of complaisant if competent time-servers. He worked to an almost unchanging daily pattern, arriving at the Dai-Ichi on the dot of 10.30 a.m., to be saluted by an honour guard and watched devotedly by large crowds of bowing Japanese citizens. He went home at 2 p.m. for lunch, and returned to the office at 4.30 p.m., staying on until the day's work was done, sometimes until midnight. He never entertained visitors at home; an occasional appearance at an official cocktail party would be all the outside world saw of him. He almost never left Tokyo and had last set foot in the continental United States in 1941.

The key figure in MacArthur's entourage, setting the tone of the whole headquarters, was the Chief of Staff, Major-General Edward Almond. By 1950 he had served for several years in the Dai-Ichi building in posts of ascending importance. He had attracted MacArthur's attention in 1946 as head of his manpower planning department, fighting against personnel cuts imposed by the Pentagon after the war; it is fair to say that had he not fought his corner tenaciously, the 8th Army would have been in an even worse state in the summer of 1950. Almond was a southerner; unlike most of the military courtiers in the headquarters he was not a member of the 'Bataan circle' who had accompanied their master in his escape from the Philippines and subsequently throughout the Pacific campaigns. He was considered by many to be hot-tempered, arrogant and vain. In the words of Professor Allan Millett, the American historian, Almond was 'endowed with intelligence and skill, yet cursed with a wretched personality'. Another senior officer who served under him recalled that he was known as 'the Big "A" – and I don't mean Almond'. He craved glory as a successful field commander, having had an unfortunate war in Italy as commander of the 92nd Infantry Division, an all-black formation formed in 1942 when combat units were still racially segregated. Once committed to battle its men, poorly led, had melted away from the firing line, and Almond frequently had to go forward in person from his command post to supervise the battle as though he were a company commander. All seeking MacArthur's opinion or approval had to go through Almond, who slavishly adapted to his master's timetable, arriving at least an hour before the general and staying on long after he had finally gone home at the end of the day.

Only one member of the inner circle was able to circumvent Almond at any time. This was Major-General Courtney Whitney, whose position was, to say the least, ambiguous. Trained as a lawyer, he had been MacArthur's personal legal adviser throughout the Pacific campaigns and had come with his master to Tokyo in 1946 as head of the Government Section in HQ Supreme Commander Allied Powers (SCAP). As such he had direct access to the chief at any time. He also continued to act as MacArthur's legal secretary, confidential adviser, and later as his fawning biographer.

The third member of the curious triumvirate serving MacArthur, and arguably the most grotesque, was Major-General Charles A. Willoughby, the head of Military Intelligence. Born Karl von Tscheppe-Weidenbach in Heidelberg, he emigrated with his parents to the United States when he was 18, became a naturalized American citizen, adopted what he believed was a suitably aristocratic anglicized name, attended the Gettysburg Military College and saw active service in the Pancho Villa expedition of 1917–18. He had been MacArthur's principal intelligence officer in the Pacific (where his often inaccurate and invariably over-optimistic forecasts were notorious) and had become one of his most intimate courtiers. His political beliefs were of the extreme right; he had long been an avowed admirer of General Franco and after MacArthur's fall in 1951 he became involved with such organizations in the USA as the John Birch Society. In appearance his bulk reminded many of Hermann Goering, on whom he consciously modelled himself. His arrogance and lordly bearing in public had long since earned him the derisive nickname

'Sir Charles' throughout the army. This toadying bully regarded himself as the living embodiment of the old Prussian military caste. During the dark months at the end of 1950 he was to wreak terrible damage upon the United Nations' army in Korea.

The junior levels of the staff at the Dai-Ichi included many men of outstanding ability; Almond, for all his faults, chose his subordinates with care. One of them, Major Al Haig, was to come to prominence later. From 1947 to 1951, Colonel James Polk, another of Almond's protégés, served on the intelligence staff of Far East Command. Occasionally, he would find himself on the fifth floor, briefing either Almond or Willoughby, when MacArthur would enter the room unannounced; the junior was normally expected to get out of sight at once, but MacArthur would often genially wave his corncob pipe, with the words 'Sit there – that's all right', and get on with business. The lower grade staff could only marvel at the servility of their seniors, whose devotion to the master had turned them into flunkeys, anxious only to please the great man and tell him what they imagined he wished to hear.

In the three years following Churchill's Iron Curtain speech at Fulton in 1946, the policy of 'containment' of the communist threat practised by Washington seemed to be working. The Atlantic Alliance was conceived as the main bulwark in Europe and the economies of the western European states were being steadily strengthened through the Marshall Plan. A special aid programme had been devised in order to signal the west's support for Greece and Turkey and to mark the free world's boundaries in the eastern Mediterranean and Asia Minor. The Berlin airlift displayed the resolve of the alliance and its readiness to go the whole way, even to war if necessary, to maintain its principles, to defend the rights of others – and its own interests. The USSR took note and recoiled; it did not relish the idea of conflict with the United States, at this time the only viable nuclear power. However, the 'containment' policy was based on the assumption that the primary threat lay in Europe and the eastern Mediterranean. No American politician at this time favoured the retention of garrisons in far-off places like Korea; in 1947 the Joint Chiefs of Staff reported to the President confirming that there was no residual American strategic interest in that country. Bearing the signatures of Admirals Leahy and Nimitz and Generals Eisenhower and Spaatz, the paladins of United States military power, it thus carried enormous weight.

Little attention therefore seems to have been paid to the Far East, where Chiang Kai-shek was regarded, until remarkably late in the day, as a credible American surrogate in the war against communism. The idea of a Soviet thrust anywhere in the east appears to have been discounted. This was mainly because foreign policy was in the hands of 'Europeans' like the Democrat Dean Acheson, whilst the old China hands, exemplified by the staunch Republican

John Foster Dulles, were temporarily in eclipse. Pentagon war plans in 1949 were still based on two scenarios: an attack on the continental United States or an invasion across the inner German border by the Russians and their eastern European allies. The outcome of this policy was the return of the US Air Force to continental Europe and the establishment of Strategic Air Command bases in England, Spain and North Africa.

In the Far East, however, by the summer of 1948 it ought to have been clear to American sinologists that they were backing a loser and that it was only a matter of time before Chiang Kai-shek's armies collapsed before Mao's communist forces. Yet even in early 1950, with Chiang's armies driven off the mainland and on to Formosa, it seemed that American Far Eastern strategy did not embrace the idea of a strong democratic South Korea providing a useful forward base, should Formosa fall to the communists. With the potential of Red China added to that of Russia's Far Eastern military strength, two inimical powers would then be placed within a few minutes' flight of Japan, now approaching an extremely delicate stage of its peace treaty preparations after being astutely groomed by MacArthur to take its place once more as a democracy on the side of communism's sternest opponents.

Service as military advisers in South Korea with KMAG, after the departure of the American garrison troops, was decidedly unpopular with the US military. Shortage of equipment and poor living conditions led to a lack of willing volunteers and the posting in of many unsatisfactory officers and senior NCOs for a job which demanded instructors of uncommon ability and perception. The main handicap for Americans was that of language. Few Koreans could be persuaded to revert to Japanese after their long servitude. The Korean tongue, one of the world's oldest, is hard to master at any time; not only does it have a complex syntax, but its Ural-Altaic roots make it radically different from Chinese or Japanese; its similarities are rather with Finnish and Magyar. There are subtle nuances of expression which have to be observed once the speaker has ascertained the exact social standing of the person he is addressing. Its simple Hanggul alphabet, devised in the fifteenth century by the Emperor Sjong, further distances it from all other neighbouring languages. Korean, unlike Japanese, lacked any kind of military vocabulary and translation posed problems. A machine-gun was 'a gun that shoots very fast' or 'gun of many loud voices'. A headlight was 'candle in shiny bowl'. There were no equivalents for military expressions such as 'phase line', 'zone' or even 'squad'. The language simply could not be mastered by Americans on the normal eighteen-month KMAG tour. Interpreters were hard to find, and in any case often argued with each other. Few Koreans were adept in English and much instruction had to be given in sign language. A simple Korean–English military dictionary was still in course of preparation in 1950 as the war started. Further problems arose over the traditional Korean tendency to circumlocution and strict adherence to the principle of saving face. Korean officers felt unable to take advice, however tactfully proffered, from American advisers of junior rank.

Under such circumstances it is surprising that KMAG achieved what it did; there were, however, some officers in its ranks who rendered outstanding service. Captain Hausman arrived in Korea in 1946 and stayed for three years, having become fascinated by the country and its people. He mastered the language and was given his head by his grateful KMAG superiors, who could not speak Korean and were unenthused by their postings. By the summer of 1949 Hausman had played a major part in the raising of eight light infantry divisions from the six brigades of the former constabulary. The quality of these troops was dubious but at least it was a start.

When the American army left in mid-1949 the ROK army lost its best source of supply. Although they had been promised a number of Chaffee reconnaissance tanks they only got light armoured cars mounting a 37mm gun, and the obsolete American 37mm anti-tank gun. Instead of the M2A2 American 105mm field howitzer with a range of more than 13,000 yards, they had to be content with the M3, a short-barrelled version designed for airborne operations, with a range of only 7,500 yards. This was 4,000 yards less than that of the Russian 76mm and 122mm guns issued to the NKPA. Even then, each ROK army regiment had only a six-gun 'cannon company' instead of a full artillery battalion. The rationale underlying this tight-fisted approach was Washington's dread that Rhee would one day live up to his sabre-rattling oratory and invade the north unilaterally, laying the United States open to the threat of involvement, outside its declared perimeter, in what could easily become a general war.

Conscientious advisers like Hausman found that the ROK army's senior officers were unwilling to abandon their Japanese-taught stereotyped procedures and attitudes. They could cope with border skirmishes but refused to master the staffwork essential for the conduct of sustained operations. Such drudgery they considered far beneath their dignity. The idea of co-ordinating the manoeuvres of more than a battalion at a time was beyond their comprehension. Hausman's unflagging enthusiasm won him many friends among the more progressive Koreans and he was adept at identifying potential leaders, many of whom were to rise rapidly to high command after the sitting tenants had failed ignominiously on the outbreak of war. So impressed was Syngman Rhee that he asked MacArthur if Hausman could be promoted general in the Korean army and allowed to serve indefinitely on long loan. His request was turned down.

The material from which the Republic's army had to be built was of very mixed quality. When Koreans returned to their country in 1945, 3,000 seasoned veterans of the Red Army came from Manchuria and 3,000 from the Kuomintang in China – the 'Kwangbok' or 'Korean Restoration' army. A total of 300,000 who had served in the Japanese army also came home. The officer corps of the new ROK army was therefore drawn from widely diverse sources, whose members tended to look askance at each other, having recently served on opposing sides. Many had to be weeded out, but the screening process was at best only partly successful.

KMAG has often been blamed for the poor performance of the ROK army in the opening stages of the war. However, its potential weaknesses had been identified in advance by enlightened KMAG officers who saw that the future of Korea's security lay in having a professionally trained army in which technical and staff skills had been thoroughly absorbed. To that end, they prevailed upon the Korean General Staff to form instructional schools in which such specialities as artillery, field engineering, signals, quartermaster and ordnance, supply and motor transport were methodically taught. Officer training was started; by 1950 a military academy had been created, based on the West Point model, and many Korean officers were undergoing instruction in the United States. No less than 13 ROK army schools were providing specialist instruction; this represented the beginnings of that training in depth which gives an army the flexibility needed to fight a serious war. All the same, KMAG's assessment of the ROK army in early 1950 was that only a third of the army's battalions could be considered battle-worthy, and it was for reasons more of political correctness than military pragmatism that Brigadier-General Roberts, head of KMAG, felt obliged to tell a congressional board that the ROK army could now 'defeat a conventional assault from the north'.

CHAPTER 3

Assault and Battery

The planners in Pyongyang were almost certainly lured into the attack of 25 June 1950 by a misreading of the mood in Washington. It seemed that the Americans had accepted, however grudgingly, the communist victory in China and, from the pronouncements of numerous eminent politicians and service chiefs, that they would also accept the subjugation of the Republic of Korea, now that American troops had been withdrawn. On 12 January 1950, when Dean Acheson made his notorious National Press Club address in Washington defining American Far Eastern policy, he had added that there was no longer an intention to guarantee any areas on the Asiatic mainland against military attack.

Kim Il-sung, encouraged by these pronouncements, aired his plans to Stalin who at first held back, knowing that it would be fatal to risk all-out war with the United States until the Russian nuclear weapon, first exploded in 1949, had been tested and put into production. But after the American troops had left Korea (despite a last-minute appeal by MacArthur, who sent General Almond to Washington to put his case for the retention of at least a token garrison in Korea), he felt safe in giving his tacit approval for an invasion, now that there was only the poorly rated ROK army to deal with.

The ROK army was not in a position to offer much more than token resistance as the summer of 1950 drew on, despite the optimistic pronouncements of KMAG's senior officers. Their ROK army training directive for the year called for four three-month training periods. It was hoped that battalion programmes would be complete by the end of March, and that formation training and full manoeuvres would follow. The task was enormous, for at the end of 1949 only 30 out of 67 battalions had completed company-level training and 11 had still not completed even their platoon training programme. The American M1 Garand semi-automatic rifle was now being issued but only 28 battalions had satisfied KMAG as to their proficiency with it. Some progress had been made in other directions; each infantry division now had its own combat

engineer battalion and signals and ordnance companies. There were as yet few
artillery units and only half of them had fired a range course. In order to spare
the army the continuing burden of anti-guerrilla operations, 10,000 police were
to be formed into 22 combat police battalions. With an increase of border inci-
dents in the first months of the year had come a significant rise in the number
of guerrilla attacks on police posts and other targets in the south. Since the
risings on Cheju and the mainland in October 1948, trained guerrillas and sabotage experts had been infiltrated across the 38th parallel by sea and land to link
up with guerrillas and mutineers from the former constabulary. By the end of
1949 the ROK army was having to mount an average of three anti-guerrilla
operations a day. Although some training value was obtained from these, they
were not good practice for general war, and unit training suffered badly. The
situation was made worse by the rapid expansion of the army from 65,000 to
over 100,000 men in 1949.

After three months, KMAG was forced to admit that the ROK army training programme was in disarray. A new schedule was patiently drawn up and
ROK army commanders urged to adopt it. It was too late; by the middle of June
only the supposedly élite Capital Division had finished its battalion-level training, together with seven battalions of the 7th Division and a solitary battalion
in the 8th. A further 30 battalions had struggled through their company training programme but 17 still had not even completed platoon exercises. KMAG
was obliged to postpone the target date for battalion training once again, to 31
July, while regimental training was to be complete throughout the army by the
end of October.

KMAG's responsibilities did not end with unit and formation training; it
had long been recognized that staff training was virtually non-existent. Junior
officers in headquarters at all levels were not much more than yes-men with
little idea of their roles. Senior commanders, most of them trained by the
Japanese, seemed to have little notion of how to train their staffs and had to be
educated themselves, especially in accepting unpalatable advice from subordinates, whom they had been accustomed to sacking on the spot. Even so, an
honest attempt had already been made to lay the foundation of a professionally
trained ROK officer corps; the first batch of US-trained ROK officers had
returned to Korea in mid-1948 and were already making their presence felt as
further batches followed them to the American command and staff schools and
to the specialist schools of artillery, engineering and infantry. At a lower level,
the army schools set up in the preceding three years by KMAG for the training of enlisted men and NCOs were now producing acceptably trained personnel. This represented a notable achievement for the often maligned KMAG,
whose personnel had struggled to overcome not only the language barrier but
also the entrenched opposition of the older Korean officers.

In North Korea, things were very different. When the Red Army departed in 1948, it left behind some advisers as instructors, and much of its weaponry and equipment. After 1949 the formation of a field army went ahead rapidly. Conscription was introduced, and the army was formed around the trained cadres of men with wide operational experience in the Chinese Communist Forces or the Red Army. Many of the pilots and technicians in the new air force had been trained in the Soviet Union.

In March 1950 there was a further infusion of Russian equipment, following Stalin's tacit permission to invade. This enabled the North Koreans to equip eight full-strength infantry divisions, two at half strength, an independent infantry regiment, a motor cycle reconnaissance regiment, an armoured brigade and five brigades of border troops. The Russians promised to deliver enough piston-engined reconnaissance, ground attack and light bomber aircraft to guarantee air superiority for the attackers. North Korea had developed a considerable industrial base and a thriving armaments industry was producing large quantities of munitions. Unlike the ROK army, the NKPA had completed its battalion training in good time and had been staging frequent regimental and divisional exercises since early in the year.

On the eve of war the ROK army was 95,000 strong, backed by 48,000 lightly armed National Police, 6,100 in a coast guard slowly growing into the makings of a navy, and 1,800 in the embryonic air force which, the Americans having declined to issue combat aircraft, possessed only ten Harvard trainers and a dozen light observation planes.

There had been plenty of hard intelligence on the North Korean build-up. Border skirmishing was intensifying and communist-led guerrillas were active in the south. The ROK General Staff considered that any attack would follow invasion routes from the north used for centuries by successive aggressors: the principal one ran from Kaesong, across the Imjin river and on to Seoul via the Uijongbu area. Another route, further east, passed through Kapyong, thence down the valley of the Pukhan river before turning west along the Han river valley and into Seoul. On KMAG advice an outpost line had been established close to the 38th parallel, to identify and delay any advance on these axes, whilst reinforcements held further to the rear were deployed to face the main thrust lines. The KMAG advisers believed that if the defenders kept their nerve and the reinforcing formations moved fast to support the blocking positions set up on the outpost line, the invaders could be halted for long enough to permit United Nations intervention and a call to the conference table.

Only days before the outbreak, the CIA were reporting the sure signs of impending invasion. North Korean frontier guards had been replaced by army units, civilians evacuated from the frontier zone, and civilian railway services suspended on strategic lines leading to the front, which were now reserved for military traffic; moreover, there were unmistakable signs of massive forward loading of munitions, fuel and other warlike stores. Details of these movements, obtained at great risk by courageous Korean agents, were referred to General Willoughby's intelligence department in Tokyo which passed it on to Washington without comment as routine information. As late as 19 June, the Far East Command intelligence summary was noting that 'Soviet advisers believe that now is the time to subjugate the South Korean government by political means, especially since the guerrilla campaign in the south has recently met with serious reverses.' It seems from this that Willoughby and his staff treated the hard-won intelligence of their Korean agents with contempt. In this they had long been tacitly abetted in Washington. As General Ridgway, soon to be commanding in Korea, but then serving in the Pentagon and privy to these intelligence reports, wrote years later: 'Our national mind was made up to liquidate this embarrassing military commitment and we closed our ears to the clashing of arms that sounded along the border as our last troops were taking ship for home.'

By the middle of June the only active UNCOK observers in Seoul were two Australians, Major Peach and Squadron Leader Rankin. Neither spoke Korean or had received any briefing in Korean affairs, but they were men of keen sensibility who realized that the demonstrations of flag-waving and banquets which were a standard feature of their tireless visits to ROK army headquarters were no more than window dressing. Other UNCOK delegates were frequently lured into compromising situations when attending political-military rallies at which they were persuaded to make indiscreet speeches associating themselves with Rhee's government and policies. In a speech in March 1950, Dean Acheson had suggested that the Soviet Union might demonstrate goodwill by obtaining entry into North Korea for UNCOK delegates.

Following a general election in the south on 30 May, in which Syngman Rhee suffered a considerable loss of support to independents and tiny splinter groups, Pyongyang responded by inviting UNCOK delegates, together with certain South Korean politicians, to a meeting near the border on 10 June – no doubt with a view to making overtures towards reunification. Rhee however immediately announced that any politicians who attended the meeting would be branded traitors; thus only three UNCOK delegates, including the two Australians, went to the rendezvous. They were stopped at the border by a ROK army general and obliged to watch helplessly as he ordered a brisk fusillade to be directed at the waiting North Koreans. It was then 3.30 in the afternoon. The North Koreans returned the fire as all kept their heads down. At 5 p.m., the scheduled time for the meeting to commence, the firing died away. The UNCOK party leader, Mr Gaillard, bravely went forward, to find the North Koreans crouching unhappily in their foxholes. He talked with them for two hours and they handed him an appeal for unification, but would accept no documents from him, becoming icily cold when they discovered that he was an American citizen. As he tried to recross the border he was pinned down for

some time by fire from the south. The next day, three North Korean representatives came across, asking to meet South Korean political leaders. They were
promptly arrested and taken before a military court. Within the week two of
them were broadcasting on Seoul radio extolling Rhee as 'the father of the
Korean nation'. The third, after a little persuasion, joined them on air a few
days later.

The last days of uneasy peace seemed unreal to observers in Seoul. John
Foster Dulles, still an exponent of an 'eastern' strategy (but in a minority
against the Acheson-led 'Europeans') visited Korea and was taken to the 38th
parallel, clad in his business suit, quaintly wearing a Homburg hat in the swel-
tering heat of the Korean summer. Looking out into the People's Republic he
saw only a vista of peaceful countryside, and was assured by his smiling ROK
army guides that in the event of an invasion, the enemy would be resoundingly
defeated before setting foot across the line.

On Friday evening, 23 June, most of the ROK army units in the frontier area
stood down for the weekend. Despite the recent rise in tension, the army's chief
of staff, General Chae, felt confident enough to allow his command to relax. At
least two-thirds of the personnel guarding the main Kaesong–Seoul route
departed for the capital. Only in the 6th ROK Division, further over to the east
below the Hwachon reservoir, was its KMAG adviser, Lieutenant-Colonel
McPhail, able to convince the divisional commander that something was in the
wind. On the Ongjin peninsula, north of the river Han, the ROK 17th
Regiment was in a particularly vulnerable position. Its only line of retreat was
by sea, and a flotilla of landing craft had been prudently beached to permit the
regiment to escape once it had performed its role of imposing delay and
maximum casualties on any invader. The 17th had been carefully selected for
this dangerous assignment and replaced another regiment, three companies of
which had mutinied before deserting to the north earlier in 1950. The commander of the 17th, Colonel 'Tiger' Kim Chong-won, a former sergeant-major
in the Imperial Japanese Army, was one of Rhee's close associates and had an
unsavoury reputation, having already been removed from one command
appointment at the insistence of KMAG. On the arrival of the 17th Regiment
in the frontier area, the North Koreans, who knew their man, strengthened
their local garrisons; immediately the level of cross-border skirmishing rose
and in May and June there were numerous clashes. It was on the Ongjin peninsula that the blow first fell. At 4 a.m. on Sunday, 25 June, after ninety minutes
of preliminary bombardment, elements of the North Korean 6th Division
began to attack the ROK army positions.

The attack spread from west to east across the 38th parallel, as a ceremonial *feu
de joie* ripples down the line of a parade. At Kaesong, the keystone of the ROK
1st Division's defensive area, only one of the KMAG advisers was in residence,

the others having gone to Seoul for the weekend. Woken by the dawn cannonade, he went outside in his pyjamas and got into his jeep to drive round the town as ROK army personnel ran aimlessly around the streets. A train had pulled into the railway station from the north and was disgorging a battalion of North Korean infantry who immediately set about anything that looked like opposition. The American prudently headed south, as bullets cracked about his jeep. Further east, the ROK 6th Division, whose commander had retained his men in post over the weekend, rushed to arms and began to fight resolutely in and around the important town and communications centre of Chunchon. In the Chorwon area, however, where a regiment of the ROK 7th Division had been posted to guard the Kapyong–Pukhan valley route to Seoul, resistance folded before troops on leave could be recalled to their units. Over on the east coast the 8th Division resisted staunchly to begin with, until rumours, followed by confirmation, informed the divisional commander that numerous landings were being made along the coast up to fifty miles to the south.

The United States ambassador in Seoul, John Muccio, heard the news at 9.30 a.m. An inspired choice for this difficult job, he had been in Korea for several years, spoke the language fluently and knew his way around the political labyrinth surrounding Syngman Rhee. He could hear explosions as the first air raids took place, and brought out the evacuation plan for American and other foreign nationals, the only fully prepared American contingency plan for Korea. Codenamed Operation 'Cruller', it was activated by the codeword 'Fireside', broadcast that evening by the local American Forces Network station. This was the cue for all American nationals to make their way at once to Inchon, where shipping had been commandeered. Muccio, having conferred with the head of KMAG, signalled Tokyo for an immediate airlift of ammunition for the ROK army, adding that it would be catastrophic were the South Koreans to be defeated simply because the United States had failed to provide enough basic military resources.

Doubts were now raised over the status of KMAG. Should its members take up arms and fight alongside the ROK army, or should they be evacuated with the American and other civilians? Muccio even proposed at one point that they should all claim diplomatic immunity, the advisers and their families taking refuge in the American embassy. It was decided in Tokyo, however, that the whole mission should leave Korea, and aircraft were sent to Kimpo airfield to lift the Americans out in between the frequent unopposed air raids. The North Korean air force had effortlessly achieved immediate air supremacy and could do what it liked. During 26 June most of the American and other civilian evacuees were put aboard an overcrowded Norwegian ship at Inchon – 700 of them on a cargo vessel with accommodation for 12 passengers. All praised the ship's crew who coped philosophically with this unexpected contingency.

On Monday the 26th, Kim Il-sung broadcast to the Korean people from

Pyongyang. He told them that the southerners had invaded the north, but that the NKPA was now counter-attacking successfully across the 38th parallel. He called for increased guerrilla activity in the south, for its workers to go on strike, and for the peasants to call for immediate land reforms; he also demanded the restoration of the People's Committees suppressed by Rhee's government. Despite vociferous claims from Kim and other North Korean leaders that the south had initiated the war by invading the north, sets of operation orders recovered from the war ministry in Pyongyang later in the year provided evidence to the contrary. They were written in Russian, and translations were taken after the originals had been photographed; these mysteriously disappeared and have never been seen again.

Meanwhile the ROK army, temporarily deprived of its KMAG advisers, was faring badly against a ferocious and well-executed North Korean assault. A powerful armoured and infantry column was sweeping all before it on the main route south through Uijongbu, heading straight for Seoul. Far out to the north-west in their isolated positions on the Ongjin peninsula, after losing an entire battalion, Colonel Kim's remaining troops managed to embark on their landing ships and sailed south. On the 26th, the ROK 2nd Division was ordered to launch a counter-attack in the area of Uijongbu in an effort to stem the armoured tide; only part of the force turned up on the start-line and the divisional commander could not make up his mind what to do, eventually beating a disorganized retreat. On the central front the ROK 6th Division held its ground at Chunchon but was finally forced to retreat on the 28th, when the units on its flanks collapsed. It saved most of its transport and guns and had inflicted heavy casualties on the NKPA 2nd Division. Elsewhere, many ROK units stood and fought courageously against overwhelming odds. With almost no anti-tank guns, the ROK infantry adopted suicidal tactics in their efforts to stop the rampaging T-34 tanks which threatened to overrun them, climbing on to their turrets with explosive charges or hurling themselves as human bombs on to the tanks to detonate satchels of explosive tied to their bodies. Many ROK army artillery units stood by their inadequate M3 howitzers until shot down at their guns, after inflicting heavy casualties on their assailants over open sights. With the return of thousands of men off weekend leave the forward units regained a degree of cohesion; but the high command was wanting and direction from the army headquarters in Seoul inept. By last light on the 28th the leading North Korean probes had reached the northern suburbs of Seoul.

Captain Vyvyan Holt, the United Kingdom diplomatic representative in Seoul, had been able to cable news of the invasion to London on the 25th but as the North Koreans entered the city he destroyed his cypher office and, with his staff, was taken prisoner. The First Secretary at the Legation was George Blake, who doubled as the station head of MI6, the Secret Intelligence Service.

He would later become notorious as a Soviet agent. Some British expatriates
had got away with Muccio and the Americans. The Anglican bishop, the commissioner of the Salvation Army and several expatriate Roman Catholic
priests, nuns and missionaries elected to remain in Seoul with their flocks and
were quickly taken away captive by the invaders, with numerous Korean clergy
and nuns, none of whom was ever seen again. The bishop, the commissioner,
and the senior Roman Catholic monsignor were lucky to survive a rigorous
imprisonment in the north.

Muccio and the remaining staff of the American embassy pulled out of Seoul
on 27 June after destroying their diplomatic radio station. With him were the
few remaining KMAG personnel including its senior officer, Colonel Wright.
Later in the day, without reference to KMAG, General Chae, the ROK army
chief of staff, and his headquarters departed hurriedly from the capital, thereby
depriving the ROK divisions in the field of their entire higher command.
Colonel Wright set out in hot pursuit, to find ROK army headquarters setting
itself up on the road to Suwon. The chief of staff, who maintained that he had
been 'forcibly carried off by his staff against his wishes', was persuaded to
return to Seoul with Wright. But irreparable damage had been done to the
morale of the ROK military, as well as to the civil population, by the unedify-
ing spectacle of the nation's top soldier cravenly fleeing the field.

The ROK army headquarters had only been back in Seoul for a few hours
when they were off again, accompanied by thousands of terror-stricken soldiers
and civilian refugees, jamming the approaches to the bridges across the Han.
ROK army engineers now blew the main bridges, still packed with fleeing soldiers and civilians; an estimated 800 of these perished. Thousands of ROK soldiers were still marooned north of the bridges, together with Colonel Wright's
KMAG headquarters, which drove out of the ancient east gate of the city,
making for the next bridge upstream, eight miles away. This too had been
blown, but KMAG got over on a raft with some of its vehicles including the
precious radio truck, now the only reliable source of contact with Tokyo. Those
members of Wright's staff for whom no places could be found on vehicles
which got over to the south bank had to march cross-country for Suwon, some
twenty miles away. As they set out, the first American fighter aircraft from
Japan appeared overhead to attack the North Korean troops entering the northern suburbs of Seoul, and to challenge the brief North Korean command of the
sky.

With the International Date Line interposing, it was still late on the evening of
Saturday the 24th when news of the invasion reached Washington in the form
of Muccio's signal, hotly followed by confirmation from MacArthur's headquarters. Dean Acheson was among the first officials to be informed; he was at
his country home after a busy Saturday in Washington but immediately

returned to the office after informing Dean Rusk, now his Assistant Secretary of State for Far Eastern Affairs, who found himself pitched once more into the affairs of the countries whose frontiers he had so arbitrarily selected back in August 1945 off a school atlas and without any reference to geographical, ethnic, military or economic factors. Acheson's immediate reaction was to get the duty staff at the Pentagon and in the State Department to contact Trygve Lie, asking him to convene an emergency meeting of the UN Security Council as early as possible on Sunday the 25th. The call went through before midnight.

Acheson now started to ring round town; the President had to be told, but Truman was out of Washington that weekend in his home town of Independence, Missouri. As it would not be possible for him to get back to the Oval Office until the following afternoon, Acheson took it upon himself to make a number of crucial decisions that were constitutionally outside his power; he authorized at once the additional military aid for the ROK army sought earlier by Muccio, directed MacArthur to task the Far East Air Force to provide overhead cover for the evacuation of American nationals from Korea, and the US 7th Fleet to cruise between Formosa and mainland China in order to discourage any attempt by Mao to invade Chiang Kai-shek's unsteady stronghold (and equally to deter Chiang from attempting to invade China proper). All this was done without consulting the Joint Chiefs of Staff and before formal approval had been obtained from Congress. It was in any case fully in keeping with Acheson's character; long known for his aloofness towards anyone he considered beneath his intellectual or social standing, he held a dim opinion (already shared by many members of the military establishment) of General Omar Bradley, the chairman of the Joint Chiefs of Staff.

Acheson had long been one of the strongest advocates of 'containment': a strategy based on the principle that if any part of the globe appeared to be coveted by the Soviet Union or one of its surrogates, United States intervention was justified, on the pretext that democracy had to be offered as the only viable alternative to communism. He held no brief for wresting North Korea back from Kim Il-sung, but equally the invasion of South Korea was to him the spearpoint of world aggression by the communists; if the two Koreas were reunited on communist terms it would trigger the next stage, which would rapidly see the end of democracy in Japan, the Philippines and the rest of south-east Asia. He believed that it would be regarded as a sign of fatal weakness if the United States recoiled from this, the first test of its resolve in the Far East. As a convinced 'European' he believed that in the event of war, the great battleground would inevitably be in western Europe or the Middle East, but that events in the Far East should not be permitted to get out of hand and affect what he regarded as the final confrontation on the north German plain. Whilst the Koreans, north and south, always thought of the conflict as a civil war between two sides seeking unification, albeit on their own terms, Acheson saw no purpose in reunification under either Rhee or Kim Il-sung. His belief in 'containment' was shared by Truman, who compared South Korea's struggle with that enacted in Greece as the Greek royalist army fought for democracy against the Greek communists after 1945, under the military tutelage of the American General Van Fleet. As long as the ROK army could offer resistance the containment could be indirect; but as the ROK army disintegrated, Truman realized that direct American, then United Nations, assistance was urgently required.

Acheson's approach to the UN upset many Congressmen who firmly believed that the American constitution had been infringed. The isolationist Republican Senator Taft spoke up, describing the Secretary of State's actions in bypassing Congress and going straight to the UN as 'a complete usurpation of the President's authority to use armed force'.

The UN Security Council met in New York on the afternoon of 25 June to consider a draft resolution hurriedly tabled by the United States calling for collective action against 'unprovoked aggression' and an immediate cease-fire by the North Koreans. Disagreement broke out among the delegates; the United Kingdom, France, Egypt, Norway and India argued that this appeared to be a civil war, that as there had been breaches of the peace for many months on both sides of the 38th parallel it could hardly be described as 'unprovoked', and that both sides should be ordered to stop fighting. This amendment, however, was rejected by Trygve Lie and Charles Noyes, the American delegate, and the original resolution passed by a 9–0 vote; the Yugoslav delegate abstained. Far more significantly, the Soviet representative Jakob Malik was not present; he was under orders from Moscow to boycott the Security Council in view of its continuing refusal – and that of the full Assembly – to admit communist China in place of Chiang's Formosan nationalist government. Had he been in attendance Malik would certainly have availed himself of the veto and the resolution would have been stillborn. In that case the Americans would have been obliged either to go to South Korea's aid alone or leave Rhee to his fate.

On the evening of 25 June, following the passing of the Security Council resolution, a top-level conference took place in Washington at Blair House. It was chaired by Truman, recalled to the capital from Missouri. Present were Acheson, Defense Secretary Johnson, and the Joint Chiefs of Staff under General Bradley, who initially advised against the committal of American ground troops; in this he was motivated by the parlous state of the army following drastic rundown post-1945 and the certainty of overstretch if resources now earmarked for western Europe were sent to the Far East. The Chief of Air Staff, Lieutenant-General Hoyt Vandenberg, believed that air power alone could quench the invasion; he favoured attacking Soviet Far East air bases with nuclear weapons, and Truman at once issued instructions for plans to be drawn up for this drastic scenario. He called on the JCS to make an appreciation as to where the USSR might strike next. There was immediate consensus that Moscow's hand lay close behind the North Korean invasion.

Truman now agonized over the appalling implications of committing American armed forces, and especially launching a nuclear strike against the Russians. 'In the final analysis,' he wrote later, 'I did this for the United Nations. I believed in the League of Nations. It failed. Lots of people thought it failed because we [the US] weren't in it to back it up. OK, now we started the UN. It was our idea, and in its first big test we just couldn't let them down. If a collective system under the UN *can* work, it must be *made* to work, and now is the time to call their bluff.' The President's authority was given for the movement of elements of the 7th Fleet to mask Formosa from the mainland, and for the US Air Force to provide air cover for the evacuation of American and other civilians from South Korea, provided that this was limited to sea and air space south of the 38th parallel.

However, a group of experts went from Tokyo to Korea at once, headed by Brigadier-General Church, to assess the situation on the ground. Church recommended the immediate insertion of American ground combat forces. UNCOK, still recommending negotiation as the proper solution, was ignored when the Security Council met again on 27 June to consider another US resolution calling on UN member states 'to furnish such assistance to the Republic of Korea as may be necessary to repel the armed attack and to restore international peace and security in the area'. The resolution was adopted, to visible relief in Washington; Britain, France, nationalist China, Cuba, Ecuador, Norway and the United States were in favour, whilst Yugoslavia was against and India and Egypt abstained. The Soviet Union was once more absent.

Tension mounted in America, haunted by a spectre of general war; even Acheson, at a meeting of the National Security Council on 28 June, advised that a very serious situation could arise if rapid success against North Korea was not achieved. The CIA was alerted to report the slightest hint that the USSR was preparing for global war, and the hawkish chiefs of the young United States Air Force, Vandenberg and Air Force Secretary Finletter, pressed for authority to attack North Korea at once. It was not forthcoming, for Truman feared rapid global escalation if the USAF's strategic bombers on Okinawa and the Marianas Islands were given their head. Aircraft of the USAF based in Japan were, however, already ranging widely across North Korea on MacArthur's orders, attacking road and rail systems as well as industrial targets and any troop concentrations they found. A fresh directive had to be drafted for MacArthur, not yet appointed United Nations commander but already acting *de facto* as such. The National Security Council met in Washington on 29 June to do this.

An offer of help came, with the authority of the British government, from the Far East Fleet, of which a portion was cruising in Japanese waters. Admiral

Turner Joy, commanding the US 7th Fleet, was pleased to receive the reinforcement of the British ships, as well as those from Australia and New Zealand which were also made immediately available by their governments. He ordered the combined fleet to sea from its Japanese ports in case a second Pearl Harbor, launched this time by the Russians, caught them at their moorings.

Truman, a provincial with little knowledge of the greater world who had begun his working life as a draper's assistant and had no pretensions to intellectual ability, possessed considerable moral courage and resolution when hard decisions had to be made. He backed his worldly-wise Secretary of State to the hilt as the crisis unfolded. Whilst the use of American ground forces was still withheld, naval reinforcements were ordered and a carrier group cruising in the Pacific was ordered to steam for Sasebo, the Japanese naval base used by 7th Fleet. Congress was directed to approve increased aid to the Philippines as well as to French Indo-China; the Chinese nationalists on Formosa were ordered to abstain from offensive operations against the mainland.

The military situation in Korea went from bad to worse. On 29 June the JCS signalled MacArthur, supplementing previous directives. He was told to limit ground force participation to communications and service units but authorized to deploy combat troops to secure an emergency exit port in the Pusan–Chinhae area. He was also given belated approval for the aerial attack of military targets in North Korea, ensuring that such targets were well clear of the Manchurian–Soviet borders. Additionally he was told to submit a 'shopping list' to Washington of any material assistance to the ROK forces which was beyond his power to provide. MacArthur was also admonished that the deployment of naval and air forces in Korean operations did not constitute permission to wage war against the Soviet Union. Should Russian forces enter the operational area he was to adopt a defensive posture and report back to Washington.

Truman went a step further by authorizing the wider use of American ground forces in Korea on 30 June with the rousing words: 'We have met the challenge of the pagan wolves.' Again, the JCS had not been consulted, although Truman, as Commander-in-Chief of all American armed forces, was acting fully within his powers. His decision was made after receiving a dire report from MacArthur, who had just returned to Tokyo from a flying visit to the front the previous day with some of his immediate entourage including Almond, Willoughby and Stratemeyer, the commander of the Far East Air Force. Met by Ambassador Muccio, Syngman Rhee, Brigadier-General Church and a team of observers, he had heard that out of almost 100,000 ROK combat troops who had theoretically been available for duty four days earlier, only 8,000 could be accounted for that morning. The enemy had now reached the north bank of the Han river and an assault crossing was imminent. MacArthur called for transport and the party had gone up the road from

Suwon airfield towards the front. From a vantage point overlooking the Han they could see that the ROK army was a spent force. The roads heading south were choked with fleeing soldiers. MacArthur, puffing his famous corncob pipe, turned to Almond with the comment: 'I've seen many retreating Korean soldiers this trip, all with guns and ammunition at their side and all smiling. I've not seen a single wounded man. Nobody is fighting.'

MacArthur knew that even the immediate commitment of American combat troops would come too late, and had privately to admit to himself that under his regime as commander of the occupying army in Japan, its infantry divisions had lapsed into a state in which they were unfit for action; yet they were all that could be brought to bear. He informed Washington of his intention to move a regimental combat team – the equivalent of a British brigade – to Korea at once. He knew that it would not be enough, envisaging it as the nucleus of a two-division build-up which would enable him to go over to the offensive as soon as possible and drive out the invader. Truman immediately cleared the sending of the combat team, but only to secure the line of communication. MacArthur fumed at the hesitation in Washington and demanded that the President be woken so he could give permission to commit the combat team to the battlefront – which Truman did.

After an early breakfast Truman conferred again with his advisers. The JCS changed their minds and recommended the despatch of more combat troops. MacArthur was authorized to commit all four of 8th Army's divisions if necessary, subject only to the need to safeguard the security of the Japanese islands. The President also gave authority for a naval blockade of North Korea. Gone was any talk of negotiating a peace, or of holding back until other UN members had agreed to contribute ground forces. America was going in as the free world's champion.

Voices of dissent could still be faintly heard in Washington. John Foster Dulles believed that if the United States challenged communism on the Asiatic mainland, as now seemed inevitable, it risked fatal confrontation with both the USSR and communist China and their virtually unlimited resources. Some UN members were still urging restraint on the United States and an attempt at peaceful settlement, but Truman now had the bit between his teeth and wanted to show his allies that Washington was totally committed to opposing the red menace wherever it manifested itself; he also felt it incumbent on him, as the self-appointed leader of the free world, to reassure his new NATO partners who might be faltering in the face of the Sino-Soviet threat. The views of UNCOK, still pressing for a negotiated settlement even at this late stage, were swept aside.

In London, Attlee immediately condemned the North Korean invasion in the House of Commons as 'undoubtedly grave' and as 'naked aggression'. At the

Foreign Office Ernest Bevin and his advisers concluded that international action was needed as a matter of urgency 'to prevent the aggressors from achieving their object, both in order to safeguard the future of the United Nations organization and to deter the Soviet Union from attempting aggression elsewhere'.

The British response was nonetheless governed by realities. The country's armed forces, it seemed, faced ever-increasing commitments with diminishing manpower. The Malayan emergency was absorbing a major portion of the army; Hong Kong had had to be reinforced, after the defeat of Chiang Kai-shek, by the insertion of the 40th Infantry Division, and on top of existing garrisons in Germany, Austria, Trieste, Egypt and North Africa there was the new burden of contribution to the Atlantic Alliance. Sir Oliver Franks, the British ambassador in Washington, favoured a placatory policy towards the North Koreans, whom he felt should not be accused at once of outright aggression but rather encouraged to go to the conference table.

Attlee's Cabinet included members who were openly disturbed by American policies in the Far East. Although they agreed that in principle something should be done to help the South Koreans in their extremity, they balked at the presence of the US 7th Fleet in the waters between mainland China and Formosa, at American military aid to French Indo-China and to the Philippines and even more at the Americans' readiness to label the invasion of the south as part of a Soviet master plan. Anxious to keep his Cabinet together, Attlee settled for condemnation of the North Koreans for an isolated act of aggression. This had the advantage, it was hoped, of persuading the Russians not to give overt assistance to the North Koreans. At the same time, the British ambassadors in Washington and at the UN were briefed to urge the Americans not to overstress the idea of a Muscovite master plot, but nonetheless to support the US resolution at the United Nations. Attlee's hand is evident here; he remembered the dreadful outcome of the British government's failure to face up to Hitler in the mid-1930s. Bevin, who despite a succession of rebuffs still cherished hopes of negotiating with the Russians, wanted to give them every chance to disassociate themselves from the North Koreans without losing face.

NATO member-state ambassadors in Washington were collectively briefed by the State Department. The Soviets, they were told, were not actually preparing to enter the war in Korea but were using Kim Il-sung as their surrogate to test the will of the western powers. It was therefore essential not to show weakness over Korea. Any sign of yielding would trigger a landslide: after Korea, Formosa; then Japan, Indo-China, Malaya and Singapore; then western Europe. The Domino Theory was receiving its first public airing. The fascinated ambassadors were assured that MacArthur was the logical choice as United Nations commander-in-chief in the theatre, and would be conducting a 'restorative, and not an aggressive' campaign.

Sir Oliver Franks signalled London that he was under pressure from George Perkins, US Under-Secretary of State for European Affairs, to come up with significant British support for the South Koreans. It was promised at once, with full parliamentary support, in spite of the reservations mentioned above. Approval was given on 28 June for British naval units to play a full operational (as opposed to 'humanitarian') role as part of the US 7th Fleet off Korea. In the Commons Winston Churchill, as leader of the Opposition, gave his party's unqualified backing to Attlee 'in what seems his inescapable duty'. The decision of Parliament was acclaimed in Washington, where Marshal of the Royal Air Force Lord Tedder, head of the British Defence Mission, went to see General Bradley on 30 June. Bradley said the promise of even a token land contingent would greatly aid the US by its 'excellent political effect in sealing even more firmly our complete unity on this issue'. This was passed at once to the Chiefs of Staff in London who referred it to the Foreign Office for comment. Whilst it was agreed that there were great political dividends to be obtained by the offer of ground forces there was a feeling, widespread in Whitehall that week, that an American military defeat might end with a unilateral decision by Washington to use the atomic bomb. The chiefs were therefore advised that any British offer was to be conditional on a guarantee that nuclear weapons would not be used without prior consultation with the British government.

The Chiefs of Staff met in Whitehall on 3 July to consider the military contribution which might be offered. They had before them a paper prepared by the Joint Planning Staff which, much more concerned with the closer threat coming from across the inner German border, opposed the sending of land or air elements, or any further naval units, as this would seriously weaken Britain's stance in western Europe. Even the despatch of a battalion from Malaya or Hong Kong, or from the largely notional Strategic Reserve in the UK, would weaken British capabilities elsewhere, especially in Malaya where the counter-terrorist campaign had reached a critical stage. The Joint Planners, whilst agreeing it was desirable to send troops to Korea, believed it was 'fundamentally unsound and unacceptable' militarily. Having digested this, the chiefs decided that consideration should be given to sending troops, but only if it was apparent that the US was seriously overstrained and had no ground forces to spare. It was also decided that if any troops were sent, they must come from the Strategic Reserve in the UK rather than from Malaya or Hong Kong. For the time being they felt it was prudent to wait and see how events developed in Korea before making a final commitment.

Three days later the Cabinet Defence Committee met to discuss the subject of troops for Korea. Shinwell, the Minister of Defence, warned that it was essential to examine the UK's capacity to defend itself wherever it was called on to do so. He was convinced that the Soviet threat was growing, and that our air defences were particularly weak. The upshot was that talks were quickly held between military advisers in Washington and London and two bomber groups and a fighter group of the USAF were moved to Britain. The arrival of this air power was, however, presented as a routine redeployment unassociated with the Korean emergency.

CHAPTER 4

Bilko Goes to War

The first American combat troops arrived in Korea on 1 July. They were from the 1st Battalion of the 21st Infantry Regiment of the 24th Infantry Division, on occupation duties in Japan. Only twenty-four hours' notice to move had been given to Lieutenant-Colonel Smith, their commanding officer. The plan was to fly the battalion to an airfield as close as possible to the crumbling front; but the weather was bad and the transport aircraft landed at Pusan, from where the 403 men of 'Task Force Smith' were taken by train and road to Pyongtaek, a town on the main Seoul–Pusan road. Two battalions of the 34th Infantry Regiment left Japan by sea on 2 July with orders to join Smith as soon as possible.

Korea came as a dreadful cultural shock to the inexperienced soldiers of 24th Division, fewer than 10 per cent of whom had seen any combat. For the most part they had been selectively drafted into the army or, if volunteers, lured by the pleasing prospect of garrison duties in Japan. Smith selected a defensive position outside the small town of Osan, astride the main road on three low hills commanding a view north towards Suwon, and ordered his men to prepare a blocking position. Digging began as darkness fell, somewhat ineffectually as the men had received no training in the preparation or siting of fieldworks, nor had they been issued with any mines or barbed wire. The ground was rocky and their light entrenching tools were inadequate. A company of field artillery was in support, but the only anti-tank weapons available were some obsolete 2.36-inch rocket launchers. Two cumbersome 75mm recoilless guns were sited on the forward slopes of the rising ground. There was no sign of the enemy or the ROK army units which were supposed to fight alongside them.

Alone, but uneasily conscious of the fact that they represented the mightiest nation of the free world, they faced the immediate future with some curiosity. Having dug their shallow weapon slits the men opened their field rations and ate them cold. It began to rain. By dawn many of the slit trenches were flooded and the soldiers were sitting miserably on the ground under their waterproof ponchos. They were cold, dirty, unshaven, baffled, and unhappy at the prospect before them. So far, all they had seen of the population was the distressing procession of refugees struggling south. The land, manured with human excrement stored in pits alongside the paddy-fields, stank to high heaven. Clouds of thirsty mosquitoes tormented the unprotected soldiers while alarmingly large unidentified insects and small reptiles crawled over them. The people spoke an incomprehensible language and clearly resented any attempt by the soldiers to converse with them in beer-hall Japanese. It would not be long before the Americans, and most other UN troops who served in Korea, regarded the hapless people of the country as debased and beneath contempt. The derogatory term 'Gook', used to describe them from the beginning, did not augur well for a campaign whose purpose was the salvation of the Korean people.

Shortly after dawn on 5 July, Task Force Smith was put to the test. A column of T-34 tanks came purposefully down the road from the direction of Suwon. Undeterred by fire from the American field guns they drove straight through the blocking position, immune to the puny anti-tank rockets. The defenders' recoilless guns, prominent on their forward slope, were quickly located by the enemy and knocked out. The tanks motored on, as lorry-borne infantry dismounted and worked their way round Smith's flanks. Enemy mortar fire plastered the American position, destroying some of the vehicles. Smith gave the order to retire on foot and the survivors began to straggle to the rear across the reeking paddy-fields, shedding equipment and weapons as ammunition ran out. The supporting gunners destroyed their 105mm howitzers *in situ*, to the disgust of Smith and his officers, and made off in the gun tractors.

That night the remnants of Task Force Smith reached Ansong, where the two weak seaborne battalions of the 34th Regiment had just arrived. They had already been advised of the fate of Task Force Smith by Brigadier-General Barth, 24th Division's senior artillery officer, who had been a horrified witness of the loss of his guns up the road. He found the 34th about to prepare a position defending the town of Pyongtaek but knew, from what had already happened to Smith's battalion, that there was every chance of another rout unless the 34th pulled back before the enemy attack developed. His advice went unheeded. As darkness fell the 34th seemed unconcerned that enemy armour was bearing down on them.

For the second night it rained hard and again the men sat miserably around in the open rather than stay in their waterlogged slits. The hours passed quietly apart from the blowing of a culvert a few hundred yards up the road by American engineers. At dawn the commanding officer toured his forward positions, ordering the men to get into their flooded trenches. Few bothered to do so, as they ate a cold breakfast out of cans. There was little sense of urgency. Suddenly a column of tanks arrived at the blown culvert. The leading crew dismounted, inspected the damaged bridge, returned to their tank, and opened fire on the Americans. There was a marked reluctance to return the fire; a sort of paralysis seemed to have set in. None of the men had ever expected to see action. In the words of the unit's candid post-combat report: 'early over-confidence changed suddenly to surprise, then to dismay, and finally to the grim realization that, of the two armies, the North Korean force was superior in size, equipment, training and fighting ability'.

Some of the Americans with combat experience tried to tell the others what to do. Many seemed stunned and unwilling to believe that enemy soldiers were firing at them. The North Korean tanks gave covering fire as their infantry poured forward and around the defenders' flanks. The mortar observer who was supposed to be controlling defensive fire went into deep shock as the result of a near miss. Men were soon moving back from the forward platoon positions, some without their packs and many without their weapons. Panic quickly set in, even though officers vainly tried to stop the rearward movement. Many of the men ran all the way to Pyongtaek, three miles down the road, where they gathered in a shambling crowd. One officer later tried to analyse the collapse of his platoon. Out of 31 men, 12 told him that their rifles would not fire. This, he found, was because they had seldom been cleaned and oiled, and the night's rain had rusted the mechanisms. Some men had tried to clean their weapons but did not know how to strip them down or reassemble them.

Back in Pyongtaek an attempt was made to sort out the demoralized batta-lion. The mortar observer, still in shock, was wandering around the streets shouting 'Rain, Rain', and could not be persuaded to say anything else. The water wagons had been lost and men were drinking stagnant water from the well-manured paddy-fields. The road to the south was covered with stragglers, many of whom had thrown away their boots; discarded webbing equipment was lying all along the route.

By last light the remnants of the unit had reached Chonan, where General Barth, still hopeful that something might be salvaged from this disaster, occu-pied a defensive position south of the town. Little digging was done as most of the troops had thrown away their entrenching tools. Officers 'liberated' tools from Korean farmers, from whom they also purchased vegetables and rice, as military supplies had run out. Rumours were rife: a train was waiting down the road which would take them all to Pusan and from there they would go back by sea to Japan. On 8 July rations appeared and all had a hot meal, the first for four days. Morale rose a little as the march south continued. By degrees, and using relays of trucks, the 34th took up a new defensive position north of the Kum river and the town of Konju. But the rot had set in; when the North Koreans came in to the attack, someone shouted, 'Let's get the hell out of here.' The rout continued.

It would be many months before the American army recovered the form it had shown in the Second World War. At the start of the Korean War the Americans paid the high price extracted from any liberal democracy whose politicians have decided that there are no votes in defence, and who cannot be persuaded by their professional advisers that nothing is as certain as the unexpected. The malaise from which these troops were suffering was due to the post-1945 reaction against anything savouring of militarism or seen as preparation for further conflict. They went into action early in July 1950 ill-disciplined, physically soft and dangerously under-trained in even basic infantry skills, bearing an alarming resemblance in many ways to the venal rabble portrayed in the Phil Silvers 'Sergeant Bilko' TV comedies. The disciplinary powers of commanding officers and NCOs had been undermined by strenuous efforts to 'democratize' the army since 1945.

Louis Heren, the experienced war correspondent of the London *Times*, was appalled at the state of the 24th and other American infantry divisions in the opening weeks of the war. Not once did he see signs of instant response to orders given in action. Following one unit into a town, he noted a platoon commander ordering his dangerously bunched men to spread out; there was no reaction. He tried again, twice, without success, 'eventually shouting petulantly, "OK . . . if you get killed it will be your own damned responsibility." Many, unfortunately, were killed that day and on others.' Heren noted a lack of basic training in simple tactics. Units seldom dug in or put up wire. There was almost no patrolling of any sort. When contact was made with the enemy there was no attempt to exercise fire control; the men simply blazed away without taking deliberate aim in the general direction of the opposition. Heren put this prodigality down to the efficiency of the American logistic system which, once established in Korea, performed daily miracles of supply for all the UN forces. This lack of fire control, however, enabled the enemy to overrun American positions with ease, heedless of the wild and unaimed firing of the defence. Defective combat discipline was most evident at night, the time usually chosen by the enemy for attacking, when inexperienced soldiers quickly lost their nerve in the dark, betraying their position by random firing.

The Americans were physically unprepared for hard campaigning. In Japan there had been virtually no route marching, battle drill practice, physical training or games. In the field, 24th Division placed its faith in mechanical transport, with which it was over-endowed. Consequently, few units could be persuaded to move off roads which became choked, then broken up, as the result of the heavy traffic. The enemy, on the other hand, moved swiftly on foot, across the hills, at night whenever possible, hiding by day to avoid detection by allied aircraft. Within weeks, the efficiency of the American supply system led to further high expectations: three times a day, even in the forward positions, troops consumed huge quantities of fruit juices, chicken, candy, hamburgers, coffee, baked beans and meat flown from the USA, defrosted and brought fresh to the very front line; such richness startled the British troops when they arrived in Korea from a country where food was still rationed. Barely two months into the war, the Middlesex Regiment, newly arrived from Hong Kong, were told that ice-cream making machines had been given a higher priority than their battalion transport vehicles for the rail move from Pusan to the front. The American soldier, wrote Heren, 'had a wardrobe which was confusingly munificent, but the roads were choked with the transport carrying it . . . nearly everything that he may have wanted was supplied except books. Instead, every unit was inundated with comic magazines.'

The reluctance of American units to close with the enemy in attack or hold their positions resolutely in defence, during the calamitous opening months of the war, stemmed from a laudably humane but in the circumstances misplaced national philosophy which held that there was 'not a yard of Korean soil worth the life of an American boy. It was better to expend millions of dollars of material rather than expose our sons and husbands unnecessarily.' The outcome of this was soon to be seen in over-reliance on massive artillery support and repeated airstrikes.

If Major-General William F. Dean, the commander of the 24th Division, imagined that the fiascos at Pyongtaek and Chonan were the low-water mark of his campaign he was wrong. The town of Taejon contained his divisional headquarters and supply dumps, well stocked with fuel, rations and ammunition. He intended to make a stand in front of this important communications centre. Two junior commanders in a unit of 24th Division later recalled their experiences.

Second Lieutenant Robert Herbert was a platoon commander in Company 'G', 2nd Battalion, 19th Infantry Regiment. He had fought with the US Marines in the Pacific campaign and subsequently obtained a commission in the US Army. Sergeant First Class Joseph Szito was the mortar section leader in Company 'H' of the same battalion. Herbert was holding a position at a road junction just outside Taejon on the south-west side of the city when four tanks approached up the road from the south. It was assumed they were the supporting tanks which had arrived in 'G' Company's area the previous evening. The tanks stopped and the crews looked around from their turrets before driving north straight past Herbert, ignoring him as he stood in the corn at the side of the road. He now realized they were North Korean T-34s; they had gone before he could do anything about them. He then saw a small party of men on foot, some carrying bazookas, hurrying in the wake of the tanks. He was surprised to see that one of them was his divisional commander. They conversed at the roadside amidst burning vehicles and bodies from an earlier attack. Herbert addressed General Dean, somewhat tactlessly, with the words, 'Sir, what the f—k is going on?' Dean laughed but said nothing. Herbert returned to the charge: 'The men will stay and fight, sir, but I have to tell them what they're doing.' Dean replied:

'We're trying to hold the ground to the west of the town till the 1st Cavalry Division can get forward and attack through us.' 'When, sir?' asked Herbert. Dean laughed again: 'As soon as they can form.' He added that the 1st Cavalry were still south of the city and that nine enemy tanks had penetrated almost to his headquarters in Taejon that morning. He exhorted Herbert to 'get the tanks if they come back' and marched back towards the city with his bazooka squad.

The tanks returned almost at once; Herbert's men hit the leader repeatedly with their bazookas but failed to halt it. The tank was now dealt with at point-blank range by a 155mm gun from a medium battery deployed, with its guns facing in all directions, between Herbert's position and the city. The gun crews, he noted, were crouching in foxholes, firing their pieces by tugging at lanyards. He asked for some of the guns to be re-laid in his direction but the artillery commander refused to do this. At this point an accurate enemy artillery concentration landed on the gun position, killing many of the gun crews. Herbert's company commander jumped into a jeep and headed off for Taejon, shouting that he was going to get hold of some tank support. Herbert suspected that he might not see him again that day. It was now 1.30 p.m. and he could see elements of the 34th Infantry streaming away south from the city. To the immediate south he also saw masses of enemy hurrying eastwards to cut off the American line of retreat. As he opened fire on the enemy with an abandoned .50 calibre machine-gun he felt that it was probably time for his platoon to go as well, but there was no sign of the missing company commander. He therefore sent a runner off to General Dean asking for instructions.

In Taejon town, Sergeant Szito had been resting in a house when, at 2 p.m., he looked out of the window to see a T-34 clanking down the street spraying the buildings with machine-gun fire. In hot pursuit came General Dean and his faithful if breathless anti-tank squad. He saw Szito gazing in fascination out of the window. 'Which way did it go?' he shouted, then vanished from view, still running. Szito, keen to find out what was happening, made his way down the street to the 24th Division command post. Here he found an unreal atmosphere of calm; visitors, including press men, were still being shown an optimistically marked battle map with assurances that all was well and that there was no cause for alarm. Coffee was being served. Barely a hundred yards away, a T-34 had been stationary and unchallenged in an alley for some hours. Displaying no identification marks it was assumed to be friendly: few members of 24th Division had ever received instruction in tank recognition. The tank's crew were lounging outside it, smoking, and one actually borrowed ten gallons of fuel from a passing American officer before starting up and driving away.

In the absence of further instructions, Herbert had left his position as swarms of enemy infantry occupied it before firing on the town and on the masses of American and ROK troops escaping to the south. The streets were jammed with convoys of trucks trying to form up. It was late afternoon when Herbert entered the town and made his way to the head of a stationary column where he found an artillery major 'in a dream' sitting in his jeep. 'Sir, we have to get moving,' said Herbert. 'OK, OK,' replied the major, who asked if anyone knew the way out of the town. At 7 p.m. the column slowly got under way. Almost at once it came under fire from buildings at the roadside. Szito and Herbert found themselves near the back of the procession. More vehicles tagged on as it edged slowly out of the burning town. At one point the column divided into two and continued along parallel streets, the two parts shooting enthusiastically at each other whenever they came into sight. One column took a wrong turn and ended up in a school yard where some fifty vehicles barged frantically at each other in their attempts to escape from the jam.

The enemy were now closing in on all sides. Szito, a man of initiative, found an abandoned 60mm mortar and a supply of bombs, with which he opened fire on the enemy. He then laid a dense smoke screen which enabled some half-tracks to get clear. They were soon blocked by another half-track whose driver had been shot dead whilst trying to shove abandoned trucks off the road. No one seemed willing to dismount and help push this vehicle to one side. An enemy mortar which was fighting a duel with Szito managed to knock out three more trucks which caught fire. At 8.45 p.m. someone gave the order to soak all the vehicles in petrol and fire them. Szito watched as the convoy went up in flames. In the school yard the artillery major who had led the column astray gave the order to take to the high ground and made off on foot with 120 men, leaving his trucks intact. General Dean also took to the hills, where he wandered for nearly a month before being captured. On his release from captivity in 1953 he was awarded the Congressional Medal of Honor.

Herbert and Szito reached Chinju, where the 19th Regiment was able to reorganize. On 26 July it was joined by the 29th Infantry Regiment, newly arrived from garrison duty on Okinawa. Herbert was unimpressed with the new arrivals, describing them as 'a mob of rounded-up service personnel' (in other words, storemen, clerks, orderlies, mechanics and messmen). On 28 July the commanding officer of the 2nd Battalion of the 19th, Lieutenant-Colonel McCrail, briefed Herbert to join a reconnaissance patrol of 60 men, commanded by Captain Barscz, which was to travel in two 2½ ton trucks. A company of the 29th Regiment had gone ahead towards the town of Hadong, some 30 miles to the south-west, to see if any enemy were there.

After about ten miles Herbert, in the leading truck, met two ROK soldiers, one of them wounded, in a jeep; they said that there were 300 guerrillas with mortars at Hadong and that the company of the 29th had been ambushed there. Soon, Herbert came across a truck containing 15 demoralized men of the 29th who said they had been overrun and lost all their equipment. A little further on he met with about fifty stragglers, on foot, coming from Hadong; most were without boots and even clothing, having been surprised and disarmed as they bathed in a creek. Barscz sent them back to Chinju in the trucks with a message for the rest of his company to join him at once to set up a roadblock. One of the sergeants of the 29th was in tears; he had fought in north-west Europe, he said, but had never seen anything like what had gone on in Hadong. A little further on, Herbert came across an officer of the 29th, in an equally emotional state, who said: 'Shit – it was a f—g disgrace; my men threw away their weapons and ran off.'

Next day saw the 2/19th in close combat with the enemy who had advanced from Hadong. Herbert deployed his platoon on high ground west of Chinju, overlooking a valley down which hundreds of refugees were streaming. Many seemed openly hostile and Herbert's platoon sergeant shot dead a 'refugee' who was signalling the platoon's position to the rapidly approaching enemy. At 5 a.m. on 31 July the battalion was attacked for four hours. By now the unit was beginning to perform as a team and morale was consequently rising. But sheer weight of numbers told and Company 'G' was compelled to wade back across a river and take up new positions as the enemy continued to press forward. An outpost was established and Herbert was ordered to take his platoon forward and dig in on the sandbanks overlooking a crossing place. When he protested that this would place him in the line of fire of the other companies he was told to obey his orders and get on with it.

After dark the enemy started to cross the river by the light of flares. Men began to wander back from the firing line and the enemy, now across the river, began to exploit the yawning gaps between the battalion's companies. Using whistles to pass messages, the enemy fought their way into the heart of the American position. Herbert's platoon had been reinforced that day with raw new arrivals, who needed watching. They were clearly shaken even by the sound of tank engines and matters were not improved when the company came under accurate fire from friendly artillery. Herbert now gave one of the new reinforcements an air recognition panel with the words: 'I don't care if you lose your weapon but for Christ's sake don't lose this!' The platoon ran back to the top of a nearby hill and formed a perimeter.

It was now 3 a.m. on 1 August. Over the radio Herbert was told that the battalion had been overrun and was withdrawing as best it could. Barscz ordered the remnants of the company back to defend the gun lines on the road back to Chinju. At the sound of engines the men took cover in a ditch as eight tanks, carrying infantry, rushed past. Firing could be heard in all directions. Herbert persuaded Barscz to keep moving. The company commander agreed and said he would bring up the rear of the column, now down to less than fifty men, 'and kick ass' to keep the men going. Many of them were now exhausted and decidedly jumpy. When friendly artillery opened up nearby one man blazed away in the direction of the guns. Stragglers from other companies were picked up on the way. As dawn broke, Barscz ordered the men to rest; from a hilltop they watched as the enemy entered Chinju, which was now well ablaze.

All Sergeant Szito's mortars had been lost at Taejon and his platoon was now fighting as a rifle section. For five days he took part in fighting around Chinju and was commissioned in the field on the 29th. Next day he was ordered to take a platoon on to high ground overlooking the river across which the enemy was expected to attack. All afternoon, in a state of extreme frustration, he watched the enemy build-up along the river. His rations were purloined by a retiring rifle company. Szito stayed on his hilltop all night but when he tried to contact battalion HQ at dawn there was no reply. The company nearest to him had promised to tell him when they retired but failed to do so. He marched back to Chinju, rejoined Company 'F' on high ground overlooking the town and was placed in command of a platoon of 30 newly arrived reinforcements.

The enemy attacked just after midnight. One platoon of the new men in Company 'F' broke at once and fled, intermingled with North Koreans. Szito's platoon opened fire, killing 'F' Company men wholesale with the enemy. In the midst of the fight the executive officer, more or less from force of habit, went off in a jeep to the rear to collect rations and returned safely. The battalion was disintegrating, and although Szito and Colonel McCrail tried to steady the men and slow them down, many kept on running. Some were guided into a school yard and sorted out. One of the senior captains was seen to jump into a jeep despite Szito's accusing shouts and to make off at high speed, finishing up in Masan, 30 miles away. Here, he was found later in the day when an exhausted Szito and the rest of the company arrived there, 'clean shaven and apparently well rested, still sitting in his jeep'. When the battalion sorted itself out, 20 miles to the east of Chinju, a roll-call revealed that 15 of the 30 new reinforcements sent to Szito's platoon were missing. Nobody knew their names; there had been no time to compile rosters at divisional, regimental or battalion level.

Szito's comments on the battalion's performance were perceptive. The commanding officer had run the battle from the rear instead of well up with his inexperienced companies. The commander of Company 'H' was at battalion headquarters throughout and not with his men. Radio communications were appalling. 'Bug-out fever' was rife and it was impossible to control the men, who tended to 'bug' after a single round of enemy fire. It was hopeless trying to fight it out with the few who stood firm; there was no alternative to going with those bugging-out in the hopes that control might be regained.

In the months to come, there would be great changes in the American army in Korea, but until its confidence had been restored there were many more disasters to be endured.

CHAPTER 5

Forming Freedom's Team

As the American forces retreated, governments around the world were studying the UN resolution and deciding if they were going to stand up and be counted. In Washington it was assumed that the United Kingdom would be quick to offer ships and troops as proof of adherence to the UN Charter and it was hoped that the Commonwealth, in the shape of Australia, Canada, New Zealand and perhaps India and Pakistan, would follow suit. This displayed a somewhat naïve view on the part of the American leadership, which had yet to appreciate the changes wrought by two world wars in the relationships between what they still believed was the revered mother country and its overseas dominions. Although in the end these did readily co-operate, there were notable changes in their approach to this new challenge. They no longer saw themselves – as had *Punch* at the time of the Boer War – as young cubs marching proudly behind the old lion; they were now nations in their own right, and not automatically sympathetic to appeals from London.

Australia responded at once by offering naval units. Her destroyers were frequent visitors to the port of Kure and one was on station there at the outbreak of the Korean War; others were to follow, to render sterling service. The Australian infantry battalion at Kure was not initially made available, having been run down to cadre strength. However, 77 (Fighter) Squadron of the Royal Australian Air Force, equipped with P-51 Mustangs based at Iwakuni near Hiroshima, was offered to the UN, as were the services of a transport flight. The New Zealand government agreed to place two frigates at UN disposal; they sailed for Japanese waters on 1 July. Both New Zealand and Australia, as Pacific basin nations, felt that they had a strong geographic interest in the Korean peninsula whilst disclaiming any strategic or economic involvement.

Canada had no interest whatever in the Far East. Its government approached Washington rather than London for advice. The head of the Canadian joint defence staff in London, however, was able to inform Ottawa on 28 June that the British government had stressed to him the importance of showing the world that NATO and the Commonwealth nations were firmly behind the United States in its positive approach to the Korean crisis. Premier Louis St Laurent was at pains to point out on 30 June, when offering three destroyers, that whilst Canada was ready to participate 'to achieve the ends of peace', it was not making war on any nation, but was taking part in a peacekeeping operation under UN direction. The last thing St Laurent wished for was to be seen as acting in collusion with the United States.

So far the Commonwealth's offers of support had been limited to naval and air force elements. On 14 July, however, as the land battle in Korea went from bad to worse, Trygve Lie appealed urgently for ground troops to be made available as soon as possible. At this time Australian politicians favoured an Australian–American alliance. They believed that the United Kingdom was too far away, and in any case too close to bankruptcy, to be of any real assistance to the distant dominion in the event of a crisis in the 'Asian fringe' which could threaten Australian security. Percy Spender, Minister for External Affairs, strongly recommended sending the Kure infantry battalion directly to Korea if its men volunteered to go, or raising a volunteer battalion in Australia. He also suggested sending the RAAF's Singapore-based heavy bomber squadron. Spender was an ardent proponent of the American connection and hoped that these offers would help to seal the bond.

The Australian Premier Robert Menzies, an avid Anglophile and royalist, was in London at this time. He attended a Cabinet meeting on 17 July at which the Korean crisis was discussed, but did not agree to sending the Japan battalion as it would be no more than a token force subsumed into a larger American formation, where it would have to be re-equipped and rapidly lose its identity. In any case, he told the British Cabinet, the battalion's men were barred under the constitution from service in Korea and were due to return home to form the training nucleus of the new Interim Army. He agreed with the prevailing British view that it was in the Middle East that Australia's contribution to Commonwealth security could most effectively be made; he accordingly signalled Canberra to keep quiet and wait until the British government had made up its mind. The New Zealand government, whose foreign policies ran on similar lines to Australia's, came to the same conclusion. It felt that the offer of two New Zealand frigates was commensurate with the size and remoteness of their country, which had residual Middle East commitments and whose army in any case was little more than a training cadre. However, the old ties of empire seem to have been stronger than in Australia. A cartoon in the *Auckland Star* at the time of the New Zealand contingent's eventual embarkation in December 1950 depicts a determined New Zealand soldier boarding the troopship with the words: 'Where Britain goes, we go'.

The Canadian Chiefs of Staff met in Ottawa on 18 July. The Chief of the General Staff, General Foulkes, argued that Canada should send a brigade group to operate 'within a Commonwealth division'. This was radical thinking, a germ of what was to mature a year later. The creation of such a brigade group would, however, denude Canada of almost all its ground forces. A special force would have to be created following a call for volunteers. In addition, the Canadian government's insistence that its troops served in Korea only as international policemen conflicted with the roles foreseen by other Commonwealth members.

Whilst the Commonwealth and other UN member nations debated their possible contributions, MacArthur's requests to Washington for reinforcement grew ever more desperate. The American Chiefs of Staff felt that the emphasis should be on English-speaking nations and that ground combat troops were urgently needed if catastrophe was to be averted.

In Australia, Spender was still urging the early despatch of infantry from Japan. He had a strong supporter in the person of Lieutenant-General Sir Horace Robertson, the Australian commander of the British Commonwealth Occupation Force (BCOF) in Japan. On 26 July the Australian Chiefs of Staff in Melbourne decided that the former 57th Infantry Battalion in Japan, the Kure battalion, recently renamed the 3rd Battalion, Royal Australian Regiment (3 RAR), should be placed at the UN's disposal, equipped as well as possible and brought to full strength with volunteers. On the same day a signal reached Canberra from the Australian Defence Liaison Staff in London; Britain had offered to send a strong brigade group, which would start to mobilize and equip at once. Spender was furious; he felt he had been trumped by London and the political benefits of what he had thought would be a splendid goodwill gesture to the US thrown away. He suspected Menzies' hand in all this. But when Menzies arrived in Washington he addressed Congress, firmly committing his country to partnership with the US 'in a great and continuing adventure towards human liberty'. This marked a watershed in Australian foreign policy and the signing of the ANZUS pact of 1951 followed, which further tied Australia and New Zealand in with America. Thus Percy Spender's studious diplomatic campaign paid off, in a progressive loosening of the London–Canberra ties.

New Zealand had actually beaten Australia to the post, for on 24 July Premier Sidney Holland informed Attlee by cable that his government had decided to send a specialist unit – probably a medium artillery regiment – to Korea, that it was intended to equip and arm it on American lines, and that it would sail from New Zealand at the end of October. Whilst it was hoped that it would eventually operate as part of a Commonwealth formation, should one be drawn up, it would otherwise become part of an American formation.

An announcement was made by the British, Australian and New Zealand governments on 26 July confirming their readiness to send ground forces. On the same day the United States asked Canada to send a brigade group. The request was accepted on 27 July. It was stressed, though, that the brigade was to serve as a *Canadian* brigade, under Canadian officers, carrying out 'Canada's obligations under the UN Charter or the North Atlantic Pact'.

In 1950 the Union of South Africa was viewed with a jaundiced eye by London. The internal policies of its nationalist government, under the intransigent Afrikaner premier Daniel Malan, indicated that a rigid policy of apartheid was about to be applied, to the detriment of the civil rights of the black and coloured population. Despite this, the South African government, whilst making it clear that it had absolutely no interest in Korean affairs, agreed on 29 July to call for volunteers to serve on attachment in all three British armed services, rather than send South African units to Korea. The British government was then spared embarrassment when the South African government changed its mind. On 4 August it offered the United Nations all the fully trained aircrew and technical personnel needed to man a fighter squadron, to be placed under US Air Force command, and was negotiating to buy 95 P-51 Mustangs from the US government. The offer was accepted and No. 2 Fighter Squadron, the celebrated 'Flying Cheetahs', was selected to represent South Africa.

The idea of a Commonwealth force for Korea took some time to evolve. New Zealand's suggestion that its artillery regiment should be associated with the Australian battalion met with agreement in Canberra. Britain then proposed that the promised United Kingdom brigade group should merge with the Australian/New Zealand contingents. This would amount to a very strong brigade group or even, with a few additions, a light division; such a formation would firmly establish a Commonwealth identity among the other UN contingents. The idea did not immediately commend itself to the Canadians, who did not wish to identify with either a Commonwealth or American formation and still saw their contribution in terms of a UN police contingent 'which happened to consist of Commonwealth troops'. They went on to suggest that it would be advantageous to include non-Commonwealth troops (as had been the case with the Canadian 2nd Army in north-west Europe in 1944–5), their preference being for the newly proffered Turkish brigade.

There were thus intra-Commonwealth divergences over the constitution of a combined formation, despite the obvious logic of bringing it about as soon as possible. There was considerable uneasiness over the likely choice of a commander, and relations with Canberra were hardly improved by the appointment of a British liaison officer, Air Vice-Marshal Cecil Bouchier, to MacArthur's headquarters as representative of the British Chiefs of Staff. Until now, General Robertson, as commander-in-chief of BCOF, had regarded himself as sole spokesman for the Commonwealth in Tokyo. Bouchier's arrival was unlikely to commend itself to the fiery Australian general, who was quick to make his feelings known. In his eyes the British had set up a direct line to MacArthur which bypassed the BCOF link, and had displayed a hurtful lack of trust in his ability as BCOF commander and Commonwealth liaison officer at Supreme Headquarters. Robertson feared that the British were secretly planning to send an all-UK contingent to Korea, to be placed unreservedly under MacArthur's command, and that he would have no authority over it.

'Red Robbo', as he was known throughout the Australian army, was a veteran of the calamitous Gallipoli campaign of 1915, when nearly 7,000 Australian troops had been killed in a series of battles overseen by British generals; during the Second World War he had seen a few months' active service in North Africa but had spent the remainder of the war in senior staff appointments in Australia, a fact which irked him. He had an alarmingly low flashpoint, and could be extremely difficult to deal with. Bouchier was perhaps not the best choice for this appointment, reluctantly emerging from retirement to go to Tokyo, where he had already served for several years under Robertson as a senior air staff officer.

Britain faced huge strategic problems after 1945. Occupation forces were required in Germany, Austria and Trieste, in the former Italian, Dutch and French empires, to see out the mandate in Palestine and to regain sovereignty over territories lost to the Japanese from 1942 onwards. The post-war government was determined to cling to what remained of empire after the departure from India in 1947, and to sustain Britain's place as one of the victorious great powers which had brought down the Axis; but this had to be done against a background of national insolvency and military rundown on a huge scale. The three pillars of British defence policy after 1945 centred on defence of the home base (including western Europe), the security of sea communications, and the maintenance of a firm grip on the Middle East, regarded as the crossroads of trade with the Empire and, because of a shortage of dollars for the purchase of American oil, the main source of Britain's petroleum supplies.

Attlee came under pressure in the first years of peace from his Chancellor, Hugh Dalton, to reimpose the 'ten-year rule' – the seriously flawed assumption that there would be no recurrence of general war for at least ten years which had dogged British defence policy between the two world wars. This was resisted, but many key development programmes were slowed down or killed off despite emergent communist threats in the Far East and rising tides of nationalism throughout Africa and Asia. There was, however, an understanding by the Chiefs of Staff that British forces would not be involved in major operations in the next three or four years. Intense pressure was placed on industry to convert from war to peace production and to make the goods so urgently needed for export. Vast American loans had to be serviced and in view of this overriding priority the service chiefs drifted into tacit acceptance of what actually emerged as a five-year rule with no rolling datelines.

The first post-war years had not been happy ones for inter-service harmony. By 1947 the naval and RAF chiefs, Sir John Cunningham and Sir Arthur

Tedder, were at least unified in detestation of Field Marshal Lord Montgomery, whose vanity and love of publicity appalled the others. Montgomery, who hated committee work and liked to be a one-man band, was neither successful nor popular as Chief of the Imperial General Staff. He was addicted to flying off around the world to visit foreign statesmen and service chiefs, returning to tell Attlee and Bevin what they should be doing in the field of foreign relations. Occasionally he was right, to everyone's fury. In 1948 he set himself against the other two chiefs, who had settled for a twelve-month National Service period, by going direct to Attlee and persuading the government to opt for eighteen months. The wisdom of this was manifest when, after the start of the Korean War, it was found necessary to raise it further to two years; the nation would not have accepted a doubling of the service period. Later in 1948 Attlee was able to kick his turbulent CIGS upstairs into European and NATO appointments. Montgomery's departure was viewed with relief in Whitehall, where he had planted one other seed which would bear later fruit: the creation of a defence overlord's post as Chief of the Defence Staff.

Attlee was now able to appoint a new CIGS. Against Montgomery's peevish protests he called General Sir William Slim out of his retirement post, on the board of British Railways. It was an inspired appointment; Slim enjoyed the respect and affection of all three services and was above all a pragmatist on excellent personal terms with the Prime Minister, a fellow veteran of the Gallipoli campaign. Lord Fraser of the North Cape became First Sea Lord and professional head of the Royal Navy and Tedder continued as Chief of the Air Staff until 1950 when he was succeeded by Sir John Slessor, another distinguished airman and a convinced believer in joint services collaboration. This triumvirate of safe hands in charge of the British armed forces enjoyed, in Emanuel Shinwell, the ardent support of a Defence Minister who respected and liked them, and was prepared to fight every inch of the way to see they got a fair deal from the government.

Shinwell, made Defence Minister in 1950, had previously been Secretary of State for War, the minister responsible for the Army, an appointment initially viewed with horror by the professional military establishment; but he was immediately seen as a breath of fresh air. In later life he confessed to his intense pride, having been jailed as a conscientious objector in the Kaiser's war, at having been appointed War, and then Defence Minister. He rapidly achieved an excellent working relationship with the service chiefs. The government's parliamentary majority after the February 1950 election was very small, so it was as well that a strong ministerial and services team was united in Whitehall, as war loomed in Korea.

There was a very disappointing response to the Security Council's resolution of 7 July calling for all UN member states to supply military forces and other aid to South Korea. This was perhaps to be expected, given the dismal situation in Korea at that time following the defeat of Task Force Smith and the rout of the 24th Division. As a result, the US Defense Department let it be known on 13 July that America could not be expected to bear the entire burden. There was an unspoken preference for contingents which could be expected to perform well in battle, such as those from Britain, New Zealand and Australia. At this stage, Pakistan was also on the Washington list. Other JCS general criteria for UN troops, based on recommendations from MacArthur's staff, were that the contingent should amount to at least a strong battalion with first reinforcements, its own artillery support, and sufficient English speakers to avoid confusion in battle. For diplomatic reasons Acheson believed that all offers should be accepted, however conditionally, and Defense Secretary Johnson agreed that the smaller nations must at least be given the opportunity to make their contribution. The JCS reluctantly agreed to accept offers of a minimum of company-sized groups; this applied in the end only to Luxembourg, whose rifle company would form part of the Belgian battalion.

Oliver Franks wrote to Attlee from Washington stressing the importance for the future of the Anglo-American alliance that Britain send at least a token ground force as quickly as possible. Slim said a token force would be no use because of the administrative effort needed to support it so far from the home base. He also opposed taking units from Malaya, where they were much needed and where their withdrawal would have a bad effect on civilian morale. He felt that the Americans did not realize the extent of the British anti-communist commitment in Malaya and recommended a public relations campaign in the US in order to redress this. Slessor, as Chief of the Air Staff, favoured strategic bombing of North Korean cities to force their troops back across the 38th parallel. He appeared to have in mind a form of 'air control', as he and his contemporaries had practised it between the wars in Iraq and on the North-West Frontier, when the civilian population were given due warning before the airstrike by means of airdropped leaflets.

Attlee, anxious to help but acutely aware of the precarious British economy and the effort needed to field a viable force for Korea, signalled Oliver Franks, asking just how important this was to the 'special relationship'. Franks answered at once; Korea had to be seen as a United Nations affair and a positive response was essential. Britain was still highly regarded as the United States' true and dependable partner despite everything; failure to produce ground troops would be seen as overt disapproval of US policy in Korea and would adversely affect the impending US appropriations for NATO defence, as well as for European reconstruction. This was little short of moral blackmail, not unusual in coalition politics, but it settled the matter. On 24 July Attlee told the Defence Committee that notwithstanding military objections to sending troops to Korea, the political, economic and psychological factors were paramount and the service chiefs must accept this. Slim had already privately concluded that nothing short of a strong brigade group would suffice; he saw this as consisting of an armoured regiment, three infantry battalions, a regiment of artillery and the proffered New Zealand medium artillery regiment as well. To send such a force at full war establishments would necessitate calling at least 2,000 regular reservists back to the colours. It would take at least two months to assemble the brigade group and prepare it for the five-week sea passage; under no circumstances was it to draw on the Hong Kong or Malayan garrisons.

Once the burden of this was signalled to Washington, Truman immediately signed an Act confirming the continuance of US military aid to 'certain free world nations', especially the western European NATO partners. Britain was irrevocably sealed into the compact. Shinwell called for a supplementary defence budget of £30 million for 1950 and a further £70 million in 1951/2. For the first time, dissenting voices were raised in Cabinet, notably that of Aneurin Bevan whose cherished National Health Service was threatened. Shinwell also called for the extension of National Service from eighteen months to two years, drawing heated protests from the left wing of the Labour Party; but Attlee, Bevin and Shinwell carried the unpalatable measure through a divided Cabinet. Many years later, as a centenarian member of the House of Lords, Shinwell recalled the private meeting between the three men before the Cabinet meeting: 'Clem, Ernie and I were determined to get this across whether they liked it or not. You see, there were people round that table whose inclinations, you might say, lay closer to the Vistula than the Thames.'

From this moment, Britain rearmed. A week later, the United States called on its NATO partners to submit shopping lists for enhancement of their armed forces and military production programmes to meet the perceived increase in the communist threat. Sir Stafford Cripps, Britain's austere Chancellor of the Exchequer, surprisingly called for even higher levels of defence expenditure and for money to set up a Civil Defence programme. It was evident that US funding would be required, as would cuts in government spending in other fields. Aneurin Bevan fiercely attacked his own government, contending that it had been British policy to give social and economic aid to countries under communist threat, but now we had adopted the American line of military confrontation, leading inevitably to an arms race. He stuck to his guns in opposing all increases in defence expenditure and resigned on this issue in 1951.

The decision to increase National Service to two years had gained the army some 50,000 men in the short term for overseas service and for a small strategic reserve. A recruiting campaign was also initiated to enlist men under the age of 30 for Korean service who had at least eighteen months' previous service, and who came to be known as 'K' volunteers.

The situation in Korea remained critical and whilst the promise of the

British brigade group was welcomed in Washington, MacArthur called for a small British contribution in the immediate future rather than a large one later on. Senior officers in Whitehall felt that, as a matter of honour, MacArthur's request must be met. On 17 August the chiefs recommended that two infantry battalions, but no tanks, should be sent from Hong Kong to Korea as a stopgap, pending the arrival of the 29th Independent Brigade Group from the UK, after which they would be returned. Attlee approved this on 23 August and orders were given for the 1st Battalions of the Middlesex Regiment and the Argyll and Sutherland Highlanders to prepare for immediate embarkation.

The first Royal Naval ships to arrive off the Korean coast were the cruiser HMS *Jamaica* and the frigates *Black Swan*, *Alacrity* and *Hart*. All had been cruising in Japan's Inland Sea in company with the aircraft carrier *Triumph*, the cruiser *Belfast* and the destroyer *Cossack* when news of the North Korean invasion reached the fleet.

Midshipman Michael Muschamp of the Royal New Zealand Navy was serving in *Jamaica*. On 2 July the ship was cruising off the east coast of Korea in company with the American cruiser *Juneau* and the frigate *Black Swan* when a flotilla of North Korean gunboats was sighted. Muschamp was asleep in the gunroom flat – the home of the midshipmen – when bells rang and bugles sounded through the ship calling all hands to action stations.

A very perturbed 18-year-old donned clothes, anti-flash gear and a tin hat in triple-quick time. I made my way to my action station on the bridge where I was 'captain's doggie', a kind of junior ADC-cum-messenger boy. I soon saw what all the fuss was about. There were six small craft, trapped between three UN warships and the shore, firing what appeared to be 20mm and 40mm cannon at *Juneau* and *Jamaica*. The two cruisers got the range of the craft and sank four within ten minutes. Another ran ashore in flames and the sixth escaped to seaward. The American Rear-Admiral in *Juneau* ordered *Black Swan* to give chase . . . Had he bothered to look in *Jane's Fighting Ships* he would have seen that frigates of that class, built during the Second World War as anti-submarine vessels, had a top speed of 18 knots while motor torpedo boats can manage twice that with ease. With her Chief Stoker sitting on the safety valve *Black Swan* did give chase but to no avail. So one-sixth of the North Korean navy lived to fight another day. Several survivors from the MTBs were fished out of the water and interrogated by our South Korean liaison officer. 'Why didn't you use your torpedoes?' 'Oh, the Russians were going to teach us how to fire them next week.' No hits had been scored on any of the UN ships. It might have been a very different story a week later.

Muschamp witnessed a tragic incident a few days after this. On 8 July, *Jamaica* went close inshore to bombard the east coast road, using her main 6-inch battery as well as close-range weapons. The ship was carrying a number of soldiers from the Hong Kong garrison on a change-of-air cruise. They had readily volunteered to act as ammunition numbers, passing ready-use shells from the deck magazines to the Bofors and Oerlikon gun crews on the upper deck. Rounding a headland the ship came under fire from three masked batteries which scored a direct hit on the mainmast, spraying the upper deck with lethal fragments, killing or wounding ten of the young sailors and soldiers serving the guns. They were the first British casualties of the Korean War and the dead were buried at sea next day, watched by a subdued ship's company.

The light fleet carrier HMS *Triumph* had joined the American naval task force off the Korean east coast within days of the North Korean invasion and her aircraft, a mix of Seafires and Fireflies, were soon in action. *Triumph* was in company with the USS *Valley Forge*, a much larger carrier which, with its Panther jets, was a source of wonder to the crew of the smaller British ship. The Seafire, a naval version of the well-tried Spitfire, was too frail for battering deck landings and the deceleration wrinkled the thin metal skin of the airframe. There were numerous crashes as pilots returned from missions over the coast. The ship was wearing out; like the Royal Navy's other light fleet carriers she had been built hurriedly during the Second World War to a Lloyds' specification with a view to possible post-war conversion as a fast merchantman. By the summer of 1950 she was finding it difficult to steam at more than 23 knots and as it required a major effort to set up the launching catapult for the Fireflies – this was before the steam catapult was in service – her crew had to work hard to maintain a high level of operational efficiency.

Triumph also carried a single Sea Otter, a biplane amphibian aircraft derived from the celebrated *Walrus*, for communications flying and, in emergency, for air-sea rescue. On 19 July an outstanding rescue was made when a US Navy Corsair fighter-bomber off *Valley Forge*, hit by enemy fire, had to ditch 120 miles from the carriers, close to the North Korean port of Wonsan and well outside helicopter range. Lieutenant Cane, the Sea Otter pilot, flew towards the scene of the ditching in poor visibility and made radio contact with two Corsairs circling protectively above the downed pilot in his dinghy. They reported that the seas were getting higher by the minute. Arriving at the scene, Cane saw that a 30-knot wind was lashing the sea into white foam, with choppy waves at least six feet high. Cane's observer, Aircrewman O'Nion, recalled the landing: 'We hit the first wave with a hell of a bang and I thought we would dive into the sea with the next one, but with consummate skill Lieutenant Cane held the nose up and we settled into a trough.' Taxiing up to the dinghy, Cane and O'Nion were warmly greeted by Lieutenant Wendell R. Muncie USN, who confessed to a feeling of awe as what appeared to be a Wright biplane threw itself on to the water. O'Nion, standing in the open fore hatch, dragged Muncie aboard after sinking the dinghy. Cane described the take-off as 'very exciting because it consisted of ploughing into the sea, banging from wave to wave, trying not to porpoise, until a wave threw the aircraft into the air with just enough airspeed to enable me to keep it there without hitting the next wave'.

In the cabin with the drenched Muncie, O'Nion recalled that 'it felt like being in a roller-coaster . . . seas were breaking over the top mainplane and the engine, which spluttered and caught again'. Landing back on *Triumph* called for superb airmanship, as the ship's fighters were ranged forward on the heaving flight deck and the crash barrier was up. Both Cane and O'Nion were decorated for this outstanding rescue. Muncie afterwards confessed that he had found the rescue far more terrifying than his ditching.

Within days of the start of the war, whilst things were going from bad to worse ashore, the North Korean air force had been driven out of the sky by the skill, aggressive tactics and superior aircraft of the US Air Force and Navy. At sea, following the destruction of the enemy torpedo boats, maritime supremacy had been achieved; a tight blockade was established around the Korean coast and even now, only three weeks after the invasion, MacArthur was beginning to think in terms of an amphibious landing in the enemy rear.

CHAPTER 6

In the Perimeter

The 27th Infantry Brigade had moved from England to Hong Kong in May 1949 to reinforce the colony's defences against the newly victorious forces of Mao Tse-tung. By the summer of 1950, the brigade consisted of the 1st Battalions of the Royal Leicestershire Regiment, the Middlesex Regiment, and the Argyll and Sutherland Highlanders; its commander was Brigadier Basil Aubrey Coad, formerly of the Wiltshire Regiment, an experienced infantryman regarded by Slim as a safe pair of hands; a 'good plain cook', as he put it. All three battalions were well below war strength and three-quarters of the officers and men were National Service conscripts, many below the age of 19. A constant turnover of National Service personnel had severely affected training. Strict economic constraints on ammunition had cut back live firing for mortar and anti-tank detachments, but the rifle companies of all 27 Brigade's battalions, hardened by vigorous practice on the hills of Hong Kong, were as fit as they could be for what awaited them in Korea.

Only two of the brigade's battalions – the Middlesex and Argylls – were to go, since the Australian battalion in Japan had now been warned for Korea. All conscripts under the age of 19 were taken off the draft and volunteers over 19 sought from the Royal Leicesters, and from the King's Own Scottish Borderers, South Staffords and King's Shropshire Light Infantry – other regiments out in Hong Kong. The small brigade thus consisted of men from a large number of units who within days had to be re-badged and absorbed into the Middlesex and the Argylls. On 25 August the two battalions went aboard the aircraft carrier *Unicorn* and the cruiser *Ceylon*, which immediately cast off and set course for Pusan accompanied by a destroyer escort. They went without a field ambulance, a field ordnance stores unit, or the normal component of RASC transport. In view of the urgency of getting them to Korea, and at the insistence of Air Vice-Marshal Bouchier in Tokyo, they also left without most of their own unit transport. For the time being, maintenance and transport in the field were to be provided by the US Army. A lack of readily available lorried transport was to dog 27 Brigade for many months. Despite the influx of volunteers from other units the battalions were well below strength. The Middlesex sailed with only 27 officers and 618 men and the Argylls were little stronger. Following on were an anti-tank battery of the Royal Artillery with 17-pounder guns, the Australian battalion, and an ordnance field park holding reserves of clothing and equipment.

The brigade arrived at Pusan on 28 August, the first United Kingdom contingent to be subjected to the standard Pusan welcoming routine: a black US Army band giving a superb rendition of the 'St Louis Blues March', troops of well-drilled Korean schoolchildren waving Union flags and singing a barely recognizable version of 'God Save the King', and ladies in colourful Korean national dress festooning the embarrassed Coad with flowers; when the pipes and drums of the Argylls marched off the ship the crowds were suitably awe-struck. These first United Nations troops to arrive were not only much appreciated as a sign of solidarity; their bearing and evident discipline promised well for the future.

At once it was found that American staff procedures were entirely different from those of the British army. The appointment of Brigade Major, or chief of staff, meant nothing to the Americans, and had to be translated to 'S3'. The resounding title of 'Deputy Assistant Adjutant and Quartermaster-General' or DAA & QMG caused even more confusion when it was found that the post was held by a junior major, whose American equivalent combined the functions of the S1 and S4. American artillery support, on which the brigade relied, followed unfamiliar radio procedures and used mils instead of degrees when adjusting fire. It was clear that much had to be learned in a very short time, for the situation ashore had reached crisis point, and the most that Brigadier Coad could hope for was that his young soldiers would not be committed to battle until they had become familiar with the ground and to working alongside the Americans and Koreans.

Recovered from the initial surprise, the American war machine reacted impressively. Early in July, MacArthur had warned the Pentagon that the North Koreans were far stronger than had been believed and that at least four more American divisions were required on the ground immediately. More naval and air reinforcements were also warned for the Far East, including a full US Marine division to augment the Provisional Marine Brigade which was in action in the Pusan perimeter by early August. At this time there was no larger Marine formation worldwide, but by stripping many embassies of their traditional Marine guards and taking drafts from the US 6th Fleet in the Mediterranean, battalions were formed into the division which was shortly to perform so outstandingly.

Chiang Kai-shek now offered 30,000 of his troops from Formosa. This offer, heavily laden with political implications, was examined at length in Tokyo by MacArthur and by the JCS. MacArthur recommended that the offer be declined on military grounds alone; he knew that the Chinese nationalists were of dubious quality, had been resoundingly defeated on the mainland, were politically unreliable and poorly led, had little or no artillery or logistic back-up and would be an albatross around his neck. Moreover, their absence from Formosa would invite invasion from the mainland. But it was important publicly to back Chiang as his presence on Formosa diverted communist Chinese forces from moving into Korea or elsewhere in the Far East. MacArthur was authorized to make contact with the nationalists and report on their potential capabilities. When he flew into Formosa he personally set the agenda without reference to the Joint Chiefs or the Department of State, and took no political or diplomatic advisers. Reaction in Washington was distinctly nervous; MacArthur replied, with a hint of irritation, that he was acting meticulously in accord with presidential directives. He added that under no circumstances would he think of extending or exceeding his authority as theatre commander and hoped that neither the President nor the Secretary of Defense had been misinformed by 'false or speculative reports from any source'. From this exchange onward, a perceptible peevishness entered relations between MacArthur and the President and his advisers in Washington.

By the end of the first week in August the ground situation in Korea had stabilized. Much of the credit for this was due to the energy of the officer appointed in mid-July to command the UN ground forces, which were henceforth to be known as 8th US Army, Korea (EUSAK). Lieutenant-General Walton H. Walker, a Texan, was 61 and on the verge of retirement when he was sent from Japan as MacArthur's field commander. He had commanded the 8th US Army in Japan for two years and was aware of its manifold deficiencies, which he had been unable to remedy. Setting up his field headquarters in Taegu within sound of the guns, he tirelessly visited front-line units, impressing on all the absolute need to stand and die rather than carry on retreating; he could see that the morale of his army was at rock bottom following its precipitate retreat and his first aim was to instil confidence. In appearance he resembled a pugnacious bulldog and his words carried weight despite what many of his subordinates recall as a curiously uncharismatic delivery.

By mid-August Walker was holding the Pusan perimeter with what was left of the ROK army, four depleted American infantry divisions, and the Provisional Marine Brigade, a total of 65,000 men. The ROKs held the eastern sector with their right flank on the sea, and American divisions were placed across the front where they could bolster the line at its most vulnerable points, notably in front of the city of Taegu. Reinforcements were beginning to arrive; the Marines brought with them their own air wing of fighter-bombers flown by

Marine pilots who were also fully experienced infantrymen able to 'read the battle' far more readily than an air force pilot flying from a distant base. The Marines also augmented the tank force now at Walker's disposal, and the 90mm guns of their heavy Pershing tanks were more than enough to deal with the North Koreans' T-34s. By moving troops from point to point by road as new threats developed, Walker was able to hold the hard-pressed line as each North Korean attack developed. What he did not know was that despite the hammering they had received in the retreat, the Americans and ROKs had taken a great deal out of the North Korean army, a fact which only became apparent later in the autumn.

A huge reinforcement programme got under way. The US Air Force's fleet of transport aircraft quickly set up a line of communication across the Pacific. Massive expansion of the Military Sea Transport Service (MSTS), involving the recommissioning of hundreds of transport, replenishment and assault ships left in mothballs since 1945, produced the sea lift which was to sustain the United Nations effort for the rest of the war. Extra combat vessels were transferred from the US 6th Fleet in the Mediterranean and the Far East Air Force was augmented by additional strategic and medium bomber squadrons.

Although Brigadier Coad had been promised a week's breathing space in which to acclimatize his troops and train anti-tank detachments on the American 3.5-inch bazooka, a great North Korean attack was launched on 1 September and 27 Brigade was sent into the line. Coad was unaccustomed to working closely with Americans; he expected perhaps too much of the American command and staff system now and in the ensuing months. Before the brigade went into action he was beset by conflicting and contradictory orders. Accustomed to working with British divisional headquarters whose staff officers were, like him, imbued with the ethos accruing from a life spent in the friendly familiarity of the regiment, and to working with officers and commanders whom he would have known for years, he found that American staff officers seldom if ever left their headquarters and ran the battle remotely off the map without personal knowledge of the problems confronting the staffs and regimental officers who were obliged to carry out their plans. Among those affecting 27 Brigade were lack of motor transport and of organic artillery support, and in Coad's personal belief, the fact that the staff who were constantly tasking him were ignorant of the terrain over which he was supposed to fight.

The brigade took over a sector of the line from an American regiment of three battalions on the extreme left of the 1st Cavalry Division, which was deployed in front of the key city of Taegu, a prized objective for the enemy. The divisional frontage extended for over 30 miles and 27 Brigade was entrusted with ten miles of it, with just two weak battalions, two artillery batteries and a platoon of tanks, all that the hard-pressed commander of 1st

Cavalry Division could produce. The brigade was also allocated a Tactical Air Control Party or TACP from the US 5th Air Force; this was an essential support arm as it would exercise direction over any tactical airstrikes requested by Coad and his battalion commanders.

Fortunately, 27 Brigade's sector overlooking the Naktong river was quiet when it moved into the line. The battalion commanders were uneasy at the huge gaps between their rifle companies, barely covered even by the long-range fire of their Vickers medium machine-guns. To make matters worse, the Middlesex, on the right flank of the brigade, found that their immediate neighbours were a 200-man unit of the ROK National Police who were untrained, poorly disciplined and only partly armed. The Middlesex took them under their wing; the battalion sanitary corporal, who had spent the war as a prisoner of the Japanese, had a fair grasp of the language in which the former Korean army had been run and his two parties of police became known as Army groups 'A' and 'B'. The officer appointed to oversee the activities of these was Major Roly Wynn of the Middlesex who found himself in virtual command of 'Roly Force', with the job of countering the infiltration of the brigade's positions by North Koreans disguised as refugees.

As desperate battles raged either side of 27 Brigade, and the enemy secured a bridgehead over the Naktong, their sector continued to be reasonably quiet, perhaps because the enemy knew that 27 Brigade was patrolling aggressively around the clock in order to dominate its sector. Coad made a point of visiting his battalions and their American supporting units every morning and one of his brigade staff officers made the rounds at least once a day. Life was complicated by the infuriating presence of hordes of uninvited visitors from the world press and minor officials of the United Nations, all of whom had to be entertained and fed; Coad never got used to the presence of press correspondents at virtually every briefing held in 1st Cavalry divisional headquarters, even at moments of acute crisis.

General Walker held off the great North Korean attack of early September. The enemy's bridgehead across the Naktong had been contained, and by 14 September their hold on the east bank had been reduced to a narrow strip. On the eastern sector of the perimeter, the enemy thrust got to within four miles of the ancient city of Kyongju before Walker rushed troops in by road to help the ROK army plug the gap. A counter-attack restored the situation and the enemy recoiled. The confidence and morale of Walker's troops, American and Korean, began to rise. Since the beginning of September the NKPA had sustained over 10,000 casualties, and the effect of air attacks on their now overstretched line of communication was beginning to make itself felt.

Throughout the month of August the air war had been prosecuted with increasing weight. B-29 Superfortress bombers of the 19th Bombardment

Group on Okinawa ranged far into North Korea with their six-ton bomb-loads attacking industrial targets, the transport system, bridges and military installations. At first there was virtually no opposition; the enemy fighter force was out of combat and anti-aircraft fire ineffective. Extravagant claims of wide-spread destruction began to emerge from Headquarters Far East Air Force, almost certainly at the instigation of senior officers of the US Air Force back in the United States. The USAF had only emerged as a separate service three years earlier, having previously been the US Army Air Corps. Just as the Royal Air Force had struggled to assert its own identity in the years after 1918, the USAF, under determined commanders like Vandenberg, Stratemeyer and the egregious Curtis LeMay, was out to prove itself, claiming that it could, if given a free hand, subdue North Korea without the assistance of the other fighting services. Events would show this to be a fallacy; the North Koreans displayed solidarity and stoicism as Stratemeyer's bombers methodically flattened their country during the next two years; the population was driven literally under-ground, but by 1953 its resolution was still evident. All the same, by the middle of September 1950, over 250 road and rail bridges in North Korea had been destroyed and in one massive raid the Pyongyang arsenal had been eliminated.

MacArthur's assessment, early in July, that at least four more divisions would be needed had alarmed the President. Within a week MacArthur's demands had swollen to an additional field army of a further four divisions with their full supporting services. A presidential mission went post-haste to Tokyo early in August, headed by Truman's special assistant and close friend Averill Harriman, supported by General Lauris Norstad of the US Air Force. In a bril-liant unscripted presentation lasting two and a half hours MacArthur deci-sively convinced them of his need for massive reinforcement; at the same time he took the opportunity to outline the 'Chromite' plan to them. It was intended as the decisive, war-winning counterstroke, a major amphibious landing well in the enemy rear, the sort of envelopment he had perfected in the Pacific. The objective of the plan was the port of Inchon, within easy striking distance of the main airbase of Kimpo and Seoul itself. It was also 180 miles behind the lines of the North Korean army investing the Pusan perimeter. MacArthur knew it to be a huge gamble, involving the removal of up to one infantry divi-sion and the Provisional Marine Brigade from Walker's hard-pressed command.

He went further, telling them of his thoughts on Formosa, assuring them that if the communist Chinese attacked the island he would fly there, assume personal command and 'deliver such a crushing defeat, it would be one of the decisive battles of the world – a disaster so great it would rock Asia, and perhaps turn back communism'. He admitted that whilst such a scenario was improb-able, he nevertheless 'went down on his knees every night and prayed that

China would attack'. The mesmerized visitors failed, it seems, to detect signs of the megalomania that would shortly consume him. On their return to Washington they endorsed every element of his demands. Harriman went even further and recommended to all and sundry, including Truman, that 'political and personal considerations should be put to one side and our government deal with General MacArthur on the lofty level of the great national asset that he is'.

In Washington, despite the awe in which he was now held, the Joint Chiefs were perturbed by the scope of MacArthur's forthcoming plans. They reminded him that he had been entrusted with almost all his country's operational combat units apart from the 82nd Airborne Division. MacArthur replied to a string of querulous JCS signals, asserting that the sea landing was the only way of wresting the initiative back and of creating the situation needed for a decisive blow against the NKPA. If he were to falter now, he said, the United Nations would be committed to a barren war of uncertain duration. The enemy, he continued, possessed a capacity for reinforcement greater than that available to the United Nations and action must be immediate. He aimed, by taking Inchon, Kimpo and Seoul, to cut the vital arteries, sinews and nerves sustaining the enemy in the Pusan area. In his view the enemy facing 8th Army in the south would then wither and die, allowing Walker a clear run, with minimal casualties, up to Seoul and beyond.

Details of MacArthur's ideas about the strategic importance of Formosa to American security now leaked out. As they clashed directly with proclaimed government policy, Truman decided to put his own views squarely before the American people, and went on air on 1 September to address the nation. He described the North Korean aggression and outlined the United Nations' response to date. He then made a number of pledges: the United States believed firmly in the United Nations; the Koreans had an inalienable right to be free; he did not want the war to grow into a general conflict, neither did he want the Chinese to be misled into entering the war on the side of the North Koreans. The United States, he emphasized, did not want Formosa or any other part of the Asiatic mainland. 'We believe', he concluded, 'in freedom for all the nations of the Far East. We do not believe in aggression or preventive war. Our men are fighting today for peace in Korea.'

CHAPTER 7

MacArthur's Master-Stroke

Planning for Operation Chromite had actually begun in the middle of July, following a visit to MacArthur by the head of the US Marine Corps, General Lemuel Shepherd, who offered to assemble a division's-worth of Marines from around the world. Armed with this promise of élite well-disciplined troops, MacArthur now ordered the formation of an independent X Corps, commanded by his Chief of Staff, Almond, who would dispose of this hastily formed 1st Marine Division and 7th Infantry Division. X Corps would be retained under MacArthur's direct command, and would not form part of 8th Army. Many interpreted this as a sign of MacArthur's waning confidence in General Walker, its commander, who had never been one of the magic circle and who did not enjoy a good relationship with him or Almond, an officer who in Walker's opinion lacked experience as a senior field commander. As Walker saw it, 8th Army, having saved the day for the United Nations, would have to slog its way out of the Pusan bridgehead and up the peninsula as Almond snatched the glory.

The commander of the 1st Marine Division, assembling in Japan as its component units and formations arrived from all quarters of the globe, was Major-General Oliver Smith, a veteran of the Pacific war, enormously respected within the Marine Corps. When he remonstrated that the Marine division would hardly be ready for the Inchon landing and had never trained collectively, Almond was unimpressed and implied that Smith was displaying 'lack of responsiveness'. The two men did not get on well together; Smith, an outstandingly brave officer who cared deeply for his men, was like Walker in that he regarded Almond as a court favourite and military adventurer who had been given X Corps by MacArthur as a reward for long and faithful service. The marine also raised the issue of weather and tides and the effect that these might have on his men, who were to carry out the initial assault.

On 23 August there was a full-dress presentation of Chromite to a distinguished audience in Tokyo. Three senior members of Pentagon staff, Admiral

Sherman, General Collins and Lieutenant-General Edwards of the US Air Force, had flown in from Washington. Admiral Doyle, who was to command the amphibious force taking the Marines ashore, shared Smith's lurking doubts over the safety of the operation; unable to suppress these he blurted out at the end of his own presentation that 'The best I can say about Inchon is that it is not impossible.'

MacArthur rose, refilled his pipe, discarded his script, and faced his audience, his back to the huge map of Inchon from which the briefing had been delivered. No one who was present would ever forget what he now said, or the electric atmosphere of high drama pervading the room: Seoul, he said, was the target. Seoul, the capital of Korea. The landing at Inchon would make its recapture possible only ninety days after it had been taken by the North Koreans. That was important. The time element was one of the fundamentals of the plan. It would seize the imagination of all Asia. 'The enemy has now concentrated more than 90 per cent of his armed forces around the Pusan perimeter and along the Naktong river . . . and they are still trying to drive Walker and his men back into the sea. To take the troops earmarked for Inchon and to give them to Walker to fight his way northward out of the perimeter would cost us a hundred thousand casualties.' The Inchon beach-head, MacArthur continued, would be the anvil on which Walker would smash the Reds from the south.

The audience was for the moment totally convinced, but in the cold light of the next morning a host of doubts assailed Collins and Sherman, who returned for final assurance. MacArthur fixed them with a level stare and simply said: 'I have the opportunity, for a five-buck ante, to win $50,000 and that, gentlemen, is what I am going to do.' Residual fears exorcized, the Washington party flew home to brief their respective staffs and assure the President that all would be well. The garrison of Inchon, consisting of two battalions of Marines and several batteries of 76mm guns, was augmented by rear area troops of low fighting ability. Numerous extra mines had been laid by the North Koreans in all the ports along the west coast in a last-minute attempt to thicken the defences, and the Inchon garrison looked to their fieldworks on Wolmi Island, which commanded the harbour and its seaward approaches.

Preparatory reconnaissance was thorough and daring. A young officer of the US Navy, Lieutenant Eugene Clark, spent two weeks ashore on the islands lining the Flying Fish Channel, right under the nose of the enemy, plotting and surveying the defences and amending the nautical charts of the approaches to Inchon. Aerial photographs were taken of Wolmi Island, where several batteries of guns were located. These were to be neutralized by naval gunfire and aerial bombing as the assault developed. The attack could only be mounted on a few days in September because of the requisite spring tides, and one of these was the 15th. Ships of the UN Fleet had been bombarding Inchon intermittently for some weeks and the intensity of their fire increased with the approach of D-Day. Diversionary landings formed part of the plan. Late on 12 September the frigate HMS *Whitesand Bay* put ashore a company of American infantry and some naval and Royal Marines personnel at Kunsan. Similar landings were taking place at other points along the coast.

With daylight on the 15th the bombardment of Inchon resumed in earnest. The enterprising Lieutenant Clark was still ashore on a small island in the channel and even switched on a lighthouse before dawn to help the navigators of the destroyers closing in to shoot the marines on to Wolmi Island.

In the main bombardment force were several British, Australian, New Zealand and Dutch warships. Midshipman Muschamp of the *Jamaica* noted events in his log as they occurred. The ship had arrived off the coast towards last light on the 13th and joined in the bombardment all day on the 14th. Naval aircraft from HMS *Triumph* were spotting and correcting the fall of shot, and results were excellent. From the bridge, where he was once more acting as 'Captain's doggie', Muschamp watched the air attack, which caused huge fires ashore. Early next morning the crew went to action stations and at 5.45 a.m. *Jamaica*'s 6-inch and 4-inch batteries went into action.

Firing continued all day and one 6-inch shell from the *Jamaica* detonated an ammunition dump ashore, to produce the most spectacular explosion of the entire action. The crew enjoyed a grandstand view as the landing craft carrying the 1st Marine Division swept past, heading for the pall of smoke hanging over the shoreline. The first wave went in on a huge flood tide shortly after dawn, overwhelming the battered garrison on Wolmi; the sea then receded for several miles, uncovering vast mudflats. A second assault wave went ashore on the afternoon tide, and the marines began to fight their way through Inchon town, now a smoking ruin. There had been virtually no sign of the North Korean air force; but on the 17th, two piston-engined fighter-bombers bravely attacked the invasion fleet anchored in the channel and its approaches. One of the aircraft attacked *Jamaica*, whose alert gunners shot it down, the first enemy aircraft to fall to allied naval fire in the war.

The preliminary bombardment had destroyed the batteries on Wolmi and demoralized the rest of the defence, and the marines got ashore with relatively few casualties. On board the headquarters ship *Mount McKinley* that night, MacArthur dined with his senior commanders and a clutch of visitors from Washington, whose curiosity had got the better of their fears over the outcome. He fulsomely praised the professionalism of the US Navy, whose expertise, gained in the hard school of the Pacific war, had not deserted them. After this, he knew that Washington would find it almost impossible to challenge his authority, and that Chromite had set a triumphant seal on his great career.

Almond's tactical headquarters was ashore by last light on D-Day and, as the marines fought their way inland towards Seoul, the 7th Division came ashore on D+5, advancing towards Seoul in the wake of the marines and south-east towards Kimpo airfield and Suwon. Almond set up his main corps headquarters on the 22nd, some three miles inland from the smoking ruins of Inchon. Kimpo was already in American hands and the 7th Division pushed towards Suwon. By the 24th one regiment of marines was across the Han and fighting its way against stiffening opposition into the western suburbs of the capital. Soon they were having to battle their way street by street. Smith, ever conscious of the need to minimize casualties and also to save as many of the city's ancient monuments as possible from avoidable damage, insisted on what seemed to his Corps commander an over-deliberate approach to the difficult business of fighting in a densely built-up area. Almond now turned 7th Division back to join in the battle for the capital; he was irritated by Smith's street-fighting techniques and began actively to interfere in the handling of the Marine division; Smith was moved to protest when Almond diverted many of the Marine Amtrak amphibian vehicles to 7th Division for the crossing of the Han from the south.

Once the dominant South Mountain, overlooking the city centre, had been taken, enemy resistance collapsed and Seoul was again in UN hands. On 29 September MacArthur brought Syngman Rhee back into his capital. To many, not least MacArthur himself, it seemed that the war was all but won.

Although X Corps was ashore at Inchon, the Pusan perimeter remained under pressure. Despite nearly 20,000 casualties sustained since it crossed the 38th parallel in June, the NKPA redoubled its efforts to break into 8th Army's bridgehead. Nevertheless, General Walker had been ordered to take the offensive on 16 September (D+1 of Chromite), drive north to link up with X Corps and destroy the fleeing remnants of what MacArthur expected to be a demoralized and broken NKPA. With its rapid growth, 8th Army was split into two corps: I Corps under Major-General Milburn, and IX Corps, commanded by Lieutenant-General Coulter. I Corps was to drive north-west as the main thrust, whilst IX Corps broke out to the south-west and cleared the country of thousands of guerrillas, who had been augmented by units of the NKPA cut off in the remote mountainous terrain of the western provinces. The ROK divisions of 8th Army were to advance up the east coast, where enemy resistance was expected to be minimal.

Although he had lost the Marine brigade to the Inchon operation, and reinforcements destined for 8th Army had been diverted to make up the numbers in 7th Division, Walker still had abundant artillery firepower with which to batter his way through the North Koreans investing him. To cope with huge predicted rates of expenditure, ammunition ships were operating a shuttle service into Pusan and the US Army Ordnance Corps had stockpiled shells and munitions of all calibres in the rear areas. EUSAK had survived a very uneasy three weeks, during which the line had come within an ace of breaking. On the east flank most of the ROK divisions were still very shaky and liable to break under pressure. Following the disasters of June and July their ranks had been filled with raw recruits press-ganged off the streets, given a few days' rudimentary training and pitched into the line. Most ROK units had no manoeuvre capability and their KMAG staff privately considered that many were barely fit for static guard duties. Having lost almost all the guns with which it had started the war the ROK army relied heavily on American artillery support. Fortunately this was available, its guns well served; on many occasions, after the ROK infantry in front of them had fled in the face of NKPA attacks, American gunners stood firm, fought as infantry from their gun pits and saved the day by their example. One ROK division had remained battleworthy despite everything. This was the 1st, under the youthful General Paik, already identified before the outbreak of war by his KMAG advisers as a potential ROK army chief of staff. Trained as an officer cadet and junior subaltern under the Japanese, he had kept his head during the worst days of the retreat from the frontier and by his personal courage had heartened his troops, whose morale was immeasurably higher than anywhere else in the ROK army.

By 15 September it was apparent that a major operation was imminent and orders to cross the Naktong reached 27 Brigade on 16 September. The defensive positions held by the Middlesex and Argylls were handed over to Major Wynn's Korean police who, it was hoped, would continue to man them even when their British overseers had departed. The brigade had been augmented from Hong Kong by an anti-tank troop with four cumbrous towed 17-pounder guns (now superfluous in the absence of enemy tanks), and a field workshops unit of the Royal Electrical and Mechanical Engineers (REME), which was extremely welcome as it enabled units to get a number of broken-down vehicles back on the road. The workshops were also able to repair a backlog of radio equipment. Even better news for Coad was that the Australian battalion from Japan would join his brigade before the end of the month.

Assault boats were to be provided by the US Army Engineers for the Naktong crossing. Although 27 Brigade was facing a complex and risky operation of war, none of its units had received training in watermanship and the Americans agreed to send some instructors. Coad ordered his battalion commanders to go forward and reconnoitre the crossing sites carefully. There now came a spate of counter-orders; the crossing site was changed, then the operation was postponed. Bad weather had grounded the close air support. The brigade was placed under command of the US 5th Cavalry in 1st Cavalry Division. Visiting divisional headquarters on the evening of the 15th Coad was met by a chaotic scene; it appeared that the assaulting troops had been attacked as they formed up and driven back off their start line. Plans were being drawn up for an immediate counter-attack to regain the lost ground. There was also a disturbing report that an enemy battalion, supported by tanks, had infiltrated to the rear of 5th Cavalry.

The morning of the 16th dawned to pouring rain. The staff of 27 Brigade waited vainly for the promised artillery support but there was an ominous silence from that quarter. Coad despatched a staff officer to find a suitable assembly area behind the 5th Cavalry in which 27 Brigade could prepare for the crossing. He found that the 5th had regained their original startline only to be driven off it again. Coad was next ordered by 1st Cavalry Division headquarters to return to his former defensive locations overlooking the river; he queried this, as his departure at this critical juncture would open a huge gap in the allied line; he was told to conform with orders and did so. Barely had the move begun when orders were countermanded and he was told to stay. Some of his units had already departed, however, and it proved extremely difficult to recall them from their hilltop positions. Major Wynn's Korean police had melted away the moment their mentors had departed on the previous day, their local commander fleeing to sanctuary in Taegu. They were rounded up and driven back into the line.

As Coad's staff worked frantically to sort out the chaos caused by careless staff work, the enemy took advantage of a situation revealed to them by their agents on the allied bank of the Naktong, and launched a series of attacks against 27 Brigade on the 18th and 19th. Their target was 'A' Company of the Argylls at the extreme left flank of the brigade, isolated on a prominent hill overlooking the river. The company had prepared carefully for such a contingency and was properly wired in, with well-sited positions giving mutual fire support. They knew it was essential to have their wire and minefields under direct observation and as the enemy approached the wire and began to cut it, the Argylls, with admirable discipline, held their fire. When the order was given they caught their attackers enmeshed in the wire, inflicting heavy casualties. Whilst the Argylls were thus occupied, the Middlesex were patrolling aggressively across the river to gain prisoners and information, and to eliminate enemy infiltrators who had reached the allied bank.

On 20 September Coad's brigade was placed under the command of the 24th US Infantry Division, whose former commander Major-General Dean was now the senior United Nations prisoner in enemy hands. He had been succeeded by the newly promoted Major-General Church. Coad and his staff thus had to deal with unknown commanders and staff as they faced their first major test. The division was under orders to carry out a crossing of the Naktong at a ferry site near Hasan-dong, a few miles south of the town of Waegwan. On the previous day, whilst establishing two crossing sites, the Americans had suffered nearly 200 casualties from artillery, mortars and heavy machine-guns; 27 Brigade was ordered to exploit these tiny bridgeheads. Coad assumed the crossing would be opposed and planned accordingly. Once across the river he was to push ahead and capture the town of Songju, nearly ten miles to the north-west. In order to make its river crossing the brigade would be relieved on the river line by a battalion of the 7th Cavalry. The relief took place without incident on the night of 20/21 September and the British battalions moved to their assembly points on the east bank.

During the afternoon of the 21st the crossings began. Instead of using assault boats, the infantry were ordered to cross the 300-yard wide river by an improvised footbridge whilst vehicles and support weapons went over on a powered raft ferry. The footbridge was a shaky structure built at short notice by the versatile US Engineers from the wreckage of a previously demolished permanent bridge. Unlike Coad, General Church had assumed that 27 Brigade's crossings would be unopposed, but the enemy were still able to bring direct and indirect fire to bear on footbridge and ferry, putting the latter out of action; the Middlesex marched over the bridge under heavy fire without their Vickers medium machine-guns and mortars, held up whilst the ferry was repaired. Colonel Man pushed ahead for Songju. The road across the river climbs gently over a saddle between high ground on both sides. The hills on the right, on the flank allotted to the Middlesex, are lower than those on the left, under which the Argylls, marching two hours behind the Middlesex, would have to pass on their way into Songju.

Coad had been promised substantial support from 24 Division once his infantry had crossed the river, in the form of some Sherman tanks, a troop of four self-propelled 105mm guns and a battalion of the heavier 155mm guns. Meanwhile, every effort was made to manhandle the Middlesex and Argylls' support weapons across the footbridge during the night of the 21st/22nd as they were essential for the next day's advance.

'D' Company of the Middlesex was commanded by Major John Willoughby, a man of imposing physical presence, a professional soldier who realized that his young conscripts needed paternalistic leadership if they were to get through what lay ahead. He commanded by example, encouraging the young conscripts of the leading platoons as they fought their way up the hills – known as 'Middlesex Hill' and 'Plum Pudding' – taking on the stubborn defenders with the bayonet. Second Lieutenant Christopher Lawrence, a recently commissioned platoon commander in 'B' Company, was the first on to 'Plum Pudding' where he found himself skylined on its summit, his six-and-a-half-foot stature making him a highly conspicuous target for every North Korean weapon which could be brought to bear. Lifted by his inspired leadership his young soldiers drove the enemy off the hill. Willoughby's company passed through 'B' Company and on to 'Middlesex Hill', nearly a thousand feet above sea level, supported by the battalion's mortars and Vickers machine-guns, now safely across the river.

1. In front of the grandiose Japanese–built railway station at Taegu, South Korean mounted infantry – until recently a ceremonial cavalry unit based in Seoul – prepare to deploy at the front. It is August 1950; invading North Korean troops are only a few miles away and the campaign has reached a critical stage. This is one of a remarkable series of pictures taken by *Picture Post* cameraman Bert Hardy. Note the misspelling of 'Taejon' on the policeman's podium

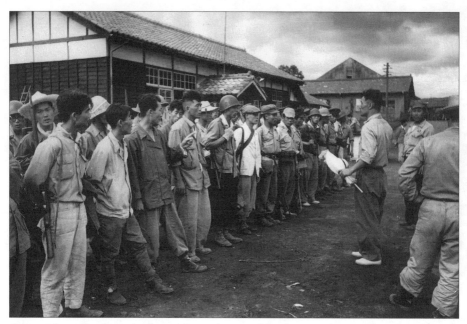

2. In order to replace the heavy losses incurred in the opening weeks of the campaign the Republic of Korea Army resorted to press-gang methods. Stragglers and civilians taken off the streets were rounded up, given a few days' hurried training and flung into the line. The ROK army's American advisers considered that these men were of use only as sentries, but they had to suffice, and their sacrifice enabled the Pusan perimeter to hold – just – until reinforcements arrived from the USA and elsewhere

3 and 4. In August 1950 the cameraman Bert Hardy, working in the Pusan and Taegu areas as the North Korean advance seemed to be about to overwhelm the South Korean and American forces, stumbled upon a number of appalling atrocities committed by the South Korean police; large numbers of 'communist sympathizers' were rounded up, driven into the countryside, and summarily shot. Similar scenes were witnessed by British troops after the fall of Pyongyang later in the year. At the time, the British government suppressed all reporting of these events, believing it would affect the morale of the troops and have a damaging effect on public opinion at home. Two of Hardy's disturbing pictures show 'political prisoners' awaiting disposal and being driven off into the countryside to their deaths

5. In August 1950, with the UN forces at bay in the Pusan perimeter, it was impossible to base combat jet aircraft on Korean soil and planes such as this Shooting Star, taking off over peasants completely heedless of the impact of modern war, were compelled to operate from airfields in Japan

6. MacArthur's masterstroke: at dawn on 15 September 1950, Bert Hardy of *Picture Post* landed at Inchon with the United States Marines. An American destroyer boldly closes with the defences to give covering fire as the landing craft approach the shore. In the background the enemy batteries on Wolmi Island are well ablaze following their bombardment by the allied fleet

7. The United States Marines, borne on a 36-foot flood tide, land on the harbour breakwater at Inchon. In the background are some of the many islands lining the Flying Fish Channel, through which the invasion fleet had to thread its way

8. United States Marines, using makeshift scaling ladders, tackle the breakwater at Inchon. The availability of these élite troops was a key factor in the success of this operation, the crowning victory of General MacArthur's long career

9. Forty-eight hours after the landing at Inchon General MacArthur, accompanied by Vice-Admiral Struble, commander of the Joint Task Force which brought off this daring operation, tours the forward positions of the 7th Marine Regiment as it advances towards Seoul

10. An American tank passes a knocked-out North Korean T-34/85 following the break-out from the Pusan perimeter in September 1950

11. On 27 September 1950 the 3rd Battalion Royal Australian Regiment embarked at Kure, Japan, for Korea. With it went the bandsmen and their instruments. Although he never played it in Korea (he gained the Military Medal as a fighting infantryman at Kapyong in April 1951), Private Dunque went to war armed with both bass tuba and Owen sub-machine-gun

12. Preparing to greet an incoming UN troopship, the 56th US Army Port Band limbers up on the Pusan dockside. Few who served in Korea would ever forget their first sight of this remarkable all-black ensemble, or its farewell serenade of 'So long, it's been good to know you' as they departed from the Land of the Morning Calm

13. The commander of the 27th Commonwealth Brigade, Brigadier Coad (*centre,* in beret) confers in the field with Lieutenant-Colonel Charles Green, commanding the 3rd Battalion Royal Australian Regiment (*right*), and a staff officer, as the brigadier's bodyguard, a soldier of the Argyll and Sutherland Highlanders, looks on. The date is 22 October 1950; a few days later, Green was killed by a chance shell fragment as he lay asleep in his tent

14. During a visit to headquarters 27 Commonwealth Brigade, General Sir John Harding, C-in-C Far East Land Forces (*left*), confers with (*left to right*) Lieutenant-Colonel Andrew Man, commanding the 1st Battalion Middlesex Regiment, Brigadier Coad, and Air Vice-Marshal Bouchier, British Liaison Officer on General MacArthur's staff

15. The despair of the refugees is reflected in the faces of these women, on the road south from Seoul in April 1951. In the severe winter of 1950–1 their plight had appalled many United Nations troops, who did what they could to succour them

16. Royal Marines
commandos, ashore on the
east coast of North Korea late
in 1950, place a demolition
charge prior to cutting the
north–south main railway

17. Men of 41 Royal Marines Commando prepare to give covering fire to a demolition
party put ashore from US naval ships on the east coast of Korea, late in 1950. They are
equipped with an American 3.5-inch rocket launcher and M-1 Garand rifles, but are
wearing their green commando berets

18. On 28 November 1950 men of the 3rd Battalion Royal Australian Regiment, clad in an *ad hoc* mix of British and American winter kit, march south in freezing weather up the 'Five-Mile Pass' as vehicles of 2nd US Division overtake them. Forty-eight hours later this section of track would be the scene of carnage as General Keiser tried to extricate his division from a huge ambush

19. The great 'bug-out'. On 30 November 1950, near the southern exit from the 'Five-Mile Pass', the shattered remnants of the US 2nd Infantry Division gather to continue the retreat. Thirty miles ahead to the south lies Pyongyang, soon to be abandoned with many of its huge dumps of fuel and equipment still intact

20. Ground crews of the South African 2nd 'Flying Cheetah' Fighter Squadron at work de-icing a P-51 Mustang in the dead of winter 1950–1. The conspicuous radiator under the centre-section of the fuselage was particularly vulnerable to ground fire, which brought down many Mustangs

21. The crew of the British destroyer HMS *Charity* cope with ice on the foredeck during the winter of 1950–1 off the Korean west coast. In the smaller warships conditions below were hardly better than on the open deck. Heating was inadequate and the interior bulkheads of messdeck and wardroom alike were permanently coated with frozen condensation

22. The crew's bodies lie on and around their Chaffee light tank following the attack on the reconnaissance company of the US 2nd Division near Chipyong-ni on the night of 13 February 1951. Only a few men from this unit survived, emerging from the surrounding countryside a few days later as the 27th Commonwealth Brigade advanced, to tell a terrible tale of surprise and massacre

23. The price of carelessness: the bodies of men from the reconnaissance company of the US 2nd Division lie amongst the vehicles and trailers in which they were trying to escape from the night attack of 13 February 1951, south of Chipyong-ni. Their unit had harboured for the night without setting adequate sentries, and was overrun. Note that the bodies have been stripped of their footwear

24. The advance towards the 38th parallel in March 1951 involved bitter fighting to dislodge Chinese rearguards from well-sited hill positions. Men of the 3rd Battalion Royal
Australian Regiment are seen manhandling their wounded down a steep slope

25. A Vickers medium machine-gun of the 3rd Battalion Royal Australian Regiment in
action during the first day of the battle at Kapyong. Note the snow still lying on the
north-facing slope, even as late as 23 April

26. During the first winter of the war, living conditions were primitive and infestation with lice and other vermin called for drastic treatment. Here, amidst much ribald comment from his colleagues, a rifleman of the Australian battalion receives a dose of anti-louse powder. Note the variegated clothing of the men; some are still in Australian standard issue, whilst others have acquired American pile caps and jackets, both prized items

27. On 23 March 1951 the 187th US Airborne Regimental Combat Team was dropped near Munsan, north of Seoul, in an attempt to cut off enemy units retreating towards the 38th parallel. The drop zone turned out to be occupied by enemy troops who resisted fiercely and an extended pitched battle developed over the next week as the paratroops pursued the enemy into the hills. In this picture, the paratroops are rallying on the ground whilst under heavy fire

28. Men of the 17th Regimental Combat Team in the 7th US Infantry Division take cover as a Sherman tank advances cautiously, its commander and driver alert for Chinese mines

On the left of the road, the Argylls were to experience one of those tragedies which can occur on any battlefield: the effects of what is ironically known as 'friendly fire'. The ground overlooking their axis of advance towards Songju was higher than 'Middlesex Hill', clearly visible on the far side of the saddle over which the road ran. There were two main features, Hills 390 (Songsan) and 282, the latter of which overlooked the road. Both were held by the enemy. The commanding officer of the Argylls, Lieutenant-Colonel Neilson, arrived in front of these features on the afternoon of the 22nd as the Middlesex fought their way on to 'Plum Pudding'. He was told by Coad, who assessed the situation in person, to go for Hill 282 before attempting to dislodge the enemy from Songsan. As a preliminary the Argylls dug in for the night on Hill 148, an outlying spur of the main mass of high ground. Nothing more could be done until the American artillery support was in position and the Forward Observation Officers (FOOs) had met up with the forward rifle companies, and Neilson decided to go ahead on the morning of the 23rd. At dawn the attack began, two rifle companies moving through Hill 148, where 'A' Company had formed a firm base. The men advancing on to Hill 282 were rewarded by coming across a party of North Koreans at their breakfast; these were disposed of and the advance continued against a now thoroughly alerted enemy. Shortly after 6 a.m. 'B' Company reported that they had taken Hill 282 and Neilson ordered 'C' Company to take the menacing bulk of Songsan.

Meanwhile, 'B' Company's wounded had to be evacuated down steep and rough slopes to the regimental aid post, located in a farmyard by the side of the Songju road. This duty fell to the battalion second-in-command, Major Kenneth Muir. Responsible for the smooth logistic functioning of the battalion in battle, as well as understudying the commanding officer in the event of his becoming a casualty, his job was admirably described by another second-in-command of a battalion in Korea, Major Digby Grist of the Glosters, as 'commanding nothing, yet responsible for just about everything'. Muir now gathered together what are inevitably known in any battalion as the 'odds and sods' – the clerks, orderlies, drivers, cooks, pipers and drummers – all fully trained combat infantrymen – and led them, with the unit stretcher bearers, up the hill towards the sound of the guns. It was now after 8 a.m., and there were ominous signs that the enemy was preparing a counter-attack; heavy mortar and artillery fire was coming down on to Hill 282, causing further casualties to the wounded awaiting evacuation. Most of them – there were now over 30 stretcher cases – had been brought down by 10 a.m. Muir returned to the hilltop to supervise the removal of the remaining stretcher cases and check the ammunition, food and water supplies, which were being humped up the hill by soldiers and Korean porters.

At this critical stage of the fight the guns of 27 Brigade's American artillery were withdrawn without consultation to meet some other contingency on 24

Division's front. The absence of their accurate fire was quickly sensed by the enemy; they increased the pressure on the Argylls, whose own 3-inch mortars lacked the range to reach the top of Songsan. Major Gillies' company was on its way to the summit but it had over 2,000 yards to go, all uphill. The North Koreans closed in on Hill 282 for the kill. 'A' Company, which had led the original advance, had been placed in battalion reserve and its men were enjoying a well-earned breakfast when they too came under attack. The Argylls were inured to desperate events, their forebears the 93rd Highlanders having stood their ground against the Russian cavalry as the 'Thin Red Line' at Balaklava in 1854. Muir was the senior officer at the critical point, on top of Hill 282. He ordered it to be held and was told that an airstrike would be coming in at noon. Fluorescent ground-to-air recognition panels were carefully laid out so that the fighter-bombers would see the Argylls. Meanwhile the enemy attack was being pressed so closely that it was impossible to use the 3-inch mortars for defensive fire on the forward slope of 282.

Shortly before midday a 'Mosquito' aircraft – a light plane carrying the airstrike observer whose job was to indicate targets for attack – appeared overhead. No radio contact could be made with him by the hard-pressed battalion but Neilson had been assured that a ground controller with a radio vehicle was also on his way forward to control the strike. In fact, this controller was so far to the rear that he could see neither Hill 282, where Muir and his men were fighting for their lives, nor Songsan, on to which the strike was supposed to be delivered. Three P-51 Mustangs appeared overhead at 1215 and, under instructions from the controller on the ground, carried out an immaculate attack on Hill 282, despite the panels laid out prominently to identify their position and a clear target description by the observer in the 'Mosquito'. Bombs, rockets, cannon and the terrible napalm, a glutinous petroleum jelly which ignited on impact with the ground, were used to devastating effect. Many of the wounded still awaiting evacuation were cremated alive.

As a huge fireball and clouds of oily black smoke erupted from the top of Hill 282 Muir rallied the survivors; Neilson offered him the option of pulling off the hill but Muir refused to do so. 'No Gooks', he said, 'are going to drive the Argylls off this hill.' Cheering on his men to the end on that seared hilltop, surrounded by the dead and dying, charging at the head of successive forlorn hopes with the bayonet, and finally working a 2-inch mortar when himself mortally wounded, he gained a posthumous Victoria Cross for his courage and devotion on that terrible day. Although Hill 282 had to be left to the enemy it was only a temporary setback. The Argylls had lost over 90 killed and wounded, but immediately re-formed as a two-company battalion; Neilson was able to report to Coad within twenty-four hours that they were once more ready for the fight.

Despite the tragic outcome of General Church's arbitrary removal of 27

Brigade's artillery support, he again declined to provide any for the next day; he was concentrating, he said, on the advance up the Kumchon road and applying all available resources there. A dismayed (and privately disgusted) Coad now found an unexpected ally. Before receiving Church's message he had encountered General Walker, who was abroad with his entourage on one of his battlefield tours; Coad told him that his brigade had been deprived of essential artillery support at a crucial moment and that the disaster to the Argylls was directly attributable to this. Walker sympathized, and immediately ordered up some anti-aircraft guns in the direct support role. He also signalled Tokyo demanding a full explanation by 5th US Air Force of the bombing of the Argylls. Coad was visited on the following day by Air Vice-Marshal Bouchier, accompanied by an abashed senior US Air Force officer. Bouchier signalled London, telling the whole sorry story. The 'Mosquito' pilot had spotted the Argylls' recognition panels and had told the distant ground controller who in turn told the fighters that as the NKPA often put out panels to confuse the fighters, they were to disregard the report from the 'Mosquito' and attack Hill 282.

The brigade got on with its business and morale remained high. The youthful soldiers, previously inclined to react nervously in the presence of the enemy, especially at night, felt that they had come through their baptism of fire with credit; they were confident in their commanders and aware that their American allies, generous as ever in their praise, admired their disciplined approach to soldiering. The sight of the Argylls on the line of march, each rifle company headed by its piper, never failed to excite comment, as did the way in which even junior NCOs were able to control the fire of their rifle sections, in contrast to the prodigal expenditure of ammunition by their allies.

For their part, the British were beginning to recognize the professionalism of the American support arms. The Naktong crossings would have proved impossible without the devotion and courage of the US Army Engineers. Commanding a company of the 3rd Combat Engineer Battalion of 24th Division, Captain Richard P. Lepke had been given orders late on 17 September for an assault crossing of the Naktong at 2.45 a.m. on the 19th. His company was to get the 21st US Infantry Regiment across. There was no time for his own commanding officer to make a bank reconnaissance and there were as yet no assault boats available in the unit; the infantry had never carried out a crossing, still less had they trained in use of the boats. Each rifle company of the 21st had been fleshed out with 100 ROK soldiers of dubious provenance and there was a dearth of interpreters. Most of the Koreans were non-swimmers and, in the absence of life-jackets, clearly apprehensive. On 18 September one boat was issued to each rifle company for familiarization, also needed by the engineers, only 10 per cent of whom had seen an assault boat since their primary training. Lepke, with his reconnaissance party, went forward to look at the crossing sites and came under heavy fire, which did not bode well for the morrow. The roads on the allied side of the river were choked with uncontrolled traffic and Lepke's company had to bring the boats 12 miles forward to the friendly side of the Naktong, crossing an intermediate river by ferry as it was too deep to ford. Progress was agonizingly slow.

The selected crossing was at a point some ten miles north of Taegu, where the Naktong flows north–south and is 400 yards wide. The near bank at one of two sites was seven feet high and had to be dug away to permit entry into the swift-flowing water. At 4 a.m., after a wait of two hours, 28 boats arrived in the infantry assembly area. The move had been difficult, as the truck drivers had kept running off rather than take the boats forward to the water's edge. Their places were taken by sappers. At dawn the first boats entered the water; in midstream they came under withering fire. Mortar bombs and shells were landing on the near bank as embarkation took place. Once on the far side, the ROK infantry refused to go ashore and had to be clubbed and kicked out of the boats. One of Lepke's warrant officers broke the butt of his carbine on a Korean's head, with little apparent effect. Even the men of the 21st Infantry were reluctant to embark until one of their NCOs shouted that 'if the sappers could take it standing up, so could the infantry'. They embarked as one man and started to cross under very heavy fire. Boats were sinking in all directions and others had drifted downstream. More were sent for. An airstrike was put in against the enemy holding the far bank; when napalm came down they 'got up and ran, and were shot down like quail'. After a short and bloody fight on the enemy bank the crossing was secured.

The engineers had lost over 40 men in the attempt. They had to support three more river crossings in that week alone, by two different regiments. Lepke recalled that during the final days of the war in Europe, the engineer battalion in which he was then serving was given three months to prepare for the crossing of the Roer river, an operation exactly like those he had just completed. The US Engineers continued to face such daunting tasks on many occasions as the advance pushed up the peninsula. As the infantry of Walker's army were not trained in mine warfare, mine operations fell to the sappers, often under extremely hazardous conditions. This was on top of their conventional roles of building, repairing and maintaining bridges (and demolishing them again as the tide of battle turned) and the endless job of keeping Korea's unmetalled roads open in all seasons. They were also responsible for setting up water points and ensuring that the water was fit to drink. Until British sappers began to arrive in the country with the 29th Brigade Group later in the year, the entire burden fell on the US Army Corps of Engineers; their performance was an outstanding example of professionalism under appalling conditions.

CHAPTER 8

The Road North

Following the Inchon landings and subsequent break-out of 8th Army from the Pusan perimeter the UN forces raced up the peninsula, past Seoul and on to the 38th parallel. Although isolated NKPA rearguards fought stubbornly to delay the allied advance it was clear that their field army had sustained a major defeat and needed to withdraw out of contact, deep into North Korea, in order to reorganize and refit.

MacArthur was certain that he would have to cross the 38th parallel in strength if he was to run his quarry to earth in the north. As yet he had no firm guidance on this from Washington but determined to get it as soon as possible. He and his staff pondered over the great wall maps in the Dai-Ichi planning room next to his office, concluding that it was feasible to land a substantial force well up the east coast. The ports of Wonsan and Iwon offered the best options. If X Corps were to be switched over to the east coast it would enjoy a relatively free run at the Yalu river, beyond the jagged central massif of the Taebaek mountains which effectively split the country into two sectors, between which there were only a handful of poor lateral tracks. If no threat was posed to the enemy on the eastern flank, MacArthur reasoned, his main drive to Pyongyang and beyond would be tied to the relatively narrow western strip favoured over the centuries by conquerors from the north.

Further advantages of east coast landings were that they posed an immediate threat to Pyongyang (barely 100 miles from Wonsan), compelling the enemy to retire at once in order to defend the North Korean capital. Capture of Pyongyang's port of Chinnampo would also ease the growing problem of supplying 8th Army over its dangerously extended lines of communication from Pusan and Inchon. The unmetalled road system in the south was disintegrating under the volume of traffic it now bore; the railways, already ruinous by midsummer 1950, were collapsing under their share of the load. Much of the permanent way, rolling stock and hundreds of locomotives had been destroyed by American air attack. A vast engineer effort would be needed to sustain the supply routes as winter drew on. MacArthur now saw another opportunity to demonstrate his strategic and tactical genius. Neither his own staff, nor potential critics at home, were keen to challenge his judgement after Chromite's sensational success.

Planning for the east coast landings began at once. On 27 September the Joint Chiefs of Staff in Washington sent MacArthur a new directive, approved by the State Department. This authorized him to continue with the destruction of the NKPA whilst watching for any signs that the Russians or the Chinese were becoming engaged. He was given clearance to cross the 38th parallel and carry out amphibious operations against the North Korean coast 'providing that at the time of such operations there has been no entry into North Korea by major Soviet or Chinese forces, no announcement of intended entry, nor a threat to counter our operations militarily in North Korea. Under no circumstances, however, will your forces cross the Manchurian or USSR borders of Korea and, as a matter of policy, no non-Korean ground forces will be used in the north-eastern provinces bordering the Soviet Union or . . . along the Manchurian border'. In the last resort, that of a massive Chinese intervention spilling into South Korea, MacArthur was 'to continue the action as long as action by your forces offers a reasonable chance of successful resistance'.

Having been told that MacArthur was planning to halt his ROK army divisions on the 38th parallel, General of the Army George Marshall, the newly appointed Defense Secretary (who had resumed the five-star rank discarded in his previous political appointment as Secretary of State), ordered EUSAK to cross the parallel at once. He had heard talk in Washington of intensive diplomatic activity involving communist China, the United Kingdom and India and felt that these nations should be sent an unambiguous signal in the form of a *fait accompli*. There was growing irritation in Washington at what was seen as Britain's conciliatory attitude towards communist China, and India's Pandit Nehru was regarded as dangerously neutralist, with strong leanings towards the communist bloc.

K.M. Panikkar, the able Indian ambassador in Peking who had access to leading Chinese politicians and military leaders, informed Nehru that the Chinese were uneasy over the approach of UN forces to their Manchurian border and were reporting infringements of Manchurian airspace by American aircraft. Nehru, who had already contacted Chou En-lai advising restraint and to avoid overreaction, passed Panikkar's information on to Bevin on 27 September. American bombs had indeed been falling, inadvertently or otherwise, on Russian as well as Chinese territory, a fact admitted by an embarrassed Acheson, who offered compensation subject to confirmation by neutral observer teams. MacArthur was advised not to embark on an all-out bombing attack on Pyongyang or similar 'sensitive' targets without approval of the Joint Chiefs. He replied curtly that he had no intention of doing so.

Once MacArthur's troops had crossed the 38th parallel there was constant reference in official communiqués to the 'liberation of occupied territory'. A euphoric air of triumphalism pervaded the Dai-Ichi building but Sir Alvary Gascoigne, the patrician British diplomatic representative, soon to be His Majesty's Ambassador to the Imperial Japanese Court, began to see MacArthur as a potentially dangerous commander who openly carped at what he saw as Washington's 'interference' and seemed bent on carrying the war across the Chinese and Russian frontiers if the situation demanded. Gascoigne was not alone in remarking the difference between the headlong advance of EUSAK into North Korea and the more moderate policies of Acheson and others who favoured a pause on the 38th parallel while efforts were made to bring the North Koreans to the conference table. John Foster Dulles wrote to MacArthur later in the autumn congratulating him on his 'stunning victory', but warning him not to heed the clamour for more decisive action from some quarters of his own Republican Party, and to exercise caution. MacArthur's apparent penchant for military adventurism disturbed not only Gascoigne in Japan; his opposite number in Moscow warned that the USSR might regard the occupation of North Korea by the UN as a cause for war and that the leaders in the Kremlin were closely watching the situation. Even if the USSR shrank from the idea of general war there was still a huge potential for propaganda and for creating diversions elsewhere, such as in Berlin or Indo-China.

On 3 October Attlee received a Foreign Office report stating that MacArthur, having dismissed the Chinese threat as bluff, intended to push forward as far as Pyongyang by 10 October; also, that the Chinese had massed some 400,000 troops in Manchuria and were capable of moving 100,000 of them into North Korea at once 'if indeed they have not done so'. In fact, the die was about to be cast: on 8 October Chairman Mao ordered Chinese troops to cross into North Korea. Attlee's government had been agonizing over the crossing of the 38th parallel but once Washington had persuaded the UN Security Council that it was operationally necessary to disarm the People's Republic of North Korea, the policy adopted in Whitehall was one of solidarity with the Americans who were, after all, shouldering the main burden of this costly campaign.

Whilst moderates of differing political affinities such as Acheson and Dulles held the lofty view that here was a chance to show the world that western democracy was able and willing to help the underprivileged nations, Syngman Rhee and his menagerie of time-serving politicians and secret police relished the prospect of having the northern provinces delivered up to them and imposing a vengeful regime, centred on Seoul, which would be anything but democratic. In the UN General Assembly doubts as to Rhee's integrity had already been expressed, notably by Britain and France; in any case, there was no personal commitment towards Rhee by the United Nations, and on 12 October the

General Assembly passed a resolution, tabled by Australia, restricting South Korean jurisdiction for the time being to below the 38th parallel. Rhee immediately protested that the UN resolution was 'wrong in principle'. Considering himself the rightful ruler of all Korea he proclaimed his determination to enforce his writ in the north whether the UN liked it or not. Although Washington believed that the occupation of the north should be a United Nations responsibility, at least for the immediate future, no effective UN management was exercised over what now transpired.

The 1st Cavalry Division recaptured Pyongyang on 19 October and Rhee's Minister of the Interior, Dr Cho Pyong-ok, was immediately flown into the city, probably with MacArthur's tacit permission. At least one reliable modern Korean source considers that US Military Intelligence was also involved. Rhee had been pressing MacArthur for some time to hold a general election for the vacant North Korean seats in the Seoul National Assembly, disregarding the UN proposals to hold nationwide elections under its supervision. The only possible reason, or excuse, for MacArthur's acquiescence to Rhee on this issue is that he thought that irreparable damage to South Korean morale would result from the adoption of any other solution.

The London *Times* correspondent, Louis Heren, had recently returned to Korea from Tokyo, where MacArthur's staff had told him that the 'Thanksgiving offensive' would be no more than a formality, that the peoples of North Korea 'were dying to be liberated' and the Chinese, having shown their strength, would retire back across the Yalu. Arriving back at the front, Heren bought a brand-new American jeep from a 'thieving but friendly transportation sergeant' for $400 and attached himself to General Gay's 1st Cavalry Division headquarters where Gay, who habitually carried a sporting shotgun, was being told how to capture Pyongyang by Brigadier 'Sheriff' Thompson, the ebullient defence correspondent of the *Daily Telegraph*. Once in Pyongyang the press corps managed to relieve the Soviet legation of its ample stocks of vodka and caviare; Heren loaded his jeep with his share and joined the queue of newsmen trying to file their stories. Ralph Izzard of the *Daily Mail* managed to contact his copytaker in Tokyo over a bad line, to be told that the victory celebrations had already started and that he need not send his story 'as the war was over'. He turned from the telephone to tell his colleagues that he had tried to pass 'the last story of the war and the buggers hung up'.

With the recapture of Pyongyang Rhee pre-empted any attempt by the United Nations to impose an equitable occupation of the north. Recruitment of a 30,000-strong 'occupation police' force got under way, attracting many brutish veterans of the Japanese-trained police who had fled to the south in 1945. The fearsome Colonel 'Tiger' Kim, last heard of as the defender of the Ongjin peninsula on the opening day of the war, was installed in Pyongyang as deputy Provost Marshal. As he hunted down communist sympathizers, Rhee promulgated an act, on United Nations Day, nullifying the land reform legislation enacted by Kim Il-sung's government. All land was to be restored to the former landowners. Nothing was done by the UN Command to reverse this or other reactionary steps now taken by Rhee's men. Administrators brought in by the American Civil Assistance Command were no better qualified than had been their predecessors in the post-war years. In Pyongyang as Colonel Kim's men set about their grisly business, public services collapsed and food distribution failed.

When Rhee had been restored to Seoul on 29 September he made an emotional speech in which he thanked MacArthur for the liberation of his country, emphasizing that the Republic of Korea, as a signatory to Article 4 of the Geneva Convention, would treat all prisoners of war accordingly: 'In victory we must, and we shall, show magnanimity . . . we must not betray ourselves into using the harsh methods which the enemy had used.' This had greatly moved American observers; but within weeks Rhee had imposed a vicious regime on the occupied north. Hard intelligence of atrocities soon reached the Foreign Office in London and was immediately brought to the attention of Dean Rusk, who conceded that these were taking place but assured Sir Oliver Franks, the British ambassador in Washington, that the US Army was investigating the allegations. By the middle of November, Cho Pyong-ok was proudly announcing the apprehension of over 55,000 'vicious red-hot collaborators and traitors'. This was probably a serious understatement.

Executions and beatings were routinely observed by horrified British troops in 27 Brigade, as were the grim convoys of trucks bearing loads of trussed prisoners into the countryside, from which none returned. Later in the year, as the tide of battle moved against the United Nations, the South Korean secret police were carrying out mass executions on a daily basis. Faced with UN protests, Cho claimed that the police were 'in the main' behaving responsibly and were 'trying to learn democratic methods'. All executions, he claimed, had taken place 'only after the full process of the law'. One Japanese source, however, credited Rhee's men with 150,000 executions during the brief period of UN occupation of the north. It is impossible to believe that these repressive policies were carried through without the knowledge, or even the tacit connivance, of the American Civil Administration whose members, as agents of the United Nations, failed to put a stop to them. When the NKPA re-entered Pyongyang they claimed to have found 2,000 prisoners shot dead in the main gaol alone and alleged that some 15,000 had been executed in the city and buried in mass graves. The hapless victims were hardly helped by the fact that virtually all UN officers and soldiers evidently despised the wretched Korean people in their extremity, for being the cause of their presence so far from home in a God-forsaken country which to all appearance fully deserved its fate.

*

General Willoughby's intelligence reports gave the impression that the UN were pursuing a demoralized and broken NKPA over the 38th parallel and into the north but this was far from being the case. The enemy had indeed sustained a reverse but was still prepared to stand and fight. NKPA generals were well trained, and their resilient and tough soldiers managed a skilful withdrawal out of contact, falling back towards the deep mountainous recesses of the north to regroup. Many of the best NKPA troops, donning peasant dress but remaining as formed units, had already vanished into the mountains of the south to join long-standing guerrilla and bandit groups harassing the UN lines of communication. By the end of 1950 it was estimated that some 40,000 NKPA troops remained in the Chollas, long the seat of opposition in the far south-west against the Japanese, now against Rhee's government. A number of important towns and local government centres in the south were firmly in guerrilla hands by mid-October; in November a large band took the town of Chunchon and for a time threatened Seoul itself. North Korea's political structure largely rested on party cells within the rural infrastructure. Guerrillas, aided by sympathizers, were therefore able to move freely even in UN-occupied areas and by the end of October some 10,000 of them were operating openly in the mountains inland from the major port of Wonsan. The growing physical separation of 8th Army, advancing on the central and western sectors of the front, from Almond's X Corps, redeployed from Inchon, put ashore at Wonsan and pressing on towards the Yalu on the east-central front, enabled the NKPA to infiltrate a whole division, the 10th, down as far as the Taegu area in November. MacArthur insisted on retaining direct command of X Corps despite the danger, already raised by Walker, of a divided command in Korea. This dispersion of effort, and the divided command, held the seeds of a dreadful reverse.

Despite the threats to his rear, MacArthur ordered Walker to continue the advance in the west. The decision to detach X Corps and land it on the east coast had created a major logistic problem. The Marine Division was re-embarked at Inchon and shipped round to Wonsan, but the 7th Division was moved overland from Seoul back to Pusan, with all its impedimenta, to board the ships despite Walker's recommendation (abruptly rejected by MacArthur) that it go by road and rail to the east coast. A heavy burden was thus placed on the 8th Army's already overstretched road transport resources, choking the inadequate roads by which all supplies had to come from Pusan. For several weeks the maintenance of 8th Army was a quartermaster's nightmare; ammunition, fuel and food supplies for the pursuit of the retiring NKPA had to be severely rationed as priority was given to the redeployment of 7th Division.

The advance into North Korea forged ahead, spurred on by Willoughby's ever-optimistic assessments of the enemy's strength. The NKPA, he maintained, was now down to 20,000 effectives and in bad order. This did not match the CIA's estimate of 132,000 North Koreans still under arms, of whom 80,000 were serving in combat formations. Not until the entry of the Chinese into the war did Willoughby's staff come to their senses and, almost overnight, adjust their NKPA battle order to eleven divisions and over 100,000 troops. But this was yet to come; as far as MacArthur was concerned the war was as good as won. No one in Tokyo seemed capable of weighing insistent reports from a variety of sources, indicating that the Chinese were now taking the UN invasion of North Korea very seriously indeed. Panikkar, India's ambassador in Peking, continued to relay information on Chinese military movements, but little heed was paid to him. The Chinese 4th Army had been widely reported by various sources as on the move to Manchuria in midsummer. British diplomatic intelligence confirmed this; the British consulate in Mukden noted the presence of crack People's Liberation Army units, many with a high content of Koreans in the ranks, training energetically in the area from mid-August onwards. In London, when the Chiefs of Staff Committee reviewed their intelligence in early October, they were convinced that Chinese intervention was imminent and urged Washington to halt MacArthur's advance past the 38th parallel; they were too late. The British government therefore settled for requesting that MacArthur be firmly discouraged from continuing his advance past the Manchurian border. In Tokyo, Air Vice-Marshal Bouchier appears to have been infected by the mood of the headquarters, signalling London that the UN offensive was 'on course and in sight of victory'.

There was already a profound difference between the British and American governments' views on the nature of the war. Attlee considered that the Chinese People's Republic was an independent agent, not tied to Moscow's apron strings, whilst Truman and his advisers believed the Chinese to be no more than Soviet surrogates and Kim Il-sung a mere Russian puppet, despite evidence showing that the NKPA had received much help from Chinese military advisers following the withdrawal of Russian troops from North Korea in 1948. Meanwhile, foreign travellers in China reported heavy military traffic by road and rail, heading towards the Manchurian–Korean border.

In fact, orders had reached the Manchurian Border Force of the Chinese People's Army as early as 5 August that it should be ready for operations by the first week in September. The Chinese General Staff were watching developments closely, and had correctly forecast the Inchon landings. On 1 October the North Korean foreign minister passed Chairman Mao a request from a worried Kim Il-sung for troop support and that night Kim personally put his case to the Chinese ambassador in Pyongyang. From now on, Peking began to plan its intervention. Marshal Lin Piao was appointed commander of a 'Chinese People's Volunteer Army' (CPVA) but pleaded sickness and the job went to Marshal Peng Teh-huai, a close friend of Mao's and former deputy commander of the People's Liberation Army (PLA). Peng immediately set up his headquarters at Mukden. Even at this stage, however, Chou En-lai was prepared to make a final effort to avoid war with the United States. He called Panikkar to his Peking office at 1 a.m. on 3 October and asked him to tell the world that China still preferred to find a peaceful means of ending the confrontation; he was well aware of his country's parlous economic position after years of war, and feared the use of American nuclear weapons should the Korean conflict get out of hand.

The British were not the only partners anxious at the conduct of a campaign which seemed to be exceeding the terms of reference set out by the Security Council. President Truman, already nettled by some of MacArthur's high-flown statements, decided that he needed to confront the general, whom he had never met. He therefore convened a top-level conference on Wake Island, in mid-Pacific. The presidential party, which included Bradley, Harriman and Frank Pace, Secretary to the Army, arrived on 14 October. MacArthur was waiting on the airport apron as the presidential aircraft came to a halt. With him were Ambassador Muccio and Admiral Arthur Radford, CinC Pacific Fleet. The general was casually dressed, in an open-necked shirt without decorations, wearing the battered service peaked cap made to his own design when he became a field marshal in the Filipino army. As Truman stepped on to the tarmac, MacArthur greeted him informally as though addressing an equal. It was noted that he did not salute his commander-in-chief. After the two men had spoken in private for a while the meeting got under way in the airport manager's house.

To read the unofficial notes and minutes conveys the impression of a mad hatter's tea-party. MacArthur opened the proceedings by forecasting the end of hostilities 'by Thanksgiving', 24 November. 'There is little resistance left in South Korea,' he went on, 'only about 15,000 men, and those we don't destroy, the winter will. We now have 60,000 prisoners of war in our compounds.' He stated that there were still some 100,000 enemy troops left in North Korea, mainly partly trained reinforcements, poorly led and equipped, 'and it goes against my grain to have to destroy them'. Describing 1st Cavalry Division's drive up the western axis towards Pyongyang, he also broke the news to his astounded audience that X Corps had gone ashore at Wonsan, and that Pyongyang would fall within the week. It was, he added, his intention to withdraw the 8th Army to Japan before Christmas, leaving a reorganized X Corps in Korea, consisting of the 2nd and 3rd Divisions plus the United Nations contingents. He intended to permit nationwide general elections as soon as possible after which all foreign military forces could be withdrawn from the peninsula. 'All occupations are failures,' he added; at which Truman nodded vigorously in agreement. The ROKs were to be left with adequate defence forces this time: ten well-equipped divisions and a 'small but competent' air force and navy. This, he felt, would be enough to secure the united country and deter any Chinese move from Manchuria across the Yalu.

Muccio spoke next, stressing the need for rehabilitation. This was the first time the United States had moved into a former communist-dominated area and there was an overriding need for re-education and information at all levels. The Koreans were tired of being pushed around and wanted to run their own country. Secretary Pace, worried at the prospect of a supplementary budget in the run-up to Christmas, asked MacArthur how much the rearming of Korea would cost and was airily promised an estimate 'accurate within 25 per cent' within thirty days.

MacArthur, gesturing with his pipe, launched into a remarkable dissertation. Of his Korean prisoners:

> They are the happiest of all Koreans . . . for the first time they are well fed and clean. They have been de-loused and have good jobs for which they are paid under the Geneva Convention . . . there is no difference in ideology and there are no North and South Korean blocs . . . we have no fear of Chinese intervention. We no longer stand hat in hand. The Chinese have 300,000 in Manchuria. Of these, no more than 100,000 to 125,000 are distributed along the Yalu river. They have no air force. Now we have bases for our air force in Korea, if the Chinese tried to get down to Pyongyang there would be the greatest slaughter . . . [The Russians] have an air force in Siberia, a fairly good one with excellent pilots equipped with some jets . . . they can put 1,000 planes in the air . . . probably no match for our air force. The Russians have no ground forces available for Korea. It would take six weeks to get them across and six weeks brings the winter.

Bradley raised the subject of further United Nations reinforcements for Korea, wondering if they were not more administrative trouble than their fighting worth justified. MacArthur agreed: 'They are useless from the military point of view and would probably never see action. From the political point of view they give a United Nations flavour.'

The meeting had lasted less than two hours and both parties immediately boarded their aircraft and flew home. On his way back to Washington Truman delivered a policy speech in San Francisco in which he was careful to assure everyone of the reasons for his unusual journey to the middle of the Pacific: 'I wanted to talk to General MacArthur. There has been speculation as to why I made this trip. There is no mystery about it. There is no substitute for a personal conversation with the commander in the field, who knows the problems there from first hand experience.' This must have sounded odd to any informed listener, as it was well known that MacArthur scarcely ever went to Korea and could in no way be described as a field commander. Although Truman kept his thoughts to himself, he must have decided that MacArthur's days in command had to be numbered. The great problem facing him as a politician, as well as constitutional Commander-in-Chief, was how to unseat the man still regarded in America as its greatest living soldier, victor of Inchon and champion of democracy, without losing his own seat in the process.

CHAPTER 9

Reinforcements

By the end of 1950 a considerable number of UN contingents were being 'fostered' by the United States Army. With the exception of the British Commonwealth's, all were placed on the American administrative system, given standard US-issue clothing and weapons, and processed, on arrival in Korea, through a well-organized reception and familiarization programme which included in-theatre training on American lines prior to being committed to operations at the front. American logistic support, however, was not free of charge; it all had to be paid for. Foreign detachments were responsible for their own reinforcements; casualties handled by the US Army medical service were evacuated to Japan, from where they were supposed to be returned when fit to their respective national organizations in Korea. Occasionally this principle failed; one subaltern of the Middlesex wounded in the Pusan perimeter was rapidly processed through Japan and on to the USA, where he was royally entertained before being returned to the British army, arriving back fully kitted out as an American army officer, including the single gold bar on his shoulder identifying him as a Second Lieutenant; this and other insignia did not long survive scrutiny by his adjutant.

The UN land forces contribution eventually amounted to four infantry brigades (three of them in the Commonwealth Division), nine individual infantry battalions, one Field Ambulance, a Norwegian Mobile Army Surgical Hospital (NORMASH), a major evacuation hospital from Sweden, and a Danish hospital ship. Some UN contingents needed considerable training on arrival and a number, found unfit for sustained front-line duties, were relegated to security roles on the lines of communication.

Some UN members sought political kudos, despatching bloated headquarters organizations to supervise and command relatively small fighting elements. These had to be diplomatically side-tracked into logistic areas or repatriated as irrelevant. Thailand originally announced that it would send a full regimental combat team, equating to a British brigade group, and a huge headquarters staff on top of it. This duly arrived even though the Thai military contribution was in the end no more than a battalion. Three hundred strong, the Thai headquarters boasted judge advocates, medical staff officers (but no field hospital), a director of finance, adjutant-general's and quartermaster-general's sections and even a Red Cross and welfare staff. All this was under command of a prince bearing the rank of major-general. It was totally superfluous and was sent to the rear to train reinforcements, which it did for a while before returning home. The soldiers of the residual battalion were to fight bravely enough in the warm season but could not take winter conditions in the line and had to be sent to the rear areas when the temperature dropped.

Another superfluous headquarters was that provided by the Royal Hellenic Army, whose élite volunteer infantry battalion arrived encumbered by an 'Expeditionary Force Headquarters' commanded by a full colonel. Unlike the similar French headquarters, the Greek force headquarters did not intrude into operational matters once it had been politely relegated to the rear areas. The French sent a battalion of seasoned veterans, complete with a 'French United Nations Headquarters in Korea' which immediately interposed itself between the battalion and the American regimental HQ to which it was assigned. This led to considerable bad blood and the surplus French manpower was not ejected from the command until December 1950. By then the French senior commander, a lieutenant-general, had demoted himself to lieutenant-colonel, commanding the battalion thereafter with great distinction.

The Turkish contribution comprised a full brigade headquarters and a regimental combat team. Exceptionally, the brigade headquarters took to the field with the combat team; its commander, Brigadier-General Yazici, was a veteran of the First World War who had pioneered armoured warfare in the reconstructed Turkish army of the 1930s. His men were a mixture of volunteers and conscripts, many of them drawn from the hardy Anatolian peasantry which had formed the backbone of Turkish armies for centuries. Before leaving Turkey Yazici was presented with a flag signed with their own blood by the pupils of Galata High School in Istanbul; it was carried into battle throughout the campaign by the brigade and taken safely home afterwards.

The Ethiopian 'Kagnew' battalion drawn from Emperor Haile Selassie's Imperial Guard was an impressive unit; the force headquarters which accompanied it was quietly detached and sent to the base area. Whilst the Filipinos enjoyed a high reputation as guerrillas, their regular soldiering was of an altogether different order and the 1,200-strong first Filipino battalion group had to be retrained from scratch before it could go into action. The greatest problem faced by the Americans was that of feeding the various UN contingents. The Turks refused any form of pigmeat, but required an extra two pounds of bread per man per day; the British, who liked much of the American troop ration, adopted a mix of this and the standard British 'composite' ration, augmented at times with fresh chilled meat from Australia and New Zealand.

Once the British government had resigned itself to sending a brigade group from the UK to Korea, in addition to those troops coming from Hong Kong, preparations went ahead. Early in July, the 29th Brigade was nominated. Its headquarters was at Colchester where it had been formed in September 1949 as part of Britain's 'Imperial Strategic Reserve'. At that time its composition reflected the vitiated state of the nation's armed forces. Apart from the brigade headquarters the only element actually at Colchester was the 1st Battalion Royal Ulster Rifles. The other battalions were the 1st Gloucestershire, only recently returned from the West Indies, and the 1st Battalion Royal Northumberland Fusiliers, hurriedly posted in from the School of Infantry at Warminster where they had been the demonstration battalion. Successive short-notice postings from one garrison to another were one of the reasons (the other being derisively low pay) for extremely poor regular army recruiting. All the battalions were only up to their lower establishment strength and included large numbers of young conscripts. The brigade's field artillery regiment, the 45th, was stationed far to the north in County Durham, its Engineer squadron at Tidworth on Salisbury Plain, and its Royal Army Service Corps company, providing ammunition, fuel, supplies and troop transport in the field, was at Newark in Nottinghamshire. Only on one occasion in 1949 had it been possible for the brigade to concentrate for collective training, and when, early in 1950, its units began to move into Eastern Command, they were in the main not the ones who had trained together the previous summer.

Even the mobilization of a brigade for Korea placed a severe strain on the British defence system. It was decided not to send combat aircraft; such jet fighters as the RAF had were needed for the air defence of the United Kingdom; the Far East Air Force, whose headquarters was in Singapore, only disposed of obsolescent piston-engined aircraft which were fully committed to the anti-terrorist campaign in Malaya or the defence of Hong Kong. The War Office convened a staff conference in Whitehall on 8 August. The agenda covered the preparation of all units involved, including provision of personnel, vehicles, weapons and clothing. It was decided to set up a battle school in Japan where reinforcements, held at a barracks near Kure, could be given refresher training before joining units in Korea. Merchant shipping had to be chartered to carry the brigade's vehicles and heavy equipment. Troopships already in service on the Far East run had to be augmented and a number of elderly passenger liners were taken into service.

The greatest upheaval, however, was generated by the need to recall several thousand reservists to the colours. Although the raising of the National Service period to two years had made extra manpower available, no conscripts under the age of 19 could be sent to Korea. All over the British Isles, men who had thankfully taken off their uniform up to five years earlier in the hope that they would never be recalled received their papers, and were soon reporting to their mobilization units in a state of disgruntlement. The regimental police sergeant of the Royal Ulster Rifles was disconcerted when a young woman appeared at the barrack gate carrying a small baby which she thrust upon him with the words: 'You've taken my bloody husband – you may as well have this one too.'

Whilst efforts were made to draw reservists from those who had most recently completed their colour service, it was necessary in many cases to recall Class 'B' men who had been in civilian life for some years. These posed the most complex welfare problems; many left young families at home, others had set up their own small businesses which now faced ruin. The system provided for a measure of flexibility and compassion, as when returned reservists clearly unfit for active service were discharged on medical grounds. Some reservists had clearly done well since leaving the army and at least one arrived at the unit guardroom in his Bentley to report for service. A taxi driver at Colchester had been jovially ferrying grumbling reservists from the railway station for some time before he too was caught and, to their great joy, joined his erstwhile passengers in uniform. Regular soldiers in the brigade's units were dismayed to find that their service had been arbitrarily extended indefinitely. Officers were recalled from the Regular Army Reserve of Officers to make up numbers. Youthful subalterns recently commissioned from Sandhurst were taken off their post-commissioning courses and confronted with their first platoons, often of recalled reservists ten years older than themselves. As the units formed up it was obvious that the latter, all of whom had served in the Second World War, had much to teach the younger officers and men around them. In some units they made up three-quarters of the total strength.

The commander of the 29th Brigade Group was Brigadier Tom Brodie, an infantryman formerly of the Cheshire Regiment, who had been one of Wingate's Chindit column commanders in Burma. Wiry and energetic, he made it his business to get around his far-flung command, mostly based in East Anglia and on Salisbury Plain. Under the strain of jettisoning young National Service soldiers and taking in a mass of total strangers, the system nearly fell apart. Had it not been for the fact that each of the battalions retained a small core of long service regulars who had been 'born to the colours', it would have been almost impossible for them to meet the challenge of battle.

As it was, the commanding officer of the Glosters, Lieutenant-Colonel Carne, and his regimental sergeant-major, had been in the regiment for twenty-five years; this was the norm throughout the army; the two had joined at the bottom of their respective promotion ladders and worked their way up together. A strong bond linked the officers' and sergeants' messes, both of which contained members bearing names which had been on the regiment's muster rolls in some cases since its formation in the wars of the seventeenth and eighteenth centuries. This core of officers and senior NCOs formed what might be termed the 'soul' of the regiment, instilling its ethos and traditions into every newcomer from whatever regiment he might come. A cockney might find himself, in the next two years, posted as a reinforcement into a Highland regiment and be in action amongst total strangers within days. Most of the Glosters' reservists came from the London area. The fact that almost every such soldier or officer was able not only to cope, but quickly to identify with his new unit, was to be of immeasurable value in the tests lying ahead. It was a phenomenon unknown (but envied) in the American army, but one with which the US Marines had long been familiar.

As the brigade's units sorted out their manning problems, they found themselves deluged with equipment of every sort. Thousands of military vehicles which had been parked in ordnance depots since 1946 were inspected and prepared for issue by the Royal Army Ordnance Corps. Clothing which appeared in quartermasters' stores seemed to have been dredged from museums; there were consignments of sealskin caps dated 1918, unused since the need for them passed with the end of the campaign in northern Russia in 1919. Boots made for an expeditionary force destined for Finland in 1940 turned out to be useless in Korea. String vests, greeted with derision on Salisbury Plain, proved invaluable in the Manchurian winter, as did 'jerseys heavy wool' – known ever after as the 'woolly pully'. The strange variety of clothing issued to 29 Brigade served to illustrate the lack of readiness for war in an extreme climate; until properly designed winter clothing was issued to Commonwealth troops in late 1951 they had to improvise as best they could, and had it not been for the unfailing generosity of their American allies their plight could have been disastrous.

Brodie was taking a much bigger formation than a normal infantry brigade to Korea, but with the usual complement of supporting arms: an armoured regiment, a field artillery regiment equipped with the well-tried 25-pounder gun, and a field squadron of the Royal Engineers. The armoured regiment was the 8th King's Royal Irish Hussars, recently equipped with the British army's new main battle tank, the Centurion. Armed with a 20-pounder gun of great accuracy, it also carried a gun-stabilizer system so highly classified that many in Whitehall dreaded the thought of losing its secrets should a Centurion fall into enemy hands; the stabilizer permitted accurate fire to be brought to bear on a target whilst the tank was on the move and was the first in service anywhere. Like all the other units in the brigade, the Hussars relied heavily on reservists and on officers and men borrowed from other regiments of the Royal Armoured Corps to bring them up to their war establishment. The newcomers found themselves in a regiment with its own carefully cultivated eccentricities; second lieutenants were addressed as 'Cornets', the antique designation of troop commanders, and all officers wore the 'tent hat', a distinctive green cap embellished with gold lace.

In addition to the normal elements of the brigade there were other units which led to 29 Brigade's 'Rolls-Royce' sobriquet. There was a squadron of Churchill 'Crocodile' tanks fitted for the flame-thrower role; these were destined never to carry out their fearsome task but were put to more conventional use in Korea. The field artillery regiment was not the only gunner unit; there was an independent battery equipped with the 4.2-inch (107mm) mortar, a weapon with extensive range, capable of firing a 9kg bomb of formidable power. As there was thought to be an air threat, a light anti-aircraft battery equipped with Bofors guns mounted on trucks was added. There was a generous provision of administrative support units. One of these was a surprising choice for service in a country boasting no more than 70 miles of metalled roads at that time: a 'Motor Ambulance Convoy' of the RASC whose vehicles, Austin ambulances of early 1940s vintage, were totally unsuited for work off tarmac. On its arrival in Korea the unit had to be reorganized and re-equipped with four-wheel drive vehicles. Its subsequent adventures were to gain it the name of 'Potter's Prostituted Pool' in honour of its commander, a notable character.

As August gave way to September, 29 Brigade trained for war in the flat scrubland of the Stamford Training Area, whose only relevance was its proximity to Colchester. Most of the brigade's vehicles and heavy equipment had been driven to the docks in Liverpool, Southampton and Tilbury, where they were hoisted aboard chartered merchantmen. Embarkation leave was given; there were surprisingly few absentees, and soon special trains were heading for Liverpool and Southampton, the main trooping ports. The departures followed a traditional pattern, with crowds of friends and relatives at the dockside, and regimental bands playing the regiments away to the far side of the world. As the ship bearing the Royal Ulster Rifles prepared to raise its gangplank, an eagle-eyed NCO spotted, amidst the cheering throng on the quayside, a notable deserter who had been unable to resist the excitement of seeing his regiment go off without him. In the last remaining seconds before sailing, a snatch party went down the gangplank, seized the protester, and brought him back to the arms of the Provost Sergeant, who welcomed him warmly aboard.

The newer troopships such as the *Empire Fowey* and *Empire Orwell* had been Nazi 'Strength through Joy' cruising ships before 1939, transporting loyal party members around Scandinavia each summer season. Taken in 1945 as prizes of war, they offered reasonably comfortable accommodation. The troop decks were in the lower regions of the ship, where the men slept on folding bunks curiously known as 'standees', and had their meals by shifts in cafeterias. In the Bay of Biscay, heavy seas reduced the lower decks to a malodorous shambles in which vomit, disinfectant, and the ever-present smell of sweaty feet greeted the troopdeck officers – normally junior subalterns, for senior officers stayed away from such distressing scenes – when they made their daily inspections and night rounds. There was no air-conditioning other than a forced draught system, and in the Red Sea life on the troop decks was infernal. In the older troopers, the men slept in hammocks which had to be folded every morning in regulation fashion and stowed in lockers, and they fed, as had the sailors of Nelson's navy, at scrubbed wooden tables on lukewarm food carried from the galleys by the troopdeck orderlies. Warrant officers and sergeants fared better and were accommodated in cabins, up to ten in each. Further up the scale, and a deck above, junior officers were packed four to a cabin. Senior officers frequently enjoyed the luxury of a single cabin.

The daily routine on a troopship to Korea consisted of physical training before breakfast, then a morning's general instruction on a wide range of subjects. Although the general level of knowledge about Korea, and even the reasons for the war, were but dimly perceived, young officers grappled manfully with the principles of the United Nations Charter which had brought them and their soldiers to this point. Instruction was also given in the recognition of North Korean tanks and the best method of attacking them, basic first aid, and what the army of 1950 persisted in describing as 'musketry'. This was popular and consisted of throwing crates over the stern and blazing away at them with rifles and Bren guns as they disappeared in the ship's wake. There were film shows in the evenings, a library, and a beer ration for the troops, a luxury denied to American troopships. For the officers, the delights of sea trooping were enhanced by plentiful duty-free liquor. Each day the passengers listened eagerly to the BBC World Service news and as October gave way to November it seemed that MacArthur had successfully completed the destruction of the North Koreans. A rapid return home, perhaps in time for Christmas, seemed more than probable.

It was rumoured that in the highest traditions of the sea, the crew of the *Fowey*, on entering the war zone, had demanded extra danger money. This at least gave rise to ironic laughter as the men lined up for their meagre trooping pay. At that time, when a second lieutenant was paid £317 a year, a private soldier's pay could be less than £3 a week. Thus rewarded, 29 Brigade Group prepared to go into battle; that is, if there was still a battle to join.

CHAPTER 10

High Hopes, Fearful Discoveries

Following their baptism of fire on the Naktong river in September, 27 Brigade had mustered on Taegu airfield, having been ordered to fly to Kimpo near Seoul and join in the pursuit of the NKPA as it fled north. Neither the Middlesex nor the Argylls had experienced such a move and were impressed by the efficiency of the US Air Force, which carried it out without the completion of a single piece of paper. Hot meals were served to the men as they awaited their turn to emplane and on arrival at Kimpo there was the supreme luxury of a field shower unit as well as plenty of good hot food. The road 'tail' took three more days to arrive; its personnel were intrigued by a roadside notice just north of Taejon beside two knocked-out T-34 tanks, proclaiming that they had been destroyed 'under the personal supervision of Major-General William F. Dean, commanding 24 Division'.

When the war erupted in June 1950 the Australian infantry battalion in the British Commonwealth Occupation Force in Japan was on the verge of moving back to Australia as part of a major reorganization of the Australian armed forces. The unit, recently retitled '3rd Battalion, Royal Australian Regiment' (3 RAR), remained an under-strength garrison unit of three weak rifle companies and a battalion headquarters, accustomed to an agreeably quiet and uneventful life in Japan. Very little field training had been done above platoon level. Although it could not be described as a particularly warlike unit, 3 RAR had a high reputation for its general bearing, the individual smartness of its men, and a particularly strong sense of unit identity. On 2 August the battalion was warned for service in Korea as part of 27 Brigade. At that time its strength was no more than 20 officers and some 500 men, well below even its peace establishment of 33 and 682. It now had to be reinforced to a war establishment of 39 and 971. As there were constitutional impediments to sending officers and men on their present engagements on active service, volunteers had to be called for. All but 26 men stepped forward and additional volunteers began to pour in from Australia. Most were seasoned veterans of the Second World War.

Battalion exercises began at once; new radios, anti-tank rocket launchers (with American instructors) and a mountain of equipment from Australia descended on the battalion lines. In two weeks the unit received a further 22 officers and 450 men including four new company commanders, the regimental sergeant-major, and, at the beginning of September, a new commanding officer, Lieutenant-Colonel Charles Green, a 30-year-old veteran of the North African, Greek, Cretan and New Guinea campaigns. He was one of Australia's outstanding young officers, whose leadership was to forge the new-found battalion within weeks into probably the finest fighting machine in Korea. Green had commanded a battalion in New Guinea at the age of 25. At the end of the war he returned to civilian life as a grazier but was accepted back into the newly formed Interim Army in 1949 as a lieutenant-colonel. As he was not a regular officer commissioned from the Royal Military College, Duntroon, he was sent to Staff College in 1950. His reputation was such that he was taken off his course to command 3 RAR.

Green soon gripped his battalion. He saw that the material was excellent, a mix of hardened veterans, young regulars and enthusiastic volunteers. Unlike reservists, unwillingly snatched back to the colours to fight a war they but dimly understood and with which they had no sympathy, the men of 3 RAR were spoiling for a fight and athirst for action, even if they, like most of the members of the brigade they were about to join, had only a dim perception of the cause of the war, or even the whereabouts of the country where their future beckoned. On 27 September the battalion sailed from Kure aboard an American transport and arrived at Pusan the following day. They drove north towards Taegu and their rendezvous with 27 Brigade, where Brigadier Coad welcomed them warmly and immediately retitled his command. Henceforth it would be known as 27 Commonwealth Brigade.

On 27 July the Canadian government had been approached by Washington and asked to provide a brigade group for Korea. Assured that Britain, Australia, New Zealand and India were also producing ground forces, it agreed, insisting that its contribution should be regarded as 'meeting its obligations under the UN Charter or the North Atlantic Pact'. Many problems had to be surmounted in creating and training this force: by the time it had been recruited, the harsh Canadian winter would be setting in; vast distances had to be covered between military installations, and apart from a token regular force, the Canadian army had been run down to mere cadre levels in the years following the Second World War.

The appointed commander for the Canadian brigade was Brigadier John Rockingham, a citizen soldier who, after a distinguished wartime career, had returned to civilian life as a company executive. He was given his head over the choice of officers for the brigade and chose well. Unfortunately, the recruiting criteria for the rank and file, who flocked to enlist in all parts of their vast country, were less exacting, and much time would later be wasted in weeding out men who had joined to escape the attentions of the Royal Canadian Mounted Police or were otherwise hopelessly unsuited to the rigours of life in Korea.

Eventually it was decided to form the brigade and train it for war in the United States, at Fort Lewis in Washington State, and here were assembled the three infantry battalions, field artillery regiment, engineers, and the squadron of Lord Strathcona's Horse who constituted the armoured element. The first battalion to set sail for Korea was in fact the least well trained; the 2nd Battalion of the Princess Patricia's Light Infantry went ahead from Seattle on 25 November when it seemed that the brigade would not be needed in Korea, as MacArthur's 'Home by Christmas' offensive had opened the previous day. The PPCLI envisaged little more than occupation duties in North Korea. On arrival at Pusan, their commanding officer, Lieutenant-Colonel Stone, came under immediate pressure from General Walker at 8th Army to get the battalion into the line to help stem the Chinese onslaught. Stone wisely declined, knowing his unit was still unfit for combat. Not until early February 1951, after two months of arduous training, did Stone inform Brigadier Fleury, the Canadian military representative in Tokyo, that he considered his battalion fully operational, and a week later it joined 27 Commonwealth Brigade.

The chaos caused to 8th Army by the extraction of the US 7th Division from its positions in the Seoul area in the second half of September and its move back to Pusan gave the North Koreans valuable breathing space as they withdrew across the 38th parallel. Walker started in pursuit as soon as he had sorted out the problems of sustaining the 8th Army over its extended line of communication from Pusan. Only when the Marine division had been extracted from Inchon was that port available as a forward entry point for ammunition, fuel and supplies. The advance north was spearheaded by I Corps, whilst IX Corps remained behind to deal with guerrilla activity in the south. 27 Brigade had a brief period at Kimpo to reorganize, before passing once more under command of the 1st Cavalry Division, already well up the road to Pyongyang.

Road conditions were appalling, and remained so. Even trunk routes in Korea were unmetalled, requiring constant attention from the hard-worked US Engineers and their graders. They were barely wide enough for jeeps to pass in opposite directions and vehicles were continually rolling off into the ditches on either side, requiring recovery trucks to winch them out. Every such incident held up traffic in both directions and five miles in the hour was a reasonable average for a battalion on the move. The washboard corrugations and potholes on the roads soon began to destroy the already ancient British and Australian transport vehicles and breakdowns were frequent. The tracked Bren gun carriers used by 27 Brigade's battalions were a liability, shedding tracks and prone to mechanical breakdown. In dry weather, choking clouds of faeces-infected dust added to the difficulty of driving and in the wet, road surfaces turned into greasy skid pans.

Brigadier Coad reported to Major-General Gay, commanding 1st Cavalry Division, for his orders and was told that the enemy was expected to make a stand along the general line of the 38th parallel and again around the important towns of Kaesong, some ten miles across the Imjin river, and Kumchon, 15 miles further on up the Pyongyang road. Gay, like Walker, had been one of Patton's protégés, his chief-of-staff in north-west Europe. The Australian official historian notes that the men of 3 RAR saw him as 'a trim small figure, [who] always wore a US Air Force flight jacket and had a worried expression on his face'. By mid-October, 27 Brigade was leading 1st Cavalry's advance north from Kumchon, and the Australians had been blooded in their first skirmishes. Far from being the broken and demoralized rabble portrayed by General Willoughby's effusive Tokyo communiqués, the NKPA was still a force to be reckoned with. Even though many of its soldiers were raw recruits, they were brave, well motivated and energetically led. Coad soon grew impatient with the woolly information passed down to him by the intelligence staff of 1st Cavalry, who were prone to 'drawing large vague circles in red crayon on their battle maps but seemed unable to produce hard and specific information as to the identity and strength of the enemy formations thus depicted'.

27 Brigade's first serious engagement came a few days later in the advance through the garrison town of Sariwon, 30 miles south of Pyongyang and known as 'the Aldershot of North Korea'. After a sharp fight the Argylls entered the town at dusk on 17 October. Large numbers of retreating North Koreans who did not know the town had fallen were also coming in from the south and southwest. The columns became hopelessly intermingled in the gathering dark. The Argylls, wearing woollen 'caps comforter' which led the enemy to think they were Russians, were greeted enthusiastically with cries of 'Russki! Russki!' The fraternization had reached the advanced stage of exchanges of cap badges and cigarettes when a Korean officer realized to his horror what had happened, and savage close-quarter fighting broke out. The Argylls' commanding officer, Lieutenant-Colonel Neilson, immediately drove south to see if a roadblock could be established to cut off any Koreans still trapped below the town. He immediately ran head-on into a five-mile column of the enemy marching north and, having spent an uncomfortable ten minutes driving through them as they loudly applauded his party, he managed to get off the main road and passed the rest of the night in a ditch, as hundreds of the enemy went by a few yards away.

The Australians had meanwhile entered the town, to find the aftermath of the Argylls' fight: some 200 North Koreans dead in the streets. Colonel Green ordered a defensive perimeter to be set up astride the road some distance north of the town and awaited the arrival of the rest of the brigade and his own administrative vehicles. Major Ferguson, his second-in-command, set up the battalion's administrative echelon in a convenient apple orchard, but instead of the unit transport heaving into sight from Sariwon town, he was joined by a marching column of enemy infantry. Ferguson called for reinforcements, then brought off a remarkable bluff, addressing the enemy battalion through an interpreter from the engine deck of an American tank. He convinced the enemy that they were surrounded and should surrender; to his surprise and relief they believed him and nearly 2,000 laid down their arms. Shortly after this, another large mob of prisoners was brought in from the north by an elated battalion of the 7th US Cavalry.

All these events had been taking place whilst Truman was meeting MacArthur on Wake Island and now that the presidential blessing (as MacArthur saw it) had been obtained, 8th Army was ordered forward to the Yalu river. 27 Brigade passed non-stop through Pyongyang on 21 October. Coad was once more under command of the 24th Division whilst 1st Cavalry stayed in Pyongyang, trying to impose some sort of order as Syngman Rhee's savage military police ran riot. As the 24th Division was still lagging some way south of the northern capital, Coad found himself in the van of 8th Army's advance. In an attempt to cut off the retreat of the NKPA from Pyongyang, MacArthur ordered a parachute landing by the 187th Airborne Regimental Combat Team on 20 October some 30 miles north of Pyongyang. There were two drop zones (DZs), one near Sukchon on the main north road, the other 20 miles further east at Sunchon. Lieutenant-Colonel Rangaraj, commanding the newly arrived Indian Field Ambulance, a parachute-trained unit, persuaded the Americans to use his unit and a field surgical detachment dropped with the 187th. Meanwhile, Coad was ordered to advance rapidly to the town of Chongju, nearly fifty miles beyond Sukchon across the Taeryong and Chongchon rivers, formidable obstacles whose bridges had long been blown.

Coad intended to clear the town of Yongyu on 22 October, then pass the Australians through to Sukchon where they expected to link with the American paratroops. Heavy traffic stalled the advance and Coad prudently called a halt; darkness was falling and they were approaching hilly country in which he was sure the enemy lay in wait. He was immediately confronted by a colonel on the staff of I Corps who ordered him to attack Yongyu at once. As Coad described the scene: 'As it was now dark I refused and asked him what he was doing. He said he had been sent up to liaise between myself and the airborne and had been with the leading company of the Argylls. He was highly excited and disappeared, but I was to see more of him ...'

It was clear that whilst the airborne landing had failed to cut off the main body of the NKPA on that axis, there were still plenty of enemy between 27 Brigade and the American parachutists, now installed in Yongyu after moving south. During the night the Argylls could hear the sounds of fighting from that direction and they were attacked themselves. At first light the Argylls took the town and relieved the airborne troops who had acquitted themselves brilliantly against heavy odds. The colonel from I Corps reappeared and ordered the Argylls to 'get on and relieve the 187th'. This time he was firmly put in his place by Colonel Neilson. The Australians now passed through the Argylls and Colonel Green had no sooner set up his battalion headquarters when it suddenly came under attack by hundreds of enemy infantry; his rifle companies were already deploying in the surrounding countryside and Green and his staff had to stand back to back to beat off the savage assault. They killed 34 of the enemy at point-blank range; four of their number were wounded. The area was alive with North Koreans trying to make their way to safety from the trap between the American airborne troops and the Australians. Coad was the fascinated spectator of what transpired as 3 RAR conducted a drive across newly harvested paddy-fields, where stooks of rice awaited collection. The battalion was armed with the antique Lee-Enfield rifle, as used in the First World War, carrying a fearsome 18-inch sword bayonet which wrought great execution in the hands of some of the world's most aggressive infantry. The enemy hid vainly in the stubble; Coad later wrote: 'I saw a marvellous sight. An Australian platoon lined up in a paddy-field and walked through it as though they were driving snipe. The soldiers, when they saw a pile of straw, kicked it and out would bolt a North Korean. Up with a rifle, down with a North Korean, and the Australians thoroughly enjoyed it.'

After this gratifying action, 27 Brigade, still leading the advance, reached the large town of Sinanju to receive a friendly welcome from the populace. The major barrier of the Chongchon river, nearly half a mile wide, lay on the far side of the town, its bridges demolished. There was a swift current and the tidal river rose and fell over 12 feet. The Middlesex were ordered to make the crossing on the flood shortly after dawn on 24 October. The boats, many of which lacked paddles, were swept upstream by the incoming tide, but the battalion managed to cross with the assistance of the local fishermen; as the tide turned, boats were drifting downstream at nearly seven knots towards the Yellow Sea, but by last light the Middlesex had secured a small bridgehead. That night was an unwelcome foretaste of what was to come. Lacking blankets, cold weather clothing, hot food or cookers, and with only the ammunition carried by the men, they tried to keep warm in their tropical clothing without even the comfort of fires as the thermometer sank below zero Celsius for the first time that winter.

As the American engineers supporting the brigade lacked the heavy equipment needed to repair the Sinanju bridges, a side-step was made into the sector of the 1st ROK Division to the east, whose commander, General Paik, allowed Coad the use of the bridge at Anju. Led by the Australians, supported by a company of American tanks, the advance continued for some six miles towards the Taeryong river, where the bridges had also been blown. An intact bridge was found upstream of the crossing and the battalion moved on despite stiffening opposition. During the night, the North Koreans attacked with infantry and T-34 tanks but were fought off. Coad realized that the opposition was strengthening as the UN forces approached the frontier area, and decided to shorten the bounds by which he was leap-frogging his battalions forward.

The limits of the allied advance were now almost in sight. The next objective was the town of Chongju and on 29 October 3 RAR began to feel its way into the enemy defences. The enemy reacted strongly with artillery, mortars, tanks and self-propelled guns whose fire was uncomfortably accurate. The Australians successfully used their 3.5-inch rocket launchers for the first time against T-34 tanks. The battle continued on 30 October; 3 RAR had stood firm against heavy enemy counter-attacks all night and the North Koreans retired after losing heavily, as the evidence of over 150 bodies in the Australian battalion area showed. By the end of the afternoon Chongju was in the hands of 27 Brigade. Coad's battalions had been on the move for five weeks and were in need of rest. The brigade went into divisional reserve and all ranks welcomed the prospect of a good night's rest.

Colonel Green of 3 RAR was exhausted and went to his tent early that evening. Shortly after sunset, six high-velocity shells, probably fired speculatively by a distant enemy tank or self-propelled gun, landed in the battalion headquarters area; one hit a tree, spraying the bivouacs with splinters. One of these hit Green, who was asleep on a stretcher, leaving a terrible wound in the stomach from which he died on 1 November. Lieutenant-Colonel Walsh, the former commanding officer, was conveniently to hand, having been assigned to a liaison post with headquarters 8th Army; his return to the battalion was viewed with some unease by all ranks, for it seemed logical that the second-in-command, the experienced Major Ferguson, should have been put in charge of the battalion he knew so well.

The spectacular advance of 27 Brigade to seize Chongju drew generous praise from the American formations under whose command it had been fighting. General Gay sent a message to Coad reflecting the opinions of many: 'It is a great pleasure to have such a unit as yours associated with the 1st Cavalry. Men of your brigade are true fighting soldiers. I send my sincerest congratulations and commendations to you and all officers and men . . . who marched 31 miles in twelve hours to deal the enemy this disastrous blow.'

If Charlie Green's death had cast a shadow over the brigade where he was much admired (especially by Coad, who kept a photograph of the young Australian on his desk for the rest of the campaign), a patrol of the Middlesex made a discovery on 31 October that was ominous in its implications for the whole character of the war. Villagers handed over two uniformed men, one of whom was a Chinese soldier. His presence confirmed rumours already current in 8th Army. In Whitehall the Chiefs of Staff were reading a Reuters' report that over 40,000 Chinese had been sent across the Yalu to safeguard the power supply to Manchurian factories. They had certainly been crossing since 12 October and were even now lying up, cunningly concealed, in the mountains, awaiting the order to attack.

With the capture of Chongju and corresponding advances further east by the ROK II Corps, the allies had reached a line on which it would have been prudent to halt and consolidate. They were now at the 'neck' of the peninsula, where it was barely 100 miles from coast to coast. Almond's X Corps occupied the port of Hungnam in the last week of October and had begun to advance inland past the major industrial town of Hamhung and on through the defiles and passes over the bleak northern mountains which led past the great Chongjin (or Chosin) reservoir. Further up the east coast the ROK Capital Division went ashore at the port of Songjin, nearly a hundred miles beyond Hungnam, and marched for the Yalu at Hyesanjin. But as the peninsula widens north of the Chongju–Hungnam line, the distance between the separate axes of 8th Army and X Corps steadily increased and the frontage broadened until, at the Manchurian and Russian borders, MacArthur would be faced with some 400 miles of mostly indefensible front. Such east–west roads as existed were no more than gravel tracks incapable of bearing the traffic of a modern army. A yawning gap some fifty miles wide opened between the right flank of 8th Army and the left of Almond's corps. The mountainous and generally trackless nature of the land enabled the enemy to infiltrate large numbers of troops round the vulnerable flanks of both forces.

For the huge Chinese forces assembled in great secrecy over in Manchuria and infiltrating into Korea, the terrain posed no insuperable problem as they were not dependent on mechanical transport. The Chinese army was accustomed to moving on foot with few motor vehicles, using large numbers of pack animals to augment human porterage. Their fighting formations moved as a matter of course across the high ground, avoiding valleys and roads wherever possible. By day they lay up, well camouflaged, never betraying their presence by fires or bad track discipline. At that time, the US 5th Air Force possessed very little in the way of photographic interpretation resources, or the Chinese might have been spotted earlier.

The 7th Regiment of the 6th ROK Division reached the Yalu on 27 October. Only two days earlier, however, a battalion of the division's 2nd Regiment was overwhelmed in a surprise ambush attack, and next day the full weight of a major counter-attack broke the remnant, which fled. Another regiment of the 6th Division was ordered to regain the lost ground and recover the abandoned guns and vehicles but suffered the same fate as the 2nd. The 6th ROK Division had thus lost two-thirds of its strength in two days. Its remaining regiment, the 7th, was marooned up on the Yalu, its line of retreat cut. Small bands of stragglers were all that returned to allied lines from the furthest points reached in the advance; one group brought a bottle of Yalu water back with them for Syngman Rhee; it was the nearest the President would get to fulfilling his dream of presiding over a united Korea.

Information pouring in from all quarters confirmed that the Chinese had indeed entered the war. Following the defeat of the 6th ROK Division, the I Corps commander, Major-General Milburn, ordered the 1st Cavalry Division to advance to the Yalu. No sooner had Gay's troops reached the town of Unsan there than they came under heavy attack. The blow fell on the night of 1 November against the 8th Cavalry Regiment as Chinese infantry, blowing bugles and whistles, erupted into the lightly held forward positions of the regiment's 3rd Battalion, scattering it completely. Brigadier Coad was summoned urgently to 24th Division's command post where he found a feverish atmosphere. General Church's first words to him were, 'Coad, the Chinese are in. World War Three has started.' 27 Brigade was ordered back to Taechon where the Middlesex were already deployed in reserve.

For three days 1st Cavalry Division was battered; then the Chinese pulled back out of contact as suddenly as they had attacked. The Americans had run headlong into what became known as the First Chinese Offensive, which was probably a trial of strength to test the resolve of the United Nations' forces; it may also have been intended as a last warning that any further advance by MacArthur would bring down a terrible retribution. By the first week of November there were at least 18 divisions of Chinese troops in Korea, some 180,000 men in all. The 13th Army Group of General Lin Piao's 4th Field Army, the élite of the People's Liberation Army, after inflicting signal defeats on the ROK II Corps as well as 1st Cavalry Division, established itself in positions where it awaited the next UN advance whilst poising itself for a decisive attack. As soon as Walker realized what was happening he sensibly withdrew his forward elements and awaited developments. They were not long in coming.

As the forward elements of 8th Army began to pull back, 27 Brigade found itself in the role of rearguard – one which was to become all too familiar in the next few weeks. On the night of 5 November, Brigadier Coad was faced with a situation which tested his character to the full. 3 RAR had been deployed to hold an important ridge overlooking the road to the south down which the withdrawal was taking place. Colonel Walsh, who had been in command less than a week, was confronted with one of the most difficult operations of war, that of breaking with the enemy when actually in contact, and at night. The Chinese were pressing down the road from the north and, as was their usual tactic, sending probing patrols round the Australians' flanks to assess the strength of the defence. Walsh, under extreme pressure and believing that he was on the point of losing his entire battalion, took counsel of his fears and, without consulting Coad who had told him to hold the position, ordered his rifle companies back off the ridge whilst they were under heavy attack. Coad immediately countermanded Walsh's order, but it was too late. There was much confusion in the dark and 3 RAR had only their pugnacity to thank for a lucky escape, losing 12 dead and over 60 wounded in the process.

At first light Coad drove forward to the battalion to find that Walsh was in a highly emotional state and appeared to have lost control of the situation. Coad relieved him of his command on the spot and appointed Major Ferguson to command in his stead. It was a painful decision to make, if only because of the political repercussions which might have resulted from the summary sacking of an Australian subordinate by a British commander; but it was hailed by all ranks of the battalion. They already had a high opinion of Coad, referring to him affectionately as 'the grey-haired old bastard', and his choice of Ferguson was subsequently fully justified. General Robertson in Japan also endorsed the removal of the luckless Walsh.

Also on 5 November MacArthur sent a report to the Security Council of the UN, claiming to have inflicted 335,000 casualties to date on the NKPA and warning that any Chinese intervention from the 'privileged sanctuary of Manchuria' would be dealt with in the same way. He also ordered General Stratemeyer to launch his heavy bombers at the Yalu bridges across which he believed the Chinese were pouring reinforcements. The Joint Chiefs forbade this, and ordered that no targets within five miles of the Yalu were to be attacked from the air. MacArthur, furious, appealed to Truman who over-turned the JCS decision. On 8 November a large force of B-29s and medium bombers flattened the border town of Sinuiju and in the following days four of the largest bridges were hit; but the bombers were forbidden to cross into Chinese airspace, and permitted to attack only the spans on the Korean side of the bridges. The anti-aircraft guns now massed around them were clearly radar-controlled and brought down many American aircraft; in any case the attacks were nugatory, for the Yalu was frozen over, permitting lorries to cross on the ice. To make matters even harder for the American bombers, they were confronted from the beginning of November by a new menace; the first MiG-15 fighters had appeared over the Yalu, operating from airfields inside Manchuria, to challenge the might of the 5th Air Force. The performance of these swept-wing jet fighters, powered by a Russian-developed version of the engines sold to the Soviet Union in the late 1940s by the British government, astonished western observers. An entirely new form of air war was about to break out in the Korean skies.

PART TWO
The Alliance in Crisis

CHAPTER 11

Enter the People's Volunteers

By the end of October numerous prisoners wearing the unmistakable uniforms of the People's Liberation Army had been taken by UN forces. All spoke of the huge numbers of 'Volunteers' massing just over the Manchurian border or already in Korea. In the first week of November, after his reverse at Unsan, Walker had drawn in his advanced elements, fearing a Chinese thrust aimed at sweeping the United Nations forces back to Pusan and to a humiliating mass evacuation by sea. On 6 November, after two urgent memoranda from the Joint Chiefs in Washington, MacArthur gave a revised assessment of the situation to the Security Council of the UN. His report stated only that 'forces other than Korean are resisting our efforts to carry out the resolutions of the United Nations . . . The continued employment of Chinese communist forces in Korea, and the hostile attitude assumed by such forces, are matters which it is incumbent on me to bring at once to the attention of the UN.'

An alarmed Security Council acted immediately on a British proposal inviting the Peking government to join its discussion of MacArthur's report. Malik, the Soviet delegate, objected at once, maintaining that it was not proper to consider accusations against the Chinese based on MacArthur's 'tendentious information'. After complaining about American infractions of Manchurian airspace, he proposed that the Peking Chinese should attend the discussions, but only if the agenda was extended beyond the war in Korea and embraced the Chinese position as a whole, including charges of American aggression against China through their support of the nationalist Chinese on Formosa. Although the British delegate at the Security Council, Sir Gladwyn Jebb, supported the idea of communist Chinese participation it was vehemently opposed by the Formosa nationalists who still represented China on the Security Council. The Soviet motion was defeated by three to two and the situation was further complicated on 15 November when Chou En-lai announced that his government would send a delegation to the UN to discuss Formosa; headed by General Wu Hsiu-chuan, the party did not arrive at Lake Success in New York

State until 28 November, when the Korean War had gone into deep crisis. Wu's party were in time for a fevered meeting of the Security Council at which the United States representative, Warren Austin, accused the Peking government of 'open aggression' in Korea, for the Chinese offensive, intended to throw the allies out of North Korea, had just started.

The South Korean foreign minister, Colonel Lim, was invited to comment on behalf of his government. Primed by Rhee beforehand, he read a bellicose statement accusing General Wu of coming to Lake Success 'with hands dripping with blood'. After claiming that Korea had been on the verge of peace when Chinese troops entered the conflict, he went on: 'I charge the Chinese communist regime with criminal, wilful, wanton and unprovoked aggression upon the Republic of Korea and with endangering the peace of the world. I demand that the regime withdraw its troops from Korea forthwith.' General Wu ostentatiously left the room as Lim began his tirade, returning to deliver a long speech protesting at communist China's exclusion from the United Nations and pointedly reminding his listeners that in the last twelve months the People's Liberation Army 'had freed every part of China except Formosa and Tibet'. He accused the American government of 'insolent aggression against numerous Asian countries' (including, curiously, the Philippines) and demanded Security Council sanctions against the United States together with the total withdrawal of American forces from Formosa and Korea to set the scene for peace talks. Sir Gladwyn Jebb advised the Peking Chinese to think carefully: passion, he said, was a bad counsellor, and he attempted to get the debate back on the rails by proposing that the Security Council adopt a UN resolution calling for the end of military operations as soon as possible. When the vote was taken, nine voted for the resolution, India abstained, and Russia used its veto, thereby nullifying the whole debate.

On 15 November Truman had reaffirmed that the United States had no aggressive aims in the Far East and a week later Bevin sent a similar message to Chou En-lai. Behind the scenes at Lake Success numerous informal meetings were taking place, notably between Gladwyn Jebb and Sir Benegaul Rao, the Indian delegate; General Wu and his delegation were handsomely entertained by the UN Secretary-General Trygve Lie at a dinner attended by Jebb, who threw his own private party for Wu next day.

On 30 November, at a White House press conference, Truman issued a statement on America's Korean policy in which he maintained that the war there formed part of a global conspiracy by the communist world and declared the United States to be the keystone of world democracy. To the consternation of the presidential staff he was then interrogated closely by the press corps, who urged him to elaborate on his earlier statement that if MacArthur was authorized to advance further in prosecution of the Korean campaign, the United Nations would 'use every weapon at its disposal'. 'Did this include the atomic bomb?' he was asked. 'That would include every weapon that we have,' replied Truman. 'Does that mean active consideration of the use of the atomic bomb?' There had always been active consideration of its use, Truman said, but he did not wish to see it used. It was 'a terrible weapon that should not be used on innocent men, women and children, who had nothing to do with military aggression'. He was pushed further: 'Do we understand that the use of the atomic bomb *was* under active consideration?' 'It always has been,' replied Truman. 'It is one of our weapons.' The President's aides were thoroughly alarmed as a now floundering Truman was led by the journalists on to dangerous ground.

There was nothing they could do to stop him answering the next volley of questions, for which he was obviously not fully briefed: 'Does that mean, Mr President, that atomic weapons would be used against military or civilian targets?' Selection of objectives or targets was for the military authorities to decide, Truman explained. He was 'not the military authority that passed on these things'. The questioning grew even more heavily loaded: 'Does that mean that we would not use the atomic bomb except on a United Nations authorization?' In his answer Truman tripped alarms in the world's chanceries: 'No. It does not mean that at all. The action against communist China depended on the action of the United Nations. The military commander in the field would have charge of the use of the weapons, as always.' A furore followed this pronouncement and the White House had to issue a supplementary press statement three hours later, emphasizing that the President had *not* given authorization for the release of nuclear weapons.

Anglo-American relations were plunged to one of their lowest points since 1945. Chiang Kai-shek's nationalists had received vast amounts of American support; but following the victory of Mao Tse-tung's communists, Britain, whose support of the nationalists had never been more than lukewarm, immediately made conciliatory approaches to Peking with a view to stimulating Anglo-Chinese trade. Conclusively bankrupted by six years of war, the United Kingdom had to seek export markets wherever they could be found in order to offset the enormous debts owed to the United States. To Attlee's government it mattered little where these markets were; Britain under Labour was committed to the creation of the Welfare State whilst maintaining her position as a world power at the United Nations and in the Security Council, as well as remaining the focus of an empire emasculated by the granting of independence to India and Pakistan. The realization of one or perhaps two of these laudable goals might have proved feasible, but not the whole package. By the autumn of 1950 the government held on by a thread after Conservative by-election gains, and the consensus which had united Parliament over the decision to send armed forces to Korea in support of the United Nations was seriously eroded.

British government policy, four months into the war, with one brigade ashore and fighting in Korea and another on the high seas, was to localize the area of conflict. China must not be forced into a corner or compelled to negotiate from a position of weakness. The advice given to the government by Foreign Office officials reflected a century of experience in dealing with the convolutions of Asian diplomacy: it was essential not to make one's opponent 'lose face'. For this reason the Chinese interpretation of MacArthur's apparent intention to go all the way to the Yalu (and, it seemed, beyond if needs be) was bound to excite the most hostile reactions in Peking. Now that Truman had apparently given MacArthur *carte blanche* to recommend, if not actually use, nuclear weapons, the Peking Chinese could hardly be expected to remain supine, and certainly there could be no question of their pulling back behind the Yalu unless major political concessions were made. These could now be nothing less than immediate admission into the United Nations in place of nationalist China.

On 6 November Attlee's Cabinet agreed that China must receive assurances that the huge hydro-electric plants in North Korea, producing much of the power for Manchuria's heavy industry as well as for the Vladivostok area of Soviet Russia, would not be attacked by UN forces. The next day, at a meeting of the British Chiefs of Staff, Field Marshal Slim suggested that in view of the reverses to the UN forces in Korea, the allies should dig in on a favourable line at the 'neck' of the peninsula, thus permitting the Chinese to set up their own *cordon sanitaire* well south of the Yalu. This might encourage them to come to the conference table without loss of face. Slim felt that the UN forces, as currently deployed on a wide frontage, would be unable to withstand a major Chinese offensive, and also that the ROK army was still likely to crumple at the first really hard enemy onslaught. The travails of the next four weeks would prove him right.

Meanwhile in Korea, the Chinese had pulled back from contact after administering a sharp reverse to the 8th Army, but were gathering themselves for the kill although the allies did not know it. MacArthur was obsessed with the concept of 'hot pursuit', chasing Chinese fighter aircraft back across the Yalu and bombing their airfields in Manchuria. He claimed that he was only calling for 'up to two or three minutes' flying time' in that airspace; but it was, for many, the thin end of a long wedge, and the British Chiefs of Staff believed that it would be used to sanction a bombing offensive against Chinese airfields, anti-aircraft defences and even industrial targets. Bevin therefore signalled Washington, voicing his opposition to 'hot pursuit'. The Canadians were prepared to compromise and recommended that pursuit should be preceded by formal warning, and then only with UN sanction. France strongly supported the British *cordon sanitaire* idea. Although Dean Acheson sensed the unease of his allies, he shrank from airing the concept in the UN in case it was interpreted by the Chinese as a sign of weakness. Attlee, deeply perturbed, called for an early summit meeting with Truman in Washington and arrangements for this were set in train.

MacArthur ordered the advance to resume after the middle of November. Lavish reinforcements were despatched to the 5th Air Force in the belief, fostered by Generals Vandenberg and Stratemeyer, that air power alone could win the war outright, even in the face of Chinese numerical superiority on the ground. If the new offensive failed, MacArthur warned Washington, he would have no alternative but to bomb Manchuria, causing even greater alarm amongst America's allies. The Joint Chiefs in Washington were still convinced that the Soviets were at the back of it all, employing the Chinese and North Koreans as their surrogates whilst plotting all-out war in other theatres; the world, they believed, was tottering on the brink of general war. The State Department took a more moderate line, but their intelligence nonetheless led them to believe that the USSR was prepared to cope with all the risks inherent in global war. There was growing irritation over the full diplomatic recognition accorded to Red China by Britain and India, and Washington nurtured dark suspicions that they would support Peking's claims for admission to the United Nations.

As the enthusiasm of America's allies waned, Acheson reluctantly sided with the hawks in Washington, warning them, however, that it was potentially dangerous to advance into the remote north-east corners of Korea close to the Soviet border and especially anywhere near Vladivostok, the Soviet fleet's principal Far Eastern base. He favoured retiring to 'a favourable line' after bringing military operations in the north to a satisfactory conclusion.

On 20 November the *New York Times* published a despatch from its Tokyo correspondent which must have given great comfort to Marshal Peng in his Mukden headquarters as he completed the plans for his impending offensive. Drawn from a Dai-Ichi press briefing it stated that an estimated 40,000 communist guerrillas, including thousands of NKPA soldiers left behind after the 8th Army's drive north, were poised to strike up the central mountain range, 'where there was only tenuous contact between the US 8th Army and X Corps on the east coast'. If ever a weak disposition of forces had been signalled *en clair* to an enemy, this was it. It presumably got through lax censorship because it was already common knowledge in Tokyo that on 24 November, its Thanksgiving celebrations over, the 8th Army was to resume its advance to the Yalu, sweeping aside any Chinese and North Korean forces in its path.

MacArthur had wanted the advance to start earlier but Walker obtained a postponement on logistic grounds; the approach of an exceptionally severe winter was hampering engineering works on the roads and railways in the south. All the railroad north of the Naktong river had to be rebuilt and even by the end of October trains were only running as far north as the Imjin river, mostly on a single line cobbled together from the former double track by the versatile US Army engineers. From Kimpo an airlift of 1,000 tons a day to Pyongyang was helping to sustain the advance, but as late as 6 November stockpiles in the forward areas were dangerously depleted. There was then only a day's supply of artillery ammunition at intensive rates of consumption and all natures of fuel were running low. A daily flow-forward of some 4,000 tons of supplies, ammunition and fuel was required to sustain further advance. The average load of rations, fuel, ammunition and ordnance stores to sustain one United Nations soldier in the field for one day was estimated at 60 pounds, compared to less than ten for a Chinese rifleman. It would only be achieved if the railroad was extended up to Pyongyang, and its port of Chinnampo, 20 miles south-west of the city, was cleared and opened.

The original starting date for the offensive of 15 November was put back to the 17th, and finally to the 24th. By then, five trains a day were reaching Pyongyang and 1,500 tons a day were being discharged at Chinnampo. Among the arrivals by rail were some of the Centurion tanks of the 8th Hussars with elements of the British 29 Brigade, ordered into 8th Army reserve, and now reaching Pyongyang by road after the long haul up from Pusan.

Walker faced an unappetizing tactical situation. The 8th Army's 70-mile front was split in two by the wide Chongchon river which rose in the rugged Taebaek mountains of the central spine and flowed south-west into the Yellow Sea. On the left, with its flank resting on the sea, was I Corps; IX Corps held the centre, and the ROK II Corps was on the right, covering the Taebaek mountains in which lurked unknown numbers of hostile guerrillas. Walker decided to play safe, moving forward cautiously on a series of phase lines, encouraging the ROKs on his right to make contact across the fifty-mile gap separating them from Almond's X Corps. This wild terrain was under constant surveillance by the US Air Force, who reported no signs of enemy activity. They had been deceived by the skilful camouflage of the huge Chinese force assembling in the Taebaek range under their very eyes.

Almond's X Corps, after its unopposed landings on the east coast, had advanced on a number of axes into the hinterland, aiming to reach the Yalu at Hyesanjin. As on 8th Army's front, the enemy remained unseen and out of contact for two weeks. By 23 November, elements of the 7th US Division had reached the river and Almond flew forward to be photographed standing proudly with his staff on the banks of the frozen river. Nearly 70 miles to the north-east, the ROK Capital Division had occupied the town of Chongjin on the coast, and the 1st Marine Division had penetrated inland from Wonsan to the area of the Chosin reservoir, a man-made lake storing water for the hydro-electric systems providing power for North Korea's industries. MacArthur had considered a plan, devised from the map rather than close knowledge of the terrain, whereby Almond would push one of his divisions due west, to take the enemy facing 8th Army in the flank. Almond was told that the first objective of this bold thrust was the town of Kanggye, an important road–rail junction which was not only the key to the North Koreans' supply system but also Kim Il-sung's emergency capital since the fall of Pyongyang.

Many years later, General Ridgway, armed with hindsight, was to write: 'I find it amazing that highly trained professionals could have approved and tried to execute the tactical plan of operations for X Corps in north-east Korea in November 1950. It appears like a pure map exercise put on by amateurs, appealing in theory but utterly ignoring the reality of a huge mountainous terrain, largely devoid of terrestrial communications, and ordered for execution in the face of a fast-approaching sub-Arctic winter.' Even the ambitious Almond had second thoughts and asked MacArthur to approve a modified plan involving a westward thrust on a more southerly axis. MacArthur agreed and gave 27 November as D-Day for X Corps. The Marines were to go west from the reservoir and 7th Division was to establish itself on the eastern shores of the lake whilst the US 3rd Division, borrowed from 8th Army, secured the road between Wonsan and the inland industrial city of Hungnam.

Almond was optimistic. He had sent a regiment up to Hyesanjin against only token opposition. Over on 8th Army's front there had been only light enemy reaction to patrols sent forward to fix the Chinese positions. The enemy's curiously passive reactions to every probe encouraged MacArthur to believe that the Chinese had no other intentions than to guard their Manchurian border.

Kim Il-sung had moved first to Sinuiju after being driven out of Pyongyang but shifted to Kanggye when the UN forces got too close for comfort. He thus escaped the bombing attack of 7 November when 79 B-29s and some 300 fighter-bombers had destroyed most of Sinuiju city; the Yalu bridges were hit over the next few days. General Stratemeyer claimed that deliberate efforts had been made to avoid damage to Sinuiju's hospitals; the rest of the city had been destroyed. It is possible that the raid was a turning point in the campaign, but not in the sense anticipated by the US Air Force's apostles of air power. It certainly hardened the resolve of the North Koreans and their Chinese allies. It is almost as if the last thing MacArthur wanted was for peace to break out at this stage, when he was confident that his forces were about to present him with a victory which would crown his long career.

The bombing continued; town after town was pulverized and torched with fire bombs. North Korea was reduced to a waste land. At Lake Success on 10 November an American spokesman at the United Nations indulged in pure hypocrisy by complaining that several B-29s had been fired on from across the Yalu during these operations, and that this 'greatly prejudiced the successful completion of the United Nations mission in Korea'. This was at the moment when the Chinese, probably considering that their troops had accomplished their aim by inflicting a series of sharp reverses on the 8th Army, were actually disengaging and pulling back from contact. It was possibly the crucial moment of the war, when a truce could have been secured; but MacArthur's determination to stick at nothing but what he saw as the total victory within his grasp drove him to order the resumption of the UN offensive as quickly as possible.

Apart from being Kim Il-sung's temporary seat of government, Kanggye also contained the joint command centre for the Chinese and North Korean forces. On paper the NKPA still consisted of 30 divisions organized into eight army corps, but most of these were at skeleton strength following the defeat of the original field army. One NKPA corps, however, was still intact, deployed in the far north-eastern sector of the front against the ROKs. There were also thousands of stragglers, South Korean dissidents and guerrillas at large in the Taebaek mountains between 8th Army and X Corps, and further south, far behind the UN lines, ready to spring into action when called. Across the Yalu in Manchuria a new North Korean army, based on the three corps which, though severely battered, had extricated themselves from the general destruction of the NKPA, was being trained and re-equipped.

The People's Liberation Army – the ground forces of the Chinese Communist Forces – was vast. Its field armies at that time totalled between two and three million men. Garrison troops accounted for a further one or two million. Behind these stood a nationwide militia totalling around five million. By 15 November there were some 250,000 soldiers of the PLA in Korea, a figure contrasting ominously with General Willoughby's first estimate of 70,000. They were concealed in the mountains facing the UN forces, awaiting the order to break cover and destroy the enemy if 8th Army's advance was resumed. Some 200,000 men of the 13th Army Group of the PLA's 4th Field Army faced Walker's 8th Army. They had entered Korea in October, days before the bombing of the Yalu bridges and, having fought successfully against American and ROK troops in the first Chinese offensive of 25 October–5 November, were confident of victory. Further over to the east the 9th Army Group had crossed the Yalu at Manpojin where the bridges were still intact. As with the 13th Army Group they used strict road discipline and camouflage to evade detection.

Willoughby's staff in Tokyo estimated that there were some 12 Chinese divisions in the field when in fact there were 30, grouped in nine armies, under the 4th Field Army commanded by Marshal Lin Piao. Born in 1908, he had served in Chiang Kai-shek's army but following conversion to communism commanded a battalion in Mao's Long March of 1934–5 from south to north China. After fighting the Japanese from 1937 he was taken to the USSR for treatment of severe wounds and served in the Red Army during the siege of Leningrad. Following the defeat of Japan he was instrumental in denying Manchuria to Chiang's troops, who tried to occupy it. In the civil war leading to Chiang's defeat and expulsion from the mainland in 1949, Lin Piao was the outstanding field commander and by 1950 undisputedly his country's leading soldier. His battle-hardened troops held the honorific title 'Iron Army'. The general headquarters of this formidable force of 'Chinese People's Volunteers' was in Mukden and its overall commander, Marshal of the PLA Peng Teh-huai, was another 'Long March' veteran and close friend of Chairman Mao.

The 9th Army Group's victims were to be Almond's two divisions, strung out in north-east Korea. Chinese morale was high. The weakness of the PLA lay in the wide range of its equipment: a mixed bag of captured stock, some Japanese, some American. There were many calibres of small arms ammunition as a result, creating huge problems for unit quartermasters. This was a marching army in which motor transport was deliberately kept back from the fighting units since it raised camouflage as well as logistic problems. Tactical doctrine was based on the hard-earned experience of years of guerrilla warfare and rapid movement on foot, usually by night. Every unit had its political officers whose task was to inculcate and maintain orthodoxy of thought in all ranks. Confident in their military ability and the righteousness of their cause, the People's Volunteers awaited the order to advance.

As the Korean War took on new dimensions in November, dissenting voices began to be heard in the Houses of Parliament in Britain. A backbench Labour cabal gave notice on 17 November of two motions for early debate, calling on the government to expedite talks with the Soviet Union in hopes of immediate agreement to halt, or at least limit, the UN advance in Korea and end the fighting as soon as possible. This immediately triggered a hostile reaction in Washington, where right-wingers saw it as a despicable pro-communist ploy. More ominously for Attlee's government, the all-party consensus at Westminster over the Korean issue was evaporating. Only two days earlier in the House of Lords that most conservative of Tory peers, Lord Salisbury, had expressed his fear that MacArthur's evident intentions could provoke escalation into general war: 'The danger in our present position was that we had, if anything, advanced too far. We had reached a point where the enemy's lines of communication were not in Korea at all and could not therefore be attacked without grave diplomatic consequences. Surely it was better in the long run to avoid such complications, even if it meant leaving a small part of North Korea unoccupied by a United Nations force.' The Labour peer Lord Chorley believed the decision to go into North Korea after Inchon was due to manipulation on MacArthur's part which played into the hands of those who believed that the United States, supported by the English-speaking world, had imperialist and aggressive designs in the Far East.

The cat was out of the bag. Next day in the House of Commons, Attlee was asked by the Conservative opposition 'if His Majesty's government would bear in mind the great importance of not becoming too much pinned down in China, or in the approaches to China, at a time when the danger in Europe is undoubtedly occupying our minds?' The pacifist Labour MP Sidney Silverman took his cue, quoting an article in the left-wing journal *New Statesman* of 11 November alleging that a special policy directive had been sent to MacArthur by the State Department some weeks earlier with the full knowledge and approval of the British government, urging him to halt the advance at the 'neck' of the peninsula and to avoid contact with the Chinese forces. This, said Silverman, had apparently been flouted. He asked Shinwell if instructions given to MacArthur were always fully complied with, and when had they been given? Shinwell declined to answer. Had he done so he would have had to admit that the United Nations had lost control over the field commander appointed by President Truman and that the whole concept of 'Unified Command' was a fiction. On 30 November, in reply to a similar question put by the *New York Times*, MacArthur brazened it out, stating categorically that he had received no instructions from 'any authoritative source that in the execution of its mission the UN Command should stop at the 38th parallel, or Pyongyang, or any other line short of the international boundary'.

The British government was in a quandary. In the view of Attlee and his Cabinet, MacArthur seemed to have been presented with a blank cheque and to be hell-bent on cashing it in the form of an overwhelming victory against the forces of communism. The surge of alarm in London, and Britain's evident wish to avert confrontation with China whilst continuing to support the USA in order to guarantee the safety of western Europe, greatly perturbed Truman and his political and military advisers and infuriated the right wing of the opposition Republican Party.

CHAPTER 12

The Dragon Strikes

On 23 November the Americans celebrated Thanksgiving Day. Rations included turkey and mince pies, which they shared with their allies, and all ranks of the Commonwealth Brigade relished the best meal they had had since arriving in Korea. The official diary of 27 Brigade for the next day reflects a sober return to the business in hand: 'Today has marked the opening of the offensive which it is hoped would reach the Manchurian border and finish the Korean War.' There had been a warning, from the Joint Chiefs in Washington, that many of America's allies were expressing alarm over the resumption of the drive to the Yalu. Despite this, MacArthur was authorized to go ahead.

The centre of the 8th Army line of battle was held by Major-General Coulter's IX Corps, consisting of the 2nd and 25th US Infantry Divisions and the newly arrived Turkish brigade, which lacked combat experience and had not undergone the full in-theatre training programme laid down by MacArthur's headquarters. The 27th British Commonwealth Brigade was also added to IX Corps after the Chinese onslaught had begun. Over to the west, Major-General Milburn's I Corps, from which 27 Brigade was transferred, consisted of the 24th US Infantry Division and the ROK 1st Division, now regarded, under its competent young commander Major-General Paik, as the best ROK formation.

As the UN attack got under way on the 24th, Milburn launched his two divisions west and north-west. Coulter retained the untried Turks at Kunu-ri as his reserve and sent his other divisions north towards Unsan, where the 1st Cavalry Division had received such a bloody nose earlier in the month. Over to the east, with their right flank anchored in the Taebaek mountains, were the three divisions of the ROK II Corps. To the rear of 8th Army lay Walker's reserves, the 1st Cavalry Division and, even further back, in the Pyongyang area, the British 29th Brigade Group, newly arrived and still forming up after its rail and road journey from Pusan.

Initially the advance seemed to be going well against only light opposition;

in reality the enemy were allowing Walker to thrust his army into the jaws of a mighty trap. On the IX Corps front, Major-General Keiser's 2nd ('Indian Head') Division led, with the 25th Division echeloned behind. On the right, however, the ROK II Corps ran into trouble at once. The enemy had identified this as the weak link and its disposition at the vulnerable flank made it all the more susceptible to the Chinese attack of 25 November. Even so, the intelligence report from 8th Army that evening, whilst acknowledging a small increase in enemy resistance, seemed optimistic that the advance would continue next day.

Shortly before midnight on the 25th the Chinese also assailed Keiser's 2nd Division, deployed across 15 miles of front with its axis lying along the Chongchon valley. The enemy had evidently reconnoitred the ground carefully; using mountain paths to outflank their victims, they moved fast on foot. Soon they had worked their way round to the rear of every American unit under attack; bugles, whistles and gongs were used for inter-unit communication and to spread confusion and alarm amongst the defence. Chinese infantry waded the freezing Chongchon river to rush the gun lines of the 61st Artillery Battalion; one battery was quickly overrun and its commander killed as he tried to rally his men. The guns were abandoned but the 23rd Infantry stood their ground as fleeing artillerymen, mingled indiscriminately with Chinese infantry, poured into their positions. Frantic messages to Keiser's headquarters indicated that command posts and administrative units were under attack in the dark, and chaos reigned. Over to the right, the 38th Infantry were also attacked and, like the 23rd, stood firm as the enemy poured round them like an incoming tide. Their commander, Colonel Peploe, organized a successful counterattack at dawn on the 26th to regain positions lost during the night.

With daylight, the commander of the 25th Division, Major-General Kean, decided that it would be unwise to resume the advance until the situation clarified, and he regrouped to await developments. The 24th Infantry, who were in an isolated position on the extreme right of the division, received an air drop of supplies that morning; as it took place the drop zone came under attack and the two rifle companies on the ground escaped as best they could, trekking eastwards across country to 2nd Division's sector. Meanwhile General Kean committed his divisional reserve, the 27th Infantry, known as the 'Wolfhounds'. Their redoubtable commander, Colonel Michaelis, was ordered to plug the hole on the right of the 25th Division. In the Second World War Michaelis had fought in the crack 101st Airborne Division in Normandy, where he was promoted colonel in the field. In Holland in September 1944 he commanded a parachute regiment and was severely wounded, his life being saved on the kitchen table of a farmhouse by an army surgeon whose glider had crash-landed near by. He was back on duty for the Ardennes offensive, driving through the German lines by jeep to play a leading role in the successful stand at Bastogne.

Whilst Michaelis tried to plug the gap in the line, Keiser was facing a fearsome situation in the Chongchon valley. First, he ordered the men of the 61st Artillery to go back and recover their guns before retiring further south. The Chongchon valley was the keystone of the defence and Keiser massed his forces there; but Colonel Peploe's 38th Regiment was out on a limb, calling for help; Keiser turned this down and left Peploe to hold his ground as well as he could. By midday on the 26th he knew he was in trouble; from his right came alarming reports, soon confirmed, that the ROK II Corps had collapsed and fled and he realized that he was now the right flank formation not only of the 2nd Division but of IX Corps and of the whole 8th Army. Peploe turned part of his regiment eastwards to cover the exposed flank as the Chinese raced to the allied rear.

Late on the evening of 25 November Brigadier Coad was warned to get ready for a possible move to the IX Corps area. By midday on the 27th Coad had reported to its headquarters where he found that 'the hysteria was quite frightening and it did not improve as the days went on'. He was told that the ROK II Corps had collapsed leaving a gap of 25 miles in the allied line through which thousands of Chinese were pouring. Coad was given a string of orders which had to be handled with great diplomacy as all were impossible to execute by a brigade which still lacked its own organic artillery, tanks or motor transport unit, for all of which it remained dependent on the Americans. Fortunately, all these orders were cancelled almost as soon as they had been issued.

By the evening of the 27th all talk at corps headquarters was of general withdrawal. During the night, both the US 2nd and 25th Divisions began to fall back and early on the 28th General Coulter sent for Coad, requiring him to send 27 Brigade to cover the withdrawal of the 2nd Division from Kunu-ri by securing the top of the pass over which its huge column of transport, tanks and artillery would have to go. Coad, aware of his brigade's lack of mobility, suggested that it would be more usefully employed establishing a firm position at Chasan, 35 miles to the south of the pass; he foresaw a precipitate general retreat as 8th Army tried to avoid encirclement, and that his brigade could secure the route south if deployed in time. All the same, the Middlesex started up towards the top of the pass; they had almost reached the summit when they came under attack from vastly superior numbers of Chinese who had won the race to the top. After sustaining numerous casualties they were compelled to retire, having no artillery or tank support.

Following Coad's suggestion that 27 Brigade would be more profitably employed further south, its three battalions were just south of the exit from the pass when there were disturbing reports that the Chinese had already cut the road to Chasan in several places. Coad was told that American trucks would be made available to carry the battalions south once they had completed the move of the corps headquarters. All morning the men waited by the roadside as sounds of battle reached them from the north, where 2nd Division was trying to fight its way south from Kunu-ri. Eventually, at 2.15 in the afternoon, Coad gave the order for the battalions to start marching south, fighting their way through any roadblocks encountered. Lifted by the sound of the Argylls' pipers, the infantry set off. It was a hard slog and few men marched less than 20 miles that night.

General Walker now intervened and ordered Coulter to commit the Turkish brigade in an attempt to cauterize the gap on the corps' right. It was ordered to the town of Tokchon and told to hold fast, if necessary driving out any Chinese who might be there already. Once there, the Turks were to maintain contact with Keiser's 2nd Division to the north-west. General Milburn then halted I Corps to safeguard its right flank. In twenty-four hours, the great 8th Army offensive, which was to have ended in outright victory by Christmas, had been stopped dead in its tracks and was recoiling. Its bemused intelligence staff altered their estimates of enemy strength opposing them yet again, this time from 54,000 to 101,000.

After dark on the 26th the Chinese 40th Army had renewed its pressure on the US 2nd Division with an attack on the 23rd Infantry. Colonel Freeman was driven out of his command post which was abandoned, but retaken the next day and its equipment recovered. Whilst Freeman and his staff were fighting for their headquarters, the 2nd Battalion of the 9th Infantry were assailed and forced back in confusion across the Chongchon river, losing most of their vehicles and weapons in the process as hundreds of men waded the icy stream to get away from an enemy who seemed to be everywhere. The survivors sought refuge in the lines of the 23rd. Colonel Sloane of the 9th called down fire from all the artillery he could contact, directing it on to the 2/9th's abandoned position. This disconcerted the Chinese and Sloane rallied the broken battalion back into the line. The enemy continued to attack after dawn on the 27th, using large numbers of mortars, heavy machine-guns and rocket launchers. The Chinese 40th Army was out to destroy the 38th Infantry as more enemy emerged from the east, having finished off the ROK II Corps. As the day wore on even the determined Colonel Peploe had to give ground. Units of the 2nd Division were becoming hopelessly mixed, adding to the problems of command and control.

The Turks' orders had been changed but, owing to difficulty in interpreting them, Brigadier-General Yazici took up a defensive position only just outside Wawon instead of seven miles to the east. Despite this misunderstanding the Turks were still in a reasonably sound position to protect an important sector of IX Corps' front and guard against infiltration from the right flank. Keiser spent most of the 28th sorting out his division and trying to conform with Coulter's instructions for a new defensive line based around Wawon. Unfortunately, the Turks, who had held off the Chinese with little difficulty, misinterpreted another instruction and fell back three miles west to Sinnam-ni at last light. The situation was grave, for Keiser had relied on the retention of Wawon. A major portion of 8th Army was in grave risk of being surrounded.

Late that evening the 7th Cavalry, moving belatedly up the road to the south to secure it as a means of retreat for the forces further north, were confronted by thousands of ROK stragglers and refugees, with whom were mixed Chinese infantry who killed many Americans before they were eliminated. A belated Army Order was issued in an attempt to channel the thousands of refugees to the flanks away from the allied lines. When one retreating ROK artillery unit stalled in the enormous traffic jam and abandoned its guns, American volunteers went forward and saved them. But the situation was hopeless and 7th Cavalry were ordered back, retiring with the survivors of 6th ROK Division.

By the 28th, only three days into the allied advance, 8th Army was in deep trouble. Over to the east the situation on X Corps' front was extremely fluid as thousands of previously undetected Chinese and NKPA troops emerged from hiding to strike at Almond's sprawling command. On Walker's right flank, the ROK II Corps had broken and the Chinese started to pour round to the rear of IX Corps. MacArthur, visibly shaken, announced abruptly that he was going over to the defensive; this was approved by the JCS, to whom he signalled on 29 November calling for the use of Chinese nationalist troops from Formosa. They could, he claimed, be in Korea within fourteen days and there could be many more of them than the 30,000 already offered by Chiang. The JCS, taken aback, replied cautiously, saying that the matter was under consideration; but they were under no illusions as to the side-effects of nationalist involvement. The British Commonwealth governments were unanimous that the Formosa Chinese were totally unacceptable as allies in Korea.

Very early on the 29th the Chinese attacked the Turks at Sinnam-ni, and they retreated to Kaechon which Keiser told them to hold in order to anchor the divisional position. For some reason, Yazici ignored repeated orders to picket the high ground overlooking the town and concentrated most of his brigade in the built-up area where it could play no useful part in the battle. His brigade was soon under heavy pressure from Chinese on the high ground overlooking the town, in which his troops were packed. The road leading north out of the town to Kunu-ri was cut and Yazici gave the order to withdraw to the west. Soon this road was choked with Turkish transport and guns, moving at a snail's pace. An American unit trying to reach Kaechon from the west found itself on the same road as the Turks going in the opposite direction, and had to turn round and go back towards Kunu-ri. The road went over a pass, where all traffic was now halted and under fire from the Chinese on the high ground. Some movement was restored by means of a brilliantly executed medium bomber strike by the USAF, using flares to locate the Chinese swarming to attack the allied column.

Keiser, still in his command post at Kunu-ri, had intended to use the Turkish brigade to secure his Main Supply Route (MSR). Colonel Peploe was in charge of the road and sorted the traffic out, but owing to the lack of interpreters it was found impossible to convey Keiser's orders to the Turks, who were now distributed widely all over the divisional area, enthusiastically fighting any Chinese they met, looking hopefully for their commanders, but totally out of Keiser's control.

Early on the 29th some Turks in a supply convoy reported in to headquarters 2nd Division at Kunu-ri. They said that they had encountered a roadblock on their way up from Sunchon. A Military Police detachment sent to investigate was ambushed and a divisional reconnaissance company sent to clear the block discovered that the countryside to the south, along 2nd Division's planned retirement route, was alive with Chinese. There appeared to be at least a battalion of enemy astride the top of the pass. The main block seemed to be near the village of Yongwon, where the road and railway ran alongside each other. To the south of the exit from the pass General Coulter was moving reserves forward to clear the way out for 2nd Division. At his command Coad sent the Middlesex up; they were ordered to assemble seven miles south of the pass and then move up at first light on the 30th whilst Keiser attacked strongly from the north with the 9th Infantry to fight his way over the top and to safety. Unfortunately the 9th's three battalions had melted away and Colonel Sloane, the regimental commander, could raise only four or five hundred men for the attack. He was directed to start at first light on 30 November; the Middlesex were to be in position at the south end of the pass by 8 a.m. but were not to attack unless ordered to do so by General Keiser. A no-fire line was agreed with the artillery commanders so that the Middlesex would not be inadvertently shelled if they had to go further forward.

It was decided to use the I Corps MSR over to the west, to evacuate as much as possible of IX Corps' remaining equipment and transport. But co-ordination with I Corps broke down and soon the road, barely adequate to supply a battalion, was choked with the vehicles and guns of the two corps as bitter altercations broke out between staff officers and military police. Keiser's staff, still at Kunu-ri, were trying to work out the movement plan for 2nd Division on the assumption that there was only one roadblock on the route south over the pass; they were wrong, for there was another and much larger one than that reported earlier by the Turks. Before dawn on the 30th, Keiser's command post was under small arms fire and the divisional column moved off, many units failing to wait for orders to do so.

The first block was only four miles south of Kunu-ri. It was attacked by tanks as Colonel Sloane of the 9th Infantry made a valiant attempt to get his troops off the road and up the hills to dislodge their tormentors, who were firing on the closely packed column below. Keiser ordered that all equipment apart from that needed to fight with was to be abandoned; cookers, office equipment and stores of every type were thrown off vehicles on to the roadside. A message was sent to the Middlesex to move up to the top of the pass; but because of the terrain there was no direct radio contact and the message had to be passed back to headquarters IX Corps. Some of Sloane's tanks forced their way over the pass and contacted the Middlesex who, as already recounted, had made one unsuccessful attempt on the previous day to get on to the summit. The tanks stayed with them in a defensive perimeter round the village of Yongwon.

With the enemy in huge numbers closing in for the kill from the north, Keiser realized that it was a case of now-or-never and gave the order to 'run the pass'. In any case it was too late to turn back and get on to the now choked I Corps MSR. Keiser, assuming that the message to the Middlesex had got through, and confident that the top of the pass would now be clear of the enemy, got his column on the road. He reversed his earlier decision and ordered that as much equipment as possible was to be recovered; any vehicle that could be coaxed into life was started up as men scrambled aboard. The rest marched by the side of the trucks, keeping under cover as much as possible.

The order to start was given at 1245 p.m. After only a mile the leading tanks ran into a new block, made by the Chinese who had slewed a tank and some half-track vehicles, abandoned the previous day by the reconnaissance company, across the roadway. The delay whilst these were removed produced a chain reaction down the column, which began to concertina. Over the top of the pass was another unexpected block but the leading tank driver barged it aside and was soon amongst the Middlesex, who were sufficiently cheered to signal back that the MSR was open and that the 2nd Division was on its way south; but they were wrong. Two regiments of Chinese had taken up positions overlooking the top of the pass and its northern approaches and were firing steadily down at the mass of stalled transport and at men frantically seeking cover in the roadside ditch and behind burning vehicles. Some men returned the Chinese fire; others sat transfixed and shocked in their vehicles until killed. There was no attempt at launching an organized counter-attack, although Colonel Peploe managed to keep his men together and got them over the pass to safety by 3 p.m.

The Chinese had brought about forty machine-guns into action and these were playing on the column like fire hoses. Men were running, walking, trying to scramble aboard the surviving tanks and half-tracks, dying in the road, crawling along the ditches. Keiser called down airstrikes but was on the verge of abandoning the remaining guns and transport when the fighter-bombers appeared, using napalm against the masses of Chinese on the high ground. Soon the bombs, rockets and cannon fire began to take effect and the enemy fire slackened off. Napalm was coming down so close to the road that vehicles were being ignited, and casualties were also sustained by 'friendly' cannon fire from the aircraft. But it was an impressive performance by skilled and courageous pilots. After two light tanks had been used to bulldoze stalled vehicles off the road the column began to move again on its dolorous passage.

Part of the 2nd Division, including Colonel Freeman's resolute rearguard, had taken the western route out of the trap, using the congested I Corps MSR, and despite the bickering for places which ensued, they fared better than the main body. Freeman's 15th Field Artillery Battalion had managed to get their guns this far, but in view of the heavy traffic, they were ordered to fire off their remaining ammunition and conducted a most gallant final shoot over open sights before reluctantly destroying their weapons.

On the south side of the pass the Middlesex rallied to succour the survivors who came through. Many vehicles bore cargoes of dead and dying men, and hundreds of wounded had to be cared for. Some of those who got through were on the verge of hysteria, firing wildly when they saw the Middlesex, hitting a number of them. The 2nd Division had sustained over 4,500 casualties between 25 and 30 November, more than a third of its strength. Sixty-four artillery pieces, hundreds of soft-skinned vehicles, most of its combat engineer equipment, and nearly half its radios had been lost. The division was no longer battleworthy and was taken out of the line to be rehabilitated. Within days, Keiser was relieved of his command.

By 30 November MacArthur's signals had lost their previous optimism. He stated that the Chinese were aiming for the total destruction of the UN forces and the capture of all Korea. To anxious signals from the JCS concerned about lack of co-ordination between 8th Army and X Corps, which was still firmly under MacArthur's (but not Walker's) control, he replied that he did not intend to put Almond under Walker's command and that X Corps, no matter what happened to 8th Army, would remain in the north-east corner of the peninsula. Thoroughly alarmed, the Joint Chiefs replied that X Corps *must* pass under Walker's command; MacArthur merely ignored them, but agreed with the Pentagon that all Korean territory north of the 'waist' could be abandoned 'except for military considerations relating to the security of the command'.

General Walker established a new defence line some twenty miles to the south of the Chongchon river. The Chinese, exhausted by their astonishing efforts and in need of resupply, did not mount a close pursuit. Only the 1st Cavalry, 24th and 25th Infantry and 1st ROK Divisions were still intact and battleworthy, as were the two British brigades. The Turkish brigade had to be re-formed and given new equipment. Although its soldiers had fought splendidly, relishing the chance to use their bayonets, too much had been asked of them in their first battle; liaison between 2nd Division headquarters and Yazici's almost monoglot staff had been virtually non-existent and although the American liaison officers had displayed great courage, their inability to speak Turkish led to continual misunderstandings and loss of control. Their experience at Kunu-ri implanted in the Turks a deep distrust of the Americans. In future, they said, they would prefer to serve alongside allies who would still be in position every morning and were prepared to stand and fight.

General Walker had to cast about for extra troops as he knew that the Chinese would soon be on the march again. He could not use the four ROK divisions deployed on anti-guerrilla duties in the rear areas, for they were if anything less reliable at this time than those of the ROK II Corps which had just bolted. Other than these he could draw on the élite 187th Airborne Regimental Combat Team, and battalions from the Philippines and the Netherlands, as well as the French battalion which, like the others, had just arrived in Korea. He felt that it would be unwise to stand and fight at this point and began to plan a phased withdrawal down the peninsula leading, in the worst case, to a complete evacuation of Korea. He saw that morale throughout the American and ROK formations was shaky and what came to be known as 'bug-out fever' was rife. This was apparent to 27 Brigade, who kept on receiving reports from 1st Cavalry Division of large numbers of enemy troops bearing down from the north. None of these reports could be substantiated and the brigade war diary reflects the irritation of Coad and his staff: 'It is the opinion that certain units are giving false information in order to extract from commanders and staffs permission or even orders for premature and quite unjustifiable withdrawal. It was just this type of excitable dishonesty which caused some unnecessary and expensive withdrawals in France in 1940.'

CHAPTER 13

Advance to the Sea

In August 1950 a special unit of the Royal Marines was quietly formed at Bickleigh camp in England. The British Chiefs of Staff had declined the offer of the First Sea Lord to send a commando unit immediately to Korea on the outbreak of the war, but he was determined to get his way. The unit drew its manpower from volunteers serving in United Kingdom-based Royal Marines units and in HM Ships serving in Japanese waters; to make up numbers, a draft of reinforcements intended for the 3rd Commando Brigade in Malaya were virtually shanghaied off their troopship at Singapore and flown to Japan to await the rest of the unit. The United Kingdom volunteers were flown out by civil airliner in civilian clothes, so as not to alarm the countries through which they passed, and they were preceded by a flurry of secret diplomatic telegrams: 'It is most important for security reasons that you and your party should do all that you can not to attract attention in Rangoon. You will be staying overnight at principal hotel and will have to be careful to avoid giving the impression of a large British Service party.' It was not explained how some forty marines, however disguised, could be insinuated into a sleepy hotel, or dissuaded from sampling the delights of Rangoon's seamy nightlife.

41 Commando assembled in Japan at Camp McGill, a US Army post near Yokosuka. The 300 men, under the youthful Lieutenant-Colonel Drysdale, were organized on an *ad hoc* basis into three troops or patrols. One troop was present at the Inchon landings, after which it went inland with the US Marines and ended up on Kimpo airfield. Two weeks later, under Colonel Drysdale, the commandos boarded the converted submarine USS *Perch* to raid enemy lines of communication on the east coast, where the key road and rail links ran conveniently close to the beach. *Perch* carried raiding craft and her torpedo tubes had been removed to provide space on the forward deck for 110 troops. This was the first of many such attacks, in which anti-tank mines were laid under railway lines before the party returned to the submarine, entertained by loud

explosions as the next train went over them. In October several successful raids were carried out from converted American destroyers.

Back in Japan the unit continued training with its American weapons and equipment, much of which was superior to standard British issue apart from the cumbersome 'Shoepak' winter boot. In the words of the US Marine historian: 'In shoepaks, perspiration-soaked feet became transformed into lumps of biting pain.' Men immobilized by bad feet could not be kept warm in the Manchurian winter by any form of clothing, and poor footwear sentenced hundreds of men to death during the forthcoming operations, when the commandos and their American comrades would be coping with temperatures down to −35°C.

On 15 November, as 41 Commando went ashore as part of the 1st US Marine Division at Wonsan, its officers and men had little inkling of the ordeal awaiting them. They were, however, pleased at the prospect of action alongside the US Marines, with whom they had so much in common: a confidence born of versatility, fitness and skill-at-arms. What was more, their respective cap badges embodied the globe, symbolizing their readiness to fight anywhere on earth.

Almond's X Corps had landed nearly a month earlier but had encountered little opposition as it probed inland. In the Pentagon the Chiefs of Staff watched their maps anxiously, noting the daily widening gap between 8th Army and X Corps. MacArthur ignored the Pentagon's instructions to use only Korean troops for the penetration and occupation of the frontier provinces; when challenged he replied airily that military necessity dictated the use of non-Korean units. Few dared dispute his decision.

As they advanced at the end of October to the Chosin reservoir over the high passes of Funchilin and Toktong, General Smith's marines suspected that they might have to retire down the same route before long. The weather was appalling and the rough road snaked up to 4,000 feet above sea level. The prudent Smith was under no illusions. He knew his cautious approach irked the impulsive Almond but he had been entrusted with the command of the best men that America could produce, and dreaded the outcome if his division was crushed in those bleak hills. He sensed that X Corps was being lured into the mountains to be cut off from the coast and destroyed piecemeal by an as yet unseen enemy. He wrote home on 15 November to General Gates of the Marine Corps, explaining what he was doing to minimize the catastrophe he foresaw. He concentrated his division in the area of Hagaru-ri, south of the reservoir and 64 miles from the port of Hungnam, placed outposts on the high ground covering the road down which he would have to retreat, and built an airstrip at Hagaru capable of taking C-47 Dakota transport aircraft. Here he established a stockpile of stores of all kinds, building a small town of huts and heated tentage for his headquarters, medical and administrative units, surrounded by defensive positions and heavily wired in. This was to be the Marine Division's operational base for the next few weeks.

By 25 November two of the division's regiments, the 5th and 7th, had been pushed forward to the north-west and were deployed around the town of Yudam-ni, 12 miles from Hagaru. From here they were ordered to move west on the 27th over the mountains and make contact with the ROK II Corps on the right flank of General Walker's advance; but before they even started to move came news of the Chinese offensive and the collapse of II Corps. The marines out at Yudam-ni had suspected the intentions of the Chinese for several days; from observation aircraft and helicopters flying over the mountains they had seen tracks in the powdery snow in all directions, betraying the hitherto unsuspected presence of a huge enemy force. They moved off westwards from Yudam-ni on the morning of the 27th as planned but that night the Chinese closed in on them. All that night, the Marine Division was under heavy attack and Smith ordered his regiments to form defensive perimeters around Yudam-ni, Hagaru-ri and at Koto-ri, ten miles further south down his MSR at the foot of the Funchilin Pass.

The other division probing into the north-eastern mountains was the 7th Infantry, commanded by Major-General David Barr, a competent staff officer with little experience of command in the field above battalion level. His division had been garrisoning the remote northern Japanese island of Hokkaido when war broke out in June and stayed there until August, being steadily drained of its trained personnel as reinforcements for Walker's hard-pressed army in Korea. It had to be hastily brought up to strength for the Inchon landing and, in default of American troops, over 8,500 untrained South Koreans were drafted in. The division had landed in mid-October further up the coast at Iwon, with orders to go for the Yalu at Hyesanjin. Almond was also given operational command of the ROK I Corps, whose units pushed on up the east coast to within 70 miles of the Soviet border.

Colonel Drysdale's men had remained at Hungnam until after Thanksgiving Day. The move up to reinforce Hagaru-ri was supposed to be non-tactical and all the unit's stores were crated and carried on trucks. The column, given the name of Task Force Drysdale, comprised 41 Independent Commando, 'G' Company of the 1st US Marines, 'B' Company 31st US Infantry and various administrative elements; a total of 922 officers and men. The column passed without incident over the Funchilin Pass and arrived at the village of Koto-ri where Drysdale was told that the Chinese had set up a roadblock between Koto-ri and Hagaru-ri, which was under attack. Drysdale was ordered to fight his way through the block. The trucks were unloaded and heavy weapons unpacked. Late in the afternoon Drysdale set out; after two hours, as darkness fell, he had gone four miles against stiffening opposition and asked General

Smith over the radio what he should do; Smith ordered him to press ahead at all costs, supported by a troop of 17 tanks, whose tank commander declined Drysdale's request to distribute his tanks down the line of soft-skinned vehicles and concentrated them at the head of the column. He then drove off and disappeared in the direction of Hagaru-ri.

The column, deprived of the tanks' firepower, was ambushed by enemy in great strength, and forced into several defensive groups along the road. Part of the force struggled ahead and reached a point within sight of Hagaru-ri, where American engineers were working under arc-lights through the night, despite continuous heavy fire, to improve the airstrip. The infantry at the rear of the column had less stomach for the fight and fell back to the relative safety of Koto-ri. Gradually, small parties from the column fought their way into Hagaru-ri. The marines towards the rear of the column had a hard time. Under the senior surviving officer, Major McLaughlin of the US Marines, they held out until 4.30 in the morning when ammunition ran out. McLaughlin ordered the survivors to make their way back to Koto-ri, where some 300 of them rallied. The Chinese ceased firing and sent some captured marines to McLaughlin with a surrender demand. He stalled for time to allow as many of his men as possible to escape into the hills before agreeing to give himself up with the survivors, of whom only 40 were unwounded. The Chinese behaved considerately, allowing the wounded to be put under cover whilst giving them all the assistance they could.

Task Force Drysdale had sustained more than 300 casualties and lost 75 vehicles but had augmented the Hagaru-ri garrison with some 300 useful soldiers. Over 230 men were unaccounted for. Less than 70 of the commandos had got through with Drysdale, and among the 61 dead and wounded was the unit's doctor. Although the tanks had left them in the lurch the US Marine truck drivers had performed magnificently. Drysdale's party now formed part of a beleaguered garrison under the 5th Marine Combat Team whose commander, Colonel Murray, appointed Drysdale to command the garrison reserve. Apart from the Chinese, the marines had to contend with the weather. The thermometer fell to below −20°C and continued to drop. A razor-like wind came in from the vast spaces of Manchuria and Mongolia, bringing frostbite to exposed flesh, and the infantryman's scourge of trench foot began to incapacitate men as the Shoepak boot revealed its shortcomings.

The men of Barr's 7th Infantry Division, many of whom were inexperienced Korean soldiers added to bring the division up to strength, were in a far worse predicament. Most were still wearing the standard issue leather boot, without even an insulated insole; many still had no gloves. Rations were short, and the division was badly under strength. The 17th Regimental Combat Team was at only 85 per cent of war establishment. Having reached the Yalu on 21 November its men were the only American troops to see the river. The 32nd

Infantry had been detached and sent up the eastern shore of the reservoir on the marines' right flank where it had set up a defensive position by 25 November. Its most vulnerable component, and most northerly unit, was Lieutenant-Colonel Don Carlos Faith's 1st Battalion, 32nd Infantry. As darkness fell on the night of 26 November Faith's men were trying to dig into the iron-hard earth some 13 miles north-east of Hagaru-ri on bleak hills overlooking the frozen reservoir. Next day they moved further north. There was warning of an attack that night but as there was no barbed wire and no trip flares the men had to hope for the best as they crouched in pairs in their slit trenches. To add to their misery, frostbite and trench foot were now claiming many victims.

After dark, the Chinese started to probe the defences, and by 3 a.m. on the 28th the battalion was under attack by many Chinese, who got into the mortar platoon's position, driving out its personnel who fell back to join a rifle company further up the hillside. The commander of the heavy weapons company was killed by a Chinese grenade while trying to organize a counter-attack to recover the abandoned mortars, but the Marine air control officer attached to the battalion took over the company. Colonel Faith sent his assistant adjutant to take over but he too was hit at once as the enemy swarmed into the battalion defences. A fighting patrol under the mess sergeant was wiped out and the company remained cut off. The enemy were attacking from all sides but the battalion was still holding out. Its Browning Automatic Rifles (BARs), the American equivalent of the British Bren gun, could only fire single shots because of the extreme cold.

A successful counter-attack at dawn on the 29th recovered the lost mortars, still intact. A skirmishing line then advanced and by last light the enemy had been driven back over a thousand yards. Morale began to return despite the numbing cold, as the battalion braced itself for another night's fighting. With the help of airstrikes by Naval and Marine Corsair aircraft, the battalion perimeter was re-established. So accurate was the air support that many targets were marked for the pilots by phosphorus grenades thrown from the defenders' slit trenches. The imperturbable Marine air controller conducted operations from battalion headquarters. That evening, Colonel McLain of the 31st Infantry Regiment was designated commander of all troops on the eastern side of the reservoir; he came forward to visit Colonel Faith and, cut off by a Chinese roadblock, remained with the 1/32nd.

At the height of the battle on the 28th, a bizarre event took place in Faith's command post. General Almond arrived in a helicopter, bearing an envelope from which he produced some medals. He then said: 'Don, I have three Silver Stars to give away. Choose two men to get them with you.' Faith turned to Lieutenant Everett Smalley, who had been wounded during the previous night's fighting and happened to be in the command post at the time. 'Smalley, come over here and stand to attention,' said Faith, who then caught sight of the headquarters mess sergeant hovering outside the tent. He too was bidden to the investiture. Smalley told a friend later that this had happened, that he had been given a Silver Star 'and didn't know what the hell for'. Disgusted, he threw the medal away, having hoped that the General had been carrying something useful, like medical supplies. Before he flew off, Almond assured Faith and his officers: 'Don't worry, Don. You're only fighting Chinese remnants fleeing north.'

As darkness fell, tired and frozen men prepared themselves for the inevitable onslaught. There were probing attacks, then silence. It was decided to pull back, taking advantage of the lull. The effects of fatigue and cold were manifest and survivors tell of the first signs of panic as the battalion assembled for its withdrawal. What followed is grimly summed up in the US Army's official report, based on interviews with those who got away: 'This action is the story of the disintegration of a highly effective military machine. It illustrates how the breakdown of the leadership structure and destruction of the chain of command transformed a military organization into a mob.'

Instead of leaving their slits silently and individually, whole sections and platoons appeared at check-points in a noisy crowd, some without weapons and equipment, alerting the Chinese who renewed the attack. Cookers were hurled off trucks to make room for the wounded. The aim was to get south and into the defensive area of the 3/31st Infantry, as yet not heavily involved. When the men of the 1/32nd Battalion gained the higher ground overlooking the road to safety they saw to their dismay that the 3/31st were being heavily attacked, their field guns firing over open sights at Chinese milling around their perimeter. The 1/32nd got on to the road running south down the eastern shore of the lake at 5.30 a.m. and started to move along it. Almost immediately they ran into a Chinese roadblock. Colonel Faith ordered one of his companies to work its way inland around the block from the east whilst he launched a diversionary frontal attack. He managed to force his way through and the retreat continued. Moving down the road, and at times across the ice of the frozen lake, Faith's men reached the illusory safety of the 3/31st perimeter at midday. Both battalions dug in as best they could in the icy ground. The artillery were down to four guns, the others having been overrun and captured.

The night was spent in a cramped perimeter measuring some 1,000 yards from east to west and 600 from north to south. It was desperately cold, and automatic weapons had to be fired to prevent seizure every fifteen or thirty minutes. Even the few men who had managed to retain their bedrolls were afraid to sleep for fear of being frozen to death. On the afternoon of the 29th there were three airdrops of ammunition and supplies. The first landed outside the perimeter and had to be fought for; the second went to the enemy; but the third was accurate. Morale began to recover as a series of devastating airstrikes took place during the afternoon. There were rumours that a special task force from 7th Division was on its way. That night the air support continued; pilots reported that they could see the enemy clearly in the bright moonlight and bombs, napalm, cannon and rockets were used to great effect.

Fear of more strikes dissuaded the Chinese from attacking on the 30th and the lull was used to improve makeshift defences. But at 10 p.m. the attacks resumed. A Chinese unit was caught in the light of flares, marching in close order down the shore road; it scattered and vanished into the hills to the east, to attack outlying company positions. Early on 1 December it began to snow and visibility fell to a few yards, enabling the Chinese to infiltrate between the rifle companies. Officers and men were utterly exhausted but some continued to provide inspiring leadership, none more than Colonel Faith, who had assumed command of what now became 'Task Force Faith' on the disappearance and presumed death of Colonel McLain.

Faith called in at the medical aid post, situated in a railway cutting and crammed with over fifty men, asking for any still capable of carrying a weapon to return to the fight. Second Lieutenant James Campbell, a machine-gun platoon commander, was one who responded; he had been hit in the face whilst assuring his surviving men that everything was under control. He crawled to the nearest weapons pit but collapsed again and was returned to the aid post, which had run out of bandages and morphine. His wounds were washed out with disinfectant and he slept for some hours. Captain Navarre the medical officer and his orderlies worked heroically under a tarpaulin screen. The jeep carrying the battalion's medical stores had gone, but at least there was still plenty of blood plasma. Parachutes from the previous day's airdrops were used as blankets and bandages for the wounded and a cook sergeant, who had managed to save two field cookers, produced hot drinks and soup.

At midday Faith decided that if he did not break out, the entire regiment would be lost. The casualties were lifted on to the remaining 22 vehicles and as a last airstrike held the enemy at bay, all remaining equipment was destroyed with phosphorus and thermite grenades. Nearly all the ammunition was gone and few men had more than a single clip of five rounds for their rifles. Faith ordered the survivors to make south for Hagaru-ri where the marines were still holding out. The column was led by a half-track carrying an anti-aircraft 'quad' of four .50 calibre heavy machine-guns. As the vehicles moved off they came under fire and the leading rifle company was hit by a friendly airstrike, covering the road with badly burned men and trucks. It was the beginning of the end. Faith, with a blanket wrapped round him and carrying his cane, walked calmly round encouraging his men to husband their ammunition and make every shot count. He then led a number of attacks against a succession of roadblocks, but was eventually hit in the kidneys and carried on to a truck. When last seen alive he had turned blue with cold. For his selfless gallantry and leadership he was posthumously awarded the Congressional Medal of Honor.

Many fugitives were taking to the ice and marching aimlessly across the lake. The Chinese left these alone, concentrating all their fire on the stalled column. A village already occupied by Chinese lay ahead and a desperate attempt was made to drive straight through. Darkness was falling as the leading vehicle was hit and overturned, spilling its load of wounded into the ditch. An artillery officer led a forlorn hope to storm the village but the attack melted away; the men had little fight left in them. At midnight the village was still full of enemy. Some officers decided to sit tight, others broke away and straggled off over the ice. About a hundred officers and men stayed with the wounded. Campbell, revived by his sleep, took part in a last attempt to smash through the village; the drivers of the first three trucks were shot dead and the column was raked by machine-guns at close range. Campbell got into a ditch, listening with horror to the screams of the helpless casualties as the burning stretcher jeeps were hit again and again. A truck driver drove his vehicle desperately at the vehicles stuck in the road, running over Campbell's foot in the process. The blazing trucks rolled over, with their loads of dead and dying, but the road stayed blocked.

It was 1.30 a.m. on 2 December when Campbell and other survivors began to make their way individually to safety. He met up with the medical orderly who had been dressing his wounds earlier. They found themselves walking across the ice and could see the trucks still burning in the village as the Chinese foraged through them. Of the 17 infantrymen in the party, only three still retained their weapons. The ice was so thick that shells were bouncing off it before exploding. The group regained the road and after two miles arrived at a Marines outpost. By 5.30 a.m. Campbell was in a medical post at Hagaru. He had been shot in the jaw thirty-six hours earlier; at the time he had felt a blow 'as though hit in the face with a baseball' but no pain. Now, he began to feel it. Afterwards, when being debriefed, he would say that 'the thing that beat us was not any overwhelming Chinese masses; it was being cut off from our supply which deprived us of the tools with which to fight'. He also noted that the Chinese, who appeared larger, healthier and less fanatical than the NKPA, were generously supplied with American-made Thompson sub-machine-guns and carried American civilian medical kits; all, he deduced, captured from Chiang Kai-shek's Kuomintang troops during the previous year's fighting in China.

MacArthur's signals to Washington at this point hardly resembled the optimistic reassurances of three weeks earlier. As early as 28 November, after barely seventy-two hours of the Chinese offensive, he was telling the Joint Chiefs that 8th Army was already so weakened that it could not be expected to stand and fight; if this was a gambit to draw more reinforcements from a Pentagon which had hardened its attitude towards further manpower expenditure it fell on barren ground. The Joint Chiefs agreed up to a point, appreciating that for the present no reliance could be placed on the demoralized ROK army and that retirement would be wise. They counselled the adoption of a strong defensive line extending from Pyongyang to Wonsan, thereby ensuring the shortest possible line at the 'neck' of the peninsula. MacArthur disagreed, claiming that this was too far north for his logistics organization to maintain the army in sustained combat, and that in any case he was now concentrating X Corps in the Hamhung area to threaten the Chinese left flank and discourage the enemy from moving into the gap between Almond's Corps and 8th Army. The Joint Chiefs demurred; the Chinese had already shown their ability to infiltrate at will, and they were increasingly worried by the apparent lack of fighting spirit in 8th Army. General Ridgway felt bound to voice his disquiet in the Pentagon map room on 3 December as things went from bad to worse. The Chiefs and the Secretaries of State and Defense glumly regarded the huge battle maps, with their sorry story of the rout of 2nd Division and the drama unfolding on the east coast, and his words were met by a stony silence, but a senior naval officer slipped him a scrap of paper bearing the words: 'Proud to know you.' The Chiefs clearly felt at this stage that almost any instruction given to MacArthur was likely to be openly challenged or disregarded.

General Collins flew to Tokyo for urgent consultation with MacArthur on 4 December and to tell him there were no prospects of short-term reinforcement. The overriding priority was preservation of the UN Command and Collins advised MacArthur that he should think in terms of the worst case and plan a phased withdrawal to the Pusan bridgehead for 8th Army, and to Wonsan and Hungnam for X Corps, and even of total evacuation. The commanders on the ground, Walker and Almond, had divergent views. Walker favoured 'deep retirement', even to the extent of giving up Seoul, and was prepared to go back to Pusan if necessary, rather than pin any faith on the ROKs. Almond was confident that he could hold Hungnam and, having been given the 3rd US Infantry Division to hold his MSR back to the coast, that he could threaten the Chinese indefinitely from this stronghold. MacArthur's staff weighed the factors and opted for a general retreat on Pusan; plans were also initiated to get X Corps out of its bridgehead and return it to 8th Army.

MacArthur visited the front on 11 December and discussed 8th Army's predicament with Walker. In the south the Naktong river defences were to be refurbished, and behind these, in case of collapse, three further lines covering the port of Pusan. Walker had already given orders for these to be prepared and an army of Korean labourers was hard at work. However, much of the material used – barbed wire, timber revetments and sandbagging – was stolen by Korean farmers as soon as it had been put in position.

Truman was pondering what to do about MacArthur's increasingly cavalier behaviour. A few days into the Chinese offensive, with 8th Army apparently on the run and X Corps about to be marooned on the east coast, MacArthur responded to criticism of his conduct of the campaign in the American press by angrily stating through his press officers that his command had done as well as it could, given the political constraint of limiting its operations to South Korean soil and airspace. An infuriated Truman issued a statement on 5 December clearly aimed at MacArthur, directing that any information made public by any executive branch was 'accurate and fully in accord with the policies of the US Government . . . Officials overseas, including military commanders, were to clear all but routine statements with their departments, and to refrain from direct communication on military or foreign policy with newspapers, magazines or other publicity media in the United States.' The Joint Chiefs passed these strictures on to MacArthur on 6 December.

Back at the Chosin reservoir, the remnants of Task Force Faith were cared for by the Hagaru garrison. The sick and wounded were flown out in a remarkable feat of airmanship by the pilots of the C–47s, despite heavy enemy fire and the perils of flying through mountainous terrain in appalling weather without the benefit of radar aids; they continued to operate round the clock, regardless of mortar and shellfire bursting around the precarious landing strip.

It was clear that the hours of the Hagaru perimeter were numbered, even though the enemy appeared reluctant to close with its determined garrison. Almond ordered Smith to destroy all the remaining heavy equipment, weapons and vehicles of the Marine Division and march south to Koto-ri whilst the 3rd Infantry Division secured the route back to the coast. Smith was horrified; this was not the way the US Marines waged war and he was determined to get as much as possible out to safety. For him it was a point of honour not to leave anything to the enemy if he was forced back to the ships. This was not a retreat, he told his men, but 'an advance in a different direction'.

Early on 1 December the two Marine regiments which had been deployed out to the west at Yudam-ni began to fight their way back to Hagaru-ri. They had 15 miles to go and the way in which they conducted their retreat was in the highest traditions of their venerable corps. The enemy could be seen on the high ground, lying in wait as the marines struggled on, but movement off the road was impossible owing to the deep snow. Whenever the weather permitted, Skyraider aircraft of the Marine Air Wing covered the withdrawal, together with fighter-bombers from the 7th Fleet cruising offshore. On the one day when flying was impossible the long column had to stick it out, pinned down on the road by intense fire from the hills. It was three days before the head of the column reached Hagaru-ri and two more before the valiant rearguard came in; at times the Chinese boldly fought their way on to the actual road, forcing the weary marines to mount a series of set-piece attacks to dislodge them.

An unbridgeable gulf had developed between the fighting marines and the staff of X Corps in their comfortable accommodation at Hamhung, where spotless napery decked the mess tables and there was plenty of good food. There were numerous tales of Almond's visits to the front, when he repeatedly demonstrated his lack of the common touch that should unite generals with their soldiers. His 'investiture' at Faith's headquarters has been cited. On another occasion he flew into the Hagaru perimeter and chatted to any marines he came across in their slit trenches; they were amazed when the immaculately dressed Almond commented, 'It's pretty cold, isn't it? When I got up this morning there was a film of ice on the glass where I put my dental plate every night.' He appeared gratified when the filthy muffled figure of the marine to whom he had been speaking responded, 'That's too f—g bad, General.'

Having recovered the 5th and 7th Marines from Yudam-ni, Smith prepared for the ordeal of getting back to Koto-ri. On 6 December the marines began to move down the road from Hagaru as the stores left behind were burnt. The marines were determined to take their dead with them, loaded aboard trucks. Also in the column were over 150 Chinese prisoners. When yet another ambush was sprung many of these ran towards the high ground in an attempt to rejoin their comrades and had to be shot down. The marines held on grimly at Koto-ri until the column was safely through, depleted by enemy fire as it marched and drove on. Fatigue and cold were bringing men to their knees and they had to be kicked into action and kept moving. After twenty-six hours all who were going to survive had reached the Koto-ri perimeter, which now contained some 15,000 men and over 1,000 vehicles. Here, the dead were buried as reverently as possible.

The final stage of the march to the sea involved crossing the Funchilin Pass, where a culvert on the road had been blown by Chinese infiltrators. Colonel Partridge, Chief Engineer of the Marine Division, was flown over the gap to assess the materials needed to bridge it. A number of bridging sections were airdropped accurately on to the site, which was made good in time for the column to cross. A piteous mass of civilian refugees dogged the tail of the column, masking the pursuing Chinese troops from the rearguards' guns. In the end the newly repaired culvert had to be blown, marooning the pathetic civilians on the wrong side, unable to flee to the coast.

Although Major-General Soule's 3rd Infantry Division had been tasked to secure the route all the way back to the sea the enemy kept inserting ambush parties past Koto-ri and at times fierce fighting broke out. The Chinese got into the town of Sudong and had to be driven out at heavy cost, with colonels and staff officers leading parties of headquarters clerks, signallers, cooks and orderlies to eliminate the intruders. At the town of Chinhung-ni, goods trains were waiting on the narrow-gauge line to take the exhausted men to Hamhung and Hungnam. Wonsan further south down the coast had already been evacuated, and Almond was under orders to get out of the X Corps bridgehead as soon as possible. The phased withdrawal and evacuation which ensued required, and got, meticulous staff work by X Corps and US 7th Fleet. By 11 December a firm perimeter had been established around Hamhung and Hungnam; this was gradually given up as the demolition works got under way.

The US Army and Marine Engineers excelled themselves. Hungnam was a major railway centre and its facilities were destroyed when no longer required for the outloading of stores and men. On 15 December a 29-span railway viaduct, 15 locomotives and 275 wagons were destroyed. The wagons were rolled on to the bridge, and the southernmost arch was blown, creating a chasm into which more wagons and locomotives were pushed. The engines had steam up and the wagons were laden with petrol. The luckless Korean railwaymen whose livelihood was disappearing in this huge bonfire were reluctant to help and had to be coerced at gunpoint to destroy their engines. The procedure was repeated span by span until the destruction reached a section of the bridge consisting of wooden spans. A locomotive and several wagons full of petrol were left there and the woodwork was ignited. The heat was so intense that the engine glowed cherry red, its whistle hooting mournfully before everything crashed through to the ground below.

Throughout the evacuation the Chinese were held at bay by the combined air power of the US Marines and Navy, whilst the 7th Fleet stood offshore giving massive gunfire support, including that provided by the 16-inch guns of the USS *Missouri*. By 15 December the Marine Division had been taken off; the 7th Division went next, followed by the ROK I Corps. In an outstanding administrative effort, 86,000 refugees were taken out by sea. By Christmas Eve only the rearguard of the 3rd Division was left ashore, embarking that night; the enemy had been so roughly handled during the final phase that no serious attempt was made to harass the embarkation. As the last ships hauled off, the port was blown up with spectacular results, large quantities of fuel and explosives having been left deliberately in their dumps to enhance the demolition charges.

CHAPTER 14

The Great Bug-Out

Having established a defensive line south of the Chongchon river in the aftermath of the disaster to the 2nd Division, General Walker took stock and realized that there was little hope of holding Pyongyang. He was authorized to evacuate the city on 2 December by Major-General Doyle Hickey, MacArthur's acting Chief of Staff in Tokyo. Anxious about the huge stockpiles of equipment, ammunition, fuel and other warlike stores in and around the North Korean capital, Walker ordered them to be backloaded or used up as far as possible before the city was abandoned. Anything left was to be destroyed where it lay.

For the time being the Chinese made no attempt to follow up, as 8th Army fell back to a defensive phase line 30 miles north of the city. The remnants of the 2nd Division and the survivors of the Turkish brigade were sent back to regroup in the area of Munsan and along the Imjin river. On his right flank Walker deployed the remains of the ROK II Corps. The redoubtable 187th Airborne Regimental Combat Team was held back in Pyongyang to guard its administrative installations and dumps as they were emptied and backloaded, a process far from complete when, on 3 December, Walker was led to believe from fresh intelligence reports that a new Chinese threat was coming from the east; lacking confidence in the ability of the ROK II Corps to hold, he decided to begin the evacuation at once, retiring to a defence line 15 miles to the south. Privately, he knew that he would have to go much further, at the very least to the line of the Imjin, before many days had passed. Orders were given to destroy all remaining stocks in the depots and by dawn on 5 December huge fires were burning around the city as the bridges over the Taedong river were prepared for demolition. Between eight and ten thousand tons of stores were burnt that day, even though the distraught Colonel Stebbkins, 8th Army's chief logistical officer, had asked for just a further twenty-four or forty-eight hours in order to get everything clear.

At this stage 8th Army was not even in contact with the enemy, who had halted to allow their slow-moving administrative tail to catch up. But panic was setting in. 'Bug-out fever' had gripped the Americans and seemed incurable. The port of Chinnampo was evacuated without interference from the enemy on the evening tide of 5 December under the cover of aircraft flying off the British carrier HMS *Theseus*, as 2,000 tons of supplies were put to the torch on the dockside. A trainload of 16 new M-46 tanks abandoned on flat cars in a railway siding had to be attacked from the air on the 6th, although later reconnaissance showed that they had apparently survived. The Indian Field Ambulance had difficulty in withdrawing across the Taedong river. The unit had arrived in Korea with six months' supplies of everything it needed, including medical stores and food, and Lieutenant-Colonel Rangaraj was determined that this would not be thrown away despite orders from 8th Army that everything was to be destroyed. His officers commandeered a goods train, filled the boiler of the locomotive with water by forming a bucket chain to the nearby river; one of his men who had been an engine driver raised steam and got the train over the Taedong just before the bridges were blown.

In both British brigades there was helpless frustration. On 3 December, after a series of orders and counter-orders from headquarters 1st Cavalry Division, the staff of 27 Commonwealth Brigade were told that Pyongyang was to be abandoned. As the war diary records: 'This news was received with amazement by officers and men in the brigade that so much ground was to be given up without a fight and at a time when there was no contact with the enemy.' On passing through the already burning city on 4 December 27 Brigade were heartened by their first sighting of the newly arrived 29 Brigade. 'The greetings exchanged between the two brigades on the way through were lively and choice and not lacking in humour,' the diarist reported. In particular, the usually critical Australians were struck by the professionalism of 29 Brigade's red-capped military policemen, immaculately turned out in battledress with white web belts, signing the routes south and calmly directing traffic as though on an exercise at Aldershot: all this against a background of an army in disorder, its units fleeing away from the front without any discernible traffic plan.

Heading south and leaving 29 Brigade as 8th Army's rearguard in Pyongyang, 27 Brigade moved over 120 miles that night, vehicle fitters bringing up the rear of the column, destroying any transport which could not be repaired on the road, off-loading their cargoes on to empty lorries which had been included in the rear details of the convoy. In the teeth of the Korean winter, fuming at the apparent lack of determination on the part of the American commanders to get to grips with the enemy, the brigade prepared for its next trial.

After landing at Pusan 29 Brigade Group had made their way north, by road and on unheated and extremely uncomfortable trains. The Glosters had seen some light skirmishing in actions against guerrillas further south but the worsening battle situation in the north put an end to training and they had deployed north of Pyongyang by 2 December, astonished spectators of 8th Army's headlong retreat. The men of the Royal Northumberland Fusiliers, Glosters and Royal Ulster Rifles stood in hastily dug positions as thousands of American and South Korean troops headed south as fast as they could go. Those who could not find places on the trucks were compelled to march, many discarding weapons and equipment as they went. The British could hardly believe what they saw. Behind them great clouds of smoke rose from burning depots in Pyongyang. Some of these were visited before they were destroyed and the Glosters helped themselves to as much of the excellent American winter clothing as they could carry, to replace the inadequate British kit issued in Colchester. There was also the chance to acquire coveted American tentage, cooking stoves and tent heaters. Louis Heren of *The Times*, evacuated by air with the rest of the press corps, had to abandon his jeep, laden with crates of vodka, at the airport.

Captain Pat Angier, second-in-command of 'A' Company of the Glosters, noted in a letter to his wife that the position the Glosters were supposed to occupy had already been outflanked. He and his men found it 'a rather disturbing experience to see, night and day, lorries and tanks and guns pelting away from the enemy'. What was even more puzzling was that there were no signs that the enemy was anywhere near the retreating mob that much of 8th Army had now become. Conditions were appalling, as Angier described:

> The morning look in my frosted metal shaving mirror showed my face thick in dust and the eyebrows pasted together. Shaving with a razor that froze at each stroke left my fingers so cold that I lost control of them . . . The greasy sausages turned to white fat soon after leaving the fire and with their taste in my mouth we set off north. I saw the Turks who had that night been in hand-to-hand combat with the Chinese. They had killed large numbers of the enemy but their captain was killed and their ammunition exhausted, their boots worn through, their transport lost. I saw officers and men fight for a drink from a filthy well bucket. They were broken.

Without firing a shot in anger Angier's battalion, with the rest of the brigade, began its long southward march on the evening of 4 December, baffled and frustrated at the lack of fight being shown by the higher command. Standing by the side of the road, the British infantry watched incredulously as the rout continued. Second Lieutenant Paddy Baxter of the Royal Northumberland Fusiliers was highly amused at one large black soldier, trekking south in a group of stragglers, constantly repeating the mantra, 'Feet, don' fail me now!' The roads were choked with thousands of civilians. Angier wrote:

> The day's journey southward across the open plain from Pyongyang could not be seen and forgotten. Full 50,000 souls pouring like lava across the fields. A continuous moving column stretching for thirty miles. Close to, it was a fearful spectacle. Men, women and children fleeing from the fear of death, rape and capture with all

they could carry. Mothers stumbling across the ploughed paddy-fields with a baby tied behind, a baby in the womb and bedding on the head.

A fortnight later the climate took its toll of Angier's company commander and he was promoted to take his place. The older reservists found life very difficult, unused as they were to the rigours of soldiering in such savage weather, and sickness began to deplete the ranks.

The 8th King's Royal Irish Hussars had landed at Pusan from the troopship *Empire Fowey* in mid-November to find that most of their Centurion tanks had already arrived, but that there was a shortage of tank-carrying flat rail cars on which they could be transported to the front. As soon as some could be mustered, 'A' Squadron was sent north. There was at this time little cause for urgency, for it seemed the impending 'Home by Christmas' offensive would put an end to the campaign and that the regiment, together with the rest of the brigade, would soon be sailing back to England. The journey from Pusan to Pyongyang took seven days, described in the unit diary as an Odyssey in itself. The squadron, with only part of its equipment and ammunition, finally managed to concentrate in an old Japanese army barracks on the western side of the city on 2 December.

The arrival of the tanks was timely, for the three infantry battalions of the British brigade felt distinctly vulnerable as they awaited the arrival of the Chinese. The Hussars were ordered forward to support the Royal Ulster Rifles north of the city and as soon as the tanks had received some overdue maintenance and were 'bombed up' with 20-pounder and machine-gun ammunition they moved forward. There were few signs that the retreating troops had been actively engaged with the enemy; there was, however, an almost tangible atmosphere of apprehension. Road discipline was non-existent, lorries frequently leaving the road for any flat ground their drivers could find in an effort to get further up the column. Major Sir Guy Lowther decided to slow down the rout and drew his tank broadside across the road. A truck approached at high speed and screeched to a halt in front of the Centurion. Lowther shouted down to the driver: 'What is your unit? Who is your commanding officer?' To which the terrified driver replied: 'I'se ain't got no unit. I'se a refugee.'

To pass the time, some of the tank crews organized a game of football on a patch of open ground at the roadside. Another American truck appeared, moving fast off the road, and halted in the middle of the football pitch. The driver urged the troopers to get on board; he was heading south and the enemy were hot on his tail. One of the players strolled over and addressed the driver, according to the British defence attaché from Seoul who happened to be present, 'in a commendably calm manner, inviting him to move on so that the game could continue'.

The Hussars, like the Glosters, were able to profit from the uninhibited looting of the 8th Army dumps. Several brand-new American trucks and jeeps were 'liberated' and loaded up with extra ammunition, as it seemed that a major battle must be imminent. As the Hussars moved back into the city and into an abandoned high school where they spent their last night in Pyongyang, the sky flared with great fires and continuous explosions as the last dumps were destroyed. There was a particularly loud one as the Hussars' remaining reserves of ammunition, still aboard a train in a nearby siding, were accidentally detonated, fortunately without casualties.

Very early on 5 December the squadron was stood-to and tank engines started. They had been run every half hour through the night in order to prevent freezing, the temperature now being so low that the issue anti-freeze was useless. Stragglers from the ROK army were still pouring south as the column moved off down the road. Immediately one of the Centurions shed a track. This was serious, as the necessary welding equipment was not available. The tanks carried highly secret gun stabilization gear and under no account could this one be allowed to fall intact into enemy hands. Brigadier Brodie ordered it to be destroyed. Whilst all movable equipment, including the breech block, gunsights and the latest armour-piercing ammunition, was removed, Lieutenant Walter Clode, the troop commander, packed the driver's and fighting compartments with explosives and propellant charges, cut the fuel lines to flood the turret, then laid a trail of petrol to what he imagined was a safe distance. He then threw a match on to it and barely made it to the safety of his scout car as the tank blew up.

The British brigade, still out of contact with the enemy, was ordered further south. The Taedong river line – in the opinion of all who had been guarding it, an ideal holding position – was abandoned without a fight. None of the Hussars was to forget the march south from Pyongyang, conducted in intense cold and a mood of blazing anger that the regiment had not been given a chance to show what its Centurions could do. 'Seldom', wrote the Hussars' regimental chronicler, 'has a more demoralizing picture been witnessed than the abandonment of this, the American forward base, before an unknown number of Chinese soldiers, as it transpired, ill armed and on their feet or on horses.'

The brigade was ordered to take up a new rearguard position at Sinmak, about 80 miles away to the south. No one knew if the unproven Centurions were capable of sustaining a road march over such a distance, for none had been run in; but in the absence of tank transporters they had to do it. Conditions were appalling; water frozen on the turret floors made it difficult to traverse the guns, and the crews, obliged to drive with all hatches opened, iced up at their posts. It was so cold that for the first three hours, running at up to 25 mph, the tank engines did not attain their running temperature. There were numerous stoppages due to fuel contamination and dust, but there were no serious mechanical problems and the journey was completed in fifteen hours, a remarkable achievement given the crews' lack of familiarity with their tanks. On the road to

Sinmak, Lieutenant Randle Cooke's tank ran over a ROK soldier, breaking his leg. Cooke dismounted to see if he could help the writhing man but was pushed aside by the Korean platoon commander who snatched Cooke's revolver and shot the luckless soldier dead on the spot. On arrival at Sinmak the squadron was exhausted, having had no sleep for thirty-six hours; but all ranks now had great confidence in their Centurions.

In the Pentagon there was dismay at the collapse of morale throughout 8th Army. One symptom of this was 'bug-out fever', the readiness of whole formations to take to the road at the mere mention of approaching Chinese forces; another was the failure of battlefield leadership at all levels. The chance to do something about this occurred with tragic suddenness on 23 December, when General Walker was fatally injured in a road traffic accident. Lieutenant-General Matthew Bunker Ridgway, serving in the Pentagon as Deputy Chief of Staff (Operations), was summoned to Tokyo for immediate briefing by MacArthur. He was now aged 55, had commanded an airborne division, then a corps, in Europe in 1944–5 with distinction, and was highly regarded by his associates in Washington where, unlike MacArthur, he was clearly identifiable as one of their 'club'. MacArthur knew him from the days when he had been Superintendent at West Point and Ridgway had been in charge of sports and physical education. He had expressed his wish to have Ridgway in command of 8th Army during the early months of the campaign and clearly preferred him even then to Walker, an officer whose career path had never brought him into contact with the 'MacArthur Ring'.

Ridgway arrived in Tokyo on Christmas Day. Coming direct from the Pentagon he was already well briefed on the dismal situation in Korea. He had not set eyes on MacArthur for many years but quickly fell under the old spell as he listened to the Commander-in-Chief's dissertation. He was to hold the enemy as far forward as possible, and to try and keep hold of Seoul for political and psychological reasons, but not to cling on to the city if it threatened to become a citadel position. MacArthur pointed out that the troops in the field were not looking after themselves properly in the administrative sense; he also went out of his way to decry the value of air support which, he said, had failed to isolate the battlefield or deny the enemy his supplies, as the proponents of air power had so stridently proclaimed. From what MacArthur had to say about the Chinese it seemed that he at last realized they were highly effective soldiers. 'They constitute a dangerous foe,' he told Ridgway. 'Walker reported that the Chinese avoid roads, using the ridges and hills as avenues of approach. They will attack in depth. Their firepower in the hands of their infantry is more extensively used than our own. The enemy moves and fights at night. The entire Chinese military establishment is in this fight.' The goal for 8th Army, in short, was to inflict 'a broadening defeat making possible the retention and security of South Korea'. There was, Ridgway noted, no longer any mention of the north. He was handed over to MacArthur's senior staff officers with the encouraging words: 'The Eighth Army is yours, Matt. Do what you think best.'

Later that day he arrived by air at Taegu to take up his crucial post. Within two days he had not only met with Ambassador Muccio and President Rhee, but had personally flown to visit all his principal subordinate commanders. What he saw and heard did not encourage him. There was, he felt, a distinct lack of the aggression and high spirits to which he had been accustomed in his airborne days. The army had to be restored to a combative mood; whether this could be done in time to save Seoul seemed doubtful. After visiting a number of American units he was agreeably impressed by the air of confidence at the first British unit he encountered, where

> a young subaltern trotted down off a knoll when he spotted the insignia on my jeep. He saluted smartly and identified himself as to name, rank and unit. Knowing that the British brigade had hardly more than a handful of men to cover a wide section of the front line, with a new Chinese offensive expected almost hourly, I asked him how he found the situation. 'Quite all right, sir,' he replied quickly. Then he added with a pleasant smile: 'It *is* a bit draughty up here.' Draughty was the word for it, with gaps in the line wide enough to march an army through.

Ridgway saw that blame for 8th Army's poor showing was to be laid at the feet not of the soldiers in the ranks, but of the politicians who since 1945 had pruned the armed forces to a dangerous level, whilst 'the workings of the Selective Service had sent into action young men who often wound up in uniform simply because they were people of little influence at home'. He also found an army which clung to the roads instead of getting on to its feet and going for the high ground like the Chinese, and took all manner of irrelevant luxuries into the field whilst failing to pay due attention to the principles of good feeding, military punctilio and personal cleanliness. The new commander of 8th Army decided to sort all this out as quickly as possible. As the year drew to its end, there were ominous signs that the Chinese, who had leisurely but methodically followed the allies down from Pyongyang to the line of the Imjin river, were preparing to renew their offensive, and that the objective for this was no less than Seoul itself.

MacArthur had, to all intents, washed his hands of responsibility for the tactical conduct of the campaign, and the astute Ridgway knew he had to make his mark at once. At main headquarters 8th Army in Taegu he found a sprawl of staff branches and ancillary services, whilst his forward tactical headquarters in Seoul was almost non-existent. He decided to move there at once to direct operations and weed out any officer who was failing in his duties, starting with his own staff. He was appalled by the lack of aggression and alertness, and of that desire to help the fighting formations which is the hallmark of good staffwork. He gave everyone a fair chance; then the axe began to fall. Divisional and regimental commanders who ran their battles from the rear were ruthlessly picked off and replaced with officers ready to get into the thick of the fight and lead by example. Realizing that 8th Army was incapable of mounting offensive operations in its present state, Ridgway ordered all formations to step up their patrolling and make aggressive contact with the enemy.

On the western sector of the front a defensive line was established on the Imjin river, but as this largely depended on the ability of ROK troops to hold it, plans were made for a two-division bridgehead around Seoul as a fall-back position, with its back to the Han river. On 29 December the enemy attacked on the central front where the groggy ROK II Corps was holding the line whilst trying to regroup following its terrible beating north of Pyongyang only a month earlier. Almost immediately it gave ground. Ridgway had few dependable reserves at his disposal and had to use the 2nd US Infantry Division, still recovering from its earlier mauling. It was shifted from near Seoul to the central front.

At last, MacArthur placed X Corps under 8th Army command and Ridgway committed it to battle; the line held. On 31 December he set up his tactical headquarters in Seoul and next morning embarked on the first of what soon became known as his whistle-stop tours; like Field Marshal Montgomery he knew the value of studied eccentricities of dress. Travelling in an open jeep, wearing full combat kit ostentatiously embellished with a pair of hand grenades, he aimed to be seen in the forward areas by as many troops as possible. As he drove north past Uijongbu he saw to his dismay what generals dread; masses of his own troops were straggling south away from the front line. The ROK army's Imjin defences had crumbled. There were reports of Chinese and North Korean attacks on the ROK III Corps far out on the eastern front. This meant that I and IX Corps – the mainstay of 8th Army in front of Seoul – were already compromised by the threat to their right flank.

Ridgway ordered both corps to retire behind the Han river; but General Milburn of I Corps, either from genuine misunderstanding or perversity, gave instructions that the two-divisional bridgehead in front of Seoul was to be held 'at all costs' by the 24th and 25th Divisions. Ridgway was furious; it was *his* prerogative to give such 'last ditch' orders, and in any case he had no intention of leaving units to fight it out in isolation until overrun; this applied particularly to politically sensitive units from other United Nations contingents, especially the 27th Commonwealth and 29th Brigade Groups, both deployed on historic invasion routes leading to the capital. The events of the next few days were to show how near Milburn came to losing both British brigades, one of them in its first battle.

The 27th Commonwealth Brigade had got clear from Pyongyang but faced a nightmare drive of almost 140 miles south. Brigadier Coad was amazed to receive the order when called to divisional headquarters. His brigade had experienced only the barest enemy contact in its present position and nobody in divisional HQ could give him any reason for this huge withdrawal. Not for the first time he was surprised at his superiors' insistence that he drive to their command posts, often over dangerous and heavily congested roads, to receive orders, instead of getting them concisely over the radio.

Coad's staff found the new location already occupied by an American regimental combat team which refused to budge, so 27 Brigade had to move a further 18 miles south. The road was cut in several places by guerrillas infiltrating down from the mountains and the MSR was blocked by columns of American transport containing infantry who seemed content to sit in their trucks whilst someone else cleared the roadblocks. The Australians set about this task with gusto, taking the chance to appropriate numerous abandoned trucks and their useful loads of tentage, clothing and rations.

IX Corps headquarters were in the ramshackle town of Uijongbu and 27 Brigade was detailed to defend it, a duty soon known as 'Palace Guard'. Called to the command post for orders, Coad found 'complete lack of control or planning . . . continually we were given jobs that other people were already doing, or three or four tasks at once which were contradictory and could not possibly be done. Morale at the headquarters was appalling. The axis was universally called the "escape route" and complete evacuation by sea was openly talked about.' On 28 December, however, Coad met Ridgway for the first time, to find him 'most refreshing. The gist of his policy was as follows: "We are at present holding a line just south of the 38th parallel. This is a political line from which I am prepared to withdraw should enemy pressure become too great. We will fall back to a line north of Seoul which we will hold against all comers."' Events were to prove that even Ridgway had been over-optimistic.

Despite earlier frustrations Coad soon received some useful help from 8th Army in the shape of an artillery observation battalion hurriedly trained in gun drill and equipped with 105mm howitzers. A company of heavy mortars from an American Chemical Corps battalion was also attached to the brigade, an association which became semi-permanent as the units stayed with 27 Brigade until the following April, resisting every attempt to have them returned to American command. After supporting the ROKs they found it refreshing to work with the British; the ROK artillerymen resented having American mortars in support as this mysteriously involved loss of face. Another valued addition to Coad's brigade was the arrival of the 60th Indian Parachute Field Ambulance, which joined in mid-December after the fall of Pyongyang. This would be a happy association, lasting until the Indians were recalled by their government in 1952 without replacement. By then they were admired by all the United Nations forces in Korea for their medical, surgical and nursing skills and their warm hospitality and courtesy to visitors who enjoyed at least a mug of superbly made tea and, if lucky, their legendary curries.

Another welcome new arrival at the front was the Expeditionary Force Institute (EFI), the active service branch of NAAFI – the Navy, Army and Air Force Institutes. This ubiquitous organization's personnel, uniformed and bearing the cap badge of the RASC in order to satisfy the requirements of the Geneva Convention, operated small Fordson shop wagons which somehow negotiated the appalling Korean roads, selling much-needed commodities like writing paper, toiletries and confectionery. Further to the rear at the army railhead at Suwon NAAFI/EFI established a depot from which huge amounts of beer and spirits were sold to unit messes; this was the envy of the American army whose personnel were reluctant victims of a bigoted temperance movement in the United States which had joined forces with evangelical women's organizations to lobby Congress, denying liquor to the fighting men. As a result, NAAFI beer and spirits became a vital currency with which dollar-starved British personnel were able to acquire virtually any item in the American military inventory. Had it not been for this, and judicious looting of abandoned US equipment, both the British brigades would have faced a terrible winter with inadequate tentage and poor winter clothing. American weapons were also acquired on a similarly informal basis. Eventually, the prize example of such bartering would be the acquisition of an American L-19 Bird Dog aircraft for the use of the commander of the 1st Commonwealth Division in exchange, it was reputed, for a case of Scotch delivered to the commander of I Corps.

A second Chinese attack on the ROKs across the frozen Imjin was launched after dark on 31 December. As in their earlier offensives they timed it to coincide with a waxing three-quarter moon. By daylight on New Year's Day, although some of the defenders were still holding out, flanking units had scattered and by last light the Chinese were across the river in strength in pursuit of the broken ROKs.

The success of this attack was no mere chance. The Chinese had carefully reconnoitred the river line by night, noting all defensive minefields, the heights of the banks and the exact locations of belts of defensive wire. Issued with hooked 25-foot poles for the neutralization of anti-personnel mines, the first assault wave of 500 men had rolled up their quilted trousers and covered their legs with lard to avoid frostbite should they fall through the ice. Every man had been told to make himself a pair of straw sandals to improve traction whilst running across the frozen river; before the attack, all ranks were treated to a hot meal and each man carried three days' dry rations and one day's fresh. Ladders had been made to assist in scaling the high banks of the Imjin, which the defenders thought were too steep to be climbed. Every possible contingency had been foreseen and it is not surprising that this professionalism enabled two assaulting battalions to defeat a division.

The artillery to support the crossing had been brought forward during the three preceding nights and carefully concealed. By dawn on 31 December over 7,500 men and 70 guns had been hidden in an area of a square mile. Senior commanders visited every unit to check their camouflage. During that day a whole Chinese division lay concealed within a mile of the water's edge. 'Not a single man, horse, rifle or weapon was exposed,' reads the Chinese post-combat report. 'Enemy planes circled low overhead all day long but were unable to detect our intentions. We thus achieved complete surprise and when enemy planes returned late in the evening we were already across the Imjin and driving into enemy territory.' At 4.40 p.m. on the 31st, as darkness fell, the Chinese guns fired for twenty minutes; three flares were then fired, the artillery intensified and the two assaulting battalions went across. More flares directed the guns to cease fire, enabling the infantry to break into the ROK positions, which had been overrun within forty minutes. By dawn on 1 January the Chinese had advanced 20 kilometres as the shattered 1st ROK Division melted away.

Coad was in Hong Kong as the new attack broke; he had been ordered there to rest and also to care for his sick wife. He was abruptly summoned back to resume command as yet another crisis threatened 8th Army. The brigade was deployed to a blocking position at Tokchon, north of Uijongbu on the main invasion route. Armed with a 'somewhat wide and vague directive' Coad deployed his Australians in Tokchon village, facing west, with the Argylls five miles back down the Uijongbu road. This proved difficult as the ROKs were already streaming south.

New orders came from IX Corps to fall back and occupy a position in defence of Seoul. The 24th US Infantry Division had apparently got wind of this order as its transport was already choking the road south from Uijongbu. No timings or staff tables were issued for this complicated move, and details were left for Coad to discuss with the staffs of Major-General Church's 24th Division and a ROK Division which to all intents was non-existent. 27 Brigade was to provide the rearguard for the retirement of IX Corps. Coad still distrusted Church for letting 27 Brigade down badly in the break-out across the Naktong river three months earlier by withdrawing artillery support at a critical moment in the battle. At least Church was good enough to tell Coad that 'he liked the British to do the rearguards as they had a steadying effect on the American soldiers'. As Coad (who tactfully kept this to himself for many months) drily noted: 'A nice compliment; but a repetition becomes tiring. Another American commander who passed through us told me his troops would not have liked to have been left behind in Seoul as we were and seemed quite surprised when told that we did not particularly relish it either.'

Coad went on to record that 'this complete lack of control by higher headquarters was a feature of the American command'. In the event, the Australians had to fight their way south from Tokchon; Colonel Ferguson and his company commanders, having gone to the rear to site new positions, were cut off by enemy roadblocks. The battalion, steady as ever under the command of its adjutant and the company seconds-in-command, got out intact with all its transport, including that purloined further north from the Americans. Coad pointed out the difficulties of acting as rearguard to the nimble ROK Division, 'as they come streaming back in all directions, usually closely followed by the enemy, and where one side ends and the other begins is a very difficult decision to take'.

The withdrawal through Seoul continued in shambolic conditions: the brigade was ordered to take up defensive positions which it had not been able to reconnoitre and dig, and at the last minute the bridge over which it was to pass to the south bank was changed, necessitating yet more reconnaissance parties. All this time, the Australians were still fighting off the pursuing enemy. Coad frequently had to visit his superior headquarters in order to find out what was happening; when he arrived at the HQ of the 25th Division on the morning of 4 January at the height of the evacuation of Seoul, he was surprised to find General Church of the 24th there as well, amid a scene of pandemonium, with a mass of excited staff officers all talking at the tops of their voices. 'There was even a woman press reporter present! 25 Division seemed to be in a muddle and was having difficulty in extricating itself. 29 Brigade had also got into trouble, and nobody seemed interested in 27 Brigade. I got an agreement from 25 Division at last for us to withdraw and I left quickly before anyone could change their minds.'

29 Brigade was indeed in trouble. In the wake of the withdrawal from Pyongyang, it had moved south into reserve north of Seoul. Brigadier Brodie may have been irked by the denial of opportunity for his brigade to display its mettle, but he enjoyed a less stressful relationship with Lieutenant-General Milburn of I Corps than did Brigadier Coad with Major-General Coulter of IX Corps. Brodie also had a far better balanced force under his command; he had the support of the 8th Hussars and their formidable Centurions, the 45th Field Regiment Royal Artillery and its 25-pounder guns, a heavy mortar battery equipped with 4.2-inch mortars and a squadron of the 7th Royal Tank Regiment with its Crocodile flame-throwing tanks. There was also a fully equipped Field Squadron of the Royal Engineers, a large Royal Army Service Corps company with abundant transport resources and supply and ammunition issuing sections.

Plenty of technical backing had been organized for the brigade including the services of a large field workshop of the Royal Electrical and Mechanical Engineers as well as the unit workshops and recovery sections spread around the combat units. The brigade had also brought to Korea a mobile laundry and bath unit of the Royal Army Ordnance Corps; the morale value of hot showers and a change of clothing, inner and outer, under field conditions during the

Korean winter was immeasurable. The officers and men of 27 Brigade may have professed disdain of the 'Rolls-Royce Brigade' but few ever lost the chance, when it occurred, to call in for a hot shower.

By the middle of December, 29 Brigade was deployed north of Seoul in what was, for the season, reasonable comfort. Sleeping bags had at last been issued to all ranks, and despite snow and fog, conditions were infinitely better than they had been up at Pyongyang. A certain amount of reorganization was carried out. The Centurions, it was decided, were not to be risked north of the Han river in case more fell into enemy hands, and they were moved south to Suwon. A scratch armoured squadron, named 'Cooper Force' after its commander Captain Astley-Cooper of the 8th Hussars, was formed from the regiment's reconnaissance troop and its Cromwell tanks; additional tanks were found by borrowing the observation post tanks of 45th Field Regiment. The role of Cooper Force was to provide close support as and when required for the infantry battalions. A troop under Lieutenant Godfrey Alexander of the Hussars was allotted to the Royal Ulster Rifles.

After celebrating Christmas Day in traditional style the brigade got down to the hard work of digging a reserve defence position for occupation by a ROK division. This work was largely carried out by Korean civilian labour under British supervision and continued for three days until news came on New Year's Day that the enemy had attacked and driven in the ROKs and that 27 Brigade was fighting hard on the Uijongbu road. The situation was already confused as 29 Brigade was ordered to occupy the defensive positions it had been preparing for the ROKs. The brigade had to be spread out into positions designed for a complete division; as a result there were unavoidable gaps. By midday on 2 January, order was emerging from chaos. A battalion of Thai infantry was attached to the brigade; it was quickly realized that they were unlikely to be of much value; they were numbed by the cold despite their American winter clothing, and in any case did not strike Brodie and his staff as of sufficient martial bearing or competence. The Thais were shepherded into a reserve position to the rear whilst 29 Brigade improved its defences energetically, knowing that the Chinese 39th and 50th Armies had been identified to their immediate front.

The I Corps line was held on the left by the US 25th Division; on the right, astride the MSR running south from Uijongbu to Seoul, was the 21st Regiment of the US 24th Division. Brodie, convinced that battle was imminent, deployed the Royal Ulster Rifles, together with Cooper Force, to defend the forward left sector of the brigade area, whilst the Royal Northumberland Fusiliers were placed to the right, their own right flank edged by the formidable range of jagged hills known to all British troops as the 'Dragon's Teeth', leading north towards Uijongbu. On the far side of these hills was the American 21st Regiment. The Glosters were held back as the brigade reserve.

Back in Seoul, the Royal Engineers of Major Tony Younger's 55th Field Squadron were preparing the demolition charges for the remaining bridges over the Han. Late on New Year's Eve Brodie issued an order of the day reflecting his personal view of the situation: 'At last after weeks of frustration we have nothing between us and the Chinese. I have no intention that this Brigade group will retire before the enemy unless ordered by higher authority to conform with general movement. If you meet him you are to knock hell out of him with everything you have got. You are only to give ground on my orders.'

The Ulsters made contact with the Americans on their left, astride the Seoul–Munsan road, where a battalion of the 35th US Infantry Regiment was deployed around the village of Koyang. Very early on 3 January, the Ulsters heard firing from that direction and the whole brigade stood to arms. It appeared that the Americans were under heavy attack and the Ulsters sent out a patrol to investigate. Shortly after it went out there was a flurry of shots and grenade explosions; the patrol had been overwhelmed by vastly superior numbers of Chinese who, using their ability to move soundlessly at night, had crept undetected almost up to the Ulsters' wire. Both the Ulsters and the Fusiliers to their right now came under heavy attack; at one point the Fusiliers' command post was overrun and the signallers manning the battalion telephone exchange were killed at their posts. Despite the confusion caused by this loss of communications the remainder of the battalion held its ground; but Chinese infantry were continually infiltrating between the rifle companies and got in among the transport lines, killing or capturing the drivers.

Over on the left of the brigade the Ulsters prepared a counter-attack against enemy who had penetrated into the battalion's position. Uniquely in 29 Brigade they had created a sub-unit known as the 'Battle Patrol', heavily armed and capable of being moved cross country at speed in the tracked weapons carriers of the support company. The attack gained a respite and heavy casualties were inflicted on the enemy by artillery fire from the 45th Field Regiment, American howitzers, the guns of Cooper Force's tanks and the 4.2 mortars of the brigade's mortar battery.

Another successful counter-attack, by the Fusiliers, took place in the afternoon, carried out by a rifle company hurriedly brought up from Seoul where it had been acting as bridge guard on the Han river. The attack was supported by the lumbering Churchill tanks of the 7th Royal Tank Regiment who had gladly forsaken their flame-throwers for the occasion. However, heavy tanks were of limited use in the close country around the 29 Brigade area, being unable to leave the narrow tracks and take to the paddy-fields. The fusiliers captured earlier in the day were freed and numerous Chinese put to the bayonet in a short but bloody fight.

During the afternoon Brodie received orders to move the brigade back across the Han that night. He issued his orders to all units at 5.20 p.m. The Ulsters and

Fusiliers were to start thinning out at 6 p.m., withdrawing through a position held by the Glosters, who had not as yet seen action. The Thais had already been despatched to the rear in order to clear the withdrawal routes. The Fusiliers managed a clean break and got away from 6.30 p.m. The trucks of 57 Company RASC were waiting for them north of Seoul and they were back across the river by the small hours of the 4th, concentrating at Suwon by dawn.

The Royal Ulster Rifles were less fortunate. Disengagement in contact with the enemy is a most hazardous operation and in this case, with an aggressive enemy swarming through the battalion area in the dark, in tumbled country with virtually no motorable tracks to the rear, the Ulsters would be fortunate to extricate themselves, especially as the Americans on the left had already pulled out under pressure. Much of the battalion's equipment was still on top of high hills and had to be manhandled down to the Koyang valley, a difficult feat at any time, now infinitely hazardous in the presence of the Chinese who were working around the flanks following the departure of the Fusiliers. 'B' Company got away safely and were followed by 'C' and 'A' Companies, under increasingly heavy enemy fire. By the time the support company, its carriers bearing the mortars and Vickers guns, had started down the track, the Chinese had already occupied the positions vacated by the other companies, from which they commanded the road back; it was now a case of running the gauntlet. The Chinese were not only in great strength on both sides of the road but had occupied a village through which the retiring riflemen had to pass, and had also followed hot on the heels of the US 27th Regiment as it pulled back down the Munsan road, further compromising the Ulsters.

No sooner had the support company column formed up at 10 p.m. when it came under fire from all directions. After only 250 yards the column was halted as carriers and vehicles skidded on the ice and veered into the paddy-fields. Twice there were roadblocks which had to be fought through. Abandoned vehicles and carriers were burning, and ahead, the village occupied by the Chinese was well ablaze, illuminating a confused battlefield. The tanks of Cooper Force stormed it but the leading tank stalled and after that, all who could still walk left their tanks and vehicles to make for the high ground to the west of the track.

Once it was clear that the Ulsters had been trapped, Ridgway intervened personally, ordering that every effort be made by Major-General Kean and his 25th Division to extricate them. Brigadier-General Michaelis of the 27th 'Wolfhounds' Infantry immediately offered to do so, but Brodie declined the offer, saying that the Ulsters 'would have to knock it out for themselves'. He reasoned that, under the circumstances, such an attempt would only succeed in losing the 27th Infantry as well, and harsh though the decision might have seemed, he was probably right. Ridgway's anxiety sprang from a political imperative; the UN Command shrank from losing a national contingent, a particularly urgent consideration following the savaging of the Turkish brigade a month earlier.

Brodie's brigade had been attacked by at least two Chinese divisions, but as these were parts of two different armies there was a lack of co-ordination in their advance which enabled the survivors of the Royal Ulster Rifles to get clear by 3.30 a.m. on the 4th. When the battalion mustered at Suwon later that morning the full extent of its losses was apparent. Cooper Force had been wiped out, losing all its tanks in the bloody night battle around the Ulsters' withdrawal route. Astley-Cooper and Alexander had both been killed; another officer, Lieutenant Probyn, descendant of a family renowned in the history of the Indian Army, died during the terrible march of the prisoners to captivity in North Korea. Survivors of the Ulsters continued to report in at Suwon for several days. Nearly 300 officers and men, including Major Blake, killed in command of the battalion, had been lost in addition to the ten tanks.

The final act as far as 29 Brigade was concerned was the blowing of the Han bridges by Major Younger's squadron of sappers. Very seldom does an engineer officer have the professional satisfaction of destruction on this scale. As 6,000 pounds of carefully placed explosive did their work, he noted with justifiable pride that of all the miles of complex wiring and fuzing, not one circuit failed.

CHAPTER 15

Winter of Discontent

By December 1950 it was high time for Attlee to go to Washington. He had counselled caution ever since the UN forces crossed the 38th parallel in September. Increasingly agitated signals via the Indian government had indicated that the Chinese were poised for a war of intervention. Now that the Chinese had joined battle, the Washington trip was essential in order to express Britain's fears that the war was about to get out of hand and to enforce consideration for its position as, in its own eyes at least, a world power.

Apart from the apparent collapse of the 8th Army in Korea there was fear in London and elsewhere of possible unilateral use of nuclear weapons by the Americans. Other UN allies were anxious at the risks to their men and critical of MacArthur's handling of the campaign. Even in Washington there was concern; Acheson, the 'westerner' who had effectively committed the United Nations to battle in Korea, now stated that China was the wrong enemy and the Soviet Union the true threat. In a singular volte-face, he favoured complete withdrawal, and redeployment in Europe to confront the USSR. Generals Marshall and Bradley recommended holding a strong defensive line at the narrowest part of Korea, and General Lawton Collins claimed that Korea was 'not worth a nickel', given Russian strength in the Far East. Many American military leaders believed that total evacuation was inevitable, and contingency plans were put in train. Others conceded that earlier British suggestions of holding a strong line and then offering to go to the conference table had merit. But in Korea the retreat was in full swing and Pyongyang about to fall.

Before departing for New York, Attlee conferred with the Commonwealth High Commissioners in London. Those of Australia and Canada insisted that firm controls be imposed on MacArthur. India supported a cease-fire, maintaining that the Chinese intervention was 'essentially defensive'. Finally the French Prime Minister, René Pleven, and his Foreign Minister Robert Schuman flew to London, stressing the need to restrain MacArthur.

The Anglo–American summit meetings took place from 4 to 8 December as the UN forces in Korea reeled back following the previous week's Chinese attack. Attlee was aware of the views of the British Chiefs of Staff who at their meeting on 1 December had heard an unusually impassioned appreciation of the situation by Field Marshal Slim: the British aim in Korea should be to help establish a firm defence line and to take part in no further offensives, even if the UN forces were in position to mount one; there should be no more reinforcement of our ground forces there; above all, no use of nuclear weapons even in dire emergency, as this would serve only to drag the Soviet Union into the war. It would help if the Americans suspended or at least reduced the strategic and interdiction bomber offensive against North Korea.

At their initial summit meeting the two leaders reviewed the general situation in the light of developments throughout the Far East and General Omar Bradley summarized the latest military situation in Korea, where things were grim. The meetings were continued on the 5th aboard the presidential yacht *Williamsburg*. Attlee was on thin ice and knew it. Acheson, trimming his sails again, did not hesitate to use moral blackmail in his efforts to stress the need for Britain to support American policy in the Far East; if the United States gave up the fight there would be an adverse national reaction in America against her European allies and popular clamour for the withholding of aid to those – by implication the British in particular – who had been party to a collapse of American arms in Korea. Attlee repeated his plea for moderation in dealing with Red China, and there was a head-on clash over Formosa.

As the meetings became acrimonious, Britain was accused of shirking the defence of Europe. Attlee noted acidly that MacArthur appeared to have been given *carte blanche* to run the Korean War as he more or less saw fit. Bradley retorted that MacArthur was doing exactly what his United Nations mandate required of him and that in any case the war could not, as the British seemed to think, be run by committee. If the allies were dissatisfied, they were at liberty to pull out and would be given every assistance to do so. If they stayed they must accept the authority of the United Nations Commander. Truman added that the United Nations had asked the United States to run the war and that he would continue to do so until ordered to stop. As a further twist, Acheson asserted that the United States would find it impossible to provide the Supreme Commander for NATO in Europe if all the member states had to be consulted before any decision was taken. The message was clear; the British should accept American predominance in Europe as well as in Asia and shut up; by implication, Britain was no longer a great power and could not expect the former deference of its ally. The myth of the 'special relationship' so carefully cultivated by Churchill was exposed as an illusion.

A bland joint communiqué stressed the unanimity of both nations on the Korea issue, the need for a negotiated settlement, and settlement of the Formosa question by peaceful means. Truman privately assured Attlee that no nuclear weapons would be used against North Korea or China. There was no agreement, however, over the admission of Red China to the United Nations (Truman admitted that it would be 'political dynamite' in the USA). Attlee failed signally to persuade the Americans that the Chinese were acting defensively in Korea or that the enemy onslaught had been triggered by MacArthur's 'Home by Christmas' offensive. It was, they believed, a pure coincidence; they remained convinced that the Chinese assault was an integral part of a world conspiracy to destroy democracy.

By mid-December it was apparent that China would only accept a political solution involving the total withdrawal of UN forces from Korea, the withdrawal of American protection from Formosa, and admission of Red China to the UN. On 19 December the UN General Assembly adopted a cease-fire resolution which went as far as providing for talks to determine the basis on which a satisfactory cease-fire could be arranged. The Chinese stance undermined this idea from the start and no agreement could be wrung from Peking. It was now that pressure was brought to bear by the United States in the General Assembly to have China declared an aggressor.

On 17 December, Truman broadcast to the American nation, declaring a state of National Emergency. Blaming the Soviet Union for the worsening international situation he affirmed the determination of the United States to uphold the principles of the UN Charter as well as his personal intention to take 'every honourable step' to avert general war. Using the constitutional power granted by the National Emergency he announced a drastic expansion of the US armed forces with the recall of thousands of reservists to a manpower level of 3.5 million, plans for the expansion of military production, and the setting-up of an Office of Defense Mobilization. Within a year, military production would increase fivefold. When the Korean War broke out the US armed forces had numbered some 1.5 million men; by the end of the year 2.5 million would be in uniform. To pay for all this, drastic economic measures were necessary: credit control, higher taxes, and a reduction in the production of non-military consumer goods.

Despite voluble dissent from his own backbenchers in Parliament over the certainty of huge increases in defence spending, Attlee revealed the full extent of the British rearmament programme at the end of January 1951. Scenting blood, the Conservative and Liberal parliamentary parties called for an immediate defence debate, Winston Churchill assuring Attlee that the government's proposals would be examined by the Tory opposition with 'fidelity, candour and goodwill'. The debate duly took place on 14 and 15 February on the motion that 'This House approves the policy of HM Government relating to defence'. Shinwell opened for the government, emphasizing that the government's position was based on collective defence as a member of NATO and other alliances. Churchill promptly tabled a motion of censure, signalling a change from the

Conservatives' previous policy of unqualified support for British involvement in the Korean War; Tory MPs attacked the Labour Party as being riddled with pacifists and fellow-travellers whose sympathies lay with the communist world, and whose attitudes had split the Labour Party from top to bottom, depriving it of authority to govern.

The censure motion failed when the Liberals voted with the government, but time was running out for Labour. The nation was weary of wartime austerity. Food rationing was still in force; on 26 January 1951 the Ministry of Food had announced a further reduction in the weekly meat ration from 10d to 8d (or about four ounces) a week per person but attempted to soften the blow by granting a supplementary issue of two pennyworth of corned beef, as housewives demonstrated against rationing outside the Palace of Westminster. On top of this the coal industry was in chaos and there were dock strikes in Liverpool and London. None of this helped the government as it sought honourably to meet its international commitments.

On 30 December, as the Chinese prepared to cross the Imjin, MacArthur replied in detail to the Washington Joint Chiefs of Staff who had asked for his views on total evacuation. He pointed out that American naval and air potential was not being fully used, that the use of Chiang's Kuomintang troops had been denied him, as had the use of guerrillas on mainland China, and that the US government needed to make a firm political declaration on the state of *de facto* war now existing between it and communist China. If this were to be done, he argued, several positive steps could be taken: the China coast could be blockaded and its ports bombarded, large numbers of reinforcements would be available in Korea from Formosa, and Chiang would be free to launch diversionary operations on the mainland.

This was no more than what he had already proposed; but now that Red China's attitudes were unambiguously hostile he felt his proposals could no longer be regarded as provocative. The Russians, he thought, might take exception but there was little to indicate that they would. They had made their own assessments and had no special concern for Peking. A forced evacuation of Korea without retaliatory action against China would only result in irreparable loss of face for the United States and the United Nations, with repercussions around the world, especially in Asia. Whilst claiming that he appreciated the need for the defence of western Europe, MacArthur believed that too much diversion of resources in that direction would forever prejudice the American and United Nations position in Asia.

Having digested these uncomfortable words the JCS replied that they felt the extreme measures proposed by MacArthur were 'inappropriate' but that certain measures could be taken to help him. He was directed to continue to defend Korean soil as the 8th Army retreated to preselected defensive lines, inflicting maximum damage on the enemy and, if absolutely necessary, to withdraw to Japan. Meanwhile there was to be no aerial reconnaissance across the Yalu.

MacArthur called for clarification on 10 January. His command was not strong enough, he claimed, to hold a position in Korea whilst simultaneously guaranteeing the security of the Japanese islands – a task for which he had already called for National Guard divisions to be sent from the USA. He pointed out that his troops were now tired, disillusioned, embittered by criticism and in low spirits. Only a few days earlier, on 6 January, he had reported adversely to Washington on the battle effectiveness of the ROK army, drawing attention to its marked inability to hold ground under pressure even when closely integrated with American forces. Given these factors he felt that his command should be evacuated as soon as possible. But if Washington's political will was up to it and it really believed in holding on in Korea it must be prepared to accept heavy casualties as well as the risk to Japanese security.

The Joint Chiefs referred the matter to Truman before replying; the policy of withdrawal by bounds still applied, as did authority to evacuate to Japan if forced to do so. Reflecting a growing concern in Washington over the handling of the campaign, Generals Vandenberg and Collins announced their immediate intention of visiting MacArthur in Tokyo.

In Korea, the line had stabilized; the Chinese, having once more outrun their logistic system, were exhausted. They had managed to get well south of the Han river before halting and by 10 January the line ran from Pyongtaek in the west, north-east to Wonju, south-east to Chechon, east to Yongwol, then northeast to Chongson and on to Samchok on the east coast. Ridgway saw the respite as a chance to restore the morale and self-respect of his battered command and stepped up his visits to formations and units; festooned with webbing equipment and grenades he was soon a familiar figure to his command.

Truman now sent MacArthur a lengthy personal message summarizing his views on the war, counselling prudence whilst the war strength of the United States was built up. He believed it was essential to offer successful resistance in Korea in order to demonstrate the free world's determination to stand together. It would also deflate what Truman seemed to think was the exaggerated political and military prestige of Red China and would buy time for the rallying of anti-communist resistance elsewhere in Asia. Truman concluded his message with a warm appreciation of MacArthur's handling of the campaign to date. Whether this message was sent with an ulterior motive, as some form of 'last chance' by an exasperated President, is hard to guess; Truman had been worrying about MacArthur since the Wake Island meeting, and the General's recent signals, swinging from triumphalism to despair, had disturbed the President, who may already have been thinking of ways in which his General could be dislodged with the minimum of political damage to the presidency.

Vandenberg and Collins conferred with MacArthur in Tokyo between 15 and 18 January. Collins emphasized that Washington believed it would be best to continue operations in Korea, without endangering 8th Army, 'as long as it was in our overall national interest to do so' and unless the USSR intervened strongly. Two more infantry divisions were to be sent to Japan to bolster security whilst operations continued in Korea. The discussions also included the delicate matter of possible evacuation, and in particular which Koreans should be given passages out to avoid summary execution.

If Ridgway's 8th Army welcomed the respite granted as the Chinese offensive lost its momentum and halted south of the Han river, its sentiments were shared by its opponents. Marshal Lin Piao had been amazed at the ease with which his 4th Field Army drove the UN forces back from the Yalu and down past Seoul. A mythology was abroad in 8th Army that it faced hundreds of thousands of drug-crazed men who attacked in suicidal human waves. The use of the word 'horde' to describe any Chinese unit was widespread, despite one astute American journalist who, at an 8th Army news conference, asked the briefing officer, 'How many hordes are there in a platoon?' In fact, the Chinese seldom attacked at more than regimental strength. They placed far more stress on fieldcraft, deception and surprise than on weight of numbers.

The US Marines were the first to recognize that the People's Liberation Army based its battlefield tactics on those evolved for sustained guerrilla war by Mao Tse-tung against the Japanese and Kuomintang armies. The Chinese excelled at movement off roads, by night, and with minimal personal equipment. The men were inured to hardship and totally at home in the Asian countryside without what the UN forces came to regard as necessities of life, such as heated tents, masses of road transport, and a rich diet of tinned and fresh rations. The Chinese soldier moved with a bag of rice, rice cakes, some dried fish, and whatever he could obtain off the land. He wore, in winter, a quilted uniform which UN personnel taken prisoner found to be as serviceable as any of their own. There were few radios in the PLA below divisional level and there was wide reliance on field telephones, runners, lamp and flare signals and the use, when in close contact with the enemy, of trumpets, bugles and whistles. For extra psychological effect, gongs and cymbals were added to the score to inculcate fear and confusion in the mind of the enemy. When used – as almost invariably they were – at night, the effect could be shattering against unsteady troops.

Careful steps were taken in all units of the PLA to ensure political conformity and this was achieved, as in the NKPA, by the use of commissars who in a sense filled the roles taken in western armies by the welfare and education officers and the chaplains. The commanders of the PLA were confident that political soundness, good military doctrine universally applied, tactics and high morale would more than compensate for lack of military hardware; to date in Korea it appeared that they were right. Even so, when the offensive ground to a halt in January 1951, Lin Piao was replaced by Marshal Peng Teh-huai and more reinforcements were drafted in from China. Drawn from the 1st and 2nd Field Armies they included the 12th, 15th and 60th Armies, forming the 19th Army Group, soon to be the best troops in the PLA. With the arrival of further reinforcements in the early months of the year the Chinese army in Korea grew to 19 Armies (each roughly equating to a UN army corps): a total of 57 divisions, of which 36 were to be used at the start of their spring offensive.

Peng Teh-huai, a close friend and confidant of Chairman Mao, was 51 years old when he took over from Lin Piao. For some months before the Chinese intervention in Korea his headquarters, as commander of the so-called 'Chinese People's Volunteers' had been in Mukden but when it was decided that Lin Piao had run out of steam he assumed direct command in the field, remaining in post until the armistice of 1953.

The Chinese army paid close attention to opponents' tactics, noting anything which could be identified as a weakness on which they could capitalize. During the winter offensive which threw the 8th Army back so dramatically they were quick to see their opportunities. Documents captured afterwards show how they defeated the 1st Cavalry Division at Unsan in November 1950: 'When the rear is cut off the UN troops will abandon all heavy equipment and weapons and retreat in a disorderly fashion . . . when encircled, they form themselves into small groups and defend themselves resolutely while waiting for reinforcements.' It was noted that the UN forces normally sought to disengage and withdraw by daylight, but one encounter with non-American troops taught them not to assume that this was always so: 'However, when all preparations have been made, or when there is no choice, they sometimes withdraw at night; an example – the disengagement of the British 29th Brigade after dusk at Pugong-ni during the 3rd phase campaign after one whole day's fierce fighting with us.' This clearly refers to the fighting north of Seoul on 4 January when the Royal Northumberland Fusiliers, who had been holding Pugong-ni on the right flank of 29 Brigade, managed the difficult manoeuvre of breaking off in contact and in the dark. The Chinese had thus already identified those United Nations troops who were prepared not only to stand and fight, but who had the skills to perform these advanced evolutions. The US Marines, the paratroops of the 187th US Combat Team, the Turks, French, Dutch, Belgian and Commonwealth contingents were all to be given similar recognition as the campaign wore on.

The Chinese were quick to recognize the strong aspects of UN tactics; they noted the precision with which air, artillery and tank support was co-ordinated, the accuracy of UN artillery, and the speed with which fire was shifted from target to target. The ability of the UN artillery to locate well-concealed

Chinese guns was attributed to the use of radar and acoustic devices; later on, the activities of light aircraft flown by trained artillery officers were to give them more trouble.

Weaknesses in American infantry tactics were identified in documents captured later in 1951: first was a lack of combat spirit:

> Their soldiers are afraid of death and lack courage. They run for cover when fired on, and few accept responsibility for security and observation. They are slow in advance, frequently halting when hearing small-arms fire, and are prone to bunching. They are incapable of fighting individually and are not accustomed to close-quarter fighting and the use of grenades . . . the majority of the US soldiers forget to pull the safety pins before they throw their grenades, which then become our weapons to throw back . . . they are unfamiliar with mountain warfare and climbing. When attacking us uphill they often have to pause to rest, presenting easy targets. They are unfamiliar with night operations, when it is expedient to penetrate and divide them. They are too heavily equipped for hill fighting and are affected by terrain and weather conditions. Afraid of being cut off in the rear, once encircled they retreat in disorder.

One Chinese report goes on to describe in detail the drills for mopping up fugitive UN troops, for which lightly equipped infantry were to be used. The systematic way in which the PLA were trained in this role explains why so few United Nations soldiers ever managed successfully to escape from captivity in North Korea, apart from the natural difficulties presented by their non-Asiatic appearance.

CHAPTER 16

Road to Recovery

The concern of Generals MacArthur and Ridgway over the morale of their command was shared by their allies. Following a visit to British troops in Korea from his Singapore headquarters, General Sir John Harding, Commander-in-Chief Far East Land Forces, wrote in some alarm to Field Marshal Slim describing what he had seen at the front. Slim's deputy, Lieutenant-General Brownjohn, replied on CIGS's behalf:

> Your remarks on American morale in Korea are most interesting and endorse similar reports that have been reaching us . . . We have now sent the Chief of the Air Staff [Sir John Slessor] to Washington. We hope he will succeed in clearing up a number of things, about which we are in the dark, and impressing on the Americans that we object to the policy of withdrawal, out of contact, without the semblance of a fight. From reports reaching us it would appear that Ridgway has already made his personality felt and that a more aggressive leadership is in evidence.

General Omar Bradley had already seen Marshal of the Royal Air Force Lord Tedder who had told Bradley bluntly that in Whitehall there was an almost complete lack of information on MacArthur's plans, or even on any thoughts the American Joint Chiefs might be entertaining as to the future of the United Nations forces. Furthermore, he conveyed anxieties over the safety of the British and Commonwealth troops entrusted to MacArthur's command. Britain's will to fight it out in Korea was undiminished, despite her desire to establish diplomatic relations with communist China. It seemed incredible to political and military leaders in London that there should be any thought of giving up altogether in Korea; the United Nations commanded the sea and air and this must be enough to guarantee the security of the UN ground forces. Furthermore, Tedder told Bradley:

> We feel you are entitled to know that reports . . . from such a wide variety of sources that they must be taken seriously, cast grave doubts on the morale and determination of some American units in Korea. We could not say this to you but for our acute sense of the importance of Anglo–American friendship and mutual confidence . . .

> There have been many instances in the history of war when good troops, including our own, have failed in determination. But we feel that this is a question of leadership and inspiration from the top, and in this connection we welcome the assumption of command by General Ridgway.

Britain's cards were on the table. After his arrival on 13 January Slessor emphasized the views of the British Chiefs of Staff. The Americans took all this in a friendly spirit, even if it must have seemed presumptuous for Britain, no longer a superpower, to criticize the military performance of democracy's champion.

Ridgway tackled the morale problem with vigour. He was shocked to be asked by officers and soldiers why they were fighting in Korea. His forthright answer, immediately promulgated around 8th Army, was 'because of the properly constituted authorities of our respective governments. Further comment is unnecessary. It is conclusive because the loyalty we give, and expect, precludes the slightest questioning of these orders.' When asked, as he frequently was, 'What are we fighting *for*?' Ridgway's reply was equally blunt: 'The real answer lies in the resolve of the free world to fight communism, a regime in which men shot their prisoners, enslaved their citizens, and derided the dignity of man; a regime which sought to displace the rule of law and to do away with the concept of God.' For Ridgway it was no longer a fight for South Korean liberty but a crusade for that of the whole free world. He knew that to regain its confidence, 8th Army must be reintroduced to offensive operations. Henceforth, any UN attack, on however small a scale, would be accompanied by massive air and artillery support, to give the infantry every chance of getting on to objectives which had first been pulverized, and with minimal casualties.

Further United Nations forces were arriving in Korea. Despite their recent bloody civil war, the Greek government had offered to send a transport flight of the Royal Hellenic Air Force, whose C-47s gave invaluable service carrying personnel and freight between Japan and Korea throughout the campaign. An infantry brigade was also offered, reduced to a battalion on MacArthur's instructions when it seemed that the victorious allies were about to reach the Yalu and win the war. This unit of specially selected volunteers with combat experience sailed from the Piraeus on 18 November 1950 after parading before the King of the Hellenes. It saw its first action when the 8th Army was once more moving forward up to the line of the Han river. The Greeks were dug in on top of Hill 381, north-west of the town of Ichon, when on the night of 29/30 January the Chinese attacked the American 7th Cavalry to which the battalion was attached. Three battalions of the Chinese 334th Regiment assailed the Greeks, who fought hand-to-hand in the dark against a determined enemy who were eventually beaten off and heavily punished by artillery as they withdrew. The Chinese, as was their habit, dragged their dead and wounded off the field but hundreds of blood trails were to be seen in the snow as dawn broke. Although only 28 Chinese dead were still lying amongst the Greek lines, it was estimated that they had killed or wounded some 800 of their attackers whilst suffering only 24 casualties themselves.

Following the evacuation of Seoul, the British 29th Brigade Group moved south to the area of Pyongtaek, where the losses sustained north of Seoul by the Hussars, Fusiliers and Ulster Rifles over the New Year were made good with reinforcements from Japan. The Glosters, who had not been seriously engaged so far, had been doing what they could to lessen the sufferings of the civilian population; the British soldier, often grossly derisive of the adult population of any country where he may find himself, invariably falls for the charms of its children. There were plenty of these to care for, as Korea now resembled a huge orphanage, with refugee waifs and strays by the hundred on the road. At Christmas, every British unit had thrown parties for local children. No one who saw the crowds of refugees could fail to be moved by them as they plodded south, away from the communists. Major Angier of the Glosters wrote perceptively of the Koreans:

> They may have dirty habits, uncertain loyalties and bad roads but they have courage and a philosophy that will stand anything and My! they need it, God help them . . . I have seen thousands of ugly mugs and scores of evil faces among them but also faces that would resemble a portrait of Christ or the Virgin Mary . . . the calm glance of a mother who will not give in though all the world is against her. The dignity of an old man in his conical black hat, with his long pipe and clothes kept spotless white amid the filth of a day's thaw. The laughing yellow dress and bright bedding bundle, carried on the black head across the snow in the bright sunshine.

Major Digby Grist, the battalion second-in-command, noted that the unit's medical officer, Captain Bob Hickey, had acquired his personal 'orphanage' where he and his orderlies tended small children who would otherwise have succumbed to disease and cold. One small girl, no older than 12, followed the battalion loyally down from Seoul to Pyongtaek, offering to do the laundry; her only words of English were 'Washy Washy', which became her adoptive name. She had with her a flock of small brothers and sisters, whom she was mothering in the absence of their parents. With the arrival on the scene of an International Red Cross team, Washy-Washy, her siblings and Captain Hickey's orphanage were taken off to what all their new friends devoutly hoped was a place of love and safety.

Major Grist was able to get around the Pyongtaek area and saw something of other United Nations contingents. The Glosters enjoyed the predicament of the Thai battalion to whom several truckloads of mines were delivered by the Americans; the Thais surrounded themselves with a vast minefield only to discover that as the mines were already primed they could not get out from it. Blissfully unaware of fuze mechanisms they had to call on the Glosters' Assault Pioneer platoon to free them.

A few days after arriving in Pyongtaek, a 'desperately cold and bleak place' according to Grist, he approached a party of refugees who were struggling up a steep embankment. One of them replied in good English to his offer of assistance. He asked who this was. 'A woman detached herself from the crowd and replied: "What do you want with me?" "It's only that you spoke English," I said lamely. "Is that so surprising? I am a teacher of English at the university." "Then you could tell us what more we can do." "Haven't you done enough? Just all go away and leave us with what's left of our country." She turned on her heel and trudged away with the rest of the refugees.'

The Glosters were within driving distance of the Turkish brigade, which had fully recovered from its earlier ordeal. Its pugnacious commander, General Yazici, was determined to show what his men could do. One afternoon the Turks reported to their American divisional headquarters that they were under attack. An offer of artillery and air support was declined and the Turks turned off their radio. Early the next morning they came on air again to report victory, with few casualties to themselves. They were asked if they had taken any prisoners. Back came the emphatic answer: none. Grist and other British officers visited the scene of this engagement; on approaching the hillside on which it had occurred they noted that the ground appeared to be covered with sheep. These turned out to be several hundred dead Chinese, the majority apparently despatched with the bayonet. A Turkish officer was cheerfully posing for a photograph in front of a heap of Chinese dead. When questioned, he replied that he had killed them himself and was going to send the photographs back to his wife and children. Sobered by this vision, the Glosters returned to their battalion.

The 8th Hussars were victims of a nervous decision, taken after the loss of Cooper Force, to evacuate all Centurion tanks from Korea. The order was rescinded after a week, but by then half the regiment's personnel had been sent to Japan. Many thought that the older Comet, Cromwell or Churchill would have sufficed for Korea. By the end of 1950, when the Hussars arrived in the country, the North Korean T-34s, which had struck such dread into the ROKs and the first American troops in Korea, had been virtually eliminated by ground and air attack. It turned out that the future for the Centurion actually lay in its use as a movable strongpoint, sited in the front line with the infantry once the battle line congealed into static warfare later in 1951. There might be no opportunities for glorious breakthroughs and exploitation, the dream pursued by proponents of tank warfare since the First World War, but the phenomenal accuracy of the 20-pounder was to prove decisive in many defensive battles once stalemate had gripped the front.

For the time being the main enemy was the climate. It was very hard to keep any vehicle going; the issue anti-freeze was of poor quality and engines froze solid unless run every hour; even hydraulic fluid had to be thawed out before movement was possible. In the tanks, turret traverse mechanisms became jammed as did the recoil systems of guns. On the night of Friday, 12 January, a temperature of −38°C was recorded, and worse was to come. The infantry fared badly, deployed in icy trenches devoid of overhead cover and in the teeth of a freezing wind howling down from Mongolia. They were committed to these appalling conditions by a ruling from on high that the defences were to be manned around the clock and that half the men in every unit were to remain awake and alert all night. Brigadier Brodie fumed at the way in which his men were subjected to conditions reminiscent of the Crimea a century earlier, when a British army, decimated by sickness and woefully ill-equipped to deal with extremes of cold, had encamped before Sebastopol. To make matters worse, whilst Ridgway's plans for a steady forward movement back to the line of the Han river were about to be implemented, Brodie was required to reconnoitre fallback positions some 25 miles to the south in case of a surprise enemy offensive. Inspection parties returned with gloomy news of almost impossible terrain with few tracks even for jeeps.

29 Brigade was deployed in a particularly bleak and exposed section of the coastal plain. Sickness increased and life became a simple question of survival, given the continuing inadequacy of the British-issue clothing. Brodie saw that the battalions were serving little useful purpose and moved them to quarters in nearby villages where there were still many habitable dwellings; the thatched farmsteads were efficiently warmed in the traditional Korean way by under-floor channels bearing the heat from wood-fired furnaces. Apart from a few disasters in which houses were burnt to the ground, the brigade was now more comfortable. Units made a number of patrols forward to the south bank of the Han river where, on 13 January, an unusual encounter took place. Two Centurions of the 8th Hussars located an enemy tank on the north bank, firing across the river from the mouth of a railway tunnel near Yongdongpo. It was destroyed, and turned out to be a Cromwell – one of those lost ten days earlier with Cooper Force. A small bit of armoured warfare history had been made: it was the first time that a Centurion had fired in anger on another tank.

General Ridgway, always a firm believer in inter-service co-operation, established a close working partnership with General Partridge of the US Air Force, and Admiral Struble, whose professionalism and enormous experience of amphibious warfare had ensured MacArthur's famous victory at Inchon. In the third week of January Partridge flew Ridgway on an aerial reconnaissance in a T-6 Harvard. Flying at times down to ground level they searched for the elusive Chinese, up to 20 miles into what was marked on 8th Army's battle maps as hostile territory. They saw no signs of enemy activity and Ridgway at once decided to move 8th Army carefully forward. He wanted to see if the Chinese had established themselves in any strength south of the Han.

The 27th Regimental Combat Team – the 'Wolfhounds' – passed through 29 Brigade on 15 January to discover that there were few enemy south of

Suwon, and a cautious general advance was ordered. Ridgway made it his business to visit as many units as possible, heartening the troops with his confident prediction that the enemy was thin on the ground and that in any case the 8th Army would 'ride with any punch' thrown by the Chinese. He carefully chose units in different divisions to head the advance in turn, and 29 Brigade found itself acting in close support of various American regiments as they pushed steadily up through Suwon.

Encouraged by the way in which the Wolfhounds' operation had gone, Ridgway ordered a more aggressive probe, Operation 'Thunderbolt', carrying both I and IX Corps past Suwon and into the towns of Ichon and Yoju. The United Nations line was thus established on the important lateral road running south of the Han river line. Progress was deliberate, as Ridgway was determined to get his infantry off the roads and on to the hills, clearing opposition thoroughly as they went.

All infantry battalions were given companies of Korean porters to assist in moving ammunition and equipment up and down the ever-steeper hills. These men proved indispensable; recruited from the Korean National Guard, they were supposedly unfit for front-line combat and many were elderly, but their devotion and courage became legendary and they welcomed the treatment they were given in the British battalions. Lieutenant-Colonel Kingsley Foster of the Royal Northumberland Fusiliers made a point of addressing his newly arrived porters through an interpreter. He told them of the traditions of his regiment, in which his father had served before him, and of the high expectations he had of the porters. They responded warmly, assuring him of their loyalty; before long a delegation approached him, asking him to stand for the presidency of their country, in which case they promised that all his battalion's porters would vote for him.

After much agonizing and back-stairs lobbying by the Americans, the General Assembly of the United Nations voted on 1 February 1951 to brand China as an aggressor nation, calling upon Peking to cease hostilities against the United Nations' forces in Korea and to withdraw its troops back across the Yalu. Predictably, the motion was opposed by members of the communist bloc and the Chinese hierarchy remained inscrutable. The Joint Chiefs in Washington and their political advisers were faced with a number of alternative courses: they could decide to reinforce the United Nations troops to the extent necessary to defeat the Chinese People's Volunteers on Korean soil and impose reunification by force; they could withdraw completely from the peninsula and hope for the best, or go firm on the existing front lines and sit out what might prove to be an indefinite military stalemate; or an attempt could be made to obtain a cease-fire agreement followed by negotiations leading to restoration of the *status quo* as existing in June 1950. Finally there was the most fearsome solution: that of inflicting decisive military and economic defeat on the Peking regime. This scenario was hurriedly dropped in favour of stalemate or cease-fire, or a combination of the two. There was nothing to be gained by extending the conflict, much as this might appeal to MacArthur and his fellow hawks. A blockade of the China coast would only be effective if it was total, and the JCS were well aware that they would never be able to carry the British and Commonwealth governments with them on this.

There was a distressing lack of consensus between the allies on what to do next. On 11 February MacArthur signalled to the Joint Chiefs his intention to order 8th Army forward until the enemy's main line of resistance was encountered or until it was clear that there was no such line south of the 38th parallel. If probes by Ridgway's troops found that the enemy was not holding ground in strength south of that line MacArthur would inform Washington and await instructions before continuing the advance. As this signal was being studied at the Pentagon, the British government's views were made clear to the JCS: no military decision should be made to recross the 38th parallel until political agreement had been achieved in the United Nations – particularly by those nations which had contributed forces to MacArthur's command. Ernest Bevin, mortally ill and about to hand over to Herbert Morrison at the Foreign Office, was particularly insistent that even minor incursions over the former border should be avoided. However, MacArthur maintained he was still operating under his original Security Council remit, and that this covered the entire peninsula. He put this to the JCS who accordingly briefed the Secretary for Defense on 27 February with three key recommendations:

1. Military operations in Korea should continue as planned until a new policy had been issued by the Department of State and passed to the Department of Defense.
2. Military and political courses were to be 'harmonized'.
3. There was to be no change to MacArthur's earlier directive, permitting him to dispose his forces either side of the 38th parallel 'as best to provide for their security'.

Only the day before these instructions were sent to MacArthur he had called for further guidance regarding the attack on the Yalu power stations, which had obsessed him for months. He was told that they were to be left alone as the original political factors still applied. Washington feared possible repercussions should the power supply to Vladivostok and other strategically delicate Soviet targets be cut off.

Before Ridgway could plan a decisive offensive he needed good intelligence on the enemy's order of battle, dispositions and state of morale; this came from a number of sources. Prisoners were remarkably ready to talk and most seemed happy to have fallen into allied hands. It had been an even worse winter for the Chinese and North Koreans than for the UN troops. Rations had been short and sickness had decimated their ranks. Early in February an accurate picture of enemy dispositions had been compiled by headquarters 8th Army. These pointed ominously to a resumption of the Chinese advance, this time well to the east of Seoul, on the central front. Much information came from exceptionally brave Korean agents infiltrated behind communist lines. The outstanding collector of this form of espionage was Colonel Polk, head of intelligence in X Corps. During the Hungnam operation in November 1950 he had found that his commander General Almond preferred to disbelieve any intelligence he found distasteful; he appeared to have learned a salutary lesson from this, and certainly placed credence in what Polk's Korean operators now told of the Chinese order of battle.

The best of Polk's informants was a recently captured Chinese medical officer, a former member of Chiang's army press-ganged into the People's Liberation Army, which was short of all forms of medical staff. He told of the ways in which all ranks of his medical unit had been subjected to seemingly endless indoctrination by the commissars, the fanatics who exercised strict political thought control over all units of the CCF; very few were taken alive unless they had obeyed orders to let themselves be captured, after which they continued to indoctrinate their fellow prisoners. This is what lay behind the great prison riots on the American-run prison islands off the Korean south coast in 1952. Regimental officers in the PLA were not so heavily politicized and most talked freely after capture once they realized they were not going to be shot out of hand.

Polk also used many native Korean agents, known as the 'Blue Boys', who were sent into the north, returning with information which in many cases was not believed until events showed that they were speaking the truth. There was a two-way traffic of agents across no man's land; Polk and his officers managed to 'turn' many captured North Korean spies, who became double agents. Some even became quadruple agents, working for several United Nations countries and receiving pay from all. As the Blue Boy network expanded it was run from headquarters X Corps (and later from 8th Army, when Polk became its head of intelligence) by one Major Jurgernsen, whose parents had been missionaries in Korea and who himself spoke fluent Korean.

By the end of the first week in February four armies of General Li Tien-yu's 13th Army Group had massed opposite X Corps on the east central front, and the 9th Army Group was detected slowly making its way forward behind the 13th, presumably for use as an exploitation force. Ridgway foresaw a major attack once they had deployed. On his left, Milburn's I Corps had edged up to the Han river line and was on the point of entering Seoul's industrial suburb of Yongdongpo, whilst other probes were pushing into the Kimpo peninsula and out towards Inchon. Milburn was told to sit tight on the south bank of the river for the time being. Further east, IX Corps was confronting a large enemy bridgehead to the south of the Han; all indications were that the Chinese would attack on the front of X Corps and the ROK III Corps to the east of this, advancing on two axes: Chipyong-ni–Changhowon–Chongju, and Hoengsong–Wonju–Chungju. Ridgway therefore ordered Almond's and the ROK Corps to stand fast and await the enemy attack until it was clear as to which axis it would take.

On the night of 11/12 February Marshal Peng gave the word to start his 'Fourth Phase' offensive. He knew there had been insufficient reconnaissance of UN positions, and unremitting aerial attack on his overstretched line of communication had left him with lower stocks of ammunition and rations in his forward areas then he would have wished. Many of his troops were sick and casualties from the appalling cold and malnutrition had been very heavy in the preceding weeks. But he was under pressure from Mao Tse-tung as well as Kim Il-sung to resume the offensive. The latter had tried a limited offensive with the NKPA in January without reference to Peng and its failure had led to acrimony and inevitable loss of face. Peng was directed to advance towards Taejon, killing up to 30,000 Americans and ROKs on the way. Success would mean the inevitable withdrawal of all other United Nations troops from further west in order to safeguard their flanks and, with any luck, bring about another precipitate rout comparable to that inflicted on the UN forces in the north only weeks before. He had failed, however, to take into account the remarkable improvement in 8th Army's morale – and thus its fighting ability – since Ridgway's arrival. Even so, Peng must have been encouraged by results in the opening days of his offensive.

The first victims were the luckless ROK III Corps far over on the right of the UN line. Chinese troops attacked its 8th Division from several directions in a well-coordinated operation. Virtually all the division's equipment was abandoned *in situ* and within hours it had suffered some 10,000 casualties and had virtually ceased to exist. The Chinese sustained their momentum, charging down on the artillery gun lines in the rear of the broken division. Almond had distributed American units in penny packets amongst the ROKs with the intention of bolstering them. However, these were in many cases so far from their parent headquarters that orders to break away did not reach them and many had to fight their way out of the trap on the following day. Suddenly realizing the gravity of the situation, Almond decided to pull back to the line of the Han river, abandoning the important road and rail junction of Chipyong-ni, and establishing a firm defensive line around the riverside town of Yoju.

Ridgway, unhappy with Almond's dispositions, ordered that Chipyong be held. But Almond no longer had the ability to do so as he sorted out his American and ROK forces, badly intermingled in the opening hours of the battle. One of the few units which had held its ground and stood to fight during the chaotic night of 12/13 February was the Netherlands battalion, at that time little more than two rifle companies; its men, however, were experienced volunteers, many having served in the Dutch East Indies. As the retreat from Hoengsong continued, the Dutch stood rearguard, fighting off vastly superior numbers of Chinese who at one stage overran their battalion headquarters, killing the gallant commanding officer as he fought shoulder-to-shoulder with his men.

Urgent adjustments were ordered to keep the Chinese away from the Han. 27 Commonwealth Brigade was deployed across the river, its headquarters in the hamlet of Tangu-ri, about five miles north-west of Yoju. The brigade was much stronger than it had been before Christmas. Apart from the welcome addition of the Indian Field Ambulance it had been joined by a field artillery regiment from New Zealand, most of whose personnel were volunteers, many having fought as gunners in North Africa and Italy during the Second World War. The regiment's 24 guns were obsolescent 25-pounders of an early vintage, but this did not deter the New Zealanders; their personal appearance would have raised eyebrows at Woolwich or Larkhill, those temples of British army gunnery, but their professionalism became legendary.

They brought with them a platoon of transport vehicles from the Royal New Zealand Army Service Corps, and the brigade was further enhanced by the formation of an *ad hoc* RASC/RNZASC transport company, soon to be joined by a Canadian ASC platoon. This was the unit that had started out from England as 78 Motor Ambulance Convoy RASC but whose subsequent employment (unrecognized even in the British official history) in a variety of roles led to it being widely known, after its jovial commander, as 'Potter's Prostituted Pool'. The drivers in the British platoon were mostly reservists who had spent the post-war years as long-distance lorry or bus drivers and knew their jobs. They needed to, for their aged Bedford three-tonners were susceptible to the extreme cold and the unsealed washboard roads of Korea were lethal to springs and suspensions. These lorries had been stored in the open for five years since 1945, and life expectancy of their puny 3.5-litre, 72-brake horsepower reconditioned engines under these conditions, where a nominal three-tonner carried up to twice its authorized payload when necessary, was measured in weeks.

In the weeks leading up to the communist build-up 27 Commonwealth Brigade, like 29 Brigade further to the west, had concentrated on surviving the appalling weather conditions; Korea's winter derives from the polar continental air mass which dictates the climate of the Asiatic land-mass; with generally high barometric pressure and low relative humidity there is surprisingly little snowfall away from the mountains; but when there is no wind the dry air is susceptible to plummeting temperatures which freeze even the main rivers so thickly that the ice can be crossed by fairly heavy motor vehicles without recourse to bridges. Night temperatures fell to the order of −30°C and the infantry were hard put to it to avoid the effects of the extreme cold. The British soldier's ingenuity came to the rescue and means were found to keep even the front-line soldiers alive; in the case of the Middlesex this was done by setting up warming centres – not unlike the *califaria* in medieval monasteries – when the rifle companies were out of the line. For the forward troops, the case was harder and resort had to be made to screened braziers in the slit trenches. By now, most officers and men in the brigade had managed to acquire, either by barter or theft, sufficient American winter clothing to keep warm; but few who spent that dreadful winter in the open would ever forget that they were still wearing their thin Hong Kong clothing when the full force of the Korean winter first hit them in November 1950. The authorities at home proffered the lame excuse that the brigade was supposed to have left Korea on the arrival of the 29th Brigade Group and was not therefore entitled to issues of tentage or winter clothing.

On 13 February, 27 Brigade passed under command of X Corps as an urgently needed reinforcement following the start of the Chinese Fourth Phase offensive. The previous two weeks had been as boring as they were uncomfortable, for yet again the brigade had been used as the 'Palace Guard', defending the headquarters of IX Corps. News of the approaching fight gave heart to all ranks. The winter had been dreary and the prospect of action offered some long-awaited excitement.

CHAPTER 17

Confidence Returns

Several factors contributed to the steady improvement which now took place in 8th Army's fortunes. Ridgway's policy of controlled offensive action, by which limited objectives were set, and in which massive artillery and air support was made available to the attacking ground forces, was designed to instil confidence. President Truman's declaration of National Emergency released huge amounts of budget support for rearmament, and recalled thousands of experienced reservists to the colours for immediate service in Korea. Their presence soon invigorated combat units whose ranks had hitherto been filled with the product of the selective draft, the underprivileged citizens lacking education and influence whose performance in the earlier battles had left much to be desired. The ROK army was beginning to reveal the effects of the training schemes put into effect after the calamitous retreats of the previous summer and winter, particularly in the matters of officer selection and technical and staff training; modern weaponry and equipment were also reaching its combat units and the motivation of all ranks was growing in strength. Back in the United States, the shortcomings of the post-1945 army were being closely studied, one of the most delicate matters on the agenda being the integration of what were still termed Negroes (or worse) into hitherto all-white combat units.

In accordance with Ridgway's offensive doctrine – and the need to pre-empt the Chinese attack which got under way further to the east on 11 February – the 27th Commonwealth Brigade found itself deploying north of the Han river on 11 February. In Brigadier Coad's absence in Hong Kong on compassionate leave, it was commanded by Lieutenant-Colonel Andrew Man of the Middlesex. As darkness fell on the 12th the infantry battalions were digging in as best they could in the frozen ground on hills either side of the road leading north towards Chipyong-ni, where it was clear that the Chinese were massing several divisions for an assault. The brigade was once more in the 2nd US Infantry Division, regrouped since its débâcle at Kunu-ri and under a new commander, Major-General Clark Ruffner, who had replaced the hapless General Keiser after a brief interregnum under Major-General McClure. The idea of renewing the association with 2nd Division was not warmly regarded in 27 Brigade, but events were to show that a change of commander, as with the 8th Army, had wrought a transformation in the division's fighting spirit.

Colonel Man was told to advance up the road from the Han river towards Chipyong-ni, now threatened by very large Chinese forces and held by the 23rd US Regimental Combat Team, which included the French battalion. The commander of the team was Colonel Paul Freeman, who had distinguished himself in the fight at Kunu-ri by keeping his command together and getting most of it to safety, as well as by his personal gallantry. On the 10th and 11th, the Australians were able to send patrols up the Chipyong road to make contact with Freeman's men, but it was clear that the Chinese were closing in on the town and that it was about to come under siege. The Americans and the French accordingly prepared for the worst, wiring in and mining their positions, sustained by an airdrop of supplies and ammunition.

An American reconnaissance unit of light Chaffee tanks and infantry in jeeps went north up the Chipyong road on the late afternoon of the 12th. On passing the forward positions of the Argylls they were warned of many Chinese in the hills ahead but pushed on confidently. Running up against opposition from Chinese who had blocked the road, the unit commander ordered a withdrawal back to the village of Chuam-ni. Instead of picketing the high ground overlooking the village they settled down for the night, lit fires, and apparently failed to post sentries. During the night the Chinese overran them. Surprise was complete and most of the Americans were caught in their sleeping bags. The war diary of the 3rd Royal Australian Regiment for 17 February tells the rest of the harrowing story. 'During the afternoon approximately 30 returned to our lines. The majority belonged to "L" Company 9th Infantry Regiment and 2nd Recce Company, both from the US 2nd Division. These units had been attacked on 13 February and suffered heavy casualties. Over 60 bodies are strewn along the road in the battalion area at present. Three light tanks and approximately 12 jeeps were abandoned by 2 Recce Company and are also in our area.'

The dead men lying along the road had tried to escape, many in their issue underwear and carrying their boots, to be run down and killed as they fled. Some had their throats cut. A few terrified survivors emerged from the surrounding countryside to tell of panic and massacre. It was a salutary lesson for all who passed that way. The bodies lay in the snow for another two days before they were picked up by American army burial parties. Any idea of pressing on up that road with a mechanized relief force for Chipyong-ni was abandoned. The steep hills either side of the road would make it impossible for supporting tanks to manoeuvre and it was clearly a task for infantry. Colonel Man accordingly ordered the Middlesex to advance, supported by the Australians, clearing the hills as they went, a slow business; but by late afternoon the brigade had advanced a mile against stiffening opposition, until a ridge, known as Point 112, had been secured. At dusk the Middlesex were ordered to dig in.

Few doubted that the Chinese would attack during the night, hoping for a repetition of their easy success at Chuam-ni. Snow lay around as the rifle companies hacked at the frozen rocky ground. The moon, which had provided generous illumination, set at 4 a.m. and within the hour the fully alert Middlesex were heavily attacked. Chinese infantry, signalled on with bugles, hurled themselves at the forward positions, supported by heavy and accurate mortar and machine-gun fire. It transpired that the two forward Middlesex companies were attacked by one of the battalions of the Chinese 119th Regiment, the rest of which was already engaged at Chipyong-ni. The young soldiers of the Middlesex kept their heads even when one of the forward platoons was overrun and captured, to be freed by a timely counter-attack.

With daylight the Chinese fell back to lick their wounds, leaving 65 of their number dead in front of the Middlesex positions as well as 14 prisoners. As was the Chinese practice, many dead and wounded had been dragged away by their comrades. Throughout the night, the New Zealand gunners had performed splendidly in their first serious engagement. Their forward observation officer (FOO), firing his carbine with one hand, was working his radio with the other to direct and correct the defensive fire. As the telephone lines from the forward posts to battalion headquarters were cut, he and his signaller became the sole method of communication between battalion headquarters and the rifle companies.

Meanwhile a fierce and decisive battle was raging around Chipyong. The town was invested by several Chinese divisions. General Ruffner planned to relieve the garrison as soon as possible, but for the moment had to resupply Colonel Freeman's beleaguered men with the ammunition, fuel and rations they urgently needed. Airdrops were accordingly carried out on the 14th and 15th as a relief column assembled. This comprised a special force, known as Task Force Crombez after its commander, Colonel Marcel Crombez of the 5th Cavalry; a company of tanks was the spearhead, backed by his three infantry battalions, engineers and artillery. It was expected that Crombez would reach Chipyong late on 15 February. The Chinese had other ideas and the task force hit fierce opposition as it forced its way north. Crombez ordered the tanks to press on, many with infantry on their engine decks. A running battle ensued, the relief force suffering heavy casualties as the tanks forced their way through a series of ambushes to reach Chipyong in the late afternoon.

Under almost constant attack, the garrison had been fighting at close quarters, often hand-to-hand, as waves of Chinese sought to capture this vital road and rail junction. Colonel Freeman, who was severely wounded, later told his story from his hospital bed in Tokyo in a radio interview: 'On the night of 12 February we were attacked by the Chinese, estimated at one to two divisions. They attacked on all sides of the perimeter . . . the French in particular did a very fine piece of work in dashing out to break up one attack before it formed and grabbing 24 Chinese by their collars.' For two days things were quieter as the Chinese were not so eager to close with the defence. 'On the morning of the 15th, things appeared to be well in hand. The Chinese were withdrawing and our air force and artillery were finishing them off.' By the morning of the 16th, calm reigned over Chipyong-ni. The besiegers had gone, leaving hundreds of dead piled on the 23rd Regiment's wire entanglements. Many Chinese who had got through the wire lay in heaps amidst the French slit trenches.

It was, though few realized it at the time, a turning point, at which the ghosts of previous disasters were laid. The American army in Korea had found its form, gained immeasurably in confidence, and never looked back after this, despite moments of acute crisis in the months ahead.

As 27 Brigade was fighting its way up towards Chipyong-ni, Brodie's 29th Brigade, further to the west, was placed under command of General Milburn's I Corps for the clearance of the Chinese bridgehead south of the Han river, east of Seoul. Some 20 miles south-east of the capital the enemy held a range of high and steep hills commanding the roads heading north in that sector. Brigadier Brodie foresaw that most of the brigade's future operations would require the infantry to scramble on to the tops of the hills, and had ordered that training be undertaken to that end. The battalions were much fitter than on arrival in Korea and were getting used to operating on light scales, nobly aided by their hardy Korean porters, who carried heavy loads on their traditional wooden 'A' frames.

The Royal Ulster Rifles had the most difficult ascent; the battalion was sent 4,000 yards out on a limb to relieve the US 5th Cavalry. So difficult was the terrain that one of the rifle companies had to be used to augment the Korean porters; the position was occupied, and patrolling began. On 15 February an Ulsters' patrol of a sergeant and three men was ambushed by the enemy. All were captured, but the sergeant and a rifleman were returned a few days later with a strange tale to tell. The Chinese, who seemed to think they were Americans, were inclined to shoot them on the spot until they produced their British identity documents, whereupon a Chinese officer unaccountably shook them warmly by the hand and released them. The third soldier, who was wounded, was retrieved a day later after a message had been sent by Korean peasants that he was still alive and hiding near by. The fourth man was retained by the Chinese and held until the armistice in 1953. The battalion, with the help of the Royal Engineers, was able to construct a hair-raising jeep track from the valley up to its forward positions after a few days to keep the rifle companies supplied. Meanwhile the Chinese prowled around the brigade's positions at night; to conserve small-arms ammunition, the battalions relied on artillery and mortar fire to keep the enemy at arm's length.

The key to the high ground still occupied by the enemy was Hill 327 which the Glosters were ordered to take. This was their first battle; apart from some skirmishing with guerrillas, they had endured a frustrating and boring winter and extremely bad living conditions. The ascent was very difficult, at times near vertical; the assaulting infantry were accompanied by their own mortar fire controllers and observation post parties from the Royal Artillery mortar battery and field regiment. The enemy resisted stubbornly but was forced off the summit as the infantry moved steadily onward and upwards, with the massive fire support of field guns and mortars, and direct fire from tanks and the Bofors guns of the brigade's light anti-aircraft battery, mounted on trucks in the valley below. The Chinese left over 50 dead in their trenches as they withdrew to the north, while British casualties were light. Colonel Carne of the Glosters may have wondered how his reservists would rise to the occasion; few had relished the prospect of returning to the colours when called back in the previous summer and it was hardly to be expected that men who had seen plenty of action during the Second World War would assault recklessly; their officers found that although circumspect in the attack, their experience showed. The other battalions of the brigade took over the lead as Brodie pushed on towards the Han river.

The final fight of this phase took place on 20 February when the Ulsters, supported by the guns of 16 Churchill and eight Centurion tanks, 16 Bofors guns, six Vickers medium machine-guns, six 3-inch mortars, 12 4.2-inch mortars, and the 24 guns of the 45th Field Regiment, scaled the topmost ridge of the range alongside the US 24th Infantry Regiment. On arrival at the top it was found that the Chinese had pulled out; the Ulsters and Americans spent an uncomfortable night high up on the summit in sub-zero weather without hot rations, bedding or blankets.

As the Chinese retired beyond the Han it was time for examination, not only of the British Commonwealth's part in operations to date, but of possible future organizations arising from the imminent arrival of the Canadian brigade. One battalion of this, the 2nd Battalion of the Princess Patricia's Canadian Light Infantry (PPCLI), known as the Princess Pat's or the Patricias, was about to join 27 Commonwealth Brigade; but the arrival of headquarters 25 Canadian Brigade, two further Canadian infantry battalions, an artillery regiment and a squadron of heavy tanks, would find three Commonwealth brigades in Korea. Under existing command arrangements they would be farmed out under American divisional commanders, some of whom had already shown little tactical aptitude and had, on several occasions, placed British units in dire peril.

There had been talk of merging the various Commonwealth contingents into a single formation as long ago as the first weeks of the war. Although the idea seemed attractive to many, the British Chiefs of Staff shrank from it; they knew that as the major contributor of ground troops the United Kingdom would be expected to provide the lion's share of administrative support for any joint division; added to that was the delicate matter of appointing a divisional commander, who the British chiefs felt should automatically come from the British army, but whose selection would need the unqualified approval of the other partners. The decision over a Commonwealth division, deferred throughout the first winter of the war, could not be postponed much longer.

London was under constant pressure from Lieutenant-General Sir Horace Robertson, the Australian commander of the British Commonwealth Occupation Force in Japan. Until the late summer of 1950 he had enjoyed unchallenged non-operational and administrative supremacy over all Commonwealth forces in the Korea–Japan theatre. Following the outbreak of the Korean War, however, he had felt his position undermined by the appointment of Air Vice-Marshal Bouchier as the personal representative of the British Chiefs of Staff to MacArthur's Tokyo headquarters. Bouchier's terms of reference, which had been made clear to Robertson from the start, should not have posed a threat to the latter's status. But Robertson was a difficult man whose personality ill suited him for coalition warfare. In the words of the Australian official history: 'At times he aroused antagonism, particularly amongst his superiors and contemporaries, for his undisguised egotism, self-assertion, and occasional vulgarity.' His short temper was legendary in Australian military circles, as was his high opinion of his own ability. He nurtured many real and imagined grudges and grievances, some of which extended back to the First World War when he had served under British generals (notably at Gallipoli), most of whom he held in contempt. In the two years prior to the invasion of South Korea he had seen his already minuscule command whittled down, and by the early summer of 1950 it looked as if it was about to wind down completely. He also had an intense dislike for what he regarded as the stiff-necked mandarins of Whitehall, who seemed to him to be insensitive – perhaps even unaware – of the sovereign claims of the dominion whose representative he was.

Robertson had pressed the Australian government to get their troops into Korea before the British as a matter of national pride, but the battalion at Kure had to be totally reorganized, manned and trained, and by the time it got to Pusan, Coad's brigade had been shipped there from Hong Kong despite Robertson's strong representations that it should go first to Japan.

If anyone can claim credit for marketing the concept of a Commonwealth division, it is Robertson. He had repeatedly signalled Whitehall in the opening weeks of the war, pointing out that whilst the Commonwealth, and Britain in particular, had little or no strategic interest in Korea, men of the United States' armed forces were laying down their lives for the United Nations' cause and it was incumbent on the Commonwealth to follow suit. Australian politicians and General Staff began to press in earnest for the formation of the division in April 1951; they accepted that most of the additional support units for the larger formation would have to come from the United Kingdom, also that the divisional headquarters would need to be fully integrated, with strong Commonwealth representation at all levels and in all branches of the staff, but that the UK would have to furnish the artillery staff, field engineers, most of the divisional signals regiment, and a share of the RASC transport column of three companies.

In the end the breakdown of Commonwealth personnel in Korea and Japan on formation of the division in the summer of 1951 was: UK 58 per cent, Canada 22 per cent, Australia 14 per cent, New Zealand 5 per cent and India one per cent. The problem of finding a British divisional commander acceptable to all was easily solved: Major-General James Cassels, in 1950 head of the United Kingdom Services Liaison Staff in Australia, was well known and popular in Australian and New Zealand military circles. Other British officers were carefully chosen for the headquarters on the basis not only of their professional competence but for their ability to mix easily and tactfully with other Commonwealth officers.

The British, who had seen plenty of the American forces during the Second World War, had come by 1945 to have a very high opinion of a tremendous fighting machine. They compared the performance of the US Army divisions in Korea to date unfavourably with that of the US Marines, who were clearly of a higher calibre. The Marine Corps had suffered huge cuts after the Pacific war in which they had earned an awesome reputation, being reduced by 1947 from four strong divisions to virtual cadre level; even the division which landed at Inchon had been hurriedly cobbled together for the occasion. The Marines also had many influential enemies in Washington including Secretary Johnson and Generals Collins and Bradley. This stemmed partly from the way in which they seemed to have evaded the progressive 'liberalization' of the US Armed Forces since 1945. Sustained by a fierce pride in their corps, they clung successfully to what many regarded as harsh disciplinary methods; above all, they had firm doctrines for virtually every aspect of their profession whilst in the Army tactical and training doctrines varied from formation to formation.

The selective draft has already been cited as one cause of the US Army's unsuitability for combat. Another stemmed from the treatment meted out to the American black population. In the southern states, segregation was still the rule in 1950, and the Civil Rights movement had barely begun to assert itself. The composition of the US Army reflected this. In the war, there had been all-black combat units – commanded by whites – whilst administrative units had frequently been mixed. General Almond had commanded an all-black division, the 92nd Infantry, in Italy; the experience had left iron in his soul; in Tokyo he had frequently said to MacArthur, when both were under pressure: 'General, nothing you did to me would disturb me emotionally, because I once commanded the 92nd Infantry Division.' It was not that the Afro-American lacked patriotism or courage; but often segregated in all-black units under mediocre white officers, and given no chance to compete for promotion on equal terms, he was frequently liable to become alienated. There were almost no black officers in the infantry above the rank of major, and many lieutenants lacked the confidence to command respect in battle. Years of subordination and denigration had deprived them of self-esteem. In 1950 the first signs of integration in military as well as civilian life were apparent; the Department of the Army's Gaillam Board studied the implications of this in the armed forces and boldly concluded that all purely black units should be disbanded and their men integrated into the army as a whole, given 'equality of treatment', and that those possessing appropriate skills be assigned to suitable posts regardless of race. This was radical for its time.

When the Korean War broke out there were still 14 all-black units in Far East Command. The oldest of these was the 24th Infantry Regiment in the 25th Infantry Division. The regiment had been declared an all-black unit in 1866 as a mark of honour for its performance fighting for the Union in the Civil War, and was originally recruited from liberated slaves. After the opening engagements in Korea, however, the commander of the 25th Division, Major-General Kean, stated that the 24th Regiment was a threat to the security of his division, being thoroughly untrustworthy in the face of the enemy, and should be replaced. Close inquiry showed that he was right. All-black units, in any case, needed 25 per cent more white officers and NCOs, the result of their men's military qualification tests being consistently lower than the army average. This was hardly surprising, given the lack of educational opportunity in their home states. But there was general agreement that one black battalion, the 3rd in the 9th Infantry Regiment (whose other battalions were all-white), had performed well in the first months, holding together in the long retreat to the Naktong during which it carried out several spirited counter-attacks. British witnesses later saw it marching south on the way back to Pyongyang, still in good order, a stern white-haired southern colonel at its head. It was found that black soldiers, integrated experimentally into white units, could and did fight well. The Gaillam Board's report went on to say that leadership played an important part and that 'no race has a mortgage on stupidity'.

Having decided to go ahead with integration the American army tackled the problem vigorously. From the start, black soldiers showed that if given good commanders they responded well, gained confidence, and rapidly became excellent soldiers, earning the unstinting admiration of their white colleagues. It was many months, however, before full integration was accomplished, following its approval by the Pentagon in July 1951. There were some residual problems; it was found that for constitutional reasons the 24th Regiment could not become 'mixed', since it had been formed by special presidential decree, sacrosanct by law. With great regret, therefore, it was formally disbanded in 1952. The proportion of non-whites to serve in newly integrated units also raised difficulties; by the end of 1950 blacks in Far East Command amounted to around 12 per cent of total strength, but the distribution was uneven, for most had long been assigned to administrative units where their military performance was not tested by the requirement to fight as infantry.

It was initially ruled that no more than 10 per cent of infantry unit personnel should be blacks, with no upper limit in 'service units' such as trucking or supply companies. The content in combat units was soon raised to 12 per cent but this too had to be adjusted upwards, as the influx of men from the selective draft brought many more blacks and Hispanics than whites. By early 1951, 8th Army contained over 17 per cent black soldiers, the demands of other theatres, especially Europe, for skilled technicians and supervisory grades taking the best of the white intake.

As the campaign wore on, the proportion of blacks in the command steadily increased until it reached nearly 20 per cent. There were restrictions which exacerbated the situation, such as that preventing the introduction of blacks into the 40th and 45th National Guard Divisions who arrived in Korea from the end of 1951. The load of absorbing blacks therefore fell more heavily on other formations in the command; at first many commanding officers resisted their introduction into hitherto all-white units, as many were clearly under-performers in terms of military competence and educational ability. In course of time, however, integration worked; it gave an enormous fillip to the cause of black consciousness and by the time of the Vietnam War the American armed forces could claim to have spearheaded the nation in the creation of a viable mixed society.

By the end of February 1951 the United Nations line had been straightened out as Ridgway's policy of slow but steady advance using massive fire support began to take effect. Procedures for calling up airstrikes had been honed to a degree where the infantry had every confidence in this form of close support. It was available from a variety of sources. Fighter-bombers, both piston and jet-engined, were stationed on airfields in South Korea and planes from the 7th Fleet and the US Marine air wings were also on call. Communications problems like those which had cost the Argylls so dear in the Naktong break-out, had been ironed out; a unit calling for an airstrike in an emergency could expect it to arrive within the hour and to deliver accurately, often within a hundred yards of friendly forces. The fighter-bombers could carry high-explosive bombs of up to 1,000 pounds, lethal to even well dug-in Chinese positions.

Rockets and cannon were effective against targets in the open; but the most spectacular weapon was napalm. This was a mixture of petroleum and a gelling agent, prepared under American supervision in Japan, dropped from low level in plastic containers holding 100 gallons of the viscous mixture, and costing approximately $40 apiece. Igniting on impact with the ground, they belched forth a mass of burning jelly, lethal against infantry or armoured vehicles, and which ran as a blazing torrent down into trenches and dugouts. Men engulfed by the fireball died instantly, as did personnel within fifty yards, their lungs deprived of oxygen, even though untouched by the flame. After a napalm strike, these could be found stone dead in their trenches, apparently untouched; their comrades caught in the flames would have been reduced in seconds to shrivelled mannikins. The dead were the fortunate ones, for burning napalm, once on the human body, stuck to it, inflicting dreadful injuries.

After the lifting of the siege of Chipyong-ni Ridgway was determined to push forward towards the town of Hoengsong on the central front, using his air and artillery power to destroy as much of the enemy army as possible in the hills to the east of Seoul. He was concerned not so much with gaining large tracts of ground but with killing as many Chinese and North Koreans as possible and, indeed, codenamed this next phase Operation 'Killer'. 27 Commonwealth Brigade was ordered to head into the mountainous terrain north-west of Hoengsong, with the ROK 6th Division on its right and 1st US Cavalry Division on its left. Coad, back from Hong Kong, welcomed the Canadians as the fourth battalion to his brigade and the Princess Patricias led with the Argylls, as the advance resumed on 21 February.

There were very few tracks, let alone roads, and the enemy rearguards clung stubbornly to the summits. The thaw started, bringing further problems as the tracks became well-nigh impassable for wheeled vehicles. Under these conditions, enormous demands were made on the Korean porters, who had to struggle over a thousand feet up hillsides, often in foul weather, carrying supplies to the alternately sodden and freezing forward rifle companies. Low cloud prevented helicopters from flying forward to evacuate casualties, who were manhandled down the steep slopes by their comrades and stretcher bearers to the regimental aid post for immediate attention before a long and often agonizing journey in an ambulance jeep for surgery at the Indian Field Ambulance. As the thaw accelerated, logistic problems multiplied; airdrops maintained supplies as pontoon bridges over the Han were swept away and the whole of IX Corps was temporarily cut off from its MSR; it also lost its new commander, Major-General Moore, killed after only ten days in post when his helicopter crashed into the river on 23 February.

MacArthur had emphasized to Ridgway that it was politically important to recapture Seoul, but the latter was confident that following the elimination of the enemy main force in the Hoengsong area the capital would fall of its own accord. He was far more concerned by an appalling breach of security on MacArthur's part which had compromised the launch of Operation Killer. Ridgway had already briefed the press corps in extreme confidence, stressing that this information was under embargo until the operation actually started. At this point MacArthur had made one of his rare visits to the front, where he held a press conference on 20 February to proclaim that a new offensive was about to start. For good measure he gave his audience the impression that Operation Killer was his own plan. Ridgway, inwardly fuming, made a mental note that when he moved on to the next phase of the advance back to the 38th parallel, to be named Operation 'Ripper', he would ask MacArthur not to come to Korea as harbinger of the offensive.

As 27 Brigade on the central front toiled northwards hill by hill, 29 Brigade stood by to cross the Han and enter the capital. At the end of February, the brigade's artillery, 45 Field Regiment, was allotted to support the 1st ROK Division, which had few field guns of its own. The British gunners were agreeably surprised by the growing competence of this formation under its energetic and professional young commander, Major-General Paik Sun-yup. Few of his officers had more than a smattering of basic English, but liaison raised few problems, because in the British system the battery commander, instead of being back at the gun position as in the American army, was physically located alongside the commander of the unit or formation his guns were supporting. This produced immediate response to any request for fire support. The Korean officer in the front-line position would turn to the British officer at his side, indicate a point on the map (the ROK officers, it was found, were extremely good map-readers) and say 'Boom-Boom'. After that, responsibility for delivering the appropriate amount of fire on target lay exclusively with the observation post officer. It was, as one of these later said, excellent training, though hardly what was taught by the School of Artillery at Larkhill.

PART THREE
On the Offensive

CHAPTER 18

Change of Management

MacArthur's wishes to carry the war over the Chinese border by means of air and even land operations might have been firmly vetoed in Washington after Attlee's earnest representations during the summit meetings of December 1950, but it seemed to many that he believed overwhelming victory in Korea would scotch, once and for all, the menace of world communism. Although such a triumph could not now be achieved by the use of ground forces alone, the unmentionable intention to use the atomic bomb was thought in Whitehall to be not far from MacArthur's mind.

The idea of using nuclear weapons had been aired in Washington as early as July 1950 at the height of the retreat to the Pusan bridgehead. The underlying rationale was that if judiciously applied, it would relieve some of the stresses on the American defence system as it tried to cope with new-found global commitments. It is even possible that MacArthur asked for the 'discretionary' power to use nuclear weapons on 9 December 1950 when it seemed that the Chinese were about to overwhelm the 8th Army. He certainly submitted what he termed his list of 'retardation targets' on 24 December, calling for the release of 26 aerially delivered free-fall nuclear devices in order to halt the Chinese advance in its tracks. Later he stated that his master plan was to drop up to 50 nuclear bombs on Manchurian targets, land up to 500,000 of Chiang's troops at the mouth of the Yalu, and create, by the use of cobalt radiation, a 'no-go' belt across the neck of the Korean isthmus which would prevent all movement there for years to come. Ridgway, on arriving at 8th Army in December 1950, also favoured the idea of using nuclears, but only as a last resort (and actually raised the requirement from 26 to 38 in May 1951). By March 1951, a number of nuclear bombs were stored at the Kadena air base on the island of Okinawa and on 5 April the Joint Chiefs in Washington secretly authorized their use if further major enemy attacks were launched at the UN ground forces, or if bombing attacks were made from Manchurian airfields against the UN forces in Korea. On the following day, Truman signed a presidential document transferring the weapons from the custody of the Atomic Energy Commission to the United States Air Force. This step, however, was overtaken by events.

MacArthur had long contended that it was time to attack the hydro-electric power systems in the northern provinces of Korea. These included the Chosin reservoir and dam, the scene of the battles of November and December 1950. Their destruction, he argued, would bring about

1. Immediate denial of substantial amounts of power to China and the USSR.
2. Denial of alternative power sources to China and the USSR in the event of general war, a contingency he regarded as inevitable.
3. Prevention of the further dismantling of North Korean power stations by the USSR, at that time desperately short of its own power generation plant and known to be stripping the North Koreans of key components for use in the power stations of the Vladivostok region.
4. Curtailment of industrial expansion in Manchuria and the Vladivostok regions.

The matter of the Yalu power complexes was addressed in Washington by the Joint Intelligence Committee. The political implications of attacking the plants along the Yalu itself were particularly sensitive. Many of America's allies were already voicing fears that any attacks on the power systems would provoke general war and in any case were well outside MacArthur's terms of reference. Destruction of the great dams was impossible with high explosive – not even with the primitive guided bomb, known as *Tarzon*, which had a 12,000-pound warhead and could be 'flown' on to its target with reasonable accuracy by a well-trained bomb-aimer. It had been used with some success against the Yalu bridges but lacked the penetrative qualities needed to breach a concrete and earth dam of the size to be tackled in North Korea. The Suiho Dam, made of reinforced concrete, was over half a mile long and 350 feet high, nearly 20 yards wide at the crest and almost 100 yards thick at the base. All the dams in the complex drew their water from reservoirs like that at Chosin, from which it was pumped in succession through a chain of power plants as the exhaust flow descended from the mountains to the level of the Yalu. About a third of the Suiho Dam's full capacity of 1.2 megawatts was exported to Vladivostok, Port Arthur and into Manchuria.

The JIC concluded that there would be little tactical advantage from breaching the dams even if it could be achieved. There would be virtually no effect on the North Korean rail system as only 90 miles of track were electrified and its signalling system could be operated manually. If the dams were breached there would be temporary flooding of the west coast ports of Antung and Sinuiju within four hours as a 70-foot tidal wave surged down the Yalu valley. It was the strategic effects, however, which carried most impact. Even these would be restricted, for much of the power formerly supplied from the complex had gone to factories in North Korea long since flattened by American strategic bombers. The factories, however, could be rebuilt if the outcome of the war was to be the beneficent occupation of North Korea by United Nations forces, whereas the dams, if destroyed, would take years to replace.

The JIC went on to consider political factors, such as the propaganda value likely to be milked by the communist world from the loss of the Yalu power complex; it also recognized that the United Kingdom and India, both already critical of Washington's policies towards communist China, would raise strong objections. On 8 November 1950, MacArthur had been informed that the Joint Chiefs approved the use of UN air power up to, but not beyond, the Yalu, but that the power complexes were to be left untouched. After considering all the factors again, the JIC recommended that a new brief be issued to UN Command conveying the desire of the Joint Chiefs that the entire Chongjin–Pujon–Hochon–Yalu river power complex 'be destroyed with maximum despatch', a volte-face on the grand scale. But before any attack could be launched there was to be a convulsively dramatic development.

On 19 March 1951 the Joint Chiefs of Staff held an informal discussion in Washington with the Secretaries of State and Defense, covering future courses of action in Korea, and to draft a presidential declaration on defence matters, with particular reference to the war in Korea. Following this discussion, a signal was sent to MacArthur, advising him in strict confidence that a presidential statement was forthcoming, concerning discussions between the opposing sides on a settlement in Korea. The mood of the United Nations, he was told, was that no further military advance should be made until diplomatic efforts had been tried to bring about at least an armistice. As this involved the commander's freedom to act tactically, he was invited to comment. His answer, in a signal of 21 March, astounded its recipients. In it, he declared that no further military restrictions should be imposed on the UN Command in Korea. Inhibitions already in force should not be increased as they would make it impossible for him to clear the north, given current enemy numerical superiority and restrictions already in place on naval and air action. The existing Commander-in-Chief Far East directive was of paramount importance as it hinged on maintaining the security of his forces and was adequate to cope with the situation.

Taken aback, but still in awe of MacArthur, the Joint Chiefs amended the presidential draft to read that the aggressors had been pushed back to their start point and thus the principal objective of United Nations intervention, that of repelling the North Korean invasion, had been attained. Further UN objectives such as unification and the establishment of a free government for the whole of Korea, should be attainable without further fighting or bloodshed. The Chinese were in effect given an invitation to cease fire and agree a settlement by negotiation. The draft went on to say that the Korean people were entitled to peace and to assistance from the rest of the world in restoring their shattered country, north and south. A settlement on these lines would also help to ease international tensions. But, concluded the draft, if the Chinese refused to negotiate, the UN would continue to fight on.

On 24 March MacArthur paid a one-day visit to the front. Before leaving Tokyo, flagrantly disregarding all earlier advice, he issued a press statement comparing relative strengths of the combatants and emphasizing the military weaknesses of communist China. If the UN was to carry the war across the Chinese border, he added, Red China would face military collapse. There was, MacArthur continued, no difficulty therefore in arriving at decisions in Korea provided the issues were resolved on their own merits without being burdened by matters such as Formosa and the admission of China to the United Nations. These, he claimed, were fundamentally political and must be sorted out in the diplomatic sphere. He, MacArthur, was ready 'to confer in the field with the enemy commander-in-chief in an earnest effort to find any military means whereby the political objectives could be achieved'.

MacArthur made a further statement on his return to Tokyo that evening, saying that he had authorized Ridgway to take the 8th Army back across the 38th parallel, 'if and when its security makes it tactically advisable'. He elaborated on the enemy's potential, saying that the Chinese did not have the industrial base for waging modern war and relied on manpower alone to gain a military decision.

> Formerly [he continued] this great numerical potential might well have filled this gap, but with the development of existing methods of mass destruction, numbers alone do not offset the vulnerability inherent in such deficiencies . . . The enemy must now be painfully aware that a decision of the United Nations to depart from its tolerant efforts through the extension of our military operations to his coastal areas and interior bases would doom Red China to the risk of imminent military collapse.

There was an immediate response from Peking radio, quick to identify the implied threat to the mainland and its hint of the use of nuclear weapons of mass destruction, and all Chinese were warned that they must 'respond to the crisis and strengthen the sacred struggle to oppose America, save Korea, and defend their country'.

In Washington, MacArthur's statements were received with incredulity and horror, especially the hints of nuclear bombardment and extension of the war to the interior of China. Whilst he was inspecting 8th Army in Korea a panicky signal, prompted by his initial press release, was on its way to him from the Joint Chiefs, emphasizing Truman's insistence that attention be drawn to the presidential directive transmitted to MacArthur on 6 December 1950 and that any future public pronouncements were to be co-ordinated as set out in that signal. 'The President also directs', continued the JCS signal, 'that if communist military leaders request an armistice in the field, you should immediately report the fact to the Joint Chiefs for instructions.' It was nothing less than a severe presidential reprimand.

Following a flurry of damage limitation meetings in Washington, an announcement was made that MacArthur's offer to meet the Chinese commander in the field had been made without prior consultation with either the Joint Chiefs or the administration. Further hurried discussions resulted in a combined statement on 25 March:

> General MacArthur is conducting United Nations military operations in Korea under military directives issued through the United States Joint Chiefs of Staff which, as the President stated in a recent press conference, are fully adequate to cover the present military situation. The political issues which General MacArthur has stated are beyond his responsibility as a field commander and are being dealt with in the United Nations and by inter-governmental consultations.

There could be no mistaking this for anything other than a final warning signal.

On 5 April, a seemingly unperturbed MacArthur informed the Joint Chiefs of his immediate plans. He would push 8th Army forward to destroy all enemy to be found south of a certain line in the general area of the 38th parallel. After securing this he intended to sit tight, patrolling forward at up to battalion strength in order to locate and assess the enemy's position. In view of logistic problems, terrain, weather and enemy dispositions, he would then make a fresh appraisal and inform the Joint Chiefs accordingly. As this signal arrived in Washington, a political bombshell exploded in Congress. Representative Joseph W. Martin, Republican leader in the House, read out a letter he had received from MacArthur replying to an earlier one in which Martin had suggested that it would be expedient to open a 'Second Front' in Asia by using Chinese nationalist troops, of whom there were some 800,000 on Formosa. In his reply MacArthur agreed that the use of nationalist troops was a good idea. Declaring that it was his policy to meet force with force, he went on:

> It seems strangely difficult for some to realize that here in Asia is where the communist conspirators have elected to make their play for global conquest, and that we have joined the issue thus raised on the battlefield; that here we fight Europe's war with arms, whilst the diplomats there still fight it with words; that if we lose the war to communism in Asia the fall of Europe is inevitable; win it, and Europe would most probably avoid war, yet preserve freedom. As you point out, we must win. There is no substitute for victory.

There was no overt reaction from the Pentagon or the White House; but moves were afoot to remove MacArthur from his post. He had shown once and for all that he was not prepared to accept the political constraints of coalition warfare, and had exposed the chasm between the policies of Secretary Marshall and himself: the former a firm believer in working out a consensus with America's allies and irrevocably committed to a 'European' strategy. This time MacArthur had wildly overreached himself. He had to go.

On the same day, unaware of the furore in Washington, Field Marshal Slim wrote to his fellow chiefs of staff. For some time he had entertained doubts as to MacArthur's handling of the campaign. Now he shared them with his colleagues:

> I may be evil-minded but I feel that MacArthur is playing his hand as he has done since the start of the war, to involve the United Nations in a real war against China. He has deliberately wrecked the attempt of the State Department and the Foreign Office to approach China to effect a truce. The State Department committed the error of telling him what they proposed. He jumped in, issued as his own half their message, and added a threat which was bound to make the approach worse than useless. He had added a bit of coat-trailing by 7th Fleet which could easily provoke an attack by a Chinese aircraft or two. He is now engaged in exaggerating the admittedly large Chinese build-up, which may or may not be intended for an offensive. He has also begun this insistence on the threat of a 'massive' Chinese air attack, to which the only answer is, he says, to bomb Manchuria, and if he does that he has achieved his object. America will then, in a state of hysteria, tear into a Chinese war with Chiang as an ally. [Slim discounted the idea of a Chinese air offensive, as suggested by MacArthur. Such an attack, he considered, could only arise in the case of Russian intervention.] But an attack by 20 to 30 Chinese bombers would have a startling effect on the unprepared UN army even if it was dealt with quickly by the US Air Force. But if we stayed on or near the 38th parallel it would be out of MiG range and the enemy bombers would be unescorted and thus cold meat . . . I regret if I am maligning MacArthur but I believe that ANY air attack by Chinese that dropped a few tons of bombs would be represented AT ONCE as the promised 'massive' attack, with a howl for retaliation on China or even retaliation without reference to Washington.

There was in fact reliable intelligence that Ilyushin jet bombers, capable of carrying a two-ton warload, were already in Chinese hands; they could attack Seoul with ease from their bases in Manchuria.

Slim's doubts would have been spectacularly confirmed had he been privy to what was afoot in Washington. The President conferred urgently on 7 April with Secretary Marshall and General Bradley. They discussed the entire world situation, but MacArthur was central to their agenda; for two days he had been the subject of fevered informal conferences in the Pentagon and on Capitol Hill. All were agreed that the matter had to be tackled. The result was a personal presidential signal for immediate despatch to MacArthur:

> I deeply regret that it becomes my duty as President and Commander-in-Chief of the United States military forces to replace you as Supreme Commander Allied Powers, Commander-in-Chief United Nations Command, Commander-in-Chief Far East, and Commanding General United States Army, Far East. You will turn

over your commands, effective at once, to Lieutenant-General Matthew B. Ridgway. You are authorized to have issued such orders as are necessary to complete desired travel to such place as you select. My reasons for your replacement, which will be made public concurrently with the delivery of the foregoing order, will be communicated to you by Secretary Pace.

On the day this signal was signed, 11 April, Truman broadcast to the nation, explaining his action: 'With deep regret I have concluded that General of the Army Douglas MacArthur is unable to give his whole-hearted support to the policies of the United States Government and the United Nations in matters pertaining to his official duties . . .'

MacArthur's reaction was to publish a statement, through his military and personal secretary, the oleaginous Major-General Courtney Whitney, to the effect that at no time had he departed from the directives he had received, nor had anyone ever specifically debarred him from making general statements on the Korean War and its implications. The Republican Party in both Houses furiously attacked Truman for sacking MacArthur. Many of its representatives and senators had long advocated the use of Chinese nationalist troops, as recommended in Martin's letter to MacArthur. Senator Joe McCarthy, high priest of the far right in Washington and instigator of the notorious campaign against any public figure suspected of even mildly liberal or 'un-American' views, described the sacking as 'perhaps the greatest victory the communists have ever won'. Senator Richard Nixon, already prominent as a McCarthyite witch-hunter of suspected fellow-travellers and 'liberals', announced his intention of introducing a resolution calling on the President to reinstate the General. The Republican Governor Dewey of New York described MacArthur as 'a towering figure of strength . . . His dismissal is the culmination of a disastrous failure of leadership in Washington, combined with a foreign policy which has lost China to the free world, brought all-out war in Korea and threatens to divide us from our allies.'

The American press, however, whether Republican or Democrat-oriented, was generally supportive of Truman's action. The *New York Herald Tribune* wrote:

The most obvious fact about the dismissal of General MacArthur is that he virtually forced his own removal. In high policy, as in war, there is no room for a divided command. Basic American policy – as defined by the Joint Chiefs of Staff, the State Department, the President, and apparently by the majority opinion of the country – has been to fight a holding war against communist aggression in the Far East in conjunction with our allies, whilst building the Alliance to a point at which it can prevent communist aggression in Europe. General MacArthur disagreed with this basic strategic concept. He believes that Asia, not Europe, is the decisive battleground . . . Here was divided command at its worst . . . With one of those strokes of boldness and decision which are characteristic of Mr Truman in emergencies, a very difficult and dangerous problem has been met in the only way it could have been met.

The London *Times* likened MacArthur to some Roman consul who, having exceeded his powers, had been dealt with by Truman with appropriate Roman severity. MacArthur was compared by others to the great Duke of Marlborough, whose fall came in like manner after he had spoken and acted indiscreetly in opposition to official government policies. The left-wing *Daily Herald* simply rejoiced.

MacArthur, by announcing that he was prepared to treat with the enemy commander in the field, when he knew full well that a presidential statement offering the enemy the chance to negotiate with the United Nations was imminent, had cut the ground from under his President's feet. It was unforgivable, and Truman acted in the only way open to him. Ridgway, ordered to assume the supreme command, flew to Tokyo and went straight to MacArthur's office. 'He received me at once, with the greatest courtesy . . . He was entirely himself – composed, quiet, temperate, friendly and helpful to the man who was to succeed him.' MacArthur's departure from Tokyo, on 16 April, was an occasion of high drama. On the previous day he had taken leave of the Emperor Hirohito and had received the Speakers of the two houses of the Diet. The eight-mile route to the airport was lined by over a million eerily silent Japanese, bowing low as the cavalcade passed as if in the presence of their emperor.

On his arrival at Washington on the 18th he received an enthusiastic welcome and the next day saw him addressing Congress. Greeted with an ovation, he spoke calmly for over half an hour, seldom referring to his text and frequently interrupted by prolonged applause. He analysed the Far East position as he saw it, and defended his policies. He could not resist a dig at Washington: 'Once war is forced on us there is no alternative than to apply every available means to bring it to a swift end. War's very object is victory – not prolonged indecision.' He went on to claim that victory had been within his grasp when the Chinese entered the conflict and that drastic decisions in Washington which would have solved the diplomatic and strategic issues had not been forthcoming. He cited all the measures with which he had canvassed the Pentagon and Capitol Hill: attacks on the Chinese sanctuary airfields across the Yalu, economic blockade of mainland China, naval blockade of Chinese ports, aerial reconnaissance of Manchuria, and the use of Chiang's nationalist troops from Formosa against the mainland. But he refrained from mentioning his earlier suggestions of using nationalist formations in Korea, or of naval bombardment of the Chinese mainland.

> For entertaining these views . . . designed to bring hostilities to an end at a saving of countless American and allied lives, I have been severely criticized in lay circles, principally abroad [a clear dig at the British government, followed by a palpable untruth], despite my understanding that from a military standpoint the above views have been fully shared in the past by practically every military leader concerned with the Korean campaign, including our own Joint Chiefs of Staff.

Although his audience cheered his every word to the rafters, the service chiefs and Truman himself, watching on television, were appalled. His peroration, carefully drafted to draw the ultimate in emotional response from an audience already geared up to near hysteria, ended with the words:

I am closing my 52 years of military service. When I joined the Army, even before the turn of the century, it was the fulfilment of all my boyish hopes and dreams. The world has turned over many times since I took the oath at West Point, and the hopes and dreams have long since vanished, but I still remember the refrain of one of the most popular barracks ballads of that day which proclaimed most proudly that old soldiers never die, they just fade away. Like the old soldier of that ballad, I now close my military career and just fade away, an old soldier who tried to do his duty as God gave him the light to see that duty.

He knew his audience like the old actor he was; they went wild and there cannot have been a dry eye in the chamber. Congressmen were fighting to get to the podium and touch MacArthur, crying out that they had just heard the voice of God. At the White House, Truman's cabinet sat stunned before the television as the telephone exchange jammed with abusive calls from voters all over the country. Only Acheson kept his head, reassuring the beleaguered President that the speech had been 'more than somewhat pathetic'. Truman, as ever homespun and down-to-earth, described it as 'a hundred per cent bullshit' and poured his scorn on the 'damn fool Congressmen crying like a bunch of women'.

MacArthur flew at once to New York and his motorcade next day through over 19 miles of packed streets is unlikely ever to be matched. There could be no doubting his popularity; 150,000 letters and 20,000 telegrams of support awaited him at his hotel. One of his bodyguards described the throng in Fifth Avenue as 'a herd of hysterical sheep'. The city's cleansing department had to remove over 2,800 tons of ticker tape and other litter from the processional route afterwards.

A month later MacArthur was called before closed sessions of the two principal Senate committees, Foreign Relations and Armed Services, to give evidence on his handling of the campaign. The heavily censored published proceedings, amounting to 2,450,000 words gathered from 13 witnesses over the 42 days it took to complete the committee's business, included his personal testimony, running to 200,000 words, covering 800 pages of the report. Under the chairmanship of the Democrat Senator Richard Russell of Georgia, the committee called a succession of expert witnesses who steadily eroded MacArthur's position. Many of his enemies, of whom Marshall was one, took the chance in private to hack at the great consul's reputation; Truman was later to say that 'Marshall gave me a rundown on MacArthur that was the best I ever did hear. He said he never was any damn good . . . a four flusher and no two ways about it.' Marshall's subtlety came to Truman's rescue, and the counter-attack got under way, headed by Acheson, who had to regain credibility following some of the comments publicly delivered about him by the general. He stressed the importance of avoiding a 'showdown' in Korea, which could lead inexorably to general war, and gradually his message caught on.

Whilst at one time it seemed that MacArthur would seek the Republican nomination at the next presidential election, it became apparent to even his most fervent supporters that he was not the man for the White House. To the end of his life he believed that he had been right and the President and his service chiefs wrong; when President Romulo of the Philippines called on him shortly after the end of the Senate hearings, he found that MacArthur still considered that he should have crossed the Yalu, but when Romulo pointed out that civilian rule was supreme and that the President was to be obeyed, the general gazed back at him in silence. 'Suddenly, I realized that the conversation was over. He didn't want facts or logic. He wanted salve for his wounded pride.'

With the first signs that the dreadful winter was giving way to spring, the front began to move forward once more. Seoul fell on 14 March as the UN forces cautiously probed across the Han and into a devastated city. The great castellated gates and ancient palaces, though battered by shellfire, had survived, as had the Japanese-built capitol, city hall and railway station. The Anglican and Catholic cathedrals, holed by shot, were still standing, but the rest of the city was in ruins, those of its inhabitants who had stayed in their homes groping around the barely recognizable streets as allied tanks and vehicles picked their way through the rubble. A few enemy stragglers and rearguards sniped vainly at the advancing troops, and as darkness fell, American tanks, giant tigers' heads emblazoned on their frontal armour, fired their main armament and machine-guns up the wide boulevards around the capitol in a Wagnerian demonstration of victory.

One North Korean formation had been fighting in the south ever since it had been cut off by the Inchon landings in the previous September. This was the NKPA's 19th Division, which marched north as the allies re-entered Seoul, found a gap in the UN lines, and rejoined the NKPA north of the Imjin river after a masterful and daring operation which did much to restore North Korean morale.

In an attempt to cut off the retreating enemy field army before it could regroup, Ridgway decided to drop the 187th Airborne Regimental Combat Team north of Uijongbu, near Munsan-ni. Although Operation 'Tomahawk', as it was codenamed, failed in its objective, it demonstrated the ability of an élite American formation to cope with a situation which almost went badly wrong. The operation had to be laid on at short notice and only four days were available for planning. The original drop zone had to be changed at the last minute as UN ground forces had got there first. The actual drop was successful and took place on 23 March, although a navigational error resulted in one battalion landing on the wrong zone, where another unit had just landed and was sorting itself out. What made the operation so critical was the fact that the 187th landed amidst a determined enemy rearguard whose positions appeared to have been prepared for some time and who were not in the least abashed by the sudden arrival of three battalions of paratroops.

Initial congestion on the overcrowded drop zones was quickly dealt with by the experienced troops. Ridgway, unable to suppress his excitement at seeing his old comrades in action again, arrived shortly after the drop in a light air-craft and joined Brigadier-General Bowen, the regimental commander, in his command post, which was under accurate sniper fire. One rifle company was pinned down for some time as it landed, but by 5.30 p.m. all initial objectives had been taken and the battalions were ordered to dig in for the night, during which the link-up with friendly ground troops was achieved. This produced some tanks for close protection, and extra transport to augment the jeeps which had been parachuted in with the infantry. The main 'ground tail' of adminis-trative support units was waiting in Uijongbu, and through the night supplies were collected from the drop zones. On the 24th, further equipment was dropped. It was raining steadily and at 4 p.m. orders were given to march east-wards into the hills, where the enemy were still dug in, overlooking the Uijongbu road. The column of some 3,500 men trudged through the night in a torrential downpour, their heavy weapons in locally commandeered oxcarts. By dawn on Easter Sunday the column had covered 20 miles and was at grips with a resolute enemy. Casualties began to mount; one battalion of the 187th suffered 137 in the first twenty-four hours.

Accounts of Operation Tomahawk by those who took part reveal the fer-ocity of the fighting. Major Mulvey, a staff officer in regimental headquarters, jumped from less than 700 feet. He was in the air for only thirty seconds and later recalled seeing the sky 'solid with parachutes', many colliding in mid-air. When 30 feet from the ground he landed on top of another soldier's canopy, which promptly collapsed. Mulvey fell the rest of the way, landing heavily on his back, breaking the wooden stock of his carbine across his left arm. For a while he lay winded, but was helped to cover as the drop zone was swept by enemy fire. Assembling his staff, he doubled them 800 yards to the regimental command post, to find it under attack by a group of enemy soldiers only 200 yards away. Before moving to a safer position, Mulvey reported the effective strengths of the regiment's units to General Bowen; a helicopter flew him out of the drop zone for closer examination and an X-ray, but he was back with his men later in the afternoon. With the arrival of the 'land tail' at dusk came a welcome issue of sleeping bags. Spirits were high; this was an élite unit of professionals who knew their job; there were no stragglers or disciplinary problems in the 187th.

Major Ross, the regiment's intelligence officer, jumped wearing a pair of gloves, which nearly killed him; his main parachute failed to open and before he could pull the rip cord of his emergency chute he had to wrench the gloves off with his teeth in the few seconds left to him. He made a vow never to wear gloves into action again. His job was the interrogation of prisoners, already arriving at the command post. From them he discovered that as the first sticks of paratroops landed, there were some 300 men of the NKPA's 36th Regiment on the drop zone. They had been about to retire north to the Imjin river where they had been ordered to form a new defensive line.

The first day of Tomahawk was full of action. As the enemy grasped the situation heavy and accurate mortar and artillery fire came down on to the drop zones. A surgical team from the admirable Indian Field Ambulance, borrowed from 27 Brigade for the occasion, was parachuted in to deal with the mounting casualties. Over 130 enemy corpses had been counted in the immediate vicinity by last light but the 187th had suffered 489 killed or wounded. Many of the latter continued to fight on after treatment. Major Ross had nearly 150 prisoners on his hands, who had to be evacuated as soon as possible. Several members of his own staff were killed by sniper fire within 200 yards of the command post. By the end of the first day two Chinese regiments had been identified in the area as well as the North Koreans. All were well dug in, with interconnected trenches and bunkers, carefully camouflaged and well supplied with 82mm and 120mm mortars. The area had also been lavishly sown with mines of various sizes; being largely made of wood they were hard to detect and caused numerous casualties to men and vehicles.

As the regiment marched into the hills, enemy resistance was vigorous. The Chinese were particularly tenacious, defending forward slopes until driven on to the reverse, where they had prepared new positions. To eject them, short artillery barrages were brought down, quickly followed up with the bayonet. The North Koreans ran from this, but the Chinese had to be winkled out individually. The men of the 187th were encouraged to use their bayonets, as the post-combat reports of individual men bear out in gruesome detail. Private 1st Class Milton Eisenhauer's company was attacking up a steep hill on 26 March against stiff opposition, the Chinese standing up in the slit trenches throwing grenades. Eisenhauer shot one of them; the man tried to crawl to safety, but Eisenhauer's sergeant, pointing his thumb down like a Roman emperor, said, 'Stick him.' Eisenhauer bayoneted the man in the shoulder, then turned him over and struck him in the stomach. Two days later one of his comrades, Private Roland LeMay, killed several Chinese with grenades, then saw a man crouching in a slit, either wounded or hiding. 'I bayoneted him in the right shoulder, and when he gave a jump I hit him in the back and in the heart.' That the 187th were able to sustain this level of close-quarter combat for days on end testifies to their worth.

Not all had gone according to plan. The appalling weather badly affected infantry weapons, notably the Garand M1 semi-automatic rifle and the Browning Automatic Rifle or BAR. One platoon reported that after seventy-two hours in the hills their Browning machine-gun, two of their BARs and ten of their M1s were out of action. One rifle company was hit by a 'friendly' air-strike because it had lost its fluorescent recognition panel; a heroic soldier from a neighbouring platoon put out his own panel but was killed whilst doing so.

The regiment marched 30 miles over extremely rough terrain by night and day against fanatical opposition. At night the temperature plummeted and snow was still falling on the higher ground. During the week it was in action – a considerable time for an airborne unit – the 187th lost over 100 killed and some 500 wounded, having been obliged to fight from the moment they landed. Few of those who took part realized that this was to be one of the last parachute operations in history. The day of the massed descent, as fondly cherished by its proponents as had been the cavalry charge of an earlier epoch, was effectively over.

As long as Ridgway was in command of 8th Army it was his understanding that its mission would have been achieved once it had demonstrably repelled the invasion of the south and restored international peace in the area. The future offered little more than the prospect of stalemate and a return to some form of *status quo*. This could obviously not be attained were the allies to dig in along the original frontier, which was militarily indefensible. Instead, a line had to be occupied which would enable the UN forces to beat off any further attempt to subdue South Korea by force. This meant going for the mountainous country north-east of Seoul and, if necessary, accepting that a significant area of South Korea below the 38th parallel had to be sacrificed; a viable UN line could then be established, running from the Imjin river mouth in the west, then following the river north-east until it reached its source in the central mountains, and across to the east coast. Ridgway's staff had carefully studied the lie of the land and were confident they had the strength to make a limited advance without exposing 8th Army to the risks attendant on a hot pursuit into North Korea, where the enemy's numerical superiority might land the UN forces in yet another catastrophic reverse.

As soon as Ridgway was called to Tokyo to succeed MacArthur, his place at 8th Army was taken by the 59-year-old Lieutenant-General James Van Fleet, who had gained a high reputation as commander of the Joint Military Aid Group in Greece, where he trained and reorganized the Royal Hellenic Army which defeated the communist insurgents in the bloody civil war. Ridgway briefed his successor in detail, with emphasis on the personalities of his corps and divisional commanders. He was determined not to emulate MacArthur's remote style of command, and aimed at retaining personal contact with the field commanders whilst in no way interfering with Van Fleet's authority. He had now received his 'riding instructions' from Washington, prepared by the Joint Chiefs with a view to preventing any further rash actions in Korea which might lead to an escalation into general war. All these he passed down to Van Fleet. Whereas MacArthur had repeatedly shown that General Walker had not enjoyed his unqualified confidence in the crucial opening months of the war, Ridgway had no doubts as to Van Fleet's competence. All the same, he gave him carefully prepared operational guidelines reflecting his own perception of the UN mission in Korea. He was also conscious of responsibilities other than to the United Nations, notably the United States' unilateral role in the defence of Japan.

Ridgway had to maintain the integrity of his multi-national command in Korea, and to continue the fight there as long as there remained, in his judgement, a reasonable chance of success. The Korean coast was to be blockaded, the front stabilized, and, if all else failed, he had to plan and execute an orderly evacuation of the peninsula on lines which had been under consideration since the previous summer. To satisfy these requirements, Ridgway placed what he considered to be 'reasonable restrictions' on the advance of the UN ground forces, until such time as he had prepared clear instructions for all three of his subordinate commanders: Van Fleet, Admiral Turner Joy and General Stratemeyer. The drafting of these took several weeks, involving as it did much consultation between the relevant headquarters.

In Washington there was still a strong belief that North Korea was primarily a Soviet client state acting on instructions from the Kremlin, and that Stalin would not accept the total defeat of his surrogate. Even a limited victory over North Korea was regarded by many as a possible trigger for all-out conflict, although subsequent intelligence showed conclusively that the Russians had no intention of being drawn into general war. The truth, had it been known, was that Stalin had only reluctantly acceded to Kim's demands for permission to invade the south after the North Korean leader had assured him that there was no risk of the conflict spreading beyond the limits of a civil war and that the NKPA was capable of getting to Pusan well before the United Nations and America could react. Whether Moscow applied pressure on Peking to join in will remain a mystery until the archives of the People's Republic and the Soviet Union have been fully revealed. If Stalin did encourage Chairman Mao to send his 'Volunteers' to the aid of North Korea it can only have been in order to gain leverage over Peking; an aim which was to prove illusory. Russian support for North Korea and China was not only minimal once the United Nations had shown some resolution, but it all had to be paid for in hard cash.

It was fear of Soviet intervention which underlay the instructions for Ridgway, under preparation in Washington in April 1951 but incomplete as Marshal Peng's 'Fifth Phase Offensive' burst on 8th Army in the last week of the month. They more or less echoed those which Ridgway was also drafting for his own subordinates and dealt with the limitation of the campaign within prescribed geographical bounds. There was a total prohibition on air or naval operations against Manchuria, Soviet territory or the North Korean power complexes in the Yalu valley. As a matter of policy, it was emphasized that 'no, repeat no, operations will be conducted within 15 miles of USSR territory' and that under no circumstances were any UN forces to cross the Manchurian or USSR borders of Korea. If Soviet 'Volunteers' became openly or covertly involved in any strength, Ridgway was ordered to report this at once to the Joint Chiefs; but if Russians were involved in only small numbers he was to proceed with operations as planned. A major Soviet attack would bring about the evacuation of UN forces from Korea and Ridgway was ordered to plan accordingly.

Finally there came an instruction which was to have far-reaching implications: 'Prisoners of war are to be handled in accordance with US Army and international regulations and conventions. Consistent with these, a comprehensive programme is to be set up for the re-indoctrination, interrogation and re-orientation of prisoners of war with a view to using them as well-trained anti-communists later.'

During the first three weeks of April, as MacArthur's long career faded away, the 27th Commonwealth Brigade was advancing up the valley of the Pukhan river, some 30 miles east of Seoul. The enemy, unwilling to yield ground without a fight, left rearguards all the way to contest the advance. Following the thaw came the first signs of spring. This is a serenely beautiful time of year in Korea, with masses of rhododendrons and azaleas bursting into flower on the hillsides. Rivers and streams, after the torrents of the melt, were once more running normally and the roads, kept open by superhuman efforts on the part of the engineers, allowed wheeled traffic to move reasonably freely. Morale was good as the advance continued and there was anticipation, in brigade headquarters as in the Middlesex and Argylls, of early relief. In Hong Kong a new headquarters, that of 28th Infantry Brigade, and two fresh battalions, the 1st King's Own Scottish Borderers (KOSB) and 1st King's Shropshire Light Infantry (KSLI), were under orders for Korea. They had been given more time for preparation than their predecessors; all national servicemen under the age of 19 had been weeded out – many with great reluctance – and replaced with older men from other battalions in the Hong Kong garrison. This meant large numbers had to change their cap badges and, for men from the south of England pitched into the KOSB, undergo the culture shock of sudden immersion in a Scottish battalion.

For the 29th Brigade Group moving north to its ordained defensive positions overlooking the Imjin river as part of Major-General Robert H. Soule's 3rd US Infantry Division, reinforcement was more of a lottery. Following their

heavy casualties in January the Royal Ulster Rifles had received over 200 reinforcements of all ranks from the depot at Hiro in Japan. The infantry here came
from all quarters. One National Service officer of the Royal Hampshire
Regiment, Second Lieutenant Denys Whatmore, arrived at Hiro in December
1950 and was appalled at what he saw when, on Christmas morning, after a vol-
untary church service and a fancy-dress football match between the officers and
sergeants, he was required to observe the hoary army tradition of waiting on
the soldiers at dinner. As he arrived at the mess hall,

> the place was a bedlam. The room was awash with beer, with more bottles standing
> by in crates. Many of the men were already the worse for wear and some were being
> sick. We carried the plates, loaded with all the traditional English Christmas fare,
> and laid them before the men. The quality of the food could not have been higher. I
> was disgusted, therefore, to see that the majority of it ended up in the waste bins.
> Men too drunk to eat simply pushed the plates away and reached for more beer. It
> was an unexpected and salutary experience and it returned forcibly to my mind
> when, a few weeks later, I saw the hungry refugees in Korea.

Less urgency was felt now that the Chinese had apparently withdrawn out
of contact. Brigadier Brodie's 29th Brigade Group welcomed the return of the
mild weather as the battalions moved on to positions which were assumed to
be only transient before a further advance took them over the Imjin and on to
the higher ground some seven miles to the north, the hump-backed hills destined to be all too familiar in the next two years.

Brodie was not happy when shown the huge sector of the front allotted to
his brigade. It extended for a distance of 17,000 yards along the south bank of
the Imjin; not only was it large enough to justify the deployment of a strong
division, but the terrain posed an insoluble problem as to the disposal of his
three British and one Belgian infantry battalions. It was physically impossible
to site these units so that they could provide mutual fire support; three of the
battalions were out of sight of each other and there were huge gaps in the
brigade area which could not be kept under constant observation by day and
night and through which an enemy army could pass undetected. The guns of
the 45th Field Regiment Royal Artillery were obliged to deploy dangerously far
forward in order to cover likely enemy lines of approach on the north bank of
the river, and the 4.2-inch mortar battery had to be parcelled out by troops in
order to give close support to the infantry battalions across the sprawling
brigade area. Very little wire and few mines were laid, as General Soule had
ruled that 3rd Division would only pause briefly on the river line before
pushing across. The nature of the ground was such that deep digging was
impossible. Most of the Glosters' slit trenches lacked overhead cover and were
barely three feet deep, with rough *sangars* of rock to give some extra protection
for the riflemen. The rifle companies were sited up to a mile from each other.
Once the positions had been reconnoitred and dug there was little for the bat-

29. Brigadier Tom Brodie (*right*), commanding the British 29th Brigade Group, briefs General Lawton Collins during the US Army Chief of Staff's visit early in 1951. Lieutenant-General Matthew B. Ridgway, commanding the 8th US Army, is on the left, characteristically festooned with field equipment and grenades

30. On the day of departure from Japan following his dismissal by President Truman, General MacArthur arrives with his wife and son at Haneda airport, Tokyo, to receive full military honours for the last time. General Matthew B. Ridgway, his successor, stands bareheaded as he shakes MacArthur's hand. With his back to the camera is the bulky figure of Major-General Willoughby, Far East Command's egregious head of intelligence, whose optimistic and inaccurate forecasts played a major part in the near-disastrous UN retreat from North Korea in December 1950

31. A Centurion tank of 'C' Squadron 8th Hussars after the battle of the Imjin in April 1951. The crew were forced to close their hatches because Chinese infantry were climbing on to the hull; the tank plunged over a steep embankment, stalled, and had to be abandoned. This photograph was taken several weeks later when British troops re-entered the area. The officer standing on the turret is Lieutenant Randle Cooke, whose gruesome experience of Korean military discipline during the evacuation of Pyongyang is described elsewhere

32. Lieutenant Atkins of the 8th Hussars and his crew survey the damage caused to their Daimler armoured car by one of the many improvised mines left behind by the Chinese as they withdrew across the Imjin river in the late summer of 1951. Often made of wood, or packed into earthenware jars, they were difficult to detect and caused damage and casualties months after being laid

YOUR BUDDIES ARE DOING FINE HERE
IN A POW CAMP

From Dickie Grenies to Mrs. Amanda Grenies of Ring Street, Howland, Maine dated February 25th 1951.

"I am in fair health and in high spirits. We are receiving excellent treatment."

COME OVER! Join your buddies here. You will go to the rear in safety and get home in one piece.

Leave Korean to the Koreans.

- - - - - USE THIS AS A SAFE CONDUCT PASS - - - - -

When you see a Korean People's Army soldier or a Chinese Volunteer soldier, lay down your gun and shout:

投 "TOW · SHONG" 降
(Surrender)

We guarantee you safe conduct and good treatment.

THE CHINESE PEOPLE'S VOLUNTEER FORCES

33. Part of a Chinese People's Army leaflet addressed to American troops, picked up in the forward area of the Commonwealth Division in the summer of 1951. Later, the Chinese introduced material aimed specifically at British personnel

34. A railway marshalling yard in North Korea under low-level attack by B-26 Invader light bombers of the 5th US Air Force. By June 1951, when this attack took place, the interdiction of communist supply routes had developed into a relentless offensive which severely affected the resupply of Chinese and North Korean field formations

35. F-86 Sabre fighters of the 5th US Air Force at dispersal. Although greatly outnumbered and outgunned by the MiG-15s used by the Chinese (which mounted cannon as against the F-86's six .50-calibre machine-guns) the superior flying ability of the American pilots enabled them to inflict heavy losses on the enemy in what became the first high-speed jet combats in history

36. Immediately after the capture of Hill 355 (Little Gibraltar) on 4 October 1951, men of the King's Own Scottish Borderers relax amidst the wreckage of the Chinese defences. In the foreground are two Chinese prisoners, watched from the right by a 'Katcom' – a South Korean soldier attached to the KOSB. At this stage, apparently unknown to the Borderers, Captain Gerke's company of the 3rd Battalion Royal Australian Regiment were less than 200 yards away over the crest. Both units were to claim that they had taken Hill 355, but it seems that the Borderers arrived on their summit at 10 a.m., some time before the Australians whose war diary reports that they were firmly on their objective by 2 p.m.

37. In October 1951 the 1st Commonwealth Division attacked the enemy-held high ground north of the River Imjin. Artillery played a prominent role in this and all subsequent operations. Here, a 25-pounder of the 2nd Regiment, Royal Canadian Horse Artillery, is in action amidst a pile of used cartridge cases, as further supplies of ammunition arrive directly on to the battery position

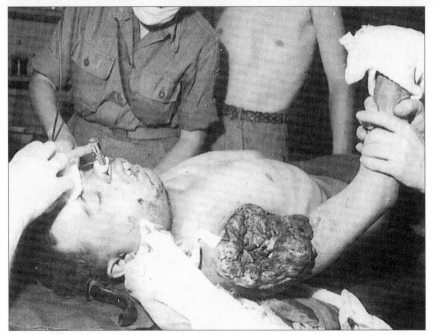

38. A badly wounded Chinese prisoner receives emergency treatment at the Norwegian MASH. His injuries are typical of those inflicted by large shell splinters

39. US Army helicopters evacuating casualties from the Indian Field Ambulance in the forward area of 27 Commonwealth Brigade, during the Kapyong battle, April 1951

40. One of the crucial developments in military battlefield medical services during the Korean War was the introduction of the Mobile Army Surgical Hospital, or 'MASH'. Here, some of the staff of the 8225th MASH pose alongside the indispensable helicopter which brought wounded men from the front line for lifesaving treatment, often within minutes of their being hit. The US Army medical services followed a more enlightened policy than the British towards the use of women nurses in the forward area, a factor which had immense morale value for the front-line troops

41. The light fleet carrier HMS *Ocean*, her full complement of Sea Fury and Firefly aircraft ranged on the flight deck, steams at full speed *en route* to Korean waters from Japan in July 1952. Apart from the small size of the deck – which is not angled as in later ships – there is only a single obsolete catapult, from which aircraft had to be launched in turn when the deck was as congested as this. The ship's maximum speed of some 23 knots also added to the difficulties of flying off and recovering aircraft

42. The flight deck of an operational carrier is one of the most dangerous places on earth. Deck crews on HMS *Ocean* rush to free the pilot of a Sea Fury which has overturned after missing the arrester wires and engaging the crash barrier

43. The enormous engineering effort required to keep the UN forces in the field was mainly borne by the US Army Corps of Engineers. A major part of their work was the construction and maintenance of adequate roads and bridges. As most of South Korea's bridges had been destroyed in the first weeks of the war, hundreds of new ones had to be built. Here, men of the 378th Combat Engineer Battalion, US Army, are installing the trackway on a bridge over the Pukhan river in November 1951

44. A rifle company of the 3rd Battalion Royal Australian Regiment, carried in Bedford 3-tonners of 78 Company RASC, crosses the Imjin river on an American pontoon bridge. It is June 1951 and as the Commonwealth Division forms up, its brigades are reaching out across the river in an attempt to make contact with the Chinese who have withdrawn to the north. Patrols such as this were a daily occurrence; from time to time the enemy responded with mortar fire but continued to avoid major confrontation

45. A meeting of senior officers on the airstrip close to HQ 1st Commonwealth Division in April 1952. *Left to right*: Lieutenant-General John ('Iron Mike') W. O'Daniel, commanding I US Corps, Major-General A.J.H. Cassels, commanding the Commonwealth Division, General Matthew B. Ridgway, Supreme Commander (complete with grenades), and General James Van Fleet, commanding 8th US Army Korea

46. In a campaign where artillery played such a key role, the accurate American 8-inch gun was widely used to tackle pinpoint targets beyond the capacity of field artillery, such as heavily protected strongpoints. The arrival of 'The Persuaders', as they were known from the inscription on their gun barrels, was invariably welcomed in the forward areas

47. A tank commander's view of an airstrike. In the area of the 'Hook' a 500-pounder lands on Chinese positions barely 400 yards ahead. The tank in this case is a Centurion of the 1st Royal Tank Regiment, which arrived in Korea in time to support the Commonwealth Division in the autumn and winter battles of 1952–3

48. The battered positions of the 1st Battalion Black Watch on the Hook after the Chinese attack of December 1952. A few months later, painstakingly rebuilt and strengthened, these defences were the scene of another grim fight when the 1st Battalion, Duke of Wellington's Regiment, fought off an even heavier attack. Many experienced veterans of the Second World War were to confirm that the violence of the Chinese bombardment on both occasions exceeded anything they had ever witnessed

49. The author reading J.B. Priestley's *Festival at Farbridge* (it was the year of the Festival of Britain) during a halt on the road from Seoul to Pusan, October 1951

50. The 60th Indian Parachute Field Ambulance, which joined the 27th Commonwealth Infantry Brigade at the end of 1950 after taking part in an American parachute assault north of Pyongyang, quickly earned a high reputation, particularly after its outstanding performance in the evacuation of the northern capital when its commanding officer, Lieutenant-Colonel Rangaraj, commandeered a goods train to bring all his medical stores to safety. This picture shows the 'waiting room' of the unit, situated amidst a group of ancient royal tombs near Suwon in the spring of 1951, as two Australian soldiers await treatment

51. Once static warfare had set in, artillery became the dominant weapon. Here, on a cold January day in 1952, gun crews of the 37th Field Artillery Battalion US Army leave the warmth of their tent for a fire mission near Kumchon in the central sector

52. The fierce Korean winter produced many ingenious forms of accommodation. Known as 'Hutchies', these invariably included the indispensable American army-issue space heater, fuelled by diesel oil or petrol, drip-fed into a stove. The erratic behaviour of these devices led to numerous fires. This partly buried 'Hutchie' was used by the ground crews of 1903 Air Observation Post Flight RAF

53. In July 1952 the 1st Commonwealth Division was visited by General Lawton Collins, US Army Chief of Staff. Seen here in a forward observation trench are (*left to right*) Brigadier Pike (Commander Royal Artillery, wearing sunglasses), Major–General Paul Kendall, commanding US I Corps, Brigadier Thomas Daly, commanding 28 Commonwealth Brigade (in bush hat), General James Van Fleet, commanding 8th US Army Korea, General Mark Clark, C-in-C Far East Command, Major–General Cassels, Commander 1st Commonwealth Division, and General Collins

54. Two RAF engine fitters service an Auster aircraft of 1903 Air Observation Post Flight. The pilots, signallers and non-technical personnel of this unit came from the Royal Artillery and the aircraft technicians from the RAF. The inter-service mix, first devised early in the Second World War, worked extremely well in practice

55. It is midsummer 1952. Under supervision of an unarmed NCO of the King's Shropshire Light Infantry, North Korean prisoners work on their new compound on Koje Island. Following the earlier riots in which the camp commandant, Brigadier-General Dodd, was taken hostage by violent prisoners, additional UN troops were sent to the island to help the American and South Korean guards restore order. The British troops soon established a curious rapport with their charges, who were to petition unavailingly for British soldiers to stay on in the garrison

56. In April 1953 the first exchange of prisoners – 'Little Switch' – took place at Panmunjon. Amongst the sick and wounded United Nations troops returned were some of the Glosters, here seen undergoing their initial debrief by a British Red Cross officer. It was noted that few of these men, despite their imprisonment in the north, showed signs of malnourishment. Interrogation in depth, however, revealed that theirs had been a far from pleasant captivity, especially in the earlier months at the hands of the North Koreans

talions to do until divisional headquarters issued patrolling instructions. For the time being it was enough to put out listening posts overlooking the fords across the river and await developments.

The apparent aimlessness of the campaign was beginning to have its effect on the morale and motivation of many of the soldiers. Major Pat Angier of the Glosters had already written home in March, noting that a number of his soldiers – miners from the Forest of Dean – had volunteered to return to work in the pits, in response to a government call to alleviate the crisis in the coal industry, as a quick way of getting home. On 11 March he added that

> I have two men who have turned sour and just refuse to obey orders at all. They are very silly and it is a pity as one of them has a nice wife and daughter. They will probably get very severe sentences. One has a bad record and may get five years in a Hong Kong prison. They have been pleaded with before all this but have got the mistaken idea that the quickest way out of the army is via prison. Also, they have the wind up.

It was not just the soldiers who were dispirited. A few days later even the stout-hearted Angier was confiding to his wife that he was feeling the pangs of separation from his family:

> Each day that goes by hardens my heart against the army. Civil and military life are so different that you have to make up your mind which you want and be decisive. I know it might be dull and boring and less money, and perhaps frustrating and set hours, but I would expect that . . . What I hope for from civil life is the end of separation, a home and garden and Sundays at home with the feeling that no one can post you or recall you here, there and everywhere (except of course, world war again!).

A few days later, however, this admirable soldier, who had served with distinction in airborne forces during the war, had recovered his spirits as he went on R and R (rest and recovery) leave in Japan. This scheme had been running for some months, enabling all ranks to get over to Japan for a week in well-appointed leave centres. Angier opted for Kure, giving him a chance for boat trips on the Inland Sea; he visited the holy island of Myajima and was enthralled by the beauty of its temple and the famous Torii arch set in the water below high-water mark. He returned to his battalion refreshed, on 15 April. 'A' Company which he commanded was deployed in the battalion's foremost position, on a low but commanding hill surmounted by the remains of an ancient castle earthwork. Castle Hill would play an important role in the impending battle. Those who manned the shallow trenches on its slopes were conscious that the old castle had been put there for a purpose many centuries before, guarding a road trodden by conquerors coming out of Asia to capture Seoul. Once again, 29 Brigade had been placed in the prime defensive position on the historic invasion road.

Angier, an enthusiastic watercolourist who spent much of his spare time painting, wrote on 17 April that 'we sit here on the parallel and although we are in the front line we are no longer in contact. It is very bad from the soldiering point of view as it is impossible to prevent the men from getting complacent and this weakness will be paid for in lives should the enemy care to counter-attack. However, I hope he will leave us in peace. It is all very strange and quite unlike a normal war.'

From the beginning of the month the brigade had been increasing the strength and depth of its patrols across the Imjin. Day after day the patrols went out, returning at last light with little to report. The Chinese might have disappeared from the face of the earth. Yet there were disturbing reports from aerial reconnaissance of a huge build-up to the north and General Van Fleet was convinced that the Chinese were about to resume the offensive. The last of the big patrols went out on 20 April. Angier described the scene as the Glosters, accompanied by tanks of the 8th Hussars under their commanding officer Sir Guy Lowther, pushed across the Imjin:

> It was a very cavalry occasion and the start across the paddy-fields and banks in the morning was just like the hunting field, tanks roaring, galloping, jumping and bogging down everywhere . . . The enemy had withdrawn and for my part I spent the day picnicking on top of a hill where they might have been. The azaleas were splendid and made the journey worthwhile, to me at any rate.

Also in the battalion that day was the newly arrived Second Lieutenant Whatmore, who had recently discarded his Royal Hampshires' cap badge for that of the Glosters. He was glad to escape from Hiro barracks, with what he described as its 'mix of disgruntled reservists and a sprinkling of regulars . . . Amongst this grousing and unashamedly embittered bunch of officers I found a new and coarser atmosphere.' Like many idealistic young officers he was eager to prove himself in a fighting battalion and quickly settled down with his new platoon. He was immediately impressed by the Glosters' Anglican chaplain, the Reverend Sam Davies; so much so that within days he had been baptized into the Church of England. He was also delighted to find in the battalion a friend from Hiro, Lieutenant Philip Curtis of the Duke of Cornwall's Light Infantry, another reinforcement officer, who had exchanged his light infantry Bugle cap badge for the Sphinx of the Glosters, together with their jealously preserved regimental peculiarity, the miniature 'Back Badge' proudly worn to commemorate the stand of the old 28th Foot at the Battle of Alexandria in 1801, when, charged from the rear by a French battalion, the colonel had ordered his rear rank to face about and deal with the threat.

Whatmore and the new arrivals lost no time in getting to know their fellow mess members. The commanding officer, Lieutenant-Colonel Carne, appeared forbiddingly remote on first acquaintance. One of the regular Glosters' officers, Major Digby Grist, described his colonel as 'a very special sort of man . . . of deep thoughts and few words who hated chatter'. Carne had spent much of his earlier service between the wars in East Africa where, instead of the vapid social life of Nairobi, he sought the deep solitude of the bush, hunting big game alone and with singular commitment. He demonstrated no evident ambition for high command and with his regimental sergeant-major, Mr Hobbs, formed the core, the living heart, of the battalion. By their very presence they and their like infused the short service members, the reservists, national servicemen and reinforcements with the sense of belonging to something with a long and honourable history and traditions which they were expected to live up to as long as they wore the Sphinx and Back Badge.

CHAPTER 19

The Fifth Phase

When Marshal Peng issued his operational orders for the 'Fifth Phase Offensive' to his army group commanders on 18 April he believed that the 27th Commonwealth Brigade was still in the van of the US IX Corps, north of Kapyong, and that the British 29th Brigade Group was defending the Imjin river line in the US I Corps sector. Having sampled the fighting power of both these formations he planned for their early destruction, assigning high-grade units to deal with them. But even as Peng's orders were being distributed, 27 Brigade had been taken out of the line, placed in reserve around the town of Kapyong, and relieved at the front by the ROK 6th Division. Its commander, Brigadier-General Chang Do-yong, had shown himself to be a skilled and courageous soldier, but unfortunately his subordinates were men of lesser calibre. His regiments continued to advance cautiously and when, on 22 April, instructions were received to halt and prepare a defensive position to meet an imminent Chinese attack, they made little effort to dig in despite the urging of their American advisers. As darkness fell the division was in disorder; some of its units were already moving to the rear in defiance of orders whilst others waited nervously to see what would happen. There was little or no attempt to prepare a solid defence.

In 27 Brigade the Argylls were to be the first to leave for Hong Kong. They handed over their vehicles and heavy weapons to the advance party of their successors, the King's Own Scottish Borderers, amid a round of farewell parties at which their pipes and drums played to appreciative audiences in the matchless highland setting of the Kapyong valley. Brigadier Coad had already left for Hong Kong where his wife was still dangerously ill, and the brigade, pending the arrival of Brigadier Taylor and the headquarters of 28 Brigade, was commanded by the deputy commander of 29 Brigade, Colonel Burke, promoted to Brigadier for the occasion.

Until it went into reserve 27 Brigade had been worked hard in a series of sharp actions against Chinese rearguards who exacted casualties on the Argylls almost up to the last minute. The Canadians of the Princess Patricias were learning fast. Their commanding officer, Lieutenant-Colonel Stone, had arrived in Korea two months earlier and whilst the battalion worked up to operational pitch in the south, he and some of his officers and senior NCOs had acquired hard-earned battle knowledge from the British and Australian battalions. Stone found that the haphazard recruiting methods adopted in Canada to raise the brigade promised for Korea had allowed undesirable elements to volunteer. Many had lurid criminal records and were more interested in escaping the police than serving the cause of freedom. Only days before embarkation one man was discovered to have a wooden leg, another was found to be over 70 years old, whilst the Korean climate soon exposed many more as being well below acceptable medical standards. Stone was still weeding these out when the PPCLI went into action for the first time.

As the advance parties of 27 Brigade left Korea for Hong Kong, their reliefs were completing their preparations for active service. Second Lieutenant Barney Henderson of the Borderers remembered it all vividly many years later:

> Hong Kong was an amazing place, throbbing with kinetic energy. My regiment had some amazing characters. First there were the Jocks – stoical and fiercely proud. The commanding officer was John MacDonald – tall, teetotal, meticulous in all he did. The adjutant's name was Fish's Tit Haig because whenever a subaltern arrived late for the daily officers' briefing and gave some silly excuse, Captain Haig would say, 'I don't give a fish's tit. You will not be late in future. Take two extra duties.'

This robust battalion left Hong Kong on 19 April aboard an American troopship (which, to the alarm of Captain Haig and most of the officers apart from Colonel MacDonald, was 'dry') and arrived at Inchon four days later, to be met by a column of British trucks and the interesting news that the Chinese offensive had started the previous night. Leaving its stores on the quayside the battalion was driven to the Kapyong area at once in case it had to reinforce 27 Brigade, depleted as it was by the imminent departure of the Argylls and Middlesex.

The situation was indeed grim, for the 6th ROK Division had collapsed on the night of 22 April, leaving a yawning gap in the UN line through which thousands of Chinese were advancing south towards Kapyong. Henderson recalled the excitement as the KOSB arrived at the front:

> Orders were given to board RASC three-tonners and move to an assembly area inland: a place called Kapyong on the central front near the source of the Pukhan river. One company was left behind at Inchon to gather up our vehicles and stores. A recipe for a grand military cock-up if ever there was one. The RASC drivers were splendid and knew where they were going. No one else did. Through Seoul, in the dark, barely a building seemed to be standing; forlorn Koreans wandering aimlessly around, devastation in every direction.

By first light on the 24th the battalion had reached its assembly area in the Pukhan valley, where two maps were issued for the entire unit. The Argylls drove off cheering in the direction of Inchon and the Borderers realized suddenly that they were very much in the war; from the hills to the north came the rumble of artillery and fugitives from the 6th ROK Division were pouring down the valley as fast as their feet could carry them. The rout was watched dispassionately by the officers and men of the brigade's administrative units, which were located, with an American MASH or field surgical hospital, along the Pukhan valley. It reminded one RASC subaltern of what he had read in school of medieval armies in full flight; soldiers in disarray, many lacking arms and equipment, some struggling manfully with parts of heavy mortars suspended on wooden yokes.

General Chang and his staff had managed to halt some of the fugitives near Kapyong but theirs was a hopeless task. The gap could only be filled by 27 Brigade, which was urgently ordered forward. The Australians, who had seen more action than any of the remaining battalions, had been looking forward to the celebration, with the New Zealanders, of Anzac Day, the annual commemoration of the landings at Gallipoli on 25 April 1915, a landmark in the histories of both countries. Arrangements had been made to observe the customary act of remembrance: a dawn vigil followed by festivities, to which the Turkish brigade, the foes of 1915, now allies serving in the US 25th Division over to the west, had been invited. All now had to be postponed.

The hapless 6th ROK Division had been supported by two New Zealand field batteries and a company of American artillery. Had some New Zealand forward observation observers been up with the ROK infantry, as was standard British practice, more warning might have been given, but shortly after dark the forward ROK positions were overwhelmed by the Chinese in a silent attack, without preliminary bombardment. The first thing the gunners knew was when all the forward ROK units went off the air as their command posts were overrun. Then came the unwelcome sounds of rifle and machine-gun fire from just in front of the gun positions. It was decided to get the guns out to safety and the batteries redeployed to a position a few miles north of Kapyong town.

Whilst they were on the move and occupying the new gun areas, the rest of 27 Brigade was alerted by General Hoge's corps headquarters, who instructed Brigadier Burke to take up a blocking position north of the gun lines, covering Kapyong itself. All three battalions – Middlesex, 3 RAR and the PPCLI – initiated their battle drills; reconnaissance parties went forward to site defensive positions for the rifle companies and company commanders reported to their commanding officers for orders. The Middlesex, somewhat disconcerted at this late call back to battle and already half packed for departure, were ordered to provide close support for the New Zealand guns, now under immediate threat from parties of Chinese infiltrating the brigade area amidst hordes of

ROK soldiery and civilians fleeing south. The Middlesex were in fact barely operational and Colonel Man, who had commanded the battalion with great determination since its arrival in Korea nine months earlier, had already left for home on expiry of his tour, to be replaced by an officer from another regiment, selected by General Robertson in Japan from the pool of lieutenant-colonels in the Hiro reinforcement depot. Burke therefore had to deploy the Australian and Canadian battalions forward, on high ground enjoying good fields of view across a sort of natural amphitheatre, but too far apart for them to support each other with fire, and hope for the best.

In the middle of the morning of the 23rd, in a desperate effort to get 6th ROK Division to stand and fight, and to encourage General Chang to hold on, Burke was ordered to send the New Zealand guns forward again. It was too late; the ROKs were no longer able to offer coherent resistance. The batteries, escorted by the Middlesex, nevertheless set forth. This meant abandoning key ground and weakening the defence at the heart of the brigade's position, where the Middlesex had been digging in. In particular it left a gap of almost three miles between the Australians on the right and the Canadians on the left.

In front of the Australian position, down in the valley, lies the hamlet of Chuktan-ni. Forward of it, on a low ridge running along and commanding the valley to the north, down which the ROK troops were still pouring, was a company of Australians. The rest of the battalion was deployed to the right, in echelon up the slopes of a massive hill feature. Colonel Ferguson's command post was sited in the valley immediately south of the main position in open ground amidst small arable fields and orchards. Close behind were the 4.2-inch mortars of the American Chemical Mortar Company which had been attached to the brigade since before Christmas. Nearly three miles to the south-west on top of another massif were the PPCLI, whose uppermost rifle company was dug in on the 500-metre ring contour. Then there was the ominous void in the centre, vacated by the Middlesex when they went forward with the guns. The two battalions dug in as well as they could, their Korean porters valiantly clambering up the steep slopes with ammunition, water and rations, using traditional 'A' frames to lift loads of up to 100 pounds.

As the enemy advanced south, Burke knew he was in a perilous position, for if the Chinese arrived before the New Zealand gunners and their Middlesex escort got back, the brigade would be destroyed where it stood. His most vulnerable unit was 3 RAR, whose battalion headquarters Colonel Ferguson had sited in the valley bottom, out of radio contact for much of the time with its own rifle companies high above on hills which effectively masked wireless signals. As a result the Australians had to pin their faith on field telephones, runners and motor cycle despatch riders. Long after the battle Ferguson was criticized by one of his officers, the formidably combative Captain Reg Saunders, the first Australian aborigine to be commissioned, who wrote:

I respected Fergie. He was a very brave man – even if I thought he was an exhibitionist because he never carried a weapon and strolled around all the time with a bloody walking stick. He always positioned his battalion headquarters in isolation from the other companies and did this again at Kapyong. He liked a neatly signposted and well laid out HQ. There was no tactical or battle HQ inside the main battalion defensive position, up with the forward companies.

The isolated rifle company on its low ridge in the valley bottom was squarely astride the enemy's line of approach from the north and thus likely to take the full impact of the Chinese attack. Mines and wire would have helped to strengthen the position, but none was available. The defence of battalion headquarters was augmented by part of the battalion's support company under the seasoned Captain Jack Gerke, with a couple of cumbersome 17-pounder anti-tank guns, 3-inch mortars, some Vickers machine-guns, and the men of the assault pioneer platoon. Close at hand was Headquarters Company, comprising signallers, clerks and orderlies, all trained infantrymen. None, however, expected to be fighting that night and preparations may have gone ahead with less urgency than those of the rifle companies. All believed that this was no more than a temporary location and that the following day would see the battalion either moving north or strengthening the present position with mines and wire.

During the afternoon of 23 April the full extent of the collapse of the 6th ROK Division was not apparent despite the steady flow of fugitives through the battalion area. Fortunately, Burke had allotted the Australians the whole of Company 'A' of the US 72nd Tank Battalion, under Lieutenant Kenneth Koch. He had already toured the brigade area and marked up his maps with the best 'going' for his 15 Sherman tanks, as well as possible routes and assembly areas, before deploying most of the tanks on the valley floor. There was additional support for the brigade in the form of extra American mortars and field artillery.

As daylight faded on the 23rd, ROK stragglers were still coming back through 3 RAR's position. The ROK divisional headquarters, or what was left of it, had been set up near Ferguson's command post, but repeated visits to it failed to elicit any information as to the disposition and condition of the ROK regiments. After dark, the New Zealand guns and Middlesex made their way safely back into the brigade area through the mass of fugitives and refugees, but then redeployed further back down the valley than their original positions. They thus imperilled the Australians, for Ferguson had expected the Middlesex to reoccupy their former area on his immediate left rear, close to his command post. His battalion was dangerously exposed and firing could already be heard from the forward companies as Chinese probing attacks began. Not all the ROKs had fled; some were rallied close to the Australian command post by one of their own warrant officers wielding a large stick, and they joined 3

RAR's anti-tank platoon, whose sergeant commented that they seemed to fear their own NCOs even more than the Chinese.

As the nearly-full moon rose over the hills, the leading tank platoon, placed dangerously ahead of the infantry in the valley, was attacked by Chinese infantry with explosive charges on long poles. They boldly clambered on to the tank hulls, killing the commanders as they showed their heads out of their hatches and hurling grenades into the turrets. The platoon commander, mortally wounded, ordered his tanks to make a fighting withdrawal and they pulled back into the Australian position where casualties could be lifted out. Making use of the moonlight the Chinese were soon assailing the Australian positions on the high ground with grenades and small arms. Using bugles and whistles to co-ordinate their attack they maintained pressure on 3 RAR through the night. Casualties were mounting, especially in 'A' Company on the forward edge of the high ground overlooking the valley.

During the night, Ferguson and his headquarters had been heavily involved as Chinese probed into the valley, setting up a roadblock a short distance to the south. The enterprising Lieutenant Koch, moving around on foot to assess the situation, ordered some of his tanks to load up with wounded, top up their fuel and ammunition, and return immediately to the fight. The situation was con-fused at Ferguson's command post, where Chinese seemed to be all round the hard-pressed defenders. The tank men had a hard night; one of the Shermans received a direct hit from a Chinese rocket launcher which killed the com-mander and wounded most of his crew. As the enemy pushed further along the valley past battalion headquarters they came across the New Zealand gun lines, to be engaged with great spirit by the gun crews, who were compelled in the small hours to withdraw to a new gun area prudently reconnoitred on the orders of the regiment's commanding officer, Lieutenant-Colonel Moodie. After a gap of little more than an hour the guns were in action from their new position. The forward observation officers, situated like the Australian battal-ion's own mortar fire controllers in the rifle company positions, had to fight alongside the infantry and one of the New Zealanders and his radio operator were killed in so doing. Communications between Ferguson and his forward companies, tenuous at best, virtually disappeared as telephone lines, lying on the surface, were cut repeatedly. During the night it became very much a company commanders' battle, and fortunately in 3 RAR these were men of resolution and experience.

By midnight the whole battalion was involved in close-quarter fighting. In the absence of orders from battalion headquarters, the rifle companies sat tight and threw off a series of attacks, often resorting to the bayonet and bare hands. The Chinese knew it was essential to take the hilltops by first light, as daylight would reveal their men milling around in the valley, easy targets for observed artillery and mortar fire as well as airstrikes. But the heavily outnumbered

Australians were immovable, although Lieutenant Argent estimated that the battalion had been attacked by up to a division-sized enemy formation. 3 RAR readily acknowledged that their survival thus far owed much to the presence of Koch's tank company, whose conduct through the night had been impeccable, unlike that of the American mortars. When these fell silent and a party was sent to investigate, it discovered that the mortarmen had abandoned their position, departing in haste along a valley heading east, leaving behind their mortars, numerous vehicles and a field kitchen.

After daylight on 24 April the battle continued. Koch estimated that his tanks had killed between 100 and 150 enemy, including an entire platoon spectacularly wiped out after they had rashly sought cover in a farmhouse which was then engaged point blank by the main armament of several tanks. Between 2 a.m. and first light, the tanks had been fighting at ranges from 15 feet to 75 yards and at times the crews were obliged to repel Chinese attacks by hurling grenades from their turrets and using their 'grease guns' – a type of sub-machine-gun – on their assailants. Later in the day it was found that the tanks had expended 162 rounds of 76mm main armament ammunition, 32,000 rounds of .30 calibre machine-gun and over 11,000 rounds of .50 calibre.

In the small hours Ferguson, having lost contact with brigade headquarters, drove back to the Middlesex position and used their radio to speak to Brigadier Burke. He was unable to give a coherent account of the battle, having been out of touch with his own rifle companies for much of the night and even for a time with his own battalion headquarters, as he walked around the valley personally directing the actions of small groups of defenders. Before leaving for the Middlesex, aware that ammunition was running low, he gave orders for his companies to pull back at first light. His impression that the command post had been overrun was probably coloured by the acute stress of the fighting around it when at the same time he could only guess what was happening to his men up on the hills. His judgement, usually very sound, may also have been affected by a Chinese mortar bomb near miss which momentarily stunned him shortly after midnight.

With daylight came the chance to sort out the confusion on the valley floor. Ferguson's headquarters was moved back alongside the Middlesex whilst Koch organized a rescue operation to recover the American mortars and their transport abandoned the previous evening. Some American sappers, who had been fighting most effectively as infantry, and personnel of the chemical mortar unit led by their commanding officer, furious at his men's conduct, recovered nearly all the mortars and some fifty vehicles. Shortly before dawn on the 24th, whilst back with the Middlesex, Ferguson had called for one of their companies to break through the Chinese roadblock to permit 3 RAR to disengage and pull back. For reasons which remain obscure this company failed to complete its mission and, following the route taken by the fleeing mortarmen the previous evening, withdrew to the east, playing no further part in the battle.

Around dawn 3 RAR's headquarters and the troops near by had been safely evacuated down the valley. Captain Gerke and his support company were unaware of this move until a battalion headquarters vehicle drove past, its driver exhorting Gerke to 'Bug out! Battalion HQ's back down the road. Watch out for Gooks on the way – they hold the high ground over there.' Gerke needed no further persuasion; getting his company on the road they ran the gauntlet of heavy, if inaccurate, Chinese fire on their way to safety, picking up a number of abandoned American vehicles as they went.

The unit in the worst predicament was Major O'Dowd's 'A' Company, sited along the ridge running up from the valley bottom, overlooking the road down which the ROK 6th Division was fleeing and in every sense the most exposed in the battalion. Snow still lay on the northern slope where they dug their shallow scrapes, and lighting fires was out of the question. The men chattered with cold as they waited for the Chinese. All night they fought off successive attacks as casualties mounted. Soon, more than fifty wounded men were sitting or lying on the reverse slope; there were no stretchers and medical supplies ran out. Chinese mortar bombs were landing amongst these unprotected casualties, wounding yet more, but they stuck it out heroically until dawn, when the attacks died away and it was possible to get them down to the regimental aid post. This had come under fire several times during the night, almost certainly by accident, for its personnel acknowledged that the Chinese never knowingly fired on the Red Cross flag, nor did they interfere with the work of the medical orderlies and bearers, or fire on the stretcher jeeps taking the wounded back down the valley, past their roadblocks to the Indian Field Ambulance.

After daybreak, determined to extricate his company, O'Dowd counter-attacked with one of his platoons. In the words of his company sergeant-major:

> Myself and a few others around company headquarters jumped up with 3 Platoon and we charged down on the Chinese. They just all of a sudden turned and ran away. They didn't feel like fighting us any more. They tried to hide in thickets or any low ground they could find down towards the creek bed. The Chinese were very stupid to stay there. We could see them and began to have a really good time. We began to pick them off while they lay on the ground or when they broke cover like rabbits. We were enjoying ourselves until our dear old major decided to stop us firing because ammunition was very scarce.

At the same time other groups of Chinese, caught in daylight in the open along the valley, were trying to make their way back to reorganize, offering good targets for the battalion's Vickers guns, which fired belt after belt of ammunition at them as they pulled back from in front of 'A' Company; in the words of one of the gun detachment commanders: 'I ordered my guns to open fire. I began counting the Chinese as they fell . . . I got to about 40 and stopped counting.'

Despite this reverse the Chinese continued to attack the rifle companies higher up the hill, who had not been so seriously troubled during the night. The sun was up and the clear weather was ideal for close air support, but none was forthcoming; the needs of 29 Brigade Group over to the west on the Imjin were given a higher priority.

It was now the turn of the Canadians to receive the attentions of the Chinese, who were steadily feeling their way round the left flank of the defence. Colonel Stone, who had been out of action suffering, unusually, from smallpox, was back in command. He and his battalion had had a grandstand view of 3 RAR's battle and during the night of the 24th his forward platoons came under attack themselves. As the day wore on, enemy pressure increased and at last light the Patricias were heavily engaged with Chinese who were intent on cutting off the withdrawal of the Australians. During the night the Chinese attacked with a battalion which for a time managed to overrun one of Stone's companies, to be ejected by a spirited counter-attack in which numbers of wounded Canadians rose to their feet and charged with the bayonet. Another company, on the point of being overwhelmed by sheer weight of numbers, called for artillery fire on its own position, to which the New Zealanders responded immediately with devastating consequences for the Chinese caught in the open. Further support was given by American medium guns which swept the Canadian position clear of the enemy in minutes.

At daybreak on the 25th the Canadians were surrounded, their withdrawal route blocked by the enemy. Stone was confident that his men, commanding magnificent views of the Kapyong valley, could bring effective fire to bear on any Chinese attempt to move along the valley bottom. He was however running short of ammunition and food, both of which were delivered accurately by parachute during the morning by four C-119 Boxcars of the US Air Force, whilst helicopters bore the wounded to safety. A successful attack by the US 5th Cavalry retook the now abandoned Australian position as Koch's tanks cleared the valley of Chinese, who had suffered such heavy losses that they retired up the valley, enabling 27 Brigade to disengage. It had been a classic example of a vigorous defence, achieved by only two battalions displaying great determination in face of a formidable threat. The Australians' company commanders in particular had shown great coolness and skill in the withdrawal of their men whilst still in contact with a determined and brave enemy. None of the New Zealand guns had been lost despite numerous occasions when their battery positions had come under small-arms fire.

Very little else was lost either; the stockpile of ammunition, rations and fuel in the brigade headquarters area, set up in the days prior to the Chinese attack, was almost entirely carried to safety by the RASC, whose three-tonner trucks were in many cases carrying up to seven tons. Several days' supplies of fresh bread were set on fire *in situ*, filling the Kapyong valley with the unusual aroma of burnt toast. Most of the tinned 'compo' rations which could not be lifted out were pitched into the Kapyong river, from which they were rescued a few weeks later for reissue to unsuspecting customers. The battle had stretched the administrative support units to the limit, placing great demands on the recovery and repair of vehicles and radios, and on mechanical transport. Not only had the newly arrived KOSB been picked up at Inchon and delivered to the brigade area, but throughout the three-day battle, huge amounts of ammunition had to be shifted from the railhead at Suwon and taken directly to the guns, a task undertaken by British, Canadian and New Zealand drivers of the RASC, RCASC and RNZASC supplemented, as they dropped with exhaustion, by their officers, headquarters clerks, even cooks, who manned the trucks and helped the gunners to unload their priceless cargoes at the gun positions.

It was time for 27 Brigade to depart. Brigadier Taylor and the headquarters of 28 Brigade assumed the proud Commonwealth title, and as he left, Brigadier Burke presented Colonel Ferguson with 27 Brigade's flag as a well-earned trophy.

CHAPTER 20

Back to Back

The 3rd US Infantry Division, commanded by Major-General Robert H. Soule, was deployed on the line of the Imjin river some 30 miles north of Seoul in what an eighteenth-century soldier would have described as the Post of Honour, the most crucial and perilous place in the line. It had been entrusted with the defence of several of the routes from the north used since time immemorial by invaders aiming to capture Seoul. General Van Fleet had directed that in the event of a major Chinese offensive the 8th Army was to fall back on the line codenamed 'Kansas', lying south of the Imjin and to some extent prepared for defence with fieldworks, wire and minefields. For the time being, however, 3rd Division was north of this line and, as it had been anticipated that there would be further forward movement across the Imjin, little attempt had been made to dig substantial fieldworks. None of the battalions of the 29th Brigade Group, which had been placed under Soule's command, was wired in, nor had anti-personnel mines been laid in any quantity. The battalions were sited far apart and incapable of giving mutual fire support. Even within battalion areas the rifle companies were deployed up to a mile from each other. This degree of dispersion did not, it appears, worry any of the senior commanders, although Brigadier Brodie was deeply apprehensive at the thought of what might happen if the Chinese elected to attack. His doubts were to be realized all too well.

Daily patrols across the Imjin, ordered by HQ I Corps with the aim of seeking out the elusive enemy, failed to produce hard information. The Chinese seemed to have pulled well back and showed no sign of regaining contact.

General Soule had a huge divisional front to cover and he placed 29 Brigade on the left on 17,000 yards of the river line, with the 65th US Infantry Regiment on the right astride Route 33, the principal road from the north. The division's frontage was not a straight one; near the point of juncture between 29 Brigade and the 65th Regiment the Imjin turns abruptly north at the point where it is joined by a tributary, the Hantan, which flows in from the east. This sharp inward kink in his line raised a tactical problem and Soule, recognizing that it was an obvious thrust point for any Chinese attack, placed his divisional reserve close at hand. Brodie also saw the danger and placed the Belgian battalion, attached to his brigade, across the Imjin at the junction where it could cover several fording places.

Soule was also worried about his flanks. To the left was the ROK 1st Division which, though regarded as the most reliable Korean formation, might yield under heavy attack. The same thought impelled Colonel Carne of the Glosters, the left-hand battalion in 29 Brigade, which found itself alongside the ROK 12th Regiment. On the right of his brigade Brodie placed the Royal Northumberland Fusiliers, who occupied high ground overlooking the Imjin and the fords close to the river junction which would be the escape route for the Belgians if forced back across the river. The Royal Ulster Rifles and 'C' Squadron of the 8th Hussars were held back in brigade reserve.

On 22 April, the day following the last big patrol over the river, there was little to suggest anything untoward, although there were signs of increased enemy movement. The Northumberlands continued with preparations for celebration of their regimental day, 23 April, when in honour of St George of England they customarily wore roses in their head-dress; in the absence of the genuine article, artificial roses had been manufactured in Japan and wearing these the battalion were to go into action on the morrow.

Patrols from the Glosters and the Northumberlands were sent across the river early on the 22nd to investigate reports of increased enemy activity, confirmed by Belgian observers in a light aircraft and by a Turkish patrol over to the right in the 25th US Division sector, who captured a Chinese survey party, complete with theodolite, whose commander confirmed that the attack would come that night. Although the Glosters and Fusiliers made contact with small parties of enemy north of the river the Chinese were so expert at concealment that it was impossible to assess their strength. Parties of them detected in the afternoon were attacked from the air and with artillery, but there was, it seemed, no cause for alarm. It was a quiet sabbath and in 29 Brigade the chaplains conducted services for congregations somewhat swollen by rumours of impending battle; the Glosters' padre, Sam Davies, celebrated the eucharist outside an old temple behind 'A' Company's position on Castle Hill, a sacrament which, as he was sadly to note, was to be the viaticum for many of his communicants.

There was little sense of urgency in divisional and corps headquarters, for it had been assumed that the Chinese would make cautious probing attacks before attempting a major river crossing. This was an unsound assumption; the enemy had been conducting covert reconnaissances for many days and, abetted by civilian agents, had plotted the positions of all 29 Brigade's units down to company level as well as the yawning gaps between them. This became apparent as the attack developed.

At last light on the 22nd Colonel Carne posted several listening patrols on the low cliffs overlooking the fords to his battalion's front. The Imjin was running low and could be waded with ease at numerous crossing points. The patrols had not long to wait. Soon after dark Chinese infantry sprang from cover on the north bank and plunged into the river. Simultaneous attacks were launched all along the I Corps frontage; over to the right in 25th Division's sector the Turks were forced back from their vulnerable forward position and a threat to Soule's right flank developed. During the night came news of the collapse of the ROK 6th Division north of Kapyong and this made Soule even more nervous for his right flank. The forward battalion of the 65th Regiment was under pressure and the Filipino battalion was soon giving ground along Route 33.

As the moon rose the Glosters' listening patrols gazed in amazement as hundreds of Chinese took to the water. Artillery fire was immediately brought down on the fords as the patrols fired steadily into the masses of infantry in the river below them. The whole brigade was alerted, slit trenches manned and ammunition issued. Checking their weapons, the battalions waited for the next stage of the attack. With up to a mile between company locations, none of which was properly wired in, it was clear that there would be a series of isolated defensive engagements all over the brigade area. Much hung on the ability of the artillery to provide defensive fire, augmented by the battalions' own support weapons – Vickers machine-guns and 3-inch mortars, as well as the heavier 4.2-inch mortars of Major Fisher-Hoch's battery.

During the night, General Soule ordered the 7th US Regimental Combat Team forward to the area of the Imjin–Hantan river junction to be available for deployment on the 23rd either to support Brodie's right flank or to augment the divisional reserve of a battalion of the 65th Regiment and a tank battalion, located on Route 33 to the east of the Belgian position. The Chinese were quick to spot the significance of the river junction and began to attack the Belgians early in the night; at the same time, once the Glosters' listening patrols had been pulled back off the river bank, the enemy began to pour infantry across the river in their sector. If 29 Brigade could be eliminated it would be possible for the Chinese to push on down Routes 5Y and 11 towards Uijongbu, cutting the retirement routes of the 7th and 65th Regiments, as well as that of Brodie's brigade, and thus destroying Soule's entire command. The stakes were indeed high.

The foremost Gloster position was that of Major Angier's 'A' Company on Castle Hill and it was the first to feel the weight of the Chinese attack. Whilst many of its soldiers had been grumbling bitterly a few days before, as Angier had described in a letter to his wife, the stimulation of action united all ranks as the enemy burst in on them. In the moonlight and the unearthly glare of star-shell fired by the gunners and mortars a furious fight broke out on the hill. The enemy had little difficulty in reaching 'A' Company's position because of the lack of wire and mines but the Glosters resisted stubbornly, the steadiness and experience of their reservists giving heart to the younger regulars and national servicemen. Angier was constantly on his feet, touring the platoons in an inferno of fire, and it was whilst doing this that he fell to enemy machine-gun fire. By first light 'A' Company was on the verge of extinction. Part of Castle Hill was firmly in enemy hands; there was a final radio call from the defenders: 'We've had it. Cheerio', before the radio went dead.

Major Grist had gone forward shortly before dawn from his 'F' echelon, sited a few miles back down Route 5Y near the southern exit from the ravine through which the narrow track ran; he took with him urgently needed supplies of ammunition for 'A' Company, which had now been driven off Castle Hill, and was saddened to find that his friend Angier and many others were already dead. He started back down the track; by the time he reached Carne's command post at Solma-ri in the shadow of Hill 235 the situation was worsening by the minute and he was ambushed as he arrived back at 'F' echelon by Chinese who had already bypassed the forward rifle companies, marched over the flank of Kamak-san, the brooding mountain which dominates the country for miles around, and cut the only road by which the Glosters could retire. Grist ordered his driver to accelerate through the ambush and passing the wreckage of his 'F' echelon area he noted that a number of his men had already been captured. Wounded in the hand, and driving on punctured tyres, Grist reached brigade headquarters and his battalion's administrative group where he rallied all available men for the relief of the besieged Glosters. Colonel Carne meanwhile remained imperturbable on the radio, having moved his command post up Hill 235 from its original position, and was calmly reporting the situation to Brodie and his staff.

Brodie's intention was to pull the Belgians back across the river when compelled to do so, using the fords covered by the Northumberlands and occupying two of their company positions, thus enabling Colonel Kingsley Foster to concentrate his battalion. He was determined to hold back his brigade reserve, the Ulsters and 'C' Squadron of the 8th Hussars, as long as possible for use only in dire emergency. This arrived sooner than expected; the loss of Castle Hill, with its commanding view over the south bank of the Imjin, and the speed with which the Chinese had ascended Kamak-san, posed a grave threat not only to the Glosters but to the entire brigade. By first light on the 23rd any hope of extracting the Glosters had already gone. The Northumberlands were also under heavy pressure. As with the Glosters their rifle companies were so far from each other that mutual fire support was out of the question, and they were not properly dug in. Only the courage and skill-at-arms of individual riflemen prevented the Chinese from overwhelming the brigade at the first push. As it was, Brodie's battalions were to exact a high price on their attackers.

Aware of the risk of losing the Belgian battalion as it came under heavy attack, Brodie ordered forward the Ulsters' 'battle patrol' in their tracked carriers, with a detachment of Royal Engineers, to secure the fords leading back from the Belgian position. No sooner had this force crossed the river than it was ambushed at close range. Two of the carriers burst into flames and the rest were abandoned, the survivors of the patrol making their way back over the ford on foot under heavy fire.

At dawn on the 23rd the Northumberlands found themselves overlooked in their position on Hill 257 by Chinese machine-guns. Despite many acts of gallantry, it proved impossible for the Northumberlands to maintain their exposed position and the Chinese took the vital high ground overlooking the fords which offered the Belgians the best hope of escape. Although they continued to hold out in their hazardous post, blinded by the smoke of scrub fires which threatened to engulf them, it was imperative to devise a rescue attempt. Shortly after 7.30 a.m. Brodie spoke with Soule on the radio and was promised help for the Belgians. A battalion of the US 7th Infantry was ordered forward to fill the void between the Glosters and the Northumberland positions. Even so, Brodie was running out of troops. By midday the Glosters were isolated, their only exit route cut in several places, and it seemed that the Belgians, on the wrong side of the river, faced annihilation.

Throughout the night 29 Brigade's gunners had given magnificent support. Major Fisher-Hoch's heavy mortars were deployed well forward, split between the Belgians, Glosters and Fusiliers. The 25-pounders of 45 Field Regiment, under Lieutenant-Colonel Maris Young, were deployed immediately behind the Northumberlands, as was 'C' Squadron of the 8th Hussars whose commander, Major Henry Huth, was even now flying back from leave in Japan. Extra protection was given by some mobile Bofors guns of the 11th (Sphinx) Light Anti-Aircraft Battery, most of whose guns were guarding the Han river bridges at Seoul against a non-existent air threat. By the middle of the morning tanks and guns were in great danger; Chinese infantry appeared on the hills overlooking the gun lines and opened fire. Bofors and 25-pounders immediately replied over open sights, but it was time to get the guns out down Route 11. The move commenced at noon.

Lieutenant-General Robertson, the commander of the British Commonwealth Occupation Force, who had gone to Korea on a routine visit a few days earlier, made his way to General Soule's headquarters on Route 33, about 12 miles north of Uijongbu, on the afternoon of the 23rd. He was courteously received, although the unheralded arrival of so senior a visitor at this moment could hardly have been welcome. Robertson spoke briefly with Brodie's liaison officer who was about to attempt a return journey to 29 Brigade bearing a personal message from General Soule, emphasizing that the brigade's position on the left flank of the division was crucial and that no ground was to be given up until the 65th Regiment had withdrawn safely down Route 33. The liaison officer confided to Robertson that he doubted if he could get back to 29 Brigade as enemy troops were reported to have cut the road. Robertson drove south to I Corps HQ at Uijongbu, passing an American infantry battalion and tanks urgently heading north on their way to assist the Belgians.

Following the attack on 'A' Company of the Glosters, it was the turn of Captain Harvey's 'D' Company, on slightly higher ground a mile to the southeast. Second Lieutenant Whatmore, the recently joined reinforcement officer, alerted his men as the sounds of battle came from Castle Hill. To the accompaniment of bugles and whistles the enemy suddenly appeared, only yards away, as flares fired by Whatmore's 2-inch mortar illuminated the scene. There had been time to put out some trip flares and as the Chinese charged into 'D' Company's position these went off to reveal what seemed to be hundreds of enemy infantry, silhouetted like spectres at point-blank range. Whatmore's men kept their nerve and in the face of their rapid fire the Chinese recoiled, to return again and again through the night. Their comrades were meanwhile passing to the rear of 'D' Company to attack 'B' Company, a further mile over to the right.

At first light on the 23rd, Colonel Carne decided to pull the battalion into a tighter position and the survivors of Angier's company, carrying their dead and wounded, made their way back from Castle Hill under cover of a series of brilliantly executed airstrikes, to join Carne at battalion headquarters on Hill 235. 'D' Company, with whom Whatmore had spent an eventful night, also pulled back, having suffered heavy casualties. Halted by airstrikes and accurate artillery fire, the Chinese went to ground for much of the day as reinforcements continued to reach them from across the river. From prisoners already taken, it appeared that the Glosters had received the full force of an attack by up to three Chinese regiments; it was clear that 29 Brigade had been singled out for destruction as a preliminary to a rapid advance on Seoul. As the Glosters regrouped and counted their losses, General Van Fleet ordered his corps commanders, Milburn and Hoge, to carry out a fighting withdrawal to the Kansas line, where they were to stand fast. The 65th Regiment began to fall back down Route 33 at noon; the Chinese, intent on resupplying their forward troops and reluctant to expose themselves to the threat of airstrikes, did not interfere with the move.

Brodie was visited during the morning by Brigadier-General Mead, Soule's Chief of Staff. Arriving at HQ 29 Brigade shortly before 10 a.m. Mead discussed the situation with Brodie who expressed concern about the numbers of Chinese reported to be all over Kamak-san and making their way to cut Route 11, the only way out for the bulk of 29 Brigade. He also drew attention to his lack of reserves, the Ulsters having now been committed to the fight. Mead immediately telephoned Soule, who agreed to allot the Filipino battalion group, as soon as it had sorted itself out following a chaotic move back down Route 33, to the 29 Brigade sector. Brodie also told Mead that he had authorized the Glosters to contract their area and concentrate around Solma-ri and, as Mead subsequently stated, 'apparently felt no particular concern about them'.

On the subject of the retirement of the Belgians Brodie suggested that they should be ordered to destroy their vehicles and heavy weapons (which included a troop of Fisher-Hoch's mortars) and fight their way out on foot; Soule disagreed and decided that an attack by the 7th Regimental Combat Team could retake the fords lost earlier in the day for long enough to permit the Belgians to escape that way. First the 7th had to storm Hill 257, the dominant feature abandoned earlier by the Northumberland Fusiliers and now held in strength by the Chinese. At 2.30 p.m. one battalion of the 7th Infantry was ready to move forward up Route 11, a narrow track to the west of, and parallel to, Route 33 from which it is separated by a range of high hills. Soon after setting out, the American battalion unaccountably turned left off the track and headed up the north-east slopes of Kamak-san, now alive with Chinese. The advance lost momentum and it was not until after 6 p.m. that the attack on Hill 257 got under way. Meeting strong opposition, it petered out. The Belgians now had to get back across to safety as best they could. Ignoring Brodie's suggestion that they abandon their vehicles they forded the Imjin at speed under heavy fire, driving and marching east until they reached Route 33. Although exhausted, the Belgians were still battleworthy and were directed to a holding position near Brodie's headquarters to reorganize.

The Filipinos did not arrive at Brodie's command post until 10 p.m. and he decided it was too late to commit them to the gap now separating the Glosters and Northumberlands. His staff had already assessed the likely performance of the Filipinos and considered them inadequately trained to bring off so hazardous an operation in the dark over strange, unreconnoitred country. Meanwhile the Glosters were taking advantage of a relative lull to replenish with ammunition from dumps left on the lower ground below Hill 235.

General Van Fleet's decision to stand on the Kansas line was based on his belief that 8th Army's enormous firepower, combined with the allies' air superiority, would halt the Chinese. Experienced as he was, he had yet to appreciate the qualities of the Chinese soldier and this almost led to the undoing of I and IX Corps. His idea was to fight off all Chinese night attacks and use his air and artillery to pulverize the enemy in daylight hours; what he did not realize was the ability of the enemy to make himself all but invisible by day. Van Fleet also believed that further withdrawal would adversely affect the morale of his army and possibly trigger off another outbreak of 'bug-out fever' such as that which had all but lost the war in the previous winter. Looking at his battle maps on the evening of 23 April, he saw that the line held, more or less intact, apart from the collapse of the 6th ROK Division north of Kapyong, where the gap was being plugged by the 27th Commonwealth Brigade. One level down the chain of command, however, General Milburn of I Corps at Uijongbu feared an imminent Chinese breakthrough on his front. The 1st ROK Division on his left was showing signs of strain; Brodie's overstretched brigade was already comprehensively infiltrated and invested by Chinese who had turned both its flanks, and the right hand of Soule's 3rd Division was falling back down Route 33.

During the night of 23/24 April the Chinese brought massive reinforcements over the Imjin and a fresh formation, their 189th Division, was pitched at the Glosters to finish them off. Two of Carne's rifle companies, heavily depleted, were still to the east of Route 5Y and by first light on the 24th were under heavy attack. Carne saw that they would be overwhelmed within hours and ordered them to join him and the rest of the battalion on Hill 235. His adjutant, Captain Farrar-Hockley, was in radio contact with Brodie's headquarters, to which he reported at daybreak on the 24th that large numbers of Chinese infantry could be seen marching south along Route 5Y, making for brigade HQ. Soon, only 'B' Company of the Glosters remained on the far side of the track and shortly after 8 a.m. Carne ordered them to make a dash for it. Covered with all the fire support that could be mustered, they set out for Hill 235, whilst under cover of a smoke screen a rescue party went down the hill to salvage anything of value from the former battalion HQ area around Solmari. Captain Hickey, the medical officer, was desperately short of plasma and other medical stores as casualties on the hill steadily mounted. Mr Hobbs, the regimental sergeant-major, led the rescue party down the hill with a group of soldiers and Korean porters, returning triumphantly with ammunition, medical supplies, rations, water and precious radio batteries. Around 400 officers and men had assembled on the hill by midday – infantry, gunners, signallers and engineers. Spirits were remarkably high and there seemed to be enough resources to fight on for at least another twenty-four hours; there was an optimistic belief that a rescue column was already fighting its way up to relieve them.

Meanwhile the Filipinos had been ordered by Brodie to advance up Route 5Y, with part of Major Huth's tank squadron. This operation might have succeeded early the previous day, but not now. Large numbers of Chinese had slipped past the Glosters in the night and were waiting for any relief column attempting to force its way along the winding track and through the narrow defile two miles south of Hill 235. Major Huth was reporting progress on the radio; by noon the leading Filipino elements had barely reached the southern entrance to the defile; resistance was increasing by the minute, and when the leading light tank entered the gorge it was disabled by a mine and slewed across the narrow track. The following tanks hung back and made no effort to go to its rescue, so two of Huth's Centurions drove up and saved its crew. Huth declined the Filipino battalion commander's invitation to take the lead; he knew the gorge was even narrower further on and that his tanks could not get through. The Filipino infantry had no further stomach for the fight and the expedition returned to brigade HQ.

According to Brigadier-General Mead's later account, Brodie had called divisional HQ on the radio asking for permission to pull the Filipinos back and to allow the Glosters to fight their way out that night. Soule, according to Mead, told Brodie to leave the Filipinos and Hussars where they were, since the Glosters would stand no chance of escape in the dark. But if any message reached the Filipinos they elected to ignore it and within two hours they fell back 5,000 yards. In fact, Major Huth, seeing that his tanks could not get through, and that the Filipinos would be unable to proceed without their support, decided on his own initiative to call the operation off.

What really worried Soule were the political consequences were he to lose a major United Nations contingent entrusted to his command. The near loss of the entire Turkish brigade in November and the narrow escape of 29 Brigade from its action north of Seoul in January haunted every American general with UN forces under his command; therefore, after the failure of the Filipino rescue attempt, Soule ordered a much stronger force to attempt the rescue on the 25th: two battalions of the 65th Regiment and a tank battalion, supported by an artillery battalion. When he called Brodie to inform him, he asked how things were with the Glosters and 29 Brigade in general. Brodie replied that they were 'pretty sticky'. This understatement was lost on Soule who, in Brodie's shoes, would surely have described the situation as verging on disastrous. In fact, 29 Brigade was about to receive the unfriendly attentions of the entire Chinese 63rd Army, all of whose three divisions were across the Imjin and at the throat of the British brigade.

As Soule assembled his new relief force, aiming to move it forward that evening, he was beset by a posse of high-ranking visitors, who arrived at his command post by air demanding to know what he was doing to sort out the situation. These were none other than Ridgway himself, who had come over from Tokyo, Van Fleet, and Milburn the I Corps commander. Soule explained that the second relief attempt was imminent and would move off as soon as it had formed up. A message was passed to Colonel Carne by Brodie; rescue was on its way, but he must hold on in his present position. Carne's reply was chilling: 'I understand my position quite clearly. What I must make clear to you is that my command is no longer an effective fighting force. If it is required that we stay here, in spite of this, we shall continue to hold. But I wish to make clear the nature of my position.'

Over on the right of 29 Brigade's area the Northumberlands and Ulsters were being forced back down Route 11, their only way of escape. The artillery had already been sent back to new gun lines near Brodie's command post but Huth's tanks and a troop of engineers remained with the infantry. By the small hours of the 25th the Ulsters were locked in close-quarter fighting as they formed the rearguard, deployed in the area of a pass over which the column was making its way south. The battlefield was lit by starshell fired by the field guns and mortars, enabling the riflemen to inflict heavy casualties on the enemy every time they attacked. With daylight, the tanks were able to give close support. The Centurions wrought great execution but their crews had no turret-mounted machine-guns with which to repel the determined Chinese infantry who employed the same tactics as those used so effectively at Kapyong, aiming to kill the commanders as they directed their tanks from open hatches. Once compelled to close down, the tanks became harder to control and several came to grief by toppling over steep banks amidst the terraced paddy-fields on the pass. Curiously, when these were recovered some weeks later, it was found that no attempt had been made to remove the highly secret gun stabilizing system.

As the battalions fought their desperate way back over the pass and down Route 11 the enemy closed in on all sides, firing at close range into the column. Captain Patchett, the Hussars' medical officer, was travelling in a half-track, trying to help the many wounded lying along the road; eventually the Chinese closed in round him and he reported on the radio that he was about to be captured; then, 'I *have* been captured', and silence. Sergeant Bill Goddard's tank, with Chinese infantry swarming all over it, was driven at speed into a farmhouse, effectively disposing of its tormentors. Another was seen to be dealing with enemy infantry hiding in the roadside ditch by running over them, its tracks weltering with blood and entrails as it drove on. As the remnants of the two battalions reached the comparative safety of the bottom of the pass, several stalled tanks were denied to the enemy by Major Huth, who had the gloomy pleasure of destroying them with his 20-pounder gun.

When the Ulsters, acting as rearguard, received the order to pull back off the pass they were grouped with the Northumberlands under command of Colonel Kingsley Foster, and the rifle companies rallied round his headquarters prior to moving off. The artillery continued to support the column with accurate fire which at times was falling within fifty yards of the rear files. Foster, disdaining advice to seek the protection of an armoured vehicle for the last stage of the retirement, insisted on staying in his jeep. The column entered the final phase of its nightmare march at 11.25 a.m. as a storm of enemy mortar fire came down from both sides. Despite the efforts of the tanks to stave off the Chinese, who were swarming down the hills on both sides of the road, control was lost. Colonel Foster was killed and men began to take to the hills on the east side of the track. Casualties were being picked up wherever possible and laid on the engine decks of the tanks, soon awash with blood as fire from all directions beat down on the column.

When it became clear that the Chinese had already cut the road to the south there was no alternative to running the gauntlet, as the hapless US 2nd Division had done at Kunu-ri. The Ulster Rifles rallied at 4 p.m. at the bottom of the escape route, where 14 officers and 240 men answered the roll-call. The Fusiliers had fared likewise. The exhausted remnants of both battalions were given a hot meal for the first time in three days and taken out of the line to refit. Apart from a few Bren guns they had lost virtually all their equipment. To all purposes the brigade was no longer effective. Recovery, however, was swift. After forty-eight hours at rest in the Kimpo area the Fusiliers and Rifles reported themselves ready once more for action.

The plight of the Glosters was worsening by the hour. General Soule's ruling on the evening of the 24th, echoing Brodie, that they had to stay where they were until the second relief attempt had been made condemned Carne and his men to death or captivity. Meanwhile Brodie continued to reassure Soule that the Glosters were still 'fairly safe', would be able to hold out for the night, and that despite the loss of some of their equipment their casualties 'did not appear to be heavy'. In fact the position on Hill 235 was grave. An airdrop of supplies and ammunition scheduled for that afternoon had to be cancelled as the enemy were now too close to the defenders and any aircraft would have been subjected to a storm of fire as it made the drop. It was therefore postponed until 7 a.m. on the 25th. But a gallant attempt was made to drop radio batteries from light aircraft, most of which, however, fell into enemy hands.

On the morning of the 25th Mead paid another visit to Brodie, arriving at 8 a.m. to find Brodie conferring in the mess tent with some of his staff officers and Colonel Harris, commander of the 65th US Infantry Regiment. When Mead expressed surprise that the relief was not already under way Harris told him that he and Brodie were in full accord, 'and that if he were left alone he was sure they could handle it'. Mead told Harris abruptly to 'get the show on the road' and stepped outside the tent so that the conference could continue. He then had words with Brodie who was concerned about the safe extraction of the Fusiliers and the Ulsters. Mead assured him that this was in hand and already in progress. Brodie was also worried about the developing threat to his rear and Mead told him that the Belgians were taking care of that, and that extra American units were deploying to cover 29 Brigade's further withdrawal down Route 33 past Uijongbu.

Although Harris had called for medium tanks to support his bid to save the Glosters he found, as had Huth the previous day, that the defile was too narrow for anything but light vehicles. The tanks were therefore sent elsewhere. With their departure went all hopes of saving the Glosters. Mead flew back to report to General Soule; it was now 9 p.m. and Brodie's headquarters was on the point of closing down in compliance with orders from 3 Division to pull back to a new location near Seoul. On Hill 235 the remaining ammunition was parcelled out among the survivors. As long as the forward artillery observers remained alive on the hill, and whilst their radio batteries held out, the guns continued to give splendid support, holding the Chinese at bay in the last hours. Major Grist got on the air to Colonel Carne from brigade HQ to tell him that Brodie considered that the Glosters had done all that was needed and were to fight their way out as best they could. Carne's voice came back calmly but faintly as his batteries died, reporting that at most the battalion could only stay on the air for another thirty minutes. At this point Brodie came into the radio vehicle and scribbled on a message pad: 'Only the Glosters could have done it.' Grist relayed the message to Carne, closed down the radio, and wept.

The time had come for the breakout. Despite continual shell fire and air-strikes the Chinese had crept up to within yards of the Glosters' positions. Captain Farrar-Hockley could hear the discordant notes of Chinese bugles sig-nalling yet another attack and called on Drum-Major Buss to respond with every call in the British army except the Retreat. Buss stood up in his slit trench to give a recital which would never be forgotten by all who heard it, silencing the Chinese musicians. A loud cheer went up from the embattled defenders. Amongst them were some 40 casualties attended to by Captain Hickey, his medical orderlies, and Padre Sam Davies. The dead were hurriedly buried where they lay. There was no hope of evacuating the wounded; the road had been cut for forty-eight hours and no helicopter would have got through. Colonel Carne, puffing his pipe, moved quietly among his men with words of encouragement. From time to time either he or Farrar-Hockley led sorties to expel any Chinese who got too close and this helped to keep spirits up. But the end was near. There was no food, little water, and ammunition was nearly gone. The last radio batteries had died and the Royal Signals detachment manning the rear link radio to brigade HQ were destroying the sets and burning their code pads.

Word was passed round for the escape to begin and men began to gather under their officers. The padre and doctor stayed on top of the hill to take their chance with the wounded. Captain Harvey set out with his group in the oppo-site direction from the others, heading north, then west, before turning south. His was the only group to get clear. Of his original 90 men only 40, including Second Lieutenant Whatmore, were still on their feet when, after being under enemy fire for much of the time, they were confronted by an American tank unit which mistakenly opened fire on them before they could be identified. Once recognized by the horrified Americans who had shot at them, Harvey and his group were taken to safety and rejoined what was left of the battalion at Yongdongpo, south of Seoul, where Major Grist was waiting for them with all the personnel who had not been committed to the battle. When the roll was called less than 170 out of 850 answered their names. Of those involved in the battle, 58 Glosters and 5 Royal Artillery personnel were killed, and 75 wounded. Just over 500 of the Glosters and 70 attached personnel, mostly gunners of the supporting mortar battery, had been taken prisoner. Thirty of these were to die in captivity.

Reinforcements were immediately sent over from Japan to bring 29 Brigade's units back to war establishment. Grist was promoted to take command of the reborn battalion, with Harvey as his adjutant in place of Farrar-Hockley, who was already proving to be an extremely awkward captive. The battalion was declared operational again in ten days and a few weeks later it paraded, with the survivors of 170 Mortar Battery, to receive the award of a United States presidential citation. As other UN detachments were to be on parade to honour them, the Glosters taught an American military band to play their regimental march and the allied detachments were coached to perform a semblance of British ceremonial drill. The new regimental sergeant-major, Mr Thackrah, was admirably suited for this, having formerly been an Irish Guards drill sergeant. In Grist's words: 'Some of our UN allies were in the habit of starting to march as soon as they were called to attention. Others had never "presented arms" in their lives. All had to be coaxed or bullied to do it our way. In the afternoon, when General Van Fleet stepped up on to the dais there was nothing untidy about our parade except the press and even if our regimental march sounded a bit unfamiliar at least we kept in step.'

Under Grist's sure touch as commanding officer, morale quickly recovered and indeed many observers found the Glosters to be a far more cheerful unit than previously. They were soon the unwilling victims of the popular press, one of whose correspondents coined the sobriquet of 'Glorious Glosters' which they have managed to live with ever since. More difficult to live with has been the popular myth that the stand was one carried out literally to the last man. This has seldom been the British way, and as Napoleon said in his *Maxims of War*: 'There is but one honourable mode of becoming a prisoner of war. That is, by being taken separately; by which is meant, by being cut off entirely, and when we can no longer make use of our weapons. In this case there are no conditions, for honour can impose none. We yield to irresistible necessity.'

The battalion did what it had been told to do, holding up the Chinese advance long enough for 8th Army to ride the punch, and as a result Seoul was not taken by the Chinese who had exhausted themselves in the attempt. An estimated 10,000 of them were killed or wounded on 3rd Division's front, most of them whilst attempting to eliminate 29 Brigade, in which they almost succeeded. An immediate inquiry into the battle and its conduct was ordered by Van Fleet, who submitted its findings to Ridgway on 26 May with a covering letter in which Van Fleet stated:

It is my opinion that all reasonable and possible courses of action open to the responsible commanders concerned were initiated in an effort to extricate the Gloucestershire battalion. Close and continuous liaison was maintained between commanders during this critical period and, as a result, maximum use was made of available resources, fire support and tactical air [cover]. The overwhelming strength and determination of the enemy's attacks, together with his initial capability for early penetration by infiltration and enveloping tactics, taxed the corps, division and brigade commanders' limited reserve capabilities to the maximum. I believe that all decisions made were tactically sound and that subordinate commanders complied with orders to the maximum extent of their capabilities. The loss of this gallant fighting unit will continue to be felt with deep regret by myself and members of this command. Its magnificent stand in the face of overwhelming odds contributed immeasurably to the maintenance of the tactical integrity of the entire US I Corps.

The Australians' stand at Kapyong had also saved the corps in which that battalion had been serving, but the action had not resulted in the loss of a United Nations contingent serving under American command and was thus not such a political hot potato. As a result, 3 RAR had to wait until the end of the year before their award of a presidential citation was announced.

CHAPTER 21

Marshal Peng's Last Throw

As silence fell over the battlefields of Kapyong and along the Imjin, Marshal Peng had to admit that his expectations had not been realized. Not only had his troops failed to take Seoul, but they had suffered alarming casualties, had once more outrun their line of communication, and had been confronted by United Nations troops who had stood their ground and slogged it out with the best that the People's Liberation Army could throw at them. Although by 29 April Chinese troops were in sight of Seoul's northern suburbs they were exhausted and short of food and ammunition. A final assault on the capital was beaten back with heavy loss. The most serious threat was an attempt to cross the Han river in small boats to the west of Seoul. Allied aircraft and artillery, augmented by the guns of the heavy cruiser USS *Toledo* anchored off the Kimpo peninsula, intervened decisively. The few men who crawled ashore on the south bank were met by a ROK marine battalion which gave no quarter. Simultaneously, an attempted crossing east of Seoul was dealt with by the American 24th and 25th Divisions, no longer the inexperienced troops sent across from Japan the previous summer and keen to restore their reputation.

Ridgway's brief tenure of command at 8th Army had borne fruit. He had ruthlessly weeded out the unfit and incompetent at all levels and the ranks were filling with experienced reservists. Lost pride and self-confidence had been amply restored. Faced by this reinvigorated army, Peng knew that he had to consolidate before launching another offensive, and that this had to be executed rapidly before the UN forces grew even stronger. He ordered his army to go to ground; concealing themselves skilfully by day and moving supplies forward by night, they patiently rebuilt their administrative system for the next phase of the attack. Units badly mauled in the first stage were reinforced with drafts who had marched down from Manchuria with the supply columns.

General Van Fleet was too seasoned a campaigner to believe that the Chinese had given up. He ordered 8th Army to look to its defences. Huge stockpiles of ammunition, fuel and supplies were established close behind the front.

Intelligence reports indicated a renewal of Chinese pressure after the first week in May and with the waxing of the moon the allies confidently awaited its start. The UN front, known as the 'No Name Line', extended from just north of Seoul, across the middle of the peninsula to a point on the east coast a few miles north of the 38th parallel. Aerial reconnaissance revealed that the Chinese were transferring units by night over to the east, no doubt seeking an easier passage of arms against ROK divisions on that sector. As the enemy in front of Seoul began to thin out the allies cautiously advanced. Thirty miles to the east, IX Corps pushed up the Pukhan valley as I Corps moved north through Uijongbu. Van Fleet applied Ridgway's policy of using massive firepower to crush resistance and spare the lives of his own troops. He had the means for this, the only problem being the supply of artillery ammunition in the vast quantities required.

As the enemy reeled under the onslaught of bomb and shell, the steady allied advance continued. Ridgway, on Washington's instructions, directed Van Fleet to push forward, posing a threat to an area on the central front where the Chinese were forming a redoubt in what was known as the Iron Triangle. Here, on a tract of plain hedged in by jagged mountains, were the enemy's main supply depots, protected by strong fieldworks in the surrounding high ground. This was Van Fleet's objective. Before the allied advance gained momentum, however, the Chinese returned to the attack. Van Fleet ordered all his troops to sit tight and hold their ground. Vast quantities of mines had been laid and thick wire entanglements set out to meet the threat, and artillery was registered on to hundreds of points where the enemy were expected to form up.

On the night of 15 May, 20 Chinese and nine North Korean divisions attacked the sector on the central front held mainly by the ROK army. Mindful of the failure of his supply system in April, Peng had ordered all his troops to carry ten days' supplies of food and ammunition. Whilst the main thrust was directed at the ROKs, a feint attack was launched in the west to divert UN forces. The weather broke and pouring rain reduced the dirt roads to quagmires, over which the allies' supply vehicles struggled to keep the guns supplied. Close air support was hampered by low cloudbases, but medium bombers of the USAF, frequently using radar, punished the enemy rear areas around the clock. After twenty-four hours the ROK 5th and 7th Divisions, posted on the hills east of Chunchon, gave way. For a few hours all hung in the balance as the Chinese, moving by night in foul weather over well-reconnoitred mountain tracks, felt their way around the defenders' flanks. Van Fleet and his corps commanders kept their heads, shifting the US 2nd Infantry and 1st Marine Divisions to the right to take the enemy thrust on its western flank. This was a race against time as the enemy salient deepened by the hour and the 2nd Division was forced back on the third day of the Chinese attack. Its new commander, Major-General Clark Ruffner, was anxious to exorcize the memory of the fiasco at Kunu-ri and had transformed his division with an infusion of battle-experienced officers and NCOs. Although it sustained over a thousand casualties in this battle the 2nd Division exacted a terrible price from its assailants whilst retiring in good order to a new position further south.

Far over on the east coast the ROK I Corps was commanded by Major-General Paik Sun-yup, the energetic and talented former commander of their 1st Division. Keeping a tight grip on the situation he rode with the punch, inflicting heavy losses on the enemy as his two divisions retired. Elsewhere, despite the near collapse of the ROK III Corps in the centre, South Korean troops were fighting with a new confidence and resolution. The long-term training plans laid down a year earlier by KMAG were at last paying off and the South Koreans showed that, given good leadership and adequate artillery support, they would stand firm. Ridgway had already spoken personally with Syngman Rhee in the strongest terms of the need to purge the ROK army of incompetent political placemen; barely a fortnight before the start of the Chinese May offensive, with only Ambassador Muccio and Van Fleet in the room, he had been extremely frank with the President, recording in his memoirs: 'I do not think that there was room for a trace of ambiguity in the straight-from-the-shoulder talk we delivered to the old warrior that afternoon.'

The enemy offensive died away, harried twenty-four hours a day from the air and mangled by allied artillery. Some elements of the Chinese and North Korean forces, striking south-west over the mountains, got within 20 miles of Seoul before they were halted and thrown back. Van Fleet was ordered to resume the advance on the Iron Triangle, the ganglion of the enemy's strategic power in Korea. It contained the terminus of a railway running from Manchuria and was the centre of a road network through which the enemy's front-line formations were sustained in the field.

On 19 May the UN high command met at the X Corps command post. Ridgway had flown over from Tokyo to be briefed by his field commanders, General Almond of X Corps, Hoge of IX Corps and Van Fleet. It was decided to open a full-scale offensive at once, with a main thrust by Hoge's corps in the centre, as X Corps watched its right flank and I Corps, advancing past Uijongbu, secured its left.

8th Army rolled forward as the enemy retired. Peng's forces had once more sustained grave losses. Over 17,000 of them lay dead and an equal number had been captured. The ROKs, who had fought stubbornly, had also taken severe losses, more than 11,000 of them killed or wounded. The advance reached the Kansas line where it halted to dig in. Van Fleet ordered the preparation of strong, semi-permanent defences; thousands of mines were laid and vast fields of wire erected. Massive fieldworks with adequate overhead cover, deep trenches and bunkers were built by army engineers. From a war of movement the campaign was about to become static, apart from limited advances to take key ground to the north of the Kansas positions.

The Commonwealth forces played their part in the return to the Kansas line. There were now three brigades: the 28th Commonwealth, 29th Brigade Group, and the 25th Canadian Brigade Group. As yet, all three were under the command of different American divisions. The three battalions of the 29th and the 8th Hussars found themselves back on the Imjin battleground of April and began the melancholy task of searching for their dead. The Chinese, it was found, had buried their own in beehive-shaped graves but the return to Gloster Valley and Castle Hill revealed many unburied British soldiers. Several of the Hussars' tanks still lay where they had been abandoned after being knocked out in the fight on Route 11. A crude wooden cross marked the roadside grave of Colonel Kingsley Foster of the Northumberlands. Once more the British dug in south of the Imjin, but this time behind substantial wire and minefields. To the north, as before the Chinese attack in April, there was no sign of the enemy, who had disengaged and moved out of contact. The front was suddenly quiet apart from the distant sounds of airstrikes far across the river as Peng's rear-guards were harried on their way.

Before returning to Tokyo, Ridgway had toured 8th Army to talk with senior commanders and their men, and to test the resolve of the UN Command. He was well pleased. His earlier purges had sharpened up the American and ROK divisions and in the corps headquarters he found none of the former pessimism and inertia which had so shocked him six months earlier. He was particularly careful to bestow lavish praise on the 2nd 'Indian Head' Division which had performed well against Peng's 'Fifth Phase Offensive', although he probably felt that their claim of inflicting over twenty times their own losses on the Chinese was hyperbolic. The production of such statistics by means of unveri-fied 'body counts', and precise figures of casualties caused by air attack (which could not possibly be quantified) was to be carried on into the Vietnam War. Ridgway was impressed by the handling of the ROK I Corps on the east coast which, though not as heavily engaged as others, had reflected the ability of General Paik, who was clearly a man to watch and easily the best of the new wave of young ROK generals. Ridgway was determined to bring the whole ROK army up to Paik's standard and directed KMAG to redouble its efforts. Technical specialists and trained staff officers were reaching ROK combat units in a steady stream and once the army was properly equipped and sustained in the field, Ridgway sensed that the South Korean soldier would be a match for his opponents.

Syngman Rhee was Ridgway's biggest problem; the old man had written to President Truman in March, and to Ambassador Muccio a month later, calling for their support in forming ten more ROK divisions. Rhee wanted to conscript 300,000 young men into a new, American-equipped army expressly to invade

North Korea, an operation he saw as the only hope of establishing his autocratic rule over the whole peninsula. In his letter to Truman he explained that this new ROK army, if backed by massive UN artillery and air power, would absolve America and its allies of the need to shed their soldiers' blood in a cause he knew was of little interest to them or their governments. In a sense he was right; but whereas the Americans had formerly considered Korea outside their Asiatic ring fence, as Acheson's press club speech back in 1950 made clear, they had belatedly realized that if the whole of Korea fell into communist hands it would form an outpost of strategic value for the Soviet Union, from which it would be possible to conduct a campaign of subversion against a newly democratic Japan. 'Easterners' in Washington such as John Foster Dulles and Dean Rusk had long made this the basis of their lobby, and even Acheson was forced to admit the importance of Korea following the North Korean invasion. Truman's closest advisers, however, were apprehensive at the thought of allowing Rhee so much military power, and counselled extreme caution, contending that Korean unity through military action increased the likelihood of general war. Truman was also advised that there should be no further advances into North Korea other than to seize tactically advantageous ground, enabling cease-fire negotiations to be made from a position of strength.

Following his visit to the front, Ridgway signalled General Collins at the Pentagon on 20 May, giving his appreciation of the situation and his views as to the efficiency of the UN Command. He stated his wish to increase the non-American content of 8th Army and this was referred to the Joint Strategic Plans Committee who submitted a report to the Joint Chiefs on 19 June. Their paper, with hindsight, appears as a mixture of objective appraisal and hopeless fantasy. It concluded that whilst the concept of a Commonwealth division for Korea was sound (and already in an advanced stage of fulfilment) the United Kingdom and other UN European allies should not be called on for further contingents in view of their need to meet their NATO responsibilities. The JCS paper went on to review existing and possible future contributions, commenting acerbically in some cases. The Australians were warmly praised for the performance of 3 RAR to date and, whilst Canberra's growing preoccupation with the Pacific basin was recognized, it was felt that their ground troop contribution might be increased, possibly up to brigade strength. (Eventually another Australian infantry battalion did arrive in Korea.) With the recent arrival of the whole of the Canadian 25th Brigade Group in Korea, no further calls could be made in that direction, as Washington intended to ask for a Canadian brigade in Germany. In view of the fighting performance of the Turkish brigade to date it was felt that a further brigade might be useful, especially if the pill were to be sweetened with generous financial inducements and the promise of American support for Turkey's early admission to NATO.

The JCS even considered an approach to Iran, in the belief that the provision of a regimental combat team for Korea would be of excellent training value for the Iranian military system as a whole. At this point the Joint Chiefs took leave of reality, proposing simultaneous approaches to Israel and the Arab states, arguing that the provision of Israeli and Egyptian brigades would be seen as 'a gesture of western confidence in their military capabilities' and in the United Nations' General Assembly as an instrument for peace in the Middle East. Continuing in this vein, the committee suggested that an approach to Pakistan would not only produce high-grade troops but also indicate American confidence in a peaceful resolution of the Kashmir crisis, which bedevilled Pakistan's relations with India. In spite of the outstanding performance of the Indian Field Ambulance, the Indian government had made it clear that it would furnish no combat units. No further approach was made to the Philippines or to Thailand whose units, according to Ridgway, had been a liability to date. The Thais had been unable to sustain operations in cold weather and the Filipinos, unprepared for the violence of the Chinese attack in April, had proved shaky and in need of further training.

The new-found strength and confidence of the UN forces was evident to friend and foe alike, bringing the first whispered suggestions of possible truce negotiations. The initial reaction in Peking to the repulse of Peng's 'Fifth Phase' was that the allies should be allowed to advance deep into North Korea so that a great counter-offensive might be launched once the UN lines of communication were stretched to breaking point and those of the Chinese People's Volunteers at their shortest, probably on a line just south of that between Pyongyang and Wonsan. Peng, however, was a realist, reporting to his masters that it would be months before his armies could deliver a decisive blow following their losses of men and *matériel* in May. From this point the Chinese high command, sensing that the UN forces were reluctant to chance another wild advance to the Yalu and content to secure advantageous ground on and round the 38th parallel, were prepared to play the same game. It also became clear that the Soviet Union, embarrassed by the failure of its North Korean surrogate to bring off the rapid and dazzling victory so confidently predicted by Kim Il-sung a year earlier, was inclined to recommend a move to the conference table.

Already in early May the Soviet delegate at the Security Council, Jakob Malik, was dropping heavy hints to this effect in New York and before the end of that month informal discussions were taking place with the aim of weighing the sincerity of the Russians' intentions. Malik, with what by the standards of the time was remarkable candour, was soon talking privately with George Kennan, a veteran American ex-diplomat who had served in the Moscow embassy. The Soviets, said Malik, wished for a peaceful ending to the Korean War as soon as possible but as they were not directly involved in the fighting, they could not participate in any armistice discussions. The best course, he argued, would be for the Americans, acting on behalf of the United Nations, to make contact with the North Koreans and the Chinese. Kennan reported all this to Acheson, who was delighted. The problem lay in getting the talks started, as the USA had no diplomatic relations with either Peking or Pyongyang, although Britain and India might be used as channels of communication with Peking. The only diplomatic representation in Pyongyang was that of nations locked into the communist bloc. Acheson therefore decided to approach the British government, which recommended immediate action to test the authenticity of the Soviet approach.

Following a broadcast by Malik, recorded for United Nations radio on 23 June, in which he stated the support of the Russian peoples for peace moves in Korea, Malik suggested that the talks should initially be held 'between the belligerents'; in other words, those actually fighting in Korea, which included the Chinese People's Volunteers. After much shuffling and indecision in Washington, where some hard-liners were opposed to any suggestion of treating with the communists, and in London, where Morrison had signally failed to grasp the subtleties of the oriental psyche so necessary when negotiating with the Chinese, Ridgway was authorized by the State Department to make a formal proposal in a broadcast from Tokyo on the morning of 30 June. Addressed to the 'Commander-in-Chief Communist Forces in Korea' it proposed a meeting on board the Danish hospital ship *Jutlandia* in Wonsan harbour. Within twenty-four hours Pyongyang had responded with a statement bearing the authority of Kim Il-sung and Marshal Peng, agreeing to hold a meeting but insisting that it took place on land, in the Kaesong area, and that it was to be held between 10 and 15 July. After further haggling the date was brought forward for an initial liaison meeting on the 8th with a view to getting down to serious negotiation on the 10th. It seemed that the end of the war was in sight.

Following the failure of the communist May offensive, the Chinese were a spent force and their North Korean allies little better. Both needed time in which to rebuild their forces, and they were unwittingly aided in this by the strategy of their opponents. Truman and his advisers were convinced that any significant advance beyond the Kansas line would risk Soviet intervention. Truman also feared that any further advance would lose him the support of most of his United Nations allies, particularly the United Kingdom. Washington's strategic guidance suddenly became obscure and lost direction.

The Chinese were hugely encouraged, once agreement to the opening of talks had been secured, that Washington had ordered an immediate end to all UN offensive operations. This was exactly what Marshal Peng and Kim Il-sung wanted, as it gave them the chance to sort out their field forces with minimal interference from the allies. At the same time they embarked on a vast programme to strengthen their lines of communication, establish great supply dumps, and dig elaborate defensive positions all along the line. It was fortunate that the last acts of Van Fleet's command before the embargo on offensive operations were to secure a number of key hill features and the towns of Kumhwa and Chorwon, forming the base of the notorious Iron Triangle. The Americans also took the communist redoubt known as the Punchbowl, after dogged fighting and with heavy losses, and dug in there for the rest of the war.

The UN delegation at the Kaesong talks was headed by Vice-Admiral Turner Joy, commander of the US Far East Fleet. Now aged 55, he had distinguished himself as a cruiser squadron commander in the Pacific war and had taken part in most of its decisive battles; more recently he was the mastermind of the planning for the Inchon landings. For the next ten months, he faced the battle of his life as senior UN delegate to the Armistice Conference. The senior South Korean delegate was Major-General Paik Sun-yup, the outstanding divisional and corps commander of the ROK army. It soon became clear that Paik had received a privy briefing from Syngman Rhee and been given an entirely different agenda from that followed by Turner Joy and his three senior American colleagues – two-star officers of the army, navy and air force respectively. Paik, to his great credit, remained loyal to the line pursued by Admiral Joy. There were at this stage no representatives from other United Nations allies. Joy and his team arrived on the appointed day at the conference site, a large shell-damaged house, to be met by the enemy representatives, Lieutenant-General Nam Il, commander of the NKPA, two more Korean generals, and the Chinese representatives: Marshal Peng's deputy Teng Hua and his chief of staff, Hsieh Fang. The two sides faced each other across a bare table with no sign of recognition or emotion, the Asians expressionless and inscrutable. For the Americans this was initially unnerving, but Joy had been briefed beforehand by Ridgway, who had seen him off from Munsan in a helicopter after telling him to be 'open, honest and dignified'.

Joy began by suggesting that both sides agreed an agenda which included measures for the separation of the combatants, the constitution of a neutral armistice commission to act as referees of the cease-fire once this had been fixed, and for the handling and repatriation of prisoners of war to be under the aegis of the International Red Cross. Joy had little or no presentiment that this last would cause more trouble than anything else in the following months. He had reason for including it as an agenda heading, however; whilst the United Nations had notified the Red Cross in Geneva of all prisoners held by them, the Chinese and North Koreans had refused to release more than the sketchiest details of the thousands of allied soldiers and civilians believed to be in their custody.

Nam Il responded with his list of points for discussion at future meetings. They included the offer of an immediate cease-fire, the setting up of a demilitarized zone 20 kilometres wide along the 38th parallel, the exchange of all prisoners and the departure of all foreign troops from the peninsula. From the outset, therefore, the demands of the two sides were incompatible. Apart from calling for a reversion to the old artificial frontier, the communists were calling for the unconditional return of all Chinese and North Korean prisoners, whether they wished to go home or not.

Admiral Joy saw at once that agreement to hold the meeting on enemy-occupied ground had allowed his opponents to score an immediate propaganda point. The communist news media were thus present in strength to film and report on this first meeting, whilst the United Nations press corps had been forbidden to accompany Joy and his party to the conference site. When Joy demanded that the UN press be allowed to enter the site, his request was refused. The admiral thereupon walked out, adjourning the talks 'until my convoy, bearing personnel of my choosing, including press representation, will be cleared to the conference site'. The talks resumed after the communists had agreed to declare a five-mile-radius neutral zone around Kaesong and the removal of all armed personnel from the UN delegates' route to the site. By 26 July it seemed that real progress was being made in these 'talks about talks'. An agenda was agreed and the Americans appeared to have succeeded in their aim of confining the talks to essentially military matters. They had not reckoned with the seemingly inexhaustible capacity of the opposition (especially the North Koreans) for diatribe, dialectics and propaganda.

Once the talks were properly under way the communists demanded categorically that the cease-fire demarcation line be set at the 38th parallel which, they claimed, was the line from which both sides had started the war. The United Nations' response was that, in view of allied air and sea supremacy, geographical concessions were required of the communists, reflecting the lines on which the opposing armies had come to rest; it was pointed out that this would mean yielding a significant amount of South Korean territory in the west. As there was no response, and to make the point about air supremacy, two heavy bombing attacks were made on Pyongyang on 30 July and 10 August. The Joint Chiefs in Washington had been reluctant to sanction these as it seemed to them that it would indicate insincerity on the part of the UN Command towards the talks. They yielded to Ridgway's insistent appeals and the attacks took place, causing much damage and heavy civilian loss of life despite the preliminary dropping of thousands of leaflets warning the population of the impending strikes. Although Washington claimed that the bombing had not been indiscriminate there were immediate murmurs of alarm in London, where the Americans' readiness to use air power in this way was attributed by some British commentators to the fact that the continental United States had never been subjected to aerial bombardment.

Some Washington officials, intent on an early end to a war which was becoming unpopular at home, pressed for acceptance of the communist line on the parallel. The Joint Chiefs, however, counselled Ridgway to insist on the current battle line. By now, only days into negotiation, Admiral Joy and his delegates knew they faced a Herculean task. As yet unfamiliar with the monumental significance of 'face' when dealing with these people, they did their best to restrain their tempers. Perhaps General Paik, accustomed to the nuances of oriental logic and ever-shifting bases of argument, was best equipped for the contest.

The two sides continued to fence with words; endless points of procedure were raised and there were frequent adjournments, often for days on end when one side or the other protested at infringements of the neutral zone. On one occasion armed Chinese troops strutted menacingly past the conference site and Joy's team walked out; on another, American aircraft inadvertently carried out an attack in the zone, killing several NKPA soldiers. The longest gap in the talks lasted for several weeks, and when they resumed on 25 October, Ridgway had already decided that further military action was required in order to bring the opposition to their senses.

CHAPTER 22

The Commonwealth Division

Following the allied advances of May, the time for forming a Commonwealth division had arrived. It had been agreed, albeit with some reluctance on Britain's part, that the administrative infrastructure (and much else) of the division would have to be provided by the United Kingdom. At least this made it easier for Whitehall to require that a British army officer be appointed in command. This raised some ghosts, for all the Commonwealth partners had experienced much dubious generalship at the hands of British commanders in two world wars. The Australians and New Zealanders had painful memories of Gallipoli and, in recent times, of Greece and Crete; the Canadians were still haunted to some extent by the loss of their battalions in Hong Kong in 1941. Fortunately, Major-General James Cassels, head of the United Kingdom Services Liaison Staff in Melbourne, had proved readily acceptable to the Australian and New Zealand contingents. A former Seaforth Highlander, he had commanded the 51st Highland Division at the Rhine Crossings in the final weeks of the war and had then commanded the 6th Airborne Division in Palestine.

Cassels' staff had to be seen to be fully integrated, reflecting the national contributions of all concerned. This was achieved with remarkably little friction. Although South Africa was regarded with distaste by Britain's Labour government, its offer of individual officers to serve in staff posts and at regimental duty attached to British units was quietly taken up. The Indian government expressed a wish early in the war for its Field Ambulance to serve under Commonwealth command and despite the obstructive attitude adopted by the British Director of Army Medical Services, this duly took place. A few British officers appeared to regard Australia and New Zealand as 'colonies' and addressed the officers from these countries in a patronizing manner; Australians in particular were quick to perceive this. Fortunately, such confrontations were rare; in many cases, associations originating during the Second World War were renewed, and another generation of young officers, fresh from Sandhurst and Duntroon, made friendships which continue half a century later.

During the run-up to the formation of the 1st Commonwealth Division in July, the separate brigades continued to pursue their operational instructions, and once the line of the Imjin had been secured, digging began in earnest on the Kansas line positions. At the same time, patrols were sent out across the river in an attempt to locate and identify the enemy to the front of I Corps of which the division was part. These efforts proved of little value, as it was clear that the Chinese had withdrawn well back from the Imjin and were eager to avoid contact.

The civilian population north of the river were still following their age-old pursuits, anxious not to become involved in the war which had seen the destruction of most of their country's infrastructure; their land had changed hands several times since June 1950 and they were wary of offending either side. By day, the wide no man's land across the Imjin was the province of allied patrols and villagers displayed placatory notices welcoming the United Nations forces. By night, there was evidence that the Chinese emerged out of cunningly hidden positions from which they had observed the British patrols during daylight hours. This was the cue for the pro-United Nations banners to come down and for red flags to replace them. In July, the villages were cleared of their inhabitants, who were removed to safer areas in the rear of the allied front. For several days, columns of British trucks were engaged on the thankless task of removing hundreds of distraught peasants and their animals from their ancestral homes, which soon became derelict and the fields overgrown. A new phase of the war had begun with this clearance of the population from the next battlefield.

As his new-found divisional headquarters trained up to operational pitch General Cassels introduced himself to his immediate superior, the new commander of the US I Corps, Lieutenant-General John W. ('Iron Mike') O'Daniel, who came with an impressive record as a combat commander in the Second World War. He at once impressed on his subordinates the need for aggression at all levels and all times. In his reports to the War Office, Cassels frequently reveals his impatience at orders from above which seemed to have little relevance. There was constant pressure to take prisoners; difficult when the Chinese refused combat and superfluous when battalions already knew which enemy units were deployed to their front. O'Daniel decreed that raids to obtain prisoners were to be undertaken at least every third day, apparently, as Cassels wrote, 'regardless of cost'. He recognized that this was part of O'Daniel's policy of 'keeping the troops sharp', also that several American units had already incurred heavy and to his mind unnecessary losses whilst trying to oblige. The commander of the 1st US Marine Division, reassuringly deployed immediately to the left of the Commonwealth Division, agreed with Cassels.

O'Daniel's rousing instructions to his commanders in the form of special orders of the day were liberally salted with injunctions to close with the enemy at every opportunity. One ended with 'The signal for combat will be "sharpen your bayonets". Use this phrase at every opportunity.' The seasonal homily for Christmas 1951 concluded with a peroration that 'With God's help and a sharp bayonet we will all fight towards peace, and will not let up until we have gained it.' Field Marshal Montgomery, fond as he was of invoking the dual aid of the Prince of Peace and the Lord God Mighty in Battle, would certainly have approved; Cassels, on the other hand, viewed the fiery O'Daniel with suspicion, as a commander ready to risk men's lives on fatuous operations lacking any real purpose. Senior Commonwealth officers visiting the division in months to come came to the same conclusion. Despite this, however, Cassels got on well with his corps commander, who was quick to acknowledge the value of the Commonwealth Division. On the rare occasions when Cassels, at O'Daniel's briefings, saw fit to point out inherent risks in a I Corps plan, his fellow American divisional commanders were fascinated by his daring, the American system discouraging any hint of dissent or constructive comment from subordinate commanders at all levels. Cassels' attitude was refreshingly new to them.

While the forward elements of the division probed out across the Imjin in search of their elusive enemy the rear areas behind them were undergoing radical change. Individual brigades lost some of their supporting elements, which were grouped together to serve the entire division. The British, Canadian and New Zealand transport companies from each brigade were formed into a divisional column, equivalent to a battalion. Its role henceforth would be to provide the 12,000 men of the division with their ammunition, fuel, rations and transport. A field bakery was opened near Seoul which produced fresh bread daily. In 28 Commonwealth Brigade 'Potter's Prostituted Pool', the *ad hoc* Commonwealth transport and supply unit which had sustained the 27th, then the 28th Brigades through the worst of the spring battles, parted regretfully with its Canadian and New Zealand platoons and prepared, in September, to go south to Pusan and work the docks; having completed one savage winter in the forward area it was not permitted to stay with the division. The brigade signals and engineer squadrons were formed into divisional regiments and the new organizations quickly settled down to give matchless support to the fighting arms.

A proper field security organization was long overdue. In the Commonwealth Division this was the responsibility of the Intelligence Corps, which had to detect and arrest hostile 'line-crossers' and persons on the Korean National Police blacklists, control the movement of civilians in the battle area, screen all refugees, and build up a reliable informer network amongst the local population. This was easier said than done, given the absence of local knowledge on the part of the NCOs involved and the impenetrable language problem.

The villages immediately behind the division, supposedly overseen by the ROK army's military police, seethed with criminal activity. Low pay drove the ROK soldiery into corrupt practices such as black marketeering, the 'staking out' of rival territories for illicit trading purposes, and the use of strong-arm tactics against anyone inclined to resist. ROK army officers appeared to be immune from civil arrest and the influence of the National Police had long vanished. A 'Stayback Line' was to be decreed in 1952 which only locally enlisted Koreans and members of the Korean Service Corps were allowed to pass beyond. Rigorously enforced in the Commonwealth Division, it was not observed in an adjoining formation, whose artillery suffered heavy losses from enemy fire directed by infiltrators who were also cheerfully making a fortune from the military brothels they managed as a profitable sideline.

Until the summer of 1951 there was little in the way of entertainment for the troops in Korea. In the 29th Brigade a number of reservists formed an excellent concert party whose open-air shows drew large audiences; a notable turn was a pair of comedians dressed as tramps whose rendition of 'We're a couple of swells' invariably included additional verses parodying well-known figures in the brigade such as 'dashing Tom' Brodie. Then professional concert parties began to appear. The Americans had the services of international stars such as Bob Hope and Marilyn Monroe who toured Korea in 1952. At first, British artistes seemed reluctant to travel so far to endure the hardships of the sweaty Korean summer, but the lead was given by the American-born harmonica virtuoso Larry Adler and many others followed, including the attractive and personable singer Carole Carr. She was required to give up to three open-air shows a day followed by informal performances in the evening, sometimes at one of the popular 'roadhouses' opened by the NAAFI. 'Once, during a show for the 5th Inniskilling Dragoon Guards,' she recounted, 'when I asked for song requests, a voice called out "Don't sing – just stand there!"' On another occasion, singing for the Welch Regiment under a tarpaulin awning during a torrential downpour, the entire canopy, borne down by the weight of water, collapsed on top of her, drawing a roar of approval from the audience, 'whether because I had carried on singing or because my dress had clung in a most revealing way – your guess is as good as mine!'

At the beginning of the war there had been considerable British press coverage, especially of the dramatic retreat into the Pusan perimeter, and *The Times* correspondent, Ian Morrison, had been killed when his jeep ran over a landmine. Nearly 20 other United Nations correspondents were to die in Korea before the armistice. Morrison's successor Louis Heren elected to distance himself from the British and Commonwealth troops, preferring the company of the Americans. For this, he was regarded with suspicion by his fellow countrymen in Korea. He did, however, secure a unique interview with MacArthur early in the war which gave a shrewd insight into the great man. Heren described him as 'a living myth, and he knew it. He played the part of a great soldier and proconsul splendidly but before the end of the interview I began to wonder how much was real and how much was play-acting . . . he did not fit into any known American mould. I decided that he was born in the wrong century. He should have been a nineteenth-century Englishman and Viceroy of India.' In the summer of 1951 when the campaign appeared to have stagnated, a number of 'temporary war correspondents' came out on short tours and frequently gave their conducting officers of the public relations staff much trouble. Randolph Churchill was notably boorish and abusive throughout his visit. This was before the days of satellite television and the British public saw only the infrequent and heavily edited newsreels screened in cinemas, up to three weeks after the events portrayed.

Before leaving England, all ranks of the British contingent had been comprehensively inoculated and vaccinated against typhoid and paratyphoid, typhus, cholera and smallpox. As Korea is a malarious zone, all were given a daily dosage of paludrine, a drug developed during the Second World War and a decisive factor in the defeat of the Japanese in Burma. With the arrival of summer in 1951 there were ominous symptoms of other tropical maladies; yellow fever injections were provided; then it was found that men were falling sick, and in some cases dying, with Japanese encephalitis or sleeping sickness and this initiated another crash immunization programme. Yet more life-threatening diseases emerged: bilharzia, caused by waterborne parasites, and the rat-borne Weill's disease. Most members of the force were introduced for the first time to hand-held aerosol sprays containing DDT for the control of mosquitoes carrying malaria as well as flies which spread dysentery. In the absence of detailed instructions, these devices were liberally used in the confined spaces of bivouac tents, to be freely inhaled by their occupants. In the rear areas, towns like Uijongbu and Tokchon were drenched with DDT delivered from light aircraft with scant regard for the human beings below. This was over forty years before the general alarm regarding 'Gulf War Syndrome' and its supposed connection with insecticides. No attempt was made to relate the subsequent illnesses of Korean War veterans to the widespread, uninstructed and uncontrolled use of DDT and its derivatives in 1951.

The Korean climate, with its huge seasonal variations of heat and humidity, levied a heavier toll than the battlefield. As early as 1919 the medical missionary Dr D. Van Buskirk noted that weather and climate affected the very traits and character of the Korean people and made life hard for the Europeans working there: 'There are many breakdowns among the foreigners in Korea. The summer climate lacks the stimulus of storms . . . and is depressing in its constant temperature and high humidity. Maintaining the homeland rate of energy consumption depletes the reserve forces and either there must be slacking of work or exhaustion . . . As a whole, occidentals in Korea look worn . . . it is not a health resort.' Van Buskirk's careful log of the Korean climate is indicative of the conditions in which the United Nations had to fight; temperature extremes varied from –40°C (–41.4°F) to 35.5°C (96°F) – a range of 76.3°C or no less than 137.4°F.

The medical officer of 3 RAR kept meticulous records even when his battalion was continually on the move and frequently in action. In the months of February and March 1951 alone he noted the following casualties: Dental, 76. Eyes, 46. Ear, Nose and Throat, 44. Respiratory, 58. Gastro-intestinal, 58. Backache, 18. Feet, 70. Unspecified (non-operational) injuries, 90. Battle casualties (dead and wounded), 57. Venereal diseases, 26. Renal tract, 14. Other medical conditions and diseases, 85. In all, the doctor recorded 652 casualties in this eight-week period who were dealt with at the regimental aid post, of whom 151 had to be evacuated. Given the fighting strength of the battalion at the time, this represented something like an 85 per cent attrition rate. During the Kapyong battle in April 1951 the Australians sustained a further 92 battle casualties, of whom 22 were killed or died of wounds, 63 wounded in action, and seven posted as missing.

Mercifully, these casualty rates were nothing like those sustained by infantry battalions almost as a matter of course in the First World War, but they caused alarm, nonetheless, when casualty lists were published in newspapers back in Australia. The whole issue of fighting in Korea for what seemed an obscure if not worthless cause, began to be raised. Most British battalions fared no better than the Australians, and a steady stream of drafts passed over to Korea from the reinforcement depot in Japan, gradually watering down the 'regimental family' character of all units.

CHAPTER 23

On to the Heights

In August 1951 the United Nations front ran inland from the mouth of the Imjin river, following the main Kansas defence line as far as the elbow caused by the sudden northward turn of the river in the area where 29 Brigade had fought so desperately in April. From here it ran north, to form a large salient, known as the 'Wyoming' line, with its head in the Chorwon–Kumhwa area, before rejoining the Kansas line in the area of the great Hwachon reservoir, thence out to the east coast. In front of the main Kansas position was an outpost line, steadily built up to include substantial earthworks, dugouts, gun emplacements, fields of barbed wire and minefields. The enemy's reluctance to offer battle enabled the allies to strengthen these forward positions without interference. To the rear, huge stocks of reserves were built up as the railheads moved forward. Engineers worked day and night to improve existing roads and build new ones, constructing semi-permanent bridges over the Imjin to replace the ferries and pontoons which had sufficed hitherto. In July these in turn were swept away by huge floods following torrential rain in the central mountains. The Imjin rose 20 feet overnight and units already established on the north bank had to rely for some days on airdrops and helicopters for resupply. Before any offensive operations could be undertaken to improve the UN position, the engineers had to build stronger bridges protected as far as possible from further flash floods.

Ridgway's directive to Van Fleet was to sit tight on existing lines but to plan local offensive actions which would help the UN delegates at the armistice talks, now moved to neutral ground at Panmunjon. In the Commonwealth divisional sector this meant seizing the high ground north-west of the angle of the Imjin bend, so that the Wyoming salient would enjoy stronger flank protection. Instructions were also given to the US Far East Air Force to step up its interdiction operations against the enemy lines of communication, and Operation 'Strangle' was duly launched. It was directed by General Otto Weyland of the US Air Force, who had succeeded Stratemeyer in June when the latter suffered a heart attack. Like all USAF officers, Weyland was a disciple of 'victory through air power' and believed in the ability of a strong air arm to secure outright supremacy over the opposing ground forces. As commander of the 29th Tactical Air Force which had supported Patton's dramatic advance across France and into Germany in 1944–5 he was convinced that his air force could extinguish the enemy's will to fight and that the UN forces need do no more than sit tight in strong defensive positions whilst aerial bombardment won the war. Weyland, a believer in personal command, frequently flew bomber missions and was to gain the Silver Star for being the first American general to be attacked by a MiG fighter.

The British Foreign Office, apprised of the plan to step up the air offensive against North Korea and aware of Weyland's addiction to strategic as well as tactical bombing, quailed at the prospect of unrestricted raids on civilian populations and sent a string of urgent telegrams to Sir Oliver Franks in Washington. After testing senior opinion in the Pentagon, Franks cabled London on 20 July advising that it would not be appropriate to express dissent at this stage; he had discovered that the supreme head of the US Air Force, General Hoyt Vandenberg, was as keen as anyone to get the temporarily stalled talks going again; but it had been too late to prevent the raids on Pyongyang. If anything these raids, combined with the iron grip of Kim Il-sung's regime, had strengthened the will of the North Koreans to fight on at all costs.

Van Fleet continued to study various options for future operations. Some of his proposals, such as large-scale amphibious landings in the enemy rear, were ruled out as beyond the capability of the UN Command. Feeling that the stalemate of the long hot summer was eroding the offensive spirit of 8th Army, he decided it was time to inject some action for the good of morale. He had his eye on certain key heights on the area of the Punchbowl, where the North Koreans were dug in on much of the rim of an extinct volcanic crater, enjoying excellent views across the X Corps rear areas. Major-General Byers, who had taken over from Almond at X Corps, was ordered to take this high ground. After the reinvigorated 2nd Division had stormed a peak known as Hill 1179, the ROK I Corps on its right made several unavailing attempts to knock the enemy off the rim of the Punchbowl. Following several bloody reverses in which the ROK marines and infantry fought most gallantly, General Paik was brought back from the truce talks to resume command of his former corps; with the aid of additional heavy American artillery the ROKs triumphantly took their objectives.

The US 2nd Division had to fight hard again in August for what became known, for obvious reasons, as Bloody Ridge. The ROKs were sent in first because Van Fleet believed they needed yet more encouragement to acquire self-confidence. They did so the hard way, attacking for over a week with artillery support that was still inadequate; recoiling in chaos, they carried an

American regiment with them. The 2nd Division went back into the attack but it seemed that little had been learned even now from the failures of the previous summer; losses were high and inexperienced American battle casualty replacements arrived in their new units in the midst of the fighting, bewildered and terrified even before they came under fire. In the words of the British official history, 'They knew no one, could scarcely tell friend from foe. Some were young officers sent to lead a platoon they joined in darkness, among whom they fell as a stranger in the first clash of the following day.'

The US Marines were thrown in next; their disciplined fighting skills enabled them to take Bloody Ridge on 5 September. Perhaps unwisely, Van Fleet continued to press forward; the next mass of high ground became infamous as 'Heartbreak Ridge' as the result of the grim fighting which continued well into October. In all these operations, and despite local reverses, the US 2nd Division played a prominent role; it was as though all ranks wanted to regain the reputation won by the 'Indian Head' during the Second World War and lost so ignominiously at Kunu-ri. With an outstanding performance by the division's French battalion, Heartbreak Ridge was wrenched from the enemy. The cost had been high; in forty days 2nd Division suffered over 6,500 casualties.

It was time for General O'Daniel's I Corps to take up the offensive. Its frontage was now the largest in 8th Army, extending from the west coast to the area of Kumhwa in the centre. The 1st Commonwealth Division, tasked with the capture of the high ground north-west of the Imjin–Hantan junction, had a key role to play. After assessing the situation to his front, General Cassels decided that it would be prudent to move a substantial part of the division across the Imjin; by occupying the ground in the bend of the river he could dominate the wide expanse of no man's land caused by the deep withdrawal of the Chinese and forestall any attempt on their part to repeat their success of April when they had materialized out of the blue to attack 29 Brigade. Early in September, Operation 'Minden' took place, enabling the division to establish itself firmly on the north side of the river.

The move appeared to take the Chinese by surprise. They responded by stepping up their patrolling and by shelling and mortaring any indiscreet movement on the part of the Commonwealth troops. Apart from sporadic Chinese shelling, the division had to put up with the attentions of an elderly Russian-built biplane which nightly flew over the Commonwealth divisional area, dropping its load of small bombs wherever lights were displayed. Known as 'Bedcheck Charlie' this aircraft and its courageous crew were regarded with something approaching affection and there was a sense of deprivation when it was reported that it had been shot down by an American night fighter (which, it was said, had also gone down, killing its crew, having stalled in its efforts to bring down so slow-flying a target). This was not the last of the 'Bedcheck' raids, and determined enemy aviators would continue to fly by night for many months to come, capitalizing on the almost complete lack of blackout precautions on the allied side of the line.

The Chinese had taken advantage of the lull to reinforce their field army with men and *matériel*, especially artillery. From August onwards there was a steady increase in hostile shell and mortar fire and patrols sent out to locate the enemy were engaged progressively nearer to friendly lines, a sure sign that the Chinese were determined to defend their new positions against all comers. Barely a night passed without a fiercely contested patrol encounter in no man's land.

Thousands of Chinese soldiers and labourers were toiling to create remarkable defensive works, tunnelling through mountains to build headquarters, field hospitals and supply dumps. There were miles of tunnels in which whole battalions could rest, secure from even the heaviest bombing or artillery fire. Field guns were placed at the forward end of tunnels cut through hills, and pulled back inside after each shot. They could be destroyed only by a direct hit on the mouth of the tunnel as they were firing and the best weapon for this proved to be the Centurion tank whose extremely accurate 20–pounder gun could 'post a letter' into a gun embrasure at ranges out to 3,000 yards. These tanks were therefore introduced into the forward infantry positions and emplaced as mobile pillboxes; this was a far cry from the cavalryman's dream of the breakout into open country, pursuit of a fleeing enemy and the disruption of his headquarters and supply systems, but it was to be a vital role for the armoured units of the allies for the rest of the war. On one memorable occasion a Centurion was borrowed by an American division on the central front in order to destroy a cleverly emplaced T-34 tank which had defied all attempts to dislodge it with artillery and airstrikes. A tank transporter was provided, on which the Centurion travelled for nearly a hundred miles across Korea. On arrival it drove into its firing position, knocked out the T-34 with its second shot and was back on the transporter before the latter's crew had finished pitching their bivouac tent.

With the completion of Operation Minden the Commonwealth Division was firmly established across the Imjin and ready for the next phase, code-named Operation 'Commando', the seizure of the high ground marking the 'Jamestown' line. A further advance beyond this, to what was known as the 'Fargo' line, was also planned if needed. To reach 'Jamestown' an advance of between six and eight thousand yards would have to be made, depending on the brigade concerned. The key to the Chinese position lay in a clutch of hills in the north-west corner of the divisional objective. From the summit of the highest of these, the 355-metre Kowang-san or 'Little Gibraltar', the Chinese commanded superb views of all the country down to and across the Imjin. It was therefore essential to drive them off this feature and from another hill, Maryang-san, some two miles due north, from where a good overview of the enemy's rear areas could be expected. The Commonwealth Division's frontage extended some nine miles, with its right flank resting on the Imjin where it flowed north–south before reaching its junction with the Hantan and turning west to run off towards the Yellow Sea. Running north–west to south–east through the divisional sector was the substantial tributary stream of the Samichon, entering the Imjin two miles west of the former Gloster crossing.

General O'Daniel entrusted the cutting edge of his attack to Cassels, who decided to use the 28th Commonwealth and 25th Canadian Brigades to take Maryang-san and Kowang-san. These were known to be held by a Chinese regiment of three battalions, well dug in and with plenty of artillery and mortar fire support. Cassels knew it would not be an easy operation; he was also aware that success had to be achieved with the minimum number of casualties. Massive fire support was therefore essential and would be provided by the 25-pounders of the three divisional field regiments under direction of the Commander Royal Artillery. Additional American artillery, some of it heavy, was also available, and the staff of Brigadier Pike, the division's senior gunner, who worked alongside Cassels, devised a careful fire plan to meet all eventualities. Further fire support would come from mortars, the guns of the 8th Hussars' tanks, now perched high up alongside the infantry, and from airstrikes. Cassels elected not to use 29 Brigade in the attack, holding it back in divisional reserve; he wished to spare its troops what could be a bloody fight when all its three battalions, still heavy with reservists, were on the point of leaving for home. Whilst he knew they were skilful and experienced, he recognized that they were unlikely to be as ardent in attack as the young regulars, volunteers and national servicemen in the other brigades.

Brigadier George Taylor, commanding 28 Commonwealth Brigade, was an experienced infantryman, accustomed to leading from the front. Commissioned in 1929 into the West Yorkshire Regiment he had played rugby football for his battalion, the army and the Barbarians, and had been an England trial-list. Deprived of action throughout the Second World War until the Normandy campaign he had been sent at short notice to command a battalion of the Duke of Cornwall's Light Infantry which had lost two commanding officers in rapid succession. Impressing his extrovert personality on his new unit he had led it with great success to the end of the war, attracting the attention and patronage of his corps commander, Lieutenant-General Sir Brian Horrocks. When, in 1950, Taylor had been sent out to Hong Kong to command 28 Brigade, Horrocks wrote to congratulate him: 'I can think of no better choice, as nobody knows more about the sharp end of the battlefield than you.' Taylor had arrived in Korea with his brigade headquarters staff immediately after the battle at Kapyong. His first task had been to settle the brigade in a defensive position and supervise the arrival of the battalions which replaced the Middlesex and the Argylls. At once he was impressed by the Australian battalion.

Taylor, a prolific letter-writer, seems to have made an arrangement with the Chief of the Imperial General Staff to report informally on events in Korea as he saw them. In an early letter to Field Marshal Slim he noted that the new battalions had settled in well and that morale was high: 'They will soon be as good, if not better, than the fine 3rd Royal Australian Battalion who fought like tigers in the last action – one section killed 55 Chinese.' He was less impressed on first acquaintance with the American 24th Division under whose command 28 Brigade was serving at the time:

> There is something the matter with them. They have as an army lost confidence in themselves and it is rather pathetic to see the trust and confidence they have in our two small brigades. Van Fleet seems a good man and a sound general and there are other good fighting men in their ranks but not enough . . . Some of their infantry is quite good in the attack. Their armour on the whole is better trained than their infantry and their engineers are excellent.

Taylor went on to list the shortcomings of his brigade's equipment, most of it worn out and obsolete. The tracked Bren gun carriers were useless (Slim heartily agreed; he thought they were deathtraps) and should be replaced by jeeps and trailers; the shoddy Sten gun was unreliable and the Australian Owen gun far better. Many more Bren light machine-guns were needed to repel Chinese night attacks, against which the slow rate of fire of the British No. 4 bolt-operated rifle was ineffective. Half the wheeled transport inherited from 27 Brigade was falling apart after nine months on Korean roads and spent much of its time in workshops.

Taylor's energetic presence was felt throughout the brigade in the months following the Chinese spring offensives as the UN forces pushed back to the 38th parallel and dug in on the Kansas line. He recognized that he had been entrusted with the command of an exceptional formation, in which British, Australian and New Zealand troops were served by the universally admired Indian Field Ambulance, and in which there was a healthy spirit of inter-unit rivalry. He was particularly pleased, after the King's Own Scottish Borderers had fought a brisk action against a stubborn Chinese rearguard, to be told by their New Zealand gunner that the KOSB 'had fought well up to the standard of the New Zealand Division in the Second World War'. From an Anzac this was indeed an accolade.

As D-day for Operation Commando approached, Cassels briefed his brigade commanders. Taylor was given the key role of capturing Little Gibraltar on 3 October; on the following day the Canadians were to clear two lower hills lying to its south so that 28 Brigade could go on to capture Maryang-san and the adjacent Hill 217. Although it is prescribed in staff colleges that there should ideally be a numerical advantage of three to one in the attackers' favour, it was not to be so on 3 October or on any subsequent days of the battle. The Commonwealth Division would be squaring up against the Chinese 191st

Division whose bayonet strength was at least equal to that of Cassels' division; Taylor's brigade would be facing the 571st Regiment, whose troops confidently awaited the assault in deeply dug positions well supported by artillery and mortars. The defenders outnumbered their attackers, but Taylor believed this would be balanced by massive artillery and air support available to him. He decided to attack in phases. On 3 October, the KOSB were to take Little Gibraltar, supported in the south by the Shropshires, and by 3 RAR to their north-east. Phase 2 was to be a set-piece attack on Maryang-san (Hill 317) by the Australians on 5 October, whilst the Northumberland Fusiliers, borrowed from 29 Brigade, would back up the Australians.

The commander of the Australian battalion was Lieutenant-Colonel Frank Hassett, who had recently taken over from Colonel Ferguson. Hassett, who had earned a fine reputation in North Africa and New Guinea, was even now only 33 years old. As a new commander he had to face up to a battalion which had been devoted to his predecessor. Naturally taciturn and not given to overt displays of emotion, he took time to overcome the innate conservatism which lurks behind the often sardonic and derisory façade of the Australian soldier. Although there were still many in the battalion who had fought under Ferguson in the bitter battle at Kapyong, there had been a major turnover of personnel as officers and men rotated back to Australia on expiry of their tours of duty. He knew that he had to rebuild the battalion quickly into the fighting machine it had been. Writing years later, he pointed out that 'the battalion was not at this stage a highly cohesive unit of the type that came later to Korea. The recent enormous turnover of personnel meant that it was basically a collection of well-trained individuals which had been strung out in a defensive position for the past three months and was quite unpractised as a unit in the battle procedures and techniques required for a battalion in attack.'

Hassett wasted no time. The men were extremely fit, well trained in the use of their personal weapons and in the minor tactics of the rifle section and platoon. He kept the battalion hard at patrolling, the best school of all for fieldcraft and low-level battle drills. However, he was beset by turmoil as the men were sent off on leave, courses and postings, whether the battalion was in or out of the line. 'I had no flexibility in the matter,' Hassett recalled. 'No less a person than the Commander-in-Chief himself, Lieutenant-General Sir Horace Robertson, had made it very clear to me that if I held soldiers back from leave or relief I would be sacked. There had been trouble about this in the past and Robertson was not one to suffer repetition.'

Hassett's rifle company commanders included such experienced warriors as Major Jack Gerke, prominent at Kapyong and earlier fights. Gerke, however, found that he was now the only officer in his company with combat experience, and he carefully distributed his few seasoned NCOs around the rifle platoons and sections to bring on the newcomers. Another company commander, Major

Hardiman, was shown his objective – the steep slopes of Maryang-san rising almost vertically, it seemed, from the valley floor – and blenched. Hassett gave him a cold beer and he cheered up. His company was well below strength, with only 72 men in all against its war establishment of 140, but it had been selected by Hassett for the key role because of the dash its men had displayed in a recent raid on the same objective. In another company, a section corporal commented that instead of his full complement of ten men he had only six apart from himself: 'We had one Bren gun. I carried an Owen gun and the remainder had rifles. Each man had two grenades and a bandolier of fifty rounds.' Hassett was to write later: 'Once casualties began to mount, platoons dropped to as low as fifteen in number . . . a bad situation even with fresh men, let alone ones weary after days of moving and fighting.'

A sense of urgency had permeated down from headquarters 8th Army to the lowliest section commander. This was to be the last chance of taking the high ground and giving the UN truce talks negotiators the bargaining power they needed. After getting his orders, Hassett privately felt that Taylor's battle plan was over-ambitious, given the shortage of manpower in all three battalions and the relative inexperience of many of the younger officers and soldiers. As it happened, his views were shared by the two British battalion commanders, each of whom privately expressed his concern to Taylor, one of them going so far as to prophesy a thousand casualties. Taylor liked to give his subordinates sufficient instructions and for them then to fight their battalions as they wished, and although he was frequently seen at the forefront of the fight, he was averse to interfering unless things went badly wrong.

His battalion commanders had got to know him well and had sized him up. In particular, his personality appears to have jarred with that of John MacDonald of the Borderers. A Calvinistic Scot, averse to tobacco and strong drink and a professional soldier to the core, he was the antithesis of Taylor, the product of an old North Country Catholic family, gregarious, extrovert, a lover of good food, wines and jovial company. There was, despite this, a curiously puritanical streak in Taylor's make-up; a few weeks earlier he had walked ostentatiously away from an open-air show given by an American concert party in which a pair of comedians put on a Rabelaisian golfing skit. If MacDonald and Hassett kept their views to themselves, Lieutenant-Colonel Moodie, commanding the New Zealand gunner regiment, was nothing if not forthright, declaring that he thought Taylor was mad.

Preparations for Operation Commando were carried out by 28 Brigade south of the Imjin, where the rehearsals could be out of sight of the Chinese who, had they possessed powerful binoculars, might have glimpsed the men of 3 RAR running up and down Kamak-san twice daily in full battle order. On 2 October the assault elements recrossed the Imjin on the massive bridges erected by the American army engineers to replace those lost in the summer floods.

Before the KOSB assault on Little Gibraltar the Australians were to occupy a lower feature, Hill 199, and the Shropshires had to take Hill 208. These were then to be used as support bases for the KOSB attack, from which observation and fire could be brought to bear on Chinese reinforcements hurrying forward to Kowang-san. The Australians were faced with a long approach march, by daylight, over exposed ground. They cleverly evaded Chinese attention by spacing their men out at 50-yard intervals, each draped with blankets to disguise the fact that they were festooned with assault gear. One of their officers recalled that it was a pleasant walk: 'a balmy autumn day and the novel idea of walking with fifty paces between each man was relaxing even with a heavy pack on one's back'. The Chinese were fooled and made no attempt to interfere. Early the next morning, Hill 199 was taken after a short sharp fight. From its summit, as the morning mist cleared, the Australians enjoyed magnificent views. They were quickly joined by a troop of Centurions and a section of Vickers machine-guns, and prepared to give fire support for the KOSBs' attack on Little Gibraltar. This, however, failed at the first attempt. The steep sides of the hill were alive with determined Chinese, whose snipers gave much trouble, forcing the advance off course. By mid-afternoon, MacDonald decided to halt the attack, consolidate, and resume next day.

The KOSB had secured a substantial foothold on the lower slopes of Kowang-san and casualties so far had not been high, thanks to good fieldcraft and some outstanding leadership by young officers and NCOs. Taylor therefore amended his original plan; Hassett, ordered to join the attack in support of the KOSB, was reluctant to commit the rifle companies he had selected for the attack on Maryang-san, and called for Gerke's company, fretting in reserve. That resolute soldier moved his men forward in order to commence the assault early on 4 October. As this got under way the Chinese found they were under attack from several directions. On the previous day the Borderers had been compelled to fight their way up the obvious route from which the attack was expected and where the Chinese had sited their strongest defences; now, Gerke's men were coming at them from the north-east as the KOSB resumed their attack from the south and east.

As the gasping Borderers scrambled up the steep slopes, egged on by their pipers, they were accompanied by their New Zealand gunner observation officers and signallers, mortar fire controllers, and personnel of the battalion's support company with Vickers guns, 3-inch mortars and ammunition; a string of porters followed bravely in their wake with yet more ammunition. The irrepressible Hussars were working their tanks up on to the high ground from which they could give close support; one of their Centurions was being guided up by an officer on foot, who paused to catch his breath. The driver was unable to hold 50 tons of steel on his brakes and the tank set off backwards, gaining speed with every yard until witnesses swore it was moving at 60 mph as it arrived at the valley bottom, to travel majestically some fifty yards up the opposite slope before coming to a halt.

On the left flank of the attack the advance of the Shropshires had gone according to plan. They were extremely fit as the result of hill training in Hong Kong before leaving for Korea and imbued with the Light Infantry habit of fast cross-country movement on foot; the prospect of a 10,000-yard approach march had not daunted them and they brushed any opposition aside *en route*. Their commanding officer, Lieutenant-Colonel Barlow, had expected that because of the difficult ground – alternating between scrub, steep slopes and valley bottoms farmed and terraced for rice – the tanks allocated for his support would find the going difficult. He was right, and the Hussars were left far behind. By last light on 3 October the KSLI were firm on their objective and athirst for further advance, but had to be restrained by Brigadier Taylor who knew that Little Gibraltar was still in enemy hands. Because of this the Canadian attack, timed for first light on 4 October, was postponed by six hours on General Cassels' orders and every gun in the divisional artillery was made available to Taylor for the support of the renewed attack.

The Borderers were determined to take Little Gibraltar at their second attempt. Colonel MacDonald selected his 'D' Company to head the attack, giving it a route up the south-western ridge leading to the summit. The company commander was Captain Robertson-MacLeod, a former Cameron Highlander who had had the misfortune in 1940 to be captured at Saint-Valéry in France when the 51st Highland Division was trapped with its back to the cliffs and compelled to surrender. Five years as a prisoner of war had not dampened his martial ardour or powers of leadership and his men followed him readily up the hillside. One of his platoon commanders, Second Lieutenant Barney Henderson, was less than two years out of Sandhurst, and as the preliminary bombardment got under way he was awestruck by the weight of high explosive landing accurately on the Chinese position. It seemed to him that the whole top of the objective had taken to the air, shrouded by dense clouds of smoke and dust punctuated by flashes of fire. The noise was incredible, drowning even the sound of the pipes: 'As we started the assault on the summit,' wrote Henderson, 'where shellfire rolled northwards on to the final slope, there was not a shrub or tree standing. I swore at that moment that I'd never be rude about gunners again.'

The Borderers moved triumphantly on to their objective at 10 a.m., unaware that the Australians of Major Gerke's company were closer at hand than they realized. Having cleared all the Chinese off the eastern slopes, Gerke's men were already consolidating in dead ground just out of sight and below the Borderers. Although they could hear the skirling of the pipes they could not see them. Both units were to claim, correctly, that they had taken Little Gibraltar, for neither would have got there without the unseen support of the other. As each group got on with the urgent drills of consolidation in their new-won positions it does not seem to have occurred to them to contact each other.

The Canadian brigade now launched its delayed attack, aiming to take the other portions of high ground. All went according to plan and by last light on 4 October there remained only the Australians' final target, the Maryang-san feature and its outlying spurs, all held in strength by Chinese who, after being driven off Little Gibraltar, were not disposed to yield a further inch of ground. Cassels saw that this was now too ambitious a project for a single battalion already well under strength, and in any case part of 3 RAR was exhausted after Gerke's Herculean efforts. Accordingly the Northumberland Fusiliers were called forward from reserve to make a diversionary attack on the left-hand side of Maryang-san, on to a spur known as Hill 217 still in Chinese hands, whilst the Australians, having set up a similar diversion against the south-east, launched their major assault from the north-east with two rifle companies. By now the Chinese had reacted swiftly to the perceived threat, rushing up reinforcements.

At first light on 5 October the Fusiliers began to work their way on to the lower slopes of Hill 217; had they known, they were heading straight for the core of the strong and unreconnoitred enemy defences, alive with determined Chinese in well-prepared fieldworks. In dense morning fog the Fusiliers ascended the steep gradients, at first taking many defenders by surprise as they burst out of the mist into the enemy positions, but as they breasted the crest-line they met fierce resistance from Chinese entrenched on the reverse slope, halting the attack as the leading company lost two of its platoon commanders and some 30 men.

Second Lieutenant Paddy Baxter, commanding one of the leading rifle pla-toons, recalled that the advance started in fog and pitch darkness; even after first light it was hard to maintain direction but suddenly, emerging from the mist, he found himself in the open on a bare hillside, surrounded by thoroughly alerted Chinese. The artillery observer moving with the leading troops called at once on his radio for fire support; as Baxter heard the muffled sound of the guns firing to his rear he had a moment's panic; perhaps he was already on the objective, with friendly fire about to engulf him and his men. He shouted for his platoon to disperse and they, who had also heard the impressive salvo from afar, needed no bidding. Seconds later a gratifying barrage descended accurately on the far side of the ridge they were about to cross.

Baxter ordered the advance to resume; he was in the heart of the enemy defences and thought he could hear a woman's voice screaming orders close at hand over the roar of battle. As his platoon continued to clear the hillside he was knocked down by a colossal blow. One of his men came over to him and said, 'You've been hit, sir.' 'I had actually noticed,' Baxter politely replied. He sensed that his wound was severe – he was to lose most of a lung – and went into deep shock. He could still hear the sounds of close-quarter fighting around him – grenades and sub-machine-guns – as his platoon continued up the hill and on to the ridge. Someone applied a shell dressing to his huge wound and stretcher bearers arrived to carry him to the regimental aid post. Immediately it seemed that his entire platoon was crowding round, offering to help with the stretcher. He tried to shout angrily at them to get on with the battle but found he could only whisper. The battalion medical officer, seeing that Baxter had been comprehensively shot in the chest, packed him off back to the Indian Field Ambulance where he was given effective first aid and their standard remedy, a cup of hot sweet tea to counter the shock, and a cigarette. He was intrigued, on inhaling, to see smoke welling up from the sucking wound in his chest. Further to the rear he received expert attention from Major Eger, chief surgeon of the Norwegian MASH, where his life was undoubtedly saved, and was delighted to find himself in the hands of a bevy of handsome Nordic nurses, for the NORMASH had a full complement of these, unlike the British army which would not allow its Queen Alexandra nursing sisters into the field in Korea.

The Northumberlands were forced back after Baxter had been wounded, and to compound this reverse, some of the supporting artillery fire hit the Fusiliers as they sought to reorganize and look to their wounded, causing yet more casualties. Whilst this was happening the Australians were steadily closing in on Maryang-san from the east, supported by three Centurions and the entire divisional artillery augmented by two American 8-inch howitzers and three batteries of 155mm guns. Above the incessant roar of these could be heard the crack of the tanks' guns, the muffled crumps of mortar fire and the steady rattle of Vickers guns as they fired belt after belt of predicted fire into and beyond the Chinese positions. The troops closing with the enemy were much heartened by this fire support. They had to make an approach march of almost a mile before reaching the foremost Chinese defences, after which they would have to fight for almost another mile through an intricate defensive system consisting of bomb-proof bunkers connected by tunnels and deep communication trenches.

The 320 Australian soldiers who brought off this remarkable feat of arms were in fact taking on two fresh battalions of Chinese infantry who enjoyed all the advantages of fighting from well-prepared positions. The approach had begun, like that of the Fusiliers, in darkness. The moon was down and there was a dense mist in the valley bottoms. Navigation was difficult and both the assaulting companies strayed off their appointed routes, but kept on heading due west, knowing that if they continued to climb they would end up some-where near the top of Maryang-san. With commendable understatement, Lieutenant Young recalled leading his company up the hill: 'Not very happily we set off, with a map in one hand, a compass in the other and trepidation over the rest of me. The fog was still dense and we proceeded slowly as map-reading under these conditions wasn't as easy as following a city street guide on a sunny day.'

The Chinese, alerted by the night-long bombardment, grimly awaited the attack in their dugouts and trenches, but as yet could see nothing through the fog and smoke. It was 10 a.m. before the mist began to disperse and by then the Australians were in amongst the defenders. A deadly firefight ensued at close range. Men on both sides were soon reduced to using fists, teeth, rifle butts, bayonets, pickhelves and entrenching tools as the fight descended to the level of a medieval brawl. Major Hardiman emerged through the mist at the head of his company to be confronted by a Chinese machine-gun which opened up at point-blank range. Hardiman was hit, reporting that 'I had the honour of escorting the wounded Chinese NCO operating the gun back to the American surgical hospital at Taegu. This took twenty-four hours and we became quite friendly, perhaps one of the few humanizing sides of war.'

From his battle headquarters half a mile behind the leading troops, Hassett anxiously monitored the progress of the battle, exhorting his company commanders as they forged ahead into the heart of the Chinese position. The mist began to clear, enabling the tanks to use their 20-pounders and machine-guns to good effect. By 5 p.m., Gerke's company, in a remarkable feat of arms hard on the heels of their work of the previous day, had taken the summit of Hill 315, leaving the rest of the high ground to be captured the next day. Meanwhile the Northumberlands were reorganizing after their reverse of the morning; no sooner had they managed to evacuate their wounded than Brigadier Taylor ordered Lieutenant-Colonel Speer, their commanding officer, to resume the attack on the following day. He then issued an additional order which would have involved the already tired, shaken and baffled Fusiliers in an eight-mile night march to a new forming-up point. Colonel Speer expostulated at this and the order was cancelled.

On 6 October the Australians continued to attack and by last light had all but taken the Maryang-san feature. The Northumberlands had once more failed, however, to take Hill 217 despite several gallant attempts, and thus part of Maryang-san was still held by the enemy. Hassett was too experienced a campaigner to believe that victory was his. Foreseeing an enemy counter-attack he spent the night resupplying his forward companies with ammunition and evacuating the wounded. This was achieved largely through the courage and devotion of his soldiers and the battalion's Korean porters.

The forward elements of the battalion were now virtually on to a feature called the Hinge, key to the entire ridge line. This fell to a rousing Australian attack on the morning of 7 October after an intensive bombardment. Hassett saw that the Chinese would have to recapture it if they aimed to regain control of Maryang-san. A counter-attack here would be decisive and the battalion dug new slit trenches facing north, at the same time laying telephone cables back to Hassett's headquarters. Rapid consolidation on any newly captured position is a maxim of war and 3 RAR did it that day according to the book. The wounded were carried to the rear, supplies of ammunition, food and water were brought up to the forward companies, and every weapon was checked and re-checked for the night's work. A rum ration was warmly appreciated.

At 8 p.m. the Chinese attacked. The first inkling for the defenders of the Hinge was when the sky to the north suddenly erupted with the flashes of what seemed to be hundreds of guns, and a devastating barrage landed squarely on the Australians. At 8.45, covered by incessant artillery and mortar fire, waves of Chinese infantry assaulted the Hinge and the rest of the Maryang feature. Despite the fury of the Chinese barrage the defenders held on. With the help of accurate artillery defensive fire, 'B' Company of 3 RAR, in the most exposed position, beat off three attacks during the night.

Their resolution proved decisive. At dawn the attacks ceased, and when in the afternoon an Australian patrol cautiously entered the Chinese positions it was to find them abandoned, together with heaps of stores and weapons. On the tumbled ground in front of the Australian positions lay the mangled remains of hundreds of Chinese. It was estimated that two battalions of them had attacked during the night, few surviving the welcome they received. At one stage Brigadier Taylor had called for the fire of the whole divisional artillery on the ground in front of the Hinge. Under a flag of truce the Chinese were permitted to remove any of their men who might yet be alive. 'Given the savagery of the fighting throughout the night,' wrote an Australian historian many years later, 'this was an impressive humane gesture. Only hours before, in the frenzy of combat, when ammunition was exhausted and weapons damaged and unserviceable, Chinese soldiers had been kicked to death or strangled by the aggressive Australians.'

The initial phase of Operation Commando was over and the Commonwealth Division had successfully taken its objectives in what was to be its one and only collective assault battle. The problem now was to hang on to them. The Australians handed Maryang-san over to the KOSB while low-flying Mustang fighter-bombers of the South African 'Flying Cheetah' Squadron savaged the enemy with rockets, napalm and cannon as they drew back from the scene of their defeat. The Northumberlands, hard hit in their last battle, left for home with the other battalions of 29 Brigade. New battalions would be joining the brigade to replace them, keen to prove their mettle as the line settled into the position it would retain, virtually unchanged, until the armistice of 1953.

In the immediate wake of Commando there was a brief interval of euphoria in the division. It had met and surmounted its first challenge and acquitted itself well; there was generous praise from General O'Daniel and Cassels had good reason to be satisfied. There had, however, been repercussions in 28

Commonwealth Brigade. Taylor was quietly relieved of his command by Cassels on 25 October. Some Australians deplored the manner of his going, for his breezy style of command had been to their taste; they let it be known that Taylor had been the victim of intrigue by a cabal of British officers within the brigade and suspicions fell initially on John MacDonald who succeeded to the command. His apparent disdain for Australians was returned by them with interest. The official New Zealand history, however, indicates that Taylor had clashed with a number of his commanding officers, especially with Hassett and with Moodie, commanding the superb New Zealand gunners, who later stated that 'We ganged up on him – we said he was a menace – no good to us.' Moodie (who seems to have been disliked by many of his own officers) passed his observations as an artilleryman to Brigadier Pike, the Commander Royal Artillery in Cassels' headquarters, who took Taylor off for an interview with the divisional commander from which he did not return. On his arrival back in London, Taylor was invited to the House of Lords for lunch by his former patron General Horrocks, who held the post of Black Rod. He told Horrocks what had transpired and, as Taylor later wrote: 'He was dumbfounded. He told me that Cassels, as a brigadier before the Rhine crossing, was himself at the point of being sacked but his divisional commander was killed by a mortar bomb and Cassels was saved.' By such chances are soldiers' fortunes decided.

Cassels went on to command the 51st Highland Division, commanded the Commonwealth Division with distinction and eventually won his Field Marshal's baton. Taylor had many admirable qualities but failed to appreciate the sensitivities inherent in a unique formation such as 28 Commonwealth Brigade. A fair and generous judgement was passed on him years later by General Sir Frank Hassett, the former commanding officer of 3 RAR, who attributed his battalion's success in Operation Commando to Taylor's leadership:

> The whole divisional attack was extremely well planned and executed. The timing of the attacks in series so as to make maximum fire support available to battalions at any given time is one example. As a battalion commander it was comforting to go into an attack with the knowledge that over 120 guns and mortars as well as tanks were in support . . . I particularly appreciated the senior commanders being well forward, fully in touch with the progress of the battle and able to make the right decisions quickly. George Taylor was a most able tactician.

There were other reasons for the aftermath of Commando being an unhappy time for 28 Brigade. Although casualties had not been unacceptably high, given the successful capture of all its objectives (58 officers and men killed, 257 wounded) the Chinese reaction was swift and casualties from their shell and mortar fire immediately started to mount. The Australians had handed over Maryang-san to the Borderers on 8 October and were moved to a quieter sector to regroup. The new occupants tried to create strong defences under continual fire by day and night as the Chinese demonstrated their mastery of the mortar, the steep trajectory of whose bombs enabled them to strike at the supposedly safe reverse slopes of the KOSB positions. Despite this harassing fire, work had to go on round the clock in expectation of a renewed Chinese night attack. Aerial reconnaissance indicated that the Chinese were building their strength for a major counter-attack on the ground taken by the Commonwealth Division, with new gun emplacements and much digging. The first test of the defences came on the night of 12 October when the Shropshires holding the high ground south-west of Little Gibraltar were attacked by a Chinese battalion after heavy artillery preparation. The defence held and the enemy recoiled with heavy loss but the warning was clear; the Borderers in their far more exposed position on Maryang-san would be next in line.

It was not auspicious that the KOSB had to face their next test only days after Colonel MacDonald had left them to command the brigade. It was apparent on the night of 3 November that something was in the wind; as the Borderers strained their eyes in the dark they could hear the sound of furious digging close at hand, where hundreds of Chinese were sapping their way towards the defences with pick and shovel. Daylight on the 4th revealed the extent of their night's work, which had gone ahead despite heavy artillery and mortar defensive fire brought down close in front of the KOSB positions. On a small eminence only a hundred yards from these was a large banner bearing the words: 'Go home Britishers or this hill will be your graveyard'. From this a deep trench snaked towards the centre of the defences; along it could be caught fleeting glimpses of hundreds of infantry moving up to attack.

An airstrike was called in, and to the cheers of the defenders, repeated napalm attacks were made on the Chinese. Australian Sea Fury aircraft from the carrier HMAS *Sydney* and South African Mustangs succeeded each other throughout the day. It seemed impossible that the enemy could launch an attack off that seared and smoking tract of ground. Any doubts, however, were resolved by the tremendous artillery barrage which descended on the Borderers. It was methodically done; instead of spreading their fire over a wide area the Chinese concentrated it in succession on selected points. The New Zealand gunners with the KOSB, visibly impressed, described this as 'the full treatment', and for most of the day an average of a hundred shells a minute landed on the Hinge, held by 'C' Company of the Borderers. Telephone lines were cut and no runner could have survived more than a few seconds in that storm of fire.

At 4.45 p.m. the Chinese rose from their trenches as the barrage abruptly stopped. Unseen by the defenders, whose heads had been kept well down, they had dug to within yards of the Borderers' wire, then camouflaged themselves and stoically borne the whole day's airstrikes before launching a frenzied assault on to the Hinge. 'C' Company were simply overwhelmed. Armed with bolt-operated rifles, which might have been useful in a different sort of war, they lacked the close-quarter firepower needed to stop such a determined infantry assault in its tracks. The New Zealand artillery observation officer and his signaller, though both severely wounded, continued to direct defensive fire, stopping only to help carry more ammunition forward to the rifle sections. The hilltop was shrouded in smoke and dust and all communications failed. It was decided to evacuate any Borderers still alive from the Hinge. Meanwhile the defenders of Hill 217 had also been driven off their position and on to the knoll between it and Maryang-san itself.

Night fell and the battlefield was eerily lit by starshell and the parachute flares of the 3-inch mortars. Hand-to-hand fighting continued but the Borderers were succumbing to sheer weight of numbers as Chinese reinforcements poured up on to the hill. One soldier, Private Speakman, though badly wounded, led repeated bayonet charges against the Chinese swarming around his section's position. Eventually a young National Service subaltern, Second Lieutenant Willy Purves, gathered together the survivors of the last two platoons on Maryang-san and led them, with their weapons and wounded, to safety.

Driven off their position by weight of numbers and an unprecedented Chinese artillery barrage, the Borderers had nothing to be ashamed of; however, they had lost ground won by the supreme effort of the Australians only a month earlier and it was never regained, remaining in Chinese hands until the armistice. The defenders' casualties were not high despite the ferocity of the battle: less than ten killed, 87 wounded and 44 missing, most of whom were taken prisoner. It was estimated, from the evidence of prisoners taken later, that the KOSB, their supporting gunners and airstrikes had inflicted over a thousand casualties on the Chinese.

On 5 November there was an attempt to recover the lost ground, particularly Hill 217 where the Northumberlands had suffered in their last attack. The battalion chosen for this was the newly arrived Royal Leicestershires, on loan from 29 Brigade. Whether through lack of experience and confidence, or the preponderance of very young soldiers in the battalion, the attack failed. The Australians were not slow to express their disgust and for a time there was a decidedly unpleasant atmosphere in what had hitherto been a happy and successful brigade. Matters were not helped when, on the same day as the Leicesters' failure, Brigadier MacDonald issued a special order of the day extolling his old battalion, in which he conspicuously failed to acknowledge the outstanding achievement of the Australians on Maryang-san, or the contribution made throughout by the New Zealand gunners.

With Maryang-san back in Chinese hands it was decided to fortify Little Gibraltar and the remaining high ground held by the Commonwealth Division. This was to be their stronghold virtually to the end. The Chinese continued to shell the division's front for the rest of November but a further attempt to dislodge the Shropshires was successfully repulsed, even though one of the forward company locations was overrun, to be retaken in a spirited counter-attack. After this the Chinese treated the division with circumspection. It was now savagely cold with the approach of the Manchurian winter, and both sides occupied themselves with preparing for sub-zero weather.

CHAPTER 24

Time for Reflection

With the Kansas line established and consolidated following the autumn battles of 1951, the war became an entrenched deadlock punctuated by artillery duels and local engagements as the Panmunjon talks dragged on. By midsummer 1952 little real progress had been made.

The communists continually raised ludicrous points of order and were quick to make wild allegations in an effort to gain advantages in the negotiations, as when the Chinese were persuaded by Nam Il to raise the subject of biological warfare. Between January and April 1952 they charged the United Nations forces with using bacteriological agents against the people of North Korea. The United States Air Force was accused of dropping containers filled with infected insects and vermin on North Korea and Manchuria in order to spread cholera, typhus and bubonic plague. Secretary of State Dean Acheson immediately called on the International Red Cross to conduct investigations behind United Nations as well as communist lines. Whilst keeping up their stream of allegations, neither the Chinese nor the North Koreans made any attempt to contact the International Red Cross in Geneva; neither did they respond to an offer by the World Health Organization to provide treatment for victims of the alleged germ attacks. There was indeed a widely held belief at the United Nations that the allegations had been made to cover up huge epidemics in Manchuria and China caused by poor sanitation, malnutrition and the collapse of health care.

Chinese photographs purporting to be of insects carrying deadly diseases were quickly exposed as crude fakes. Microscopic pictures stated to be of 'meningitis and gangrene germs' were dismissed by the experts as either 'fake photos of utterly innocuous bacteria or meaningless blotches'. A photograph purporting to be of a canister used for dropping germ agents depicted a device commonly used for dropping propaganda leaflets. The germ warfare allegations rebounded on the North Koreans, who lost face and hurriedly dropped the subject from their agenda.

Admiral Joy soon learned how to comport himself and became a tough negotiator, combining Job-like patience with a strong will. The repatriation of prisoners of war remained the governing factor, with the communists demanding that all prisoners be returned to their country of origin. Joy met them head-on, insisting that the UN would demand that prisoners be given a free choice over repatriation and that the current front be accepted as the basis of the truce line once this became effective, although this meant giving up a significant area of the former Republic of Korea on the western sector, including the important town of Kaesong. The communists pressed for the 38th parallel, and the return to the *status quo ante* before the North Korean invasion, knowing full well that this line was totally indefensible and that acceptance of the 38th parallel would have been nothing less than abject surrender on the part of the United Nations Command. Joy had to contend also with siren voices in Washington, and even within Ridgway's Tokyo headquarters, advocating an all-out advance to the Yalu, but even General Mark Clark, who succeeded Ridgway in 1952, was to recognize that the United Nations did not have the manpower, even if it had the will, for such an enterprise.

When it became apparent that the truce talks were going to be long drawn out, a base camp was set up at Munsan, 14 miles south of Panmunjon. Here, the world's press were accommodated in a special train, and messes and clubs set up for use by the UN delegates and important visitors. As the months lengthened into years, the Munsan camp developed into a miniature township.

Attempts at psychological warfare were made by both sides from early in the campaign, but the new semi-static conditions gave many more opportunities than hitherto. One United Nations attempt featured a cartoon depicting a group of downcast Chinese soldiers; the text in translation read: 'Chinese men, Korean land. Soviet Russian guns and rifles. Eating local grain, drinking cold water. Pulling all the strength from your guts. By day a prisoner, by night a slave. Chinese–Soviet friendship – till death you will never leave the field. Chinese–North Korean friendship – cold water and borrowed food.' On the reverse of the leaflet was a picture of cheerful, well-nourished Chinese troops, smoking, playing volleyball, and the text read: 'Chinese men, Korean land. Not seeing Soviet arms but eating white rice in UN Army camp. Passing time usefully – by day you smoke, have sport. At night your sleep is sweet, you don't have to die. You have no worries or fears. Eating good meals, your body is strong and healthy.'

Another allied leaflet carried a picture of a blackboard bearing the following message: 'A year ago, the army invaded South Korea. A year later it had been forced back to its starting position. In a year, 1,176,750 casualties and nothing in return. Every day you go in fear of losing your life. Wake up and use your intelligence – come over to the UN lines. Then you can stop being part of this war and find life for yourselves.' This was backed by a simple profit-and-loss account: 'Remember the anniversary. June 1950 to June 1951. Dead and wounded, 1,176,750. Prisoners, 162,398. Loss of material cannot be counted.'

Both sides distributed their leaflets by leaving them in prominent 'dead letter' boxes in no man's land and, in the allied case, by dropping them in thousands from aircraft. Communist propaganda was mainly directed at the Americans and ROKs. It ranged from crudely printed 'safe conduct passes' to sophisticated messages using the statements of captured UN soldiers who had been 'turned', often with photographs of individuals or groups apparently enjoying the delights of captivity in North Korea. A recurrent theme was 'Your families want you back'. Others showed photographs of President Truman playing golf, or wealthy New York families such as the Vanderbilts enjoying themselves at society functions. 'Why fight for these people?' was the general theme. One example, supposedly written by a Private 1st Class Henry C. Comer of the United States Army, was entitled 'How the Chinese treated me'. Another, aimed at British troops, consisted of a letter purporting to be from a father to his son, held in a Chinese prison camp, begging British soldiers not to risk their lives for Yankee dollars. It went on: 'I am glad you are out of danger, being a prisoner. The other soldiers are having a rotten time and still there is no sign of the government breaking with America who are [*sic*] the cause of this trouble. They are going to cause a world war and Britain is doing just what they want them to do.'

Many British reservists and regulars had to be retained in service after their normal term had expired, a measure forced on the War Office by the chronic recruiting deficiencies of the army at this time. Their eventual replacement by younger soldiers appreciably lowered the average age of British units in the Commonwealth Division. Battalions arriving in Korea from the middle of 1951 had a far higher National Service content than those of the previous autumn, and required further training before going into the line. A divisional battle school was therefore set up, in which junior NCOs and officers were familiarized with the techniques found effective in Korea. The reputation gained by the Commonwealth Division in the defensive battles ahead was in no small measure due to the high quality of instruction given in this unit.

By this stage of the campaign, the Americans were becoming used to the diverse character of the Commonwealth units. For a start, they did not appear to wear uniform, if by that is meant uniformity of dress. In the 28th Commonwealth Brigade, the KSLI wore dark green Light Infantry berets bearing the distinctive Bugle cap badge. The KOSB wore green jungle hats emblazoned at the front with a patch of Leslie and Buccleuch tartan. The Australians wore their equally distinctive bush hats, while all New Zealand vehicles and equipment bore the emblem of the fern leaf and there were numerous representations of the Kiwi, a bird unknown to the Americans.

Although the propaganda leaflets addressed to British troops had little effect on the men of the Commonwealth Division (who quickly found another more practical use for them) there were signs of rising disquiet at home, orchestrated by left-wing groups. The communist-dominated World Peace Congress attempted to convene an international 'Partisans of Peace' conference in Sheffield as early as November 1950. This was roundly condemned by Attlee in a speech to the Foreign Press Association on 1 November, as well as by Archbishop Fisher of Canterbury, and the British Council of Churches. All made the point that whilst the World Peace Congress was voluble in its espousal of universal peace, it had not published or uttered a word of condemnation against North Korea's invasion of the south. The conference had to be transferred from Sheffield to Prague after only one day, as several hundred delegates were either refused British visas or were turned away on arrival in England. Amongst these oddly assorted notables was Dmitri Shostakovich the composer; but Pablo Picasso, another delegate, was given permission to enter the United Kingdom. Some 1,750 delegates found their way to Prague, where they duly rubber-stamped a series of motions condemning the United States and its allies.

The ranks of the Labour Party began to display unsteadiness under fire in the summer of 1951. The government's overall majority in the Commons was down to five and many MPs on the government back-benches were openly critical of the conduct of the war, seen by them as an American adventure into which Britain had been dragged by moral blackmail. On 11 July 1951 the left-wing journal *Tribune* published a pamphlet entitled 'One Way Only'. It set out to be a socialist analysis of current world problems featuring articles by three former government ministers who had recently resigned on matters of principle: Aneurin Bevan, Harold Wilson and John Freeman. All had contended in their resignation speeches that Britain could not afford the rearmament programme on which Attlee and Shinwell had embarked. They believed that the enormous cost of raw materials for this could only be met by reductions in the workers' standards of living, and that the best way of combating the spread of communism was to set up huge development plans in the Third World, especially in the backward areas of Asia. War, they claimed, was not inevitable, but could be if an arms race was allowed to develop. A supreme effort must therefore be made to reach an accommodation with the USSR within two years. The underprivileged peoples of the undeveloped world had every right to complete their own revolutions and it was the duty of Britain's socialists to convince her allies that economic aid was more appropriate than counter-insurgency operations. They also held that rearmament should be paid for, not out of inflation, but by means of unspecified 'socialist controls'.

The government was swift to respond. On 27 July 1951 Shinwell released a press statement stressing that it was government policy to build up sufficient armed strength to bring the Russians to the conference table. He rejected outright the 'arguments in certain quarters' (in other words, the left wing of the

Labour Party) that British government defence plans were excessive. The manpower of the Soviet home forces, he pointed out, was 4.6 million, with over a million more in East Germany and eastern European satellite states. There were 117 active Soviet divisions and 40 anti-aircraft divisions – all capable of doubling in size on mobilization. Of the 22 divisions in East Germany, 18 were armoured.

The Labour government, under pressure from the disenchanted in its own ranks, could not survive much longer with its tiny majority, so Attlee gambled and went to the country. On 25 October the Conservatives were returned to power under Winston Churchill with a majority of 18 over all parties combined, and 27 over Labour. Churchill appointed himself Minister of Defence, as in his wartime premiership; he immediately called Lieutenant-General Sir Ian Jacob back from his retirement post at the BBC to be his personal Chief of Staff and the contact between Cabinet and the professional heads of the fighting services. Anthony Eden became Foreign Secretary and Brigadier Anthony Head, as Secretary for War, was the army's new political master.

There were immediate problems to be faced other than that of the war in Korea. Earlier in the month the Egyptian parliament had unilaterally abrogated the 1936 Anglo–Egyptian treaty and scrapped the Anglo–Egyptian condominium over the Sudan. There were anti-British riots in all Egyptian cities in which a number of expatriates were brutally murdered. The incoming Tory government confronted an economy in deep trouble. R.A. Butler, the new Chancellor, announced heavy cuts in imports, a reduction to £50 of the tourist allowance to most countries, restrictions on new building, the raising of the bank rate from 2 to 2.5 per cent, and a swingeing tax on excess profits. The dollar deficit was astronomical and the national balance of payments had deteriorated even further than had been expected.

Butler met with immediate opposition from the Chiefs of Staff when he called for a downward revision of the Navy, Army and Air estimates. They countered with the unpalatable facts that apart from the Korean commitment, forces were needed to maintain a naval presence in the Atlantic and Mediterranean, the Suez Canal Zone (where recent events threatened the vital sea route to the Far East and Australia), and to maintain garrisons in Gibraltar, Malta, Hong Kong, Aden and Singapore – all of them essential to the security of the imperial lines of communication. In addition there was the protection of sea trade world wide, and the build-up of the British Army of the Rhine to four divisions, two of them armoured, in fulfilment of NATO requirements.

No sooner had Churchill been returned to power than he announced his intention of going to Washington for urgent discussions with President Truman. His enthusiasm for an early meeting with the President lay in his wish to rekindle the 'special relationship' he had fostered with Roosevelt over the years. Churchill was now 77 and the oldest Prime Minister since Gladstone. He was in declining health and had already confided to his private secretary that he intended to serve for no more than a year before handing over to Anthony Eden, his heir apparent. When, on 11 December 1951, he announced to the Cabinet his intention of going to Washington 'to re-establish the intimate relationship', there was consternation in Downing Street. The idea of the Atlantic crossing in the depth of winter (Churchill's doctor had forbidden him to fly) aroused little enthusiasm among the senior civil servants and service chiefs who were called on to produce ideas for a vast agenda, ranging over the Cold War, operations in Korea, allied policy in the Middle East, American backing for British defence commitments in NATO, and atomic energy. The punishing schedule prepared by Churchill would have daunted men half his age, including as it did an address to Congress and a session with the Canadian government in Ottawa.

The Washington meetings were not a success. The patrician Churchill found little or no common ground with Truman, the former draper's assistant, who in turn tended to dismiss Churchill's ideas in midstream; the old statesman's orotund delivery was not warmly received by the Missouri politician, used as he was to more direct speech. Korea, Churchill found, was treated as a minor issue compared with the other weighty matters on the agenda.

Back in Whitehall the military staffs were in the throes of drafting their contributions to the Conservatives' first Defence White Paper. Published in February 1952, it was essentially an examination of the last Labour review of 1951 in which, despite vociferous protests from the party's left wing, a huge increase of defence expenditure had been announced in order to meet Britain's new-found treaty obligations, the chief of which lay in Europe. Even before the Conservatives returned to power it had been apparent that this programme, the most that the nation could afford without reversion to a war economy, was over-ambitious and would be subject to delays. The national balance of payments had reached crisis point, plunging deeper into the red every day. The 1952 White Paper was therefore an attempt to come to terms with a number of unpalatable facts. One of these was that of recruitment for the armed forces. A shortage of regulars had already made itself felt in Korea and the government now offered inducements such as improved pay and better conditions of service to remedy the situation. As a further inducement, resettlement schemes for service men and women were set up, to teach appropriate civilian skills on termination of longer-service engagements.

Defence expenditure had to be brought under control whilst meeting ever-increasing demands from Korea and from the anti-terrorist campaign in Malaya. The £304 million of the 1949/50 Army Estimates was expected to swell to £521 million by 1953. This was principally the result of unexpected commitments in the Canal Zone where it had been necessary to reinforce the garrison following Egypt's unilateral abrogation of the 1936 treaty. Malaya had

to be further reinforced following the assassination of the governor, Sir Henry
Gurney. An augmented division was tied down in Hong Kong and garrisons
had to be provided in Austria, Trieste, around the Mediterranean and in the
West Indies. The burden on the taxpayer was likely to become insupportable
and it was decided to extend the timescale of the Labour government's defence
programme. Even so, there were doubts that the forces being built up would be
financially sustainable; exports were falling off alarmingly as Britain's former
customers went elsewhere for cheaper goods. In December 1952 Churchill
would be forced to announce that there would be no further increases in
defence expenditure, and yet another defence review had to be initiated.

The political scene was also changing in Washington as Churchill's government grappled with its inherited problems in London. A presidential election
campaign was gathering momentum and it soon became apparent that the
Republicans would win. Having toyed with the idea of inviting MacArthur to
stand as their candidate, the party caucuses thought again and asked General
Dwight Eisenhower to run. The prospect delighted many in Britain, not least
Churchill. Eisenhower was regarded as an old friend and likely to look with
favour on his erstwhile allies. Disillusionment would come later, in 1956 after
the fiasco of the Suez expedition.

   In Tokyo, Ridgway was succeeded as Commander-in-Chief UN Forces by
General Mark Clark in May 1952, and left to take over from Eisenhower as
NATO Commander-in-Chief in Europe. General Clark was no stranger to
British leaders. Handsome, charming and incurably egocentric, his appointment was viewed with dismay by Field Marshal Lord Alexander, whom
Churchill had invited to be Minister of Defence in March, an appointment he
had accepted against his better judgement. As Supreme Allied Commander in
the Italian campaign of 1943–5 Alexander had found the American a difficult
subordinate; Clark, commanding the US 5th Army, had flouted Alexander's
operational instructions, making a theatrical entry into Rome instead of
enveloping and destroying the German forces in his operational area. Clark,
perhaps scenting trouble following a visit by Alexander to Tokyo and anxious
to establish a good working relationship, asked for the appointment of a senior
Commonwealth officer as his Deputy Chief of Staff. After discussion in
Whitehall and consultation with the Commonwealth countries involved, it was
agreed that a British officer should go, and Major-General Shoosmith, a
gunner, was selected. It was emphasized that he would not be the channel for
passing the views of the British Chiefs of Staff to the UN Command; this
would remain the responsibility of the United Kingdom Liaison Staff in
Washington. Neither would he supplant Air Vice-Marshal Bouchier, the
Chiefs of Staffs' liaison representative at UN Command.

   Shoosmith was comprehensively briefed in London before leaving for

Tokyo. He was told that the enemy forces in Korea now totalled some 940,000 of whom 675,000 were Chinese. 437,000 of these and 90,000 North Koreans were deployed in the forward areas, about 147,000 more than in the previous autumn. The enemy had many more tanks and self-propelled guns than in 1951 and, though deployed defensively in depth, were capable of mounting an offensive at little or no notice. More than 400 MiG fighter aircraft had arrived on Manchurian airfields since the previous winter, but as they were obliged to operate from Chinese soil owing to the effective destruction of all North Korean airfields, they did not pose a threat to the UN ground forces. Although the UN allies enjoyed mastery of the seas around Korea, small enemy amphibious operations were still taking place and, despite continuous naval bombardment, the enemy's coastal defences had been methodically improved.

At Panmunjon, Shoosmith was told, agreement had been reached on all but two of the articles in the draft armistice agreement. The sticking points centred on the disposal of the thousands of Chinese and North Korean prisoners, held in camps on islands off the South Korean coast, who refused to be repatriated once an armistice was signed. The Chinese and North Korean delegations to the talks were adamant that repatriation must be total and compulsory. The effects of this debate had already been reflected in large-scale prison mutinies on the islands. General agreement had been reached on a demarcation line following the approximate course of the existing front lines; land and air forces were to remain for the time being at current levels, with the rotation of up to 35,000 personnel a month; there was to be no restriction on the repair of military airfields after an armistice; neutral inspections would be limited to ground, sea and airports of entry and to the main centres of communication in Korea; there was to be no aerial inspection of North Korea; and there was an agreed recommendation to call a political conference within three months of the signing of an armistice to discuss, among other matters, the withdrawal of foreign forces from Korea.

Shoosmith also received briefings on British governmental policy towards the Korean War. Britain felt that as the original UN objective had been to oppose the North Korean invasion and, later, Chinese intervention, the establishment of a more or less stable front in the area of the 38th parallel could be said to have achieved this. Assuming that an armistice agreement was reached, it would be necessary to ensure that there was no recurrence of North Korean aggression and, above all, that war did not spread beyond the borders of Korea. It was to be understood that no further land operations would be undertaken without prior consultation between Washington and London. The Commonwealth Division was thus committed to static operations on its present ground until the end of the campaign.

If, however, aerial attacks were made on UN forces in Korea from bases outside Korea, HM Government agreed in principle that retaliatory action would be taken against these bases. However, as such action ran the risk of escalating the war, Britain reserved the right not to commit itself in advance and to judge the situation in the light of events. But in the last resort the Americans reserved the right to go it alone in dire emergency, even if British consensus was not forthcoming. If the Panmunjon talks broke down, Mark Clark or his successor would be given discretionary powers to increase the tempo of operations in Korea if militarily desirable, advancing as far as the 'waist' of the peninsula (but no further). He would also be authorized to bomb the Yalu dams, completing the destruction of the North Korean power system. There was in fact only one of these across the Yalu itself – the Suiho dam, half of which was in China. The others were in North Korea. The British government pressed for a qualification: that Manchurian airspace would not be infringed and that the Chinese half of the Suiho remained untouched. This was something the Americans could not guarantee.

The British had agreed to contribute to any UN occupation force left in Korea following an armistice, and to persuade the other Commonwealth countries to do likewise. In the event of a resumption of hostilities following an armistice breakdown, Britain was pledged to give prompt and effective military support to help restore the situation; but war with Russia was to be avoided at all cost. The enemy build-up since October 1951 had been considerable and if a decisive defeat were to be inflicted on the enemy, it would require substantial UN reinforcements; there would also be increased Chinese air activity if hostilities broke out again, and if this required airstrikes on the Manchurian airfields there was a lurking dread in Whitehall that this would impel the Americans to employ what they euphemistically referred to as 'weapons of mass destruction'. As far as London was concerned this could only mean nuclear weapons, and Shoosmith was left in no doubt that he was to make it clear that the British government had to be consulted if America so much as contemplated the use of these.

Weighed down with his briefings, Shoosmith set out for Tokyo where he immediately saw Air Vice-Marshal Bouchier to assure him that he was in no way there to replace him. Bouchier was in any case nearing the end of his eventful tour. After nearly two years in post he departed for England in October 1952 to resume his retirement.

PART FOUR
Final Confrontations

CHAPTER 25

Tests of Strength

O nce static warfare had set in, the artillery of both sides came into its own. Since the earliest days of the war the NKPA had skilfully handled its excellent Russian guns, in many ways superior to anything the Americans could field. Although huge stockpiles of artillery ammunition existed in the United States, they were depleted at an alarming rate during the first twelve months in Korea. During its attacks on Bloody Ridge in August and September 1951 the American 2nd Division's artillery alone fired off 153,000 rounds, one of its battalions achieving a record output of 14,425 rounds in twenty-four hours from 24 guns. As the enemy dug ever deeper emplacements, much ammunition was wasted in attempts to destroy these, which were immune to anything less than a direct hit by an 8-inch howitzer shell with a delayed fuze; these impressive guns, known as the 'Persuaders' from the motto inscribed on their barrels, were brought well forward at times to engage targets with direct fire.

Ridgway had to appeal to the Joint Chiefs in the autumn of 1951, demanding increased supplies of ammunition to compensate for the lack of guns at his disposal, and urging the abandonment of the lower scales of daily expenditure per gun based on Second World War figures, when the numbers of guns allotted to the field army had been much higher than in Korea. From 8th Army, General Van Fleet added his weight; he contended that his artillery, compared with the amount available in the latter stages of the war in Europe, was short by no less than 70 field artillery battalions. Both he and Ridgway agreed that liberal use of artillery saved the lives of their own troops. Despite this, ammunition had to be rationed at the end of 1951; this did not immediately affect the Commonwealth Division, whose 25-pounder guns were sustained from wartime stocks shipped hurriedly out to Korea from the United Kingdom.

Whilst the allies grappled with ammunition shortages the Chinese were continually building up their artillery. By spring 1952 they had deployed nearly 900 guns in the forward areas. Despite the difficulty of maintaining supplies in the face of allied air supremacy, the Chinese rates of fire steadily increased; in April

1952 they were firing some 2,400 rounds a day, but only two months later this had risen to over 6,800. In the ferociously contested battles for Sniper Ridge on the IX Corps sector, key features changed hands several times; in each case artillery was decisive in forcing off the high ground whoever currently held it. Van Fleet decided to use the massed artillery of I, X and IX Corps to overwhelm the enemy guns, but this massive counter-battery fire only succeeded in destroying 39 of the Chinese field pieces.

In the Commonwealth Division's sector, Chinese artillery was almost impossible to locate and destroy. This was due to shortage of specialist counter-mortar and counter-battery staffs and the equipment necessary to pinpoint enemy firing positions. Improvised methods had to suffice until the arrival of a specialist locating battery in the summer of 1952; a 5.5-inch medium battery was added to the divisional artillery at the same time. The Commonwealth gunners had deployed in the open throughout the first year of the war, but once Operation Commando had been completed and the line stabilized, there was a rude awakening; as early as 4 November 1951 a battery of the New Zealand field regiment was relaxing in its position when some 35 shells landed amongst them. In the words of one of their men, quoted by the official historian: 'Most of us were just sitting about at the time . . . believe me we were all making for earth in one hell of a hurry. A lot of us like myself didn't have a hole dug, but by the powers, it wasn't long before we did have, and we'd only just have time for one or two shovelfuls between each shell.' This alarming experience, which fortunately caused few casualties but destroyed a number of vehicles and tentage, was taken to heart.

Life for soldiers of the Commonwealth Division in the static conditions following Operation Commando was similar to that in all other UN formations. The winter of 1951/2 was bitter but at last there was an adequate supply of winter clothing for the front-line troops. In sub-zero temperatures the engines of all vehicles froze solid unless started and run every half hour through the night. Rifle oil froze, and men's hands stuck to the cold metal of their weapons and equipment. Cases of frostbite and trench foot occurred unless junior leaders were vigilant; those who were not risked severe disciplinary action. It seemed to most that the cold was a more ruthless foe than the Chinese.

By January 1952 temperatures of −30°C were commonplace. When in the line, battalions did their best to alleviate the conditions by constructing 'hutchies' or lean-to dwellings and dugouts on the reverse slopes of the forward positions, where men could rest when not in their fire trenches, warmed by American-issue petrol space heater stoves and protected from enemy fire. With the turn of the seasons the dry cold of the Manchurian winter was replaced by the humid sub-tropical heat of the Korean summer. This meant either clouds of infected dust in dry weather, or monsoon-like downpours causing flash floods, which washed away bridges and reduced the unsealed dirt roads to quagmires. Summer also brought the stench of corruption and excrement, and myriads of insects.

Routine in the front line bore a strong resemblance to that on the Western Front of 1914–18. It had been ordained by headquarters I Corps that no man's land was to be dominated by night, and this meant constant patrolling. As patrols were frequently out all night a great proportion of the entire battalion was deprived of sleep; those involved in support had to remain alert, whether artillerymen, mortar and machine-gun personnel of the battalion's support company or the crews of the Centurion tanks deployed amongst the forward infantry positions. Some of these were fitted with powerful searchlights for illumination of the battlefield. The 8th Hussars had been able to take some of their tanks right up to Pyongyang in the first dreadful winter and had used their mobility to save 29 Brigade from extermination in the dramatic Imjin battles of April 1951, but their successors, the 5th Royal Inniskilling Dragoon Guards, who were followed in turn by the 1st Royal Tank Regiment, were obliged to function as semi-static strongpoints. When the enemy attacked it was usually at night, and the Centurion's searchlight was used in conjunction with 20-pounder canister shell whose grapeshot was deadly to men in the open. The infantry continually added to their protective fields of wire and mines, and the defence was further underpinned by the artillery's pre-planned Defensive Fire or DF targets, carefully ranged beforehand on likely enemy forming-up positions and approach routes.

The enemy responded aggressively to allied patrolling as both sides sought to dominate no man's land and take prisoners. Ambushes set on winter nights often failed because the 'snatch party', having lain motionless and silent for hours in the appalling cold, were unable to rise to their feet to seize their victim when the ambush was sprung. In the summer, the short nights were almost as unendurable; the waiting men were beset by ferocious insects and, on many occasions, by rats and venomous snakes. There was the constant threat of enemy ambush, or of a sudden flurry of artillery and mortar fire against any group of men caught in the open by the spectral light of flares. It speaks volumes for the adaptability and courage of the young conscripts who formed the greater part of every British battalion in the last two years of hostilities that they coped with this strange and dangerous existence with humour and patience. The experience of one battalion at this time serves to describe the life of them all.

The 1st Battalion of the Durham Light Infantry arrived in Korea in the summer of 1952. They fought no major battles nor were subjected to any major Chinese assaults, but the attrition of patrolling and of periodic bombardment cost them 17 killed and 151 all ranks wounded during their tours in the line. Lieutenant-Colonel Jeffreys, their commanding officer, kept a meticulous log of his battalion's experiences. A large proportion of his men were recruited from County Durham; many had been miners and, like other battalions raised in colliery areas, they knew how to dig. Jeffreys found his national servicemen excellent material; the junior subalterns had been given a good grounding at Eaton Hall Officer Cadet School where, in the Duke of Westminster's vast Victorian country palace outside Chester, a generation of young men were subjected to the disciplines of the parade ground by Foot Guards instructors (respectfully known as Drill Pigs), as well as the rudiments of their trade. Conscript officers for the Royal Artillery and Royal Armoured Corps went to Mons Officer Cadet School at Aldershot where they made the acquaintance of the fabled Regimental Serjeant-Major Brittain of the Coldstream Guards. After less than a year's service they were in Korea and in charge of 30 young soldiers.

The Durhams' National Service platoon commanders, as in every other British battalion, were of a very high order, maturing notably after only a few weeks in the front line. Of the battalion's junior ranks, well over half were national servicemen. There had been initial doubts as to the staying power of young conscripts, but Jeffreys found that they learnt quickly; they soon showed that 'they could match the endurance and fitness of the robust Australians in 28 Brigade, or the brave resourceful field-craftsman that their enemy the Chinese infantryman had proved to be'. Within weeks these young men had become 'imperturbable, mature, self-reliant fighting men; tough, with bags of spiritual strength'. Nearly half the battalion's corporals – in charge of a ten-man rifle section and frequently leading patrols in no man's land – were national servicemen and six of them were promoted to sergeant. To Jeffreys' sorrow, none could be persuaded to sign on as long-service regulars, whose pay was still derisory. Also, they were put off by the prospect of an arid two-year tour of duty in Egypt, the battalion's next destination.

As in every other British battalion the regular officers and NCOs were the backbone. The quality of the officers was assured by the fact that the best of the Light Infantry Brigade were clamouring to get to Korea, if only to escape the boredom of successive postings to Germany or Egypt. The regular junior ranks tended to be of mixed quality and good regular corporals were in short supply. A very high quality junior rank entry in the years immediately prior to the Second World War ensured that the experienced senior NCOs and warrant officers were excellent. As with the junior ranks, however, the pay offered to NCOs in the early 1950s, comparing most unfavourably with that available in the other Commonwealth contingents, was too low to retain the best men.

Maintenance of morale and professional standards was essential in the forward positions and went hand in hand. It was all too easy in Korea to become dirty and dispirited, and rigorous attention was paid in the Durhams to personal cleanliness, shaving, waste disposal and sanitation. High standards were not universal, even in the Commonwealth Division. The Canadian brigade, on the admission of one of its own commanders, was notoriously slack over the disposal of waste, the worst offenders being the French-Canadian Royale 22e Regiment, the 'Van-Dooz', who habitually threw empty ration cans and cartons out of their trenches, thereby betraying their position; on one occasion when they handed over their section of the line to an incoming Australian battalion, its commanding officer remarked sourly in the war diary that 'it was like taking on an open midden'. The Canadians, it appeared to the British, Australians and New Zealanders, did not quite fit in with the rest of the division; although relations with them at personal level were cordial, and whilst none begrudged the fine reputation gained earlier by the Princess Patricias, or the undoubted expertise of the Royal Canadian Horse Artillery, the Canadians seemed to keep others at arm's length. To many they seemed very American, steeped in a culture which owed less to Anglo-Saxon roots than to those of the great republic whose neighbours they were and whose culture they had now absorbed, far more than perhaps they themselves realized.

In all British battalions, trenches were swept clean and inspected daily, ammunition stacked neatly in bays in the sides of the trenches, and meticulous attention paid to cleanliness of weapons and equipment. Close attention was also paid to food; prepared whenever possible near the front line at platoon level by the battalion's Army Catering Corps and regimental cooks, it was eaten communally by platoons as a means of fostering corporate unit spirit, rather than cooked centrally and laboriously carried forward to the trenches in insulated containers. The rations were excellent; by mid-1951 the efficiency of the American logistic system ensured that an unbroken supply of fresh food reached the UN forces in Korea and, for new drafts accustomed to meagre rations in the United Kingdom, a new world of huge steaks, poultry, whole hams and salad vegetables grown by the US Quartermaster Corps in its hydroponic farms in Japan, came as a revelation. This fresh food was augmented by the standard British composite, or 'compo' ration, whose popularity rested on the inclusion of prosaic tinned items such as stew, baked beans, steak and kidney pudding, rich fruit cake, the inevitable bully beef, and a generous supply of strong tea. This mix of American fresh food and the staples of British army rations proved successful; there was considerable bartering between American units, who coveted the 'compo' puddings, and Commonwealth quartermasters seeking to increase the intake of fresh steaks, turkeys and chickens on festive occasions. No British army prior to the Korean War can have been so well fed in the field.

Across the UN line from coast to coast defensive positions were progressively wired in and heavily mined. Communication trenches were soon six to eight feet deep, with radiating fire positions on forward slopes. Dugouts on the reverse slopes housed platoon and company headquarters; these had at least five feet of overhead cover, prefabricated in concrete by the Royal Engineers and installed by the battalion's own assault pioneers. The British army had to re-learn the techniques of building substantial fieldworks, ignored since 1945. As any movement above ground during daylight drew instant enemy artillery or mortar fire it was essential to dig. Jeffreys calculated that once the Durhams had completed their defences, casualties during an enemy bombardment amounted to one for every 100 shells or mortar bombs received, and would have been even lower if all the fire trenches had been covered in.

Constant patrolling sought to locate the enemy, assess his intentions, and deny him the ability to approach so close that he could easily launch the night attacks he favoured. Listening patrols of two or three men lay out silently, keeping watch on the enemy lines. Fighting patrols led by subalterns or senior NCOs went out with the intention of bringing the Chinese patrols to battle and of taking prisoners. Standing patrols of four or five men, with radios, were placed in front of the main position to give early warning of enemy attack; they usually had a telephone line back to the company position behind them, so that artillery and mortar fire could be brought down instantly to defeat any hostile move. These patrols were capable of fighting until ordered in to the main position and constituted a form of outpost line. Young NCOs excelled at this hazardous work. If a standing patrol was forced in, the company on its immediate front stood to – all hands would be roused silently to man the fire trenches. The Durhams, however, preferred to reinforce a threatened standing patrol rather than call it in. Twice during their tour of duty, they were required to carry out full-blooded trench raids; these were only attempted when ordinary patrolling had failed to deliver any prisoners, and were high-risk undertakings. One raid failed because the targeted enemy position was empty on that night; the other, carried out at company strength, succeeded, but the assaulting platoon lost 15 men whilst overrunning the enemy position. The Chinese went to ground and the raiders, who had to pause and collect their own dead and wounded, narrowly escaped further losses by getting clear just before enemy artillery and mortars were unleashed on to the target area.

The battalions which did best under these conditions were those which relied on ruthless battle discipline of a sort which Jeffreys believed 'had gone out of fashion with the "democratic" approach favoured by some commanders'. By the middle of 1952 co-operation between artillery and infantry had reached a very high level in the division, for the gunners shared command posts right down to company level with 'their' infantry, for whom they felt a strong familial attachment. As telephone lines were invariably the first things to be lost in a heavy enemy bombardment – even when buried three feet underground – the gunners, who were highly proficient in its use, relied on radio. The British system placed great responsibility on junior gunner officers at the gun positions, whilst their troop and battery commanders were right forward with the supported units. The artillery regimental commanding officer placed himself alongside the supported brigade commander, and the divisional Commander Royal Artillery or CRA – a brigadier – was the gunnery adviser to the divisional commander and consequently a key member of his headquarters. The system was extremely flexible, guaranteeing almost instantaneous response to any call for help from an infantry unit in any of the Commonwealth Division's brigades. In dire emergency the entire weight of the divisional artillery could be brought down on a single target by a forward observer within three minutes; a similar situation in an American division would require up to twenty minutes to obtain a comparable response. In the opinion of the British, the American system was top-heavy; the weight of command lay too far to the rear and the staff was master, not servant, of the fighting troops.

In an American infantry division the commander, a major-general, was assisted by a brigadier-general as assistant commander, a full colonel as chief of staff, and two lieutenant-colonels responsible respectively for intelligence and operations. Each division normally consisted of three regiments commanded by full colonels, who were given little delegated power and tended to be overawed by the array of senior officers at divisional headquarters. A British division was also commanded by a major-general, supported by a lieutenant-colonel as General Staff Officer Grade 1 (GSO1) and departmental staffs covering the other branches such as intelligence, operations, manpower and logistics. Staff officers of all grades made it their business to visit the units on every possible occasion, thus establishing mutual confidence between head-quarters and subordinate formations and units. This was a conscious reaction to widespread accusations arising from the 1914–18 war when front-line sol-diers saw little of the despised 'gilded staff' whose members were alleged (often unfairly) never to have been near the front line. The three brigades were com-manded by brigadiers, fully briefed on their commander's plans and policies but given a great deal of autonomy in carrying them out. There were no con-flicting orders from an all-powerful divisional staff once battle was joined, when it became the staff's job to do all they could to support the fighting command-ers. The effect of the American structure was to stifle initiative at all levels of command, a characteristic noted frequently by Brigadier Coad in the early months of the campaign.

In the artillery of the Commonwealth Division, which became the dominant fighting arm after the autumn of 1951, the key man was probably the troop com-mander, one of two in each eight-gun battery. He would have had about six years' service, which meant that most of the troop commanders in the division had seen active service in the Second World War. He had trained his men and knew them personally, and was well versed in infantry and armoured tactics. Not only was he fully qualified as a forward observation officer but he could also act as the artil-lery adviser to the infantry company commander with whom he lived when in the line. His battery commander lived with the battalion commander. When

British troop commanders found themselves supporting American infantry units they discovered that their company commanders were often of less than three years' service and had little power of discretion or initiative in the running of their units.

In addition to the FOOs there were also the pilots of 1903 Air Observation Post Flight, Royal Air Force, all of them primarily expert artillery officers, whose ability to bring down fire, switch targets in mid-shoot, and co-opt the support of guns from neighbouring allied formations, vastly enhanced the fire support of the Commonwealth Division. The Air OP Flight had joined the Commonwealth Division as it formed in the summer of 1951, and 1913 Light Liaison Flight, whose aircraft were flown by officers and NCOs of the Glider Pilot Regiment, arrived some weeks later. Both units were based on an airstrip close to the banks of the Imjin, within half a mile of Fort George, the location of the Commonwealth divisional headquarters. Although the Light Liaison Flight's primary role was the provision of an aerial taxi service between the division and other headquarters and back to Kimpo airfield outside Seoul, its pilots soon found themselves augmenting the Air OP's surveillance and reconnaissance tasks; aircraft of both units were flown boldly up to five miles behind the enemy front line in order to find the cunningly concealed gun positions from which the Chinese harassed the Commonwealth forward areas. The presence of an Auster over the battlefield soon resulted in cessation of enemy fire, for the skill of the pilots in pinpointing targets, and directing accurate artillery fire, was quickly realized. In addition to maps, pilots carried annotated aerial photographs on which were marked all known hostile gun positions, headquarters and supply areas.

An impressive array of artillery was available in support of the Commonwealth Division; its three regiments of 25-pounders had been augmented by 5.5-inch guns and an additional battery of 4.2-inch mortars. There was plenty of American heavier artillery within range, available on call: this included 8-inch and 240mm howitzers, whose shells, if achieving a direct hit, could defeat the strongest Chinese bunker. When engaging targets well behind enemy lines, American 'Long Toms' – 155mm long-barrelled guns with a range of some 15 miles – were often used, but they were so inaccurate that the aerial observer often had to land for refuelling in the midst of a sortie before obtaining a 'target round'. There seemed to be unlimited supplies of ammunition for the Commonwealth Division's artillery and its expenditure was prodigal; one Air OP pilot spotted a company of Chinese infantry in the open and brought down on them the fire of no less than 72 25-pounder guns – all three of the division's gunner regiments – firing 11 rounds apiece. Having undergone several such experiences the Chinese responded by deploying hidden anti-aircraft guns in their forward area. By flying at six or eight thousand feet pilots were reasonably safe from the lighter 40mm guns, but still extremely vulnerable to the radar-controlled 85mm guns placed further to the enemy rear. Even a near miss from one of these would be lethal to a light aircraft, and the appearance of their characteristic black shell-bursts anywhere near an Air OP was the cue for a rapid departure into safer airspace. On occasion the Austers were taken up to 10,000 feet in order to gain views of the Chinese rear areas and escape the attentions of the anti-aircraft guns.

The Korean War was notable for the large-scale introduction of the helicopter. A few small Sikorskys had been used by the Americans in Burma in 1945 for liaison and casualty evacuation, and the first operational use after that, albeit on a modest scale, had been by the Royal Air Force in Malaya. Light helicopters were used by the American army in Korea from the beginning and they proliferated thereafter; senior commanders were able to visit forward units in a fraction of the time it would have taken to negotiate the roads, and hundreds of soldiers owed their lives to the prompt appearance of stretcher-fitted helicopters which carried them rapidly from regimental aid posts to the extraordinarily effective American mobile field hospitals, subsequently commemorated with remarkable fidelity in the book, film and then television series *MASH*. These were staffed by surgeons skilled in all forms of traumatic and life-saving operations, and by female nurses whose very presence so close to the front was a boost to morale.

One such MASH was located in the Pukhan valley at the time of the Chinese spring offensive of 1951. The officers of a neighbouring British unit, finding that in common with all American units in Korea this MASH had little or no access to alcohol, stimulated fraternization with gifts of NAAFI whisky and welcomed the doctors and nurses to their tented mess on every possible occasion. To signal their appreciation the Americans invited the British to a party which got under way the night the Chinese Fifth Phase Offensive opened. As the guests arrived they passed the entrance to the tent in which the surgeons were already hard at work, as helicopters brought in the first wounded; in the harsh light of the theatre lamps they presented a lurid picture, working up to their elbows in blood to keep pace with the stream of casualties. The party was in an adjacent tent, its gaiety in no way diminished by the surgical drama only a few yards away. Guests, curious as to how the Americans were going to surmount the problem of providing enough drink for visitors from several United Nations units, soon found that the 'Uncle Sam's fruit cup', being ladled from an up-ended searchlight reflector bowl into enamel mugs, consisted of American tinned fruit salad awash in pure surgical alcohol. If the desired effect was to create an instant bacchanale, it was triumphantly achieved. A British subaltern addressed the nurse in charge of the ladle as 'Sister', as he would her British equivalent in the Queen Alexandra's Nursing Corps. This was a mistake; the nurse rounded on him furiously: 'See here, Limey. Don't "Sister" me. I am a Lootenant and don't you forget it.'

Larger helicopters were introduced into Korea at an early stage, proving invaluable in the rescue of allied pilots from inside enemy territory. By 1952 US Army and Marine cargo helicopter units were equipped with the Sikorsky S-55; on occasion these were used to lift infantry companies complete with their support weapons and equipment to the tops of mountains, saving hard labour and time. Had the war not developed after mid-1951 into a stalemate they would have been used to confer enhanced mobility on the ground forces. Even the most ardent proponents of airborne warfare were compelled to see that the day of the massed parachute and glider descent into enemy-held territory was unlikely ever to be repeated. The helicopter's ability to move troops rapidly to the point where a tactical decision was required, to deliver them as formed bodies ready to go immediately into action, sustaining them in the field and if necessary lifting them to another objective, had endowed the foot soldier and his supporting weaponry with the greatest single enhancement of his battlefield mobility since infantry had been mounted on horseback in the seventeenth century.

CHAPTER 26

The Secret War

As the opposing armies fought up and down the Korean peninsula another campaign, hidden from the world's press, had been taking place. As the Americans and South Koreans retreated towards the Pusan bridgehead in the opening weeks of the war the need for stay-behind parties became apparent. There was, however, no organization for setting these up. The Central Intelligence Agency, set up by Congress in 1947 at Truman's insistence with the aim of conducting strategic intelligence operations abroad, had an office in Tokyo. Although Truman ordered MacArthur to allow the CIA to operate in Far East Command, neither he nor Willoughby, his intelligence chief, were well disposed towards what they regarded as 'Washington spooks' and offered as little assistance as possible, forbidding their staffs to deal with the CIA except through Willoughby himself. In July 1950 the CIA, undeterred, increased their Tokyo staff and Lieutenant-Colonel Kramer of the US Marine Corps, appointed to run their Korean operation, set up his training base on the island of Cheju, off the South Korean coast. A converted destroyer, the USS *Horace A. Bass*, modified to take over 150 raiding personnel, was made available to Kramer for the transport of landing parties and underwater demolition teams. The submarine *Perch* was soon added to Kramer's fleet; it could carry 100 raiders, with their inflatable boats. It was intended that *Bass* would operate in the shallow waters off the west coast, whilst *Perch* operated off the east. Kramer set up a top secret advanced base on an island near Pusan, from which the civilian population was evacuated.

As the retreat continued, stay-behind parties were recruited by 8th Army from North and South Korean volunteers. Little use was made of them until after the Inchon landings. They were run from 8th Army by the Counter-Intelligence Corps of the US Army, whilst clandestine warfare cells were set up in the headquarters of I and X Corps. The cell in HQ I Corps consisted of a Tactical Intelligence Liaison Office or TILO, with a small Anglo-American staff of officers and NCOs experienced in clandestine operations. The Britons were all former intelligence or SAS personnel.

As the lines stabilized following the UN advance into North Korea the organization expanded. Safe houses were set up all over South Korea for training purposes and three methods of penetrating into the north were practised: boat landings, line crossing and parachuting. From December 1950, following the Chinese offensive, numerous sea landings were made along the Han estuary and amongst the hundreds of small islands along the west coast of North Korea. These were relatively easy to approach because of the lack of North Korean coastwatchers. Line crossers went out with allied foot patrols and were left behind enemy lines, having agreed the locations for their recovery later by other patrols. This was a dangerous business, and several agents were shot by mistake by the friendly forces sent to retrieve them. In the first year there were few parachute insertions owing to lack of equipment.

In the early days the passage of intelligence to the rear was slow and unfiltered. Lack of liaison between the services compounded difficulties and in the autumn of 1950 the Far East Command Intelligence Liaison Committee was set up, reporting directly to Willoughby in Tokyo. A special unit was formed to control all 8th Army's intelligence activities; known as 'Combined Command Reconnaissance Activities, Korea, 8240th Army Unit' (CCRAK or, more popularly, 'Seacrack'), its base was in Pusan. By January 1951 it had been decided to open Special Forces bases on two islands off the North Korean west coast, Yongpyong-do and Cho-do. There was an immediate objection from the CIA which, unknown to Willoughby's staff, was already operating undercover from both. The CIA's appeal was upheld in Washington, thereby further straining official relations with Far East Command. As if two separate intelligence organizations were not enough, the US Air Force produced a third, a detachment of the 6004th Air Intelligence Squadron, whose functions were sabotage, demolition and guerrilla operations. Its commander got in touch with the CIA's partisans on Cho-do and started to lay on operations independently of 8th Army's intelligence branch, which believed the Air Force unit was there purely to obtain air intelligence, operate a fighter control and early warning radar, and to help shot-down pilots. It was some months before this was sorted out and demarcations were agreed; henceforth the US Air Force would stick to air intelligence, using its radars at Cho-do on the west coast and Yo-do, a small island just off Wonsan harbour on the east coast.

A major clandestine operation preceded the Inchon landings. On 1 September 1950 the British destroyer HMS *Charity*, escorted by the cruiser HMS *Jamaica*, landed parties of Korean partisans on the islands lining the Flying Fish Channel leading into Inchon harbour. The landings were made at dawn; when a lone North Korean sentry spotted the boats in the dim light he opened fire but immediately received a single 6-inch round from *Jamaica* which silenced him. When the enemy garrison on the next island saw the cruiser bearing down on them they hoisted a white flag. By the time the main landing took place on 15 September, most of the offshore islands in the Inchon area had been taken. The majority of those put ashore were ROK soldiers but they were joined by numerous volunteers and the Americans soon trained many Korean civilians for this hazardous work.

As the UN advance pushed north after Inchon, the allies found unexpected evidence of resistance to the Pyongyang regime, particularly in the province of Hwanghae-do, in the south-west of North Korea, where the abolition of private land ownership had proved surprisingly unpopular. The conscription decrees of 1947 had also driven many young men into the hills rather than join the NKPA and they were waging a successful guerrilla war against the government. Hundreds of partisans emerged from the mountains with the arrival of the UN forces, and thousands of known communists and their supporters were summarily executed. When the tide turned in November 1950 the guerrillas took to the offshore islands, to be warmly welcomed by the UN-backed partisans and irregulars already installed there.

Ridgway, unlike his predecessor Walker, was keen to harness the patriotism of the irregulars and ordered his intelligence staff to provide all the weaponry they needed. A 'Miscellaneous Division' of 8th Army's staff was set up under Colonel John McGee; a West Point graduate, he had been captured in the Philippines by the Japanese, escaped when the ship carrying him to Japan was torpedoed and spent the remainder of the war as a highly successful leader of Filipino guerrillas. He established a firm base on the island of Paengnyong-do off the west coast of North Korea where the ROK navy was already running a refugee camp. Strongly fortified, the island became the headquarters of Partisan Command. Its long beaches were suitable as an airstrip capable of taking C-47s, and tank landing ships could get in with heavy loads. From here McGee ran dozens of partisan groups on islands all up the west coast, manned by 'regiments' bearing the names of the mainland districts from which they had been recruited. The Americans devised an efficient training organization which by sheer improvisation, and without formal training manuals, gave the irregulars a workable command structure with its own flexible operating procedures. Leaders were democratically chosen from among leading citizens such as mayors, police chiefs, local government officers and school teachers. They all had to satisfy the selection panels as to their courage, hardihood and readiness to risk death on a daily basis. Weapons came from many sources, mainly American but with a strong leaven of captured material of Russian and Chinese origin.

Once trained, the irregulars had to be landed on the mainland. This meant coping with huge tides, which left miles of glutinous mud at low water, and demanded the intimate local knowledge of the helmsmen on the fishing boats which had to be used, for no helicopters were available. The boats were powered by 'hot-head' diesels, primitive and noisy but requiring little maintenance. For landings close inshore where silence was necessary, 'wiggle boats' propelled by oars, or sailing junks were used. Later came special boats with the tophamper of sailing junks but high-speed planing hulls and powerful diesels giving speeds of over 25 knots. Once safely ashore, the radios, ammunition and supplies were carried on 'A' frames or in the 'honey buckets' used by peasants to carry human ordure to manure the fields. Messages were often carried in the dungbags suspended below the tails of oxen to conserve every fragment of organic fertilizer.

Early in 1951 McGee began to plan for parachuted deep penetration operations. A new secret headquarters was established in Pusan with the cover name of '8th Army Liaison Office for Oceanic Research', and its students were referred to as 'harbour engineer trainees'. McGee had already directed several sea landings along the east coast to sabotage the coast road and rail links, using ROK marines and an American demolition team, but the North Koreans had quickly repaired the damage. A second attempt was made in March 1951, using US Army Rangers and partisans. This time part of the force was to be dropped by parachute. The target was a railway tunnel well inland on the key railway line leading cross-country from the east coast.

Codenamed 'Virginia', the drop took place on the night of 15/16 March. Conditions over the drop zone were bad, with thick cloud, an unexpected squall, and thick snow on the ground. It was bitterly cold in the plane and most of the party were airsick. The actual drop was calamitous, landing seven miles adrift owing to faulty navigation. The party arrived on the ground in four scattered groups; fortunately there were no landing injuries and all the kit was recovered. But no one knew where they were. As the groups made contact with each other the full force of a winter storm broke on them; the intense cold killed the radio batteries and contact was lost with the mission control aircraft circling high overhead. After a fearsome cross-country march the party arrived at their target on the 18th. The reconnaissance party, wearing NKPA uniforms, reported that the tunnel was in use as a barracks for a Chinese engineer battalion and heavily defended. It was clearly impractical to proceed with this target, but the radio was still not working and the mission control plane could not be consulted.

Back at base, the entire party was written off as lost on 21 March. However, after a council of war they had decided to march east and blow up a tunnel near the shore; reaching it on 23 March they discovered that this too was full of Chinese troops. They buried their loads of explosive with a time fuze, and marched on towards where they thought an allied ship might be offshore. Five days later their radio suddenly came to life and contact was made with a light observation aircraft which had been listening out on the 'Virginia' frequency. Supplies were dropped to the party that night but the enemy had picked up the trail.

Patrolling off the coast, also listening for signals from 'Virginia', were the British destroyer *Alacrity* and the American cruiser *St Paul*. These relayed signals to the task force further out to sea, which had two helicopters each capable of lifting two American or three Korean passengers at an extreme radius of 40 miles. Taking off from a tank landing ship and escorted by fighters from the carrier USS *Coral Sea* the helicopters flew inshore on 30 March; by this time the ground party were surrounded and under heavy fire. The first helicopter was shot down within 200 yards of the landing site; the second managed to rescue a few men one at a time by using its rescue sling before the landing zone was overrun. The few survivors made for the hills, taking with them the gallant pilot of the shot-down helicopter. He and the other surviving American became detached from the Korean group and marched for the Diamond Mountains, which lay between them and the allied lines. The pilot, feeling that he was holding the other up, surrendered at a police post; he had been marching in his flimsy aircrew clothing and fur-lined flying boots. The other American was captured the next day, only two miles from friendly lines. Both survived their subsequent captivity, although abominably treated. Two Korean members of the group who succeeded in regaining allied lines were subsequently identified as double agents and executed by the ROK authorities after interrogation.

During the winter of 1950/1 many heroic small actions were fought by Korean partisans as the United Nations forces fell back from the Yalu. Some units volunteered to stay behind and set up partisan groups in the heart of North Korea. One such group, codenamed 'Donkey', acted on intelligence which had reported an important meeting of communist officials in a village police station. They lay up on the night of 20/21 March 1951 near the village; next day they observed the arrival of numerous high-placed military and civil personnel. After dark, as the meeting got under way, they cut the telephone lines to the village and attached explosive charges to the doors and windows of the building. When these went off, a merciless killing party went in to finish off all who had survived the explosions. The bodies of 27 officials, police and army officers and their wives, were counted. All the police vehicles were set alight, five oxcarts of ammunition and weapons were seized, and surplus rations were distributed to the delighted local population.

Helped by a friendly garage mechanic, the group next attacked an army vehicle park; then, on the night of 18/19 April, it took on its biggest target, the town of Sinchon where 1,700 citizens were imprisoned in a warehouse on suspicion of being UN supporters. The military vehicle park was fired, and the police station destroyed with all inside it; of the captives, only 400 were fit enough to make a getaway. These left with the partisan group; those who could not travel were killed a few hours later when the Chinese and North Korean army attacked the warehouse, thinking the partisans were still there.

The escape of the 'Donkey' group was hampered by the liberated civilians, and the pursuit caught up before it reached the safety of the hills. In the subsequent fire-fight over fifty of the partisans died, as did most of the civilian escapers.

'Donkey', undeterred, broke up into small groups, moved 30 miles, and recommenced operations. Using stolen NKPA uniforms they set up roadblocks to obtain supplies. As most of the drivers were civilians working under duress they were set loose, but any found carrying a party card were shot on the spot. In May 1951 'Donkey' was still active in the Sinchon area, blowing bridges, ambushing convoys and cutting communications. On 11 May it attacked a mining complex, freeing hundreds of political prisoners working there. The Chinese now sent in two divisions of troops to hunt the group down. By early in July it had been reduced to a core of 15 men, who were able to get offshore later in the month to an island held by another 'Donkey' group.

British raiding forces had been present since early in the campaign. After their harrowing experiences on the north-eastern sector with the 1st US Marine Division in November 1950, the Royal Marines of 41 Commando reorganized in Japan, where they prepared for further operations. Colonel Drysdale devised a series of raids on the Korean east coast with the aim of cutting the vulnerable railway and road link from Manchuria to Hungnam and down to Wonsan. On 2 April 1951, 21 officers and 226 men of the commando set out to cut a vulnerable length of rail track on the Korean east coast. A cruiser and two destroyers had been allotted for gunfire support of what was intended to be a daylight demonstration of United Nations strength. The American carriers *Philippine Sea* and *Boxer* were to provide close air support and six minesweepers accompanied the force. The commando was also given an American reconnaissance team for the control of naval gunfire and air support as well as an underwater demolition team.

After two careful rehearsals, the force assembled off the Korean coast and moved in towards the beach early on 8 April. The covering force went ashore first, followed by the demolition engineers who placed explosive charges which produced a gap in the railway over 100 feet long and 16 feet deep. Before withdrawing to the boats after over eight hours ashore, dozens of anti-personnel mines were laid. The entire operation had been achieved without losing a man. As the ships put out to sea, the gratifying sound of detonating anti-personnel mines could be heard ashore as the North Koreans attempted to repair the damage to the embankment.

Following this raid, the commando was put ashore on the island of Yo-do inside Wonsan harbour, a great natural anchorage whose mouths, over ten miles apart, encompass a bay littered with islands of varying size. A number of these were occupied by UN forces; one of them, Hwangto-do, lay under three miles from the coastal batteries guarding the entrance to the inner harbour. Of the other four occupied islands, Yo-do was the largest, with its own 400-yard airstrip. Much of Wonsan Bay was regularly swept for mines, allowing boldly handled American destroyers to enter the harbour and provide fire support for the marines. Wonsan was thus placed under siege, denying it as a forward base for the communists on the eastern sector of the front. By the autumn of 1951 the commandos had some 800 ROK marines under command and were carrying out frequent nuisance raids to 'keep the coast alive', as their new commanding officer, Lieutenant-Colonel Grant, put it. They were finally pulled out in December to Sasebo for disbandment. Theirs had been an eventful tour of duty; some personnel went to the 3rd Commando Brigade in Malaya, the rest returned to England where formal disbandment took place in February 1952. They had taken part in some 18 amphibious landings in addition to the Inchon operation; 31 of their number had been killed in action and a further 19 surviving prisoners returned from communist prison camps in 1953. Their influence had been out of all proportion to the size of the unit, which seldom exceeded a strength of 300.

If the naval coastal patrols and the commando raids were more or less public knowledge, covert operations continued throughout the campaign on both coasts. With the enthusiastic support of General Van Fleet, Far East Command allotted more support than ever to the 'Miscellaneous Group' which had steadily evolved from its modest origins around Pusan. Colonel McGee discovered in mid-1951 that the various South Korean groups were waging war against each other. The partisans, it transpired, were true warriors, itching to get at the enemy, whereas the irregulars were led by a man who avoided action himself and regarded his men as a private army, for use in building up his own political base whilst purloining supplies and weapons destined for the aggressive and spirited partisans. McGee took steps to arrest this anarchy. He was determined that the best of the newly available equipment should go to the partisans, especially the most prized items, converted air-sea rescue launches fitted for armament and capable of a range of 700 miles at 20 knots.

The British contribution to special operations was considerable. A small SAS liaison detachment was based on the island of Kanghwa-do. Captain Ellery Anderson, a Royal Ulster Rifles officer detached to McGee's command early in 1951, was sent to command a semi-permanent base on the mainland of North Korea. Codenamed 'Spitfire' its operational area extended from just south of the 38th parallel for 80 miles to the north. The northern boundary was the Wonsan–Pyongyang road, and the area covered some 4,800 square miles of sparsely populated mountainous terrain. A main dropping zone (DZ) was set up in the upper Imjin valley, close to the river's source. McGee's intention was to run 'Spitfire' with a mixed team of American, British and Korean personnel.

One of Anderson's first recruits for the 'Spitfire' team was Second Lieutenant Leo Adams-Acton of the Royal Northumberland Fusiliers. He had gone to Korea with his battalion but his thirst for adventure, combined with ability to speak Cantonese (he had been brought up in China), better suited him for special operations than life in the battalion. McGee believed him to be fully SAS-trained, which he was not; Adams-Acton also omitted to tell him that he was not even a parachutist. On his own initiative he made some practice jumps with the Americans and attended specialist sabotage classes before setting out to join Anderson. Mindful of the disastrous experience of the 'Virginia' operation, McGee issued Adams-Acton's party with extra radios of a type which the enemy could not monitor, while pathfinders, under Anderson, would secure the DZ and mark it properly before calling Adams-Acton in.

The pathfinders landed at 10 p.m. on 18 June, an auspicious date for the British army, marking as it does the Battle of Waterloo. Anderson was injured on landing, but the DZ was quickly cleared for the supply drop which followed. A base camp was set up in the hills a few miles away in an area shunned by the locals who believed it to be haunted by the spirits of hundreds of Chinese prisoners and their Japanese guards who had died there of bubonic plague during the Second World War.

Anderson's party made an astonishing discovery; only a short distance from the DZ they found a series of cunningly concealed rest camps for use by Chinese troops during daylight hours. Their locations were accurately fixed and passed to headquarters and a devastating bombing attack was made on them within twenty-four hours. Anderson and his men watched spectacular explosions as dumps were ignited, and later saw Chinese being thrown in their hundreds into massed graves. Two days later another series of camps was dealt with in the same way. The Chinese, realizing they were under observation, began to scour the countryside. Anderson and other casualties of the initial jump were taken out by helicopter on 23 June.

Fearing that their location had now been compromised the rest of the advance party moved to a new area where they were joined by Adams-Acton and the main body three days later. Adams-Acton's inexperience as a parachutist resulted in a badly cut knee on landing; Fusilier Mills, his signaller, and most of the others ended up in trees, and the supply drop which followed them down was widely scattered. After four days, Adams-Acton's knee was badly infected and penicillin had to be dropped to him. On the night of 5/6 July the supply drop pilot could not locate the DZ in the dark and circled overhead until daylight before finding it, thereby revealing the party's presence to the enemy already scouring the area. Burying much of their kit, the entire group took to the mountains; almost at once the scouts ahead of the main body were ambushed. When Adams-Acton arrived on the scene he could see only fourteen pools of blood in the enemy's ambush position; of his own scouts there was no sign. All his supply caches, complete with reserve radios and stores, had fallen into enemy hands.

On the night of the 10th Adams-Acton made radio contact with an aircraft overhead but his batteries failed during the conversation and he decided to march the survivors out to allied lines. As the crow flies the distance is about 70 miles, but the cross-country route adopted by Adams-Acton involved a journey of 150 miles through hostile territory. He left a message in a pre-arranged dead-letter drop, buried all surplus gear and set off. That night, another radio party was dropped by parachute, found the letter box, and followed Adams-Acton. After two weeks on the march they were within earshot of the battle line. They were hiding in a disused bunker when a party of North Korean soldiers stumbled upon them. Adams-Acton ordered his men to escape and took on the Koreans single-handed with his pistol, shooting four before closing with the others, using his gun as a club; his men, hearing the fight, came back to his rescue, killed the remaining enemy, and continued their march south. At dawn on the 25th they crossed no man's land; hearing an American patrol blundering through the thicket ahead, they identified themselves unmistakably by shouting 'Hold your fire, assholes; friendlies coming through'. After debriefing at headquarters 8th Army they were flown to Japan. Adams-Acton was awarded an immediate Military Cross for his outstanding performance.

To avoid further compromises of special operations by daylight supply drops, a specialist airdrop unit was formed in Far East Air Force, which rendered excellent service for the rest of the war. However, it was clear that the insertion of identifiably non-Asian troops deep behind enemy lines raised insuperable problems, whereas Koreans could easily pass for anyone. They could also exist for weeks on simple rations without detriment to their health; five or six men could subsist for three weeks on 100 pounds of rice and ten pounds of dried fish. The same weight of American field rations would sustain one man for a mere eighteen days. From now on, it was decided, no American or British operators would go on long-term mainland missions although they would be used for coastal raiding parties.

The South Korean partisans carried out 158 attacks in July and August 1951 in which they killed 1,200, wounded 2,000, and captured 150 enemy troops. Several trains deep inside North Korea were destroyed, together with 150 lorries and several key bridges. However, opposition was growing, for several communist divisions had been deployed in the counter-guerrilla role. In September the enemy struck back at the islands off the west coast occupied by the various 'Donkey' groups. Some of these were less than a mile offshore and could be reached by walking across the sandbanks at low tide. 'Donkey 4' was on the twin islands of Yuk-do and Ojak-do; another island, Yongui-do, was held by 'Donkey 8'. The enemy attacked all three on the night of 6/7 September.

Their plan was to send infantry wading across from the mainland as intensive mortar fire kept the defenders' heads down. At Yuk-do the defences had been cunningly prepared; mutually supporting machine-gun bunkers had been carefully sited, roofed with layers of railway sleepers. Two belts of wire had been prominently laid above high water, easily visible from the mainland. What the attackers did not know was that inside the inner wire belt were dozens of buried napalm and high explosive charges. The garrison also had mortars zeroed on to the wire and the beaches. The attack came as no surprise as agents on the mainland had kept the defenders well primed. The North Koreans estimated that it would take them an hour to wade the thousand yards to Yuk-do. It took them three to get to the wire, and as they reached it, the defenders fired dozens of parachute flares to illuminate the exhausted attackers as they floundered in the mud. Those who managed to crawl through the outer wire perished on the napalm mines. At dawn, the defenders counted 286 bodies on the shore; many more had been washed away by the tide now covering the killing zone. 'Donkey 8' had fared less well; although the attack was eventually repelled, the defenders lost their American commander and many others.

Having been told that he could not be sent on further deep penetration missions, Adams-Acton was reassigned to training duties. He did not care for this and approached McGee's successor, Colonel Koster, asked for a more active role and was posted to 'Leopard' group on the west coast island of Paengnyong-do. Arriving there on 15 September he was sent first to Cho-do, but found this too quiet, and asked for a posting as 'Leopard' liaison officer to one of the 'Donkey' groups on the remoter islands; assigned to 'Donkey 15' on the island of Taehwa-do, he arrived there with his signaller, Sergeant Brock, on 1 October and quickly made friends with the Korean commander, Kim Ung-su, a kindred spirit afire with aggression. They impulsively planned a raid on two small islands 12 miles to the north and five from the mainland. These were thought to be only lightly held but when the partisans landed early on 9 October, the North Korean police garrison put up a stiff fight, losing ten killed and 12 wounded before surrendering. The partisans shot the wounded on the spot. There was no resistance on the other island. Adams-Acton and his new friend sat down to plan a more ambitious operation: the recapture of the important island of Sinmi-do.

Tragically, the plan was betrayed. On 13 October the Chinese and North Koreans sent reinforcements from the mainland to the threatened island. By midnight several hundred Chinese infantry lay in wait. The partisans sailed into a trap; fortunately the Chinese fire was inaccurate and the landing parties managed to get back to their junks with fewer than 20 casualties. The Chinese, scenting victory, began to land on many of the partisan-held islands. Adams-Acton and Kim concentrated their force on Taehwa-do, where they dug strong defences. A CIA patrol boat arrived off the island on 29 November to evacuate

American and British personnel in the event of a successful enemy attack. The Chinese, using a number of captured American 105mm field guns, shelled the island from the mainland on the following night. At the same time, Chinese troops came ashore from motor junks. When asked to give some fire support the commander of the CIA boat steered away from the scene.

By 2 a.m. the enemy were all round Adams-Acton's command post, a substantial bunker in the middle of the island. He made radio contact with HMS *Cossack* and called down fire on his own position; this helped to deter the enemy who were closing in on all sides, when the destroyer's 4.7-inch guns scored a direct hit on the roof of the command bunker, collapsing it on its inmates. Their radio went off the air at 2.19 a.m. as the island fell. The Chinese dug Adams-Acton and his naval colleague Lieutenant Lankford, together with their signallers, out of the wrecked bunker. All four were taken to Sinuiju on the Yalu for interrogation and were initially treated in a civilized manner; their fortunes changed for the worse, however, when they were handed over to the North Koreans a few weeks later. After many vicissitudes and considerable mistreatment following several ill-judged escape attempts, Adams-Acton was shot dead in the course of another attempt, only weeks before the armistice in 1953.

After the fall of Taehwa-do the partisan movement lost much of its momentum. The enemy counter-intelligence organization had improved considerably, many Koreans had been 'turned' (one of the reasons for the betrayal of Adams-Acton's plans) and this was not sufficiently appreciated by those at 8th Army headquarters responsible for covert operations. Most of the islands off the west coast in partisan hands, however, managed to hold out until the armistice of 1953 when their garrisons were withdrawn to the south.

CHAPTER 27

Naval Operations

The prompt British and Commonwealth naval response at the outset of the war owed much to the fortuitous presence of several units of the Royal Navy and Royal Australian Navy in Japanese waters. Their early involvement in bombardment of the east coast roads and railways has already been described.

Although the North Korean war plan had included numerous amphibious landings behind the retreating ROK forces, these were quickly dealt with by allied naval supremacy. The presence of strong American and Commonwealth naval forces close inshore reassured the ROKs that they had powerful allies, and the ability of the fleet to provide them with heavy and accurate fire support did much to sustain their morale. With mastery of the sea off both coasts, the allies ensured the safety of the sea lanes from Japan to Korea. Tank landing ships of the War Department Fleet and chartered merchant ships operated a ferry service throughout the campaign, carrying troops and freight across the Straits of Shimonoseki to Pusan. The former Yangtse river steamer *Wusueh* was chartered from the firm of Swire and Butterfield in Hong Kong and converted to house the Flag Officer Second-in-Command Far East Fleet and his staff in Sasebo harbour where, rechristened and commissioned as HMS *Ladybird*, she served as the Commonwealth naval headquarters ship until the end of the war. With living accommodation for a crew of around 200 officers, ratings and marines, she provided space for communications and cypher staffs, their equipment, briefing rooms, and the admiral's map room.

Although shore bombardment, coastal patrols, minesweeping and the support of special forces activities occupied much of the naval effort throughout the war, a key naval contribution was that of naval aviation. American, British and Australian carriers operating as part of Task Force 77 off the Korean east coast, and others working off the west coast, were able to provide rapid-reaction close air support in the early months when most land-based air support had to fly from bases in Japan. It was only after September 1950 and the subsequent allied advance up the peninsula that airfields fell into UN hands on which piston and jet-engined attack aircraft could be based.

There were considerable differences of scale between the big American carriers and the light fleet carriers used by the Commonwealth navies off Korea. Apart from the limited size of their flight decks, the latter carried aircraft initially of Second World War vintage, such as the Seafire, flimsy and prone to structural damage following heavy deck landings, and the Firefly, whose weight meant that even when the ship was steaming at 23 knots – about the best that a light fleet carrier could manage – a catapult launch was required. The situation was somewhat improved after the first relief of carriers on station when it became normal to use a mixed complement of robust Sea Fury fighters and Fireflies.

The British light fleet carriers were ill suited for operations off Korea; built hurriedly during the war and far slower than comparable American ships, their relatively light construction led to damage in heavy seas. They pitched and rolled abominably in a heavy swell, and their single catapult – which required three hours to rig – made launching a Firefly strike a long-drawn-out affair; furthermore, the catapults had only a month's operational life before major overhaul. The steam catapult pioneered by the Royal Navy, and soon adopted world-wide, was not yet fully developed and none was fitted to the light fleet carriers. Accommodation for the ships' companies and air groups was horribly cramped, poorly heated in winter and without air-conditioning in the stifling Korean summer. When an admiral came aboard with his staff, matters became even worse. Several of the carriers showed alarming signs of wear and tear after only weeks on station; both *Theseus* and *Triumph* experienced failures of their stern glands with resultant flooding along the propeller shafts. None of the Commonwealth carriers boasted armament heavier than Bofors guns and it was fortunate that the allies enjoyed virtual mastery of the air throughout the campaign, except within the operational range of the Chinese MiG fighters flying from their sanctuaries across the Manchurian border.

Supporting the Commonwealth naval aviation was the repair and ferry carrier HMS *Unicorn*. Built with extra decks in order to accommodate additional hangar space, her appearance was oddly top-heavy. She was fortunately on station in the Far East in the summer of 1950 and in the following years proved an inestimable asset, one of her first tasks being to transport the Middlesex Regiment from Hong Kong to Pusan. During the next three years she was used frequently as a troop and cargo ship as well as in her primary role of floating workshop and aircraft ferry plying between Singapore, Hong Kong, Kure and Sasebo. Like all other naval ships, *Unicorn* had to be fitted into a complex programme of refits at the Far East Fleet's home base in Singapore. Vice-Admiral Andrewes' staffs and their successors therefore had to cope with a host of non-operational matters whilst maintaining a balanced fleet in support of the United Nations.

Many British and Australian naval aircrews underwent extraordinary experiences during their operational tours. On 26 October 1951, five Fireflies with full warloads were catapulted off HMAS *Sydney*. Their target was a railway tunnel near Chaeryong, south of Sariwon, well inside enemy lines in North Korea. It was to be attacked using bombs fuzed at 25 seconds, placed as accurately as possible into the tunnel's mouth. At this time, all United Nations aviators faced heavy ground fire; only the previous day one of *Sydney*'s Sea Furies had been hit by anti-aircraft fire over the Han estuary and had to make a forced landing on a sandbank, the pilot rescued almost immediately by the frigate HMS *Amethyst*. On the 26th, the Fireflies found their target without difficulty but one was immediately hit by ground fire. Its pilot made a creditable crash landing in paddy-fields some three miles from the target, and an American rescue helicopter was called for. At once enemy troops were spotted moving to the scene.

A dramatic race now took place; whilst the helicopter was on the way in failing light, the remaining Fireflies circled protectively above. Within minutes they were joined by several Meteor fighters of 77 Squadron RAAF and four Sea Furies. The downed pilot and his observer calmly collected their survival gear and personal weapons before leaving the aircraft; it was known that Chinese and North Korean soldiers were under orders to fire at the cockpits of downed UN aircraft in order to stop the crews using their radios. The plane had landed just before 4 p.m.; comforted by the knowledge that the helicopter was on its way the two airmen saw that the enemy were getting close and by 5.15, as night closed in, they were firing their Owen sub-machine-guns at Chinese infantry. The Meteors, short of fuel, had to pull off and return to base. Whilst dropping a message assuring the survivors that rescue was on the way, the flight commander's Firefly was hit by ground fire but managed to get to safety at Kimpo. Then the Sea Furies had to leave.

The rescue helicopter, crewed by American naval airmen, was meanwhile close at hand, having exceeded its designed maximum airspeed by some 20 knots. Under heavy fire, it landed alongside the downed airmen at 5.25. By now the enemy were less than 25 yards away and the helicopter crewman leapt out and shot two of them. The final take-off in gathering darkness was dramatic, the enemy having crept up to within ten yards. As the machine became airborne the resolute crewman shot another Chinese soldier who was about to open fire at less than ten yards' range. By the time the helicopter reached Kimpo it was pitch dark; it had flown well over a hundred miles in each direction to bring off this daring rescue. There were to be many more in the following two years; the Korean War saw helicopters saving hundreds of aircrew from death or captivity. No praise can be too high for the American helicopter pilots and crewmen who made it a point of honour to snatch downed allied airmen from under the guns of the enemy, often deep into hostile territory or out at sea.

Operating from the light fleet carriers was a fraught business. Under the pressures of active service it is hardly surprising that hair-raising crashes were frequent; aircraft often returned to the carrier suffering from battle damage, and adverse weather conditions added to the perils. This was before the advent of the angled deck or sophisticated approach lights and everything depended on the pilot, directed by the 'batsman' with his manual signals, making a positive engagement with his arrester hook on to the rows of wires positioned across the rear end of the constricted flight deck. If the approach was too high the batsman waved the pilot away for another attempt, but there were many occasions when aircraft failed to hook on and careered towards the bows, where further aircraft were parked under protection of the crash barriers. At the best of times the flight deck of a carrier engaged in flying operations is one of the most lethal places on earth; on active service, in poor weather and visibility, and in high seas, the danger factors increase out of all proportion. Landing a damaged aircraft under such conditions, often with the pilot's windscreen obscured by ice and salt spray, demanded the highest standards of skill and courage. Despite this an extremely high level of operational flying was sustained; HMAS *Sydney*, which replaced the British carrier HMS *Glory* in the autumn of 1951 off the east coast, flew 89 sorties in one day – at the time a record – and in the next two months flew a total of 1,000 operational missions. In one eight-day period her aircraft flew 401 sorties, hit 14 bridges in bombing attacks, sank 14 junks and destroyed three railway tunnels.

To gain supremacy over the inshore waters on both coasts it was necessary for United Nations ships to venture close to shore batteries; on occasions this could lead to embarrassing mishaps: on 8 January 1951 the enthusiasm of the captain of the Thai frigate HMTS *Prasae* took his ship close inshore whilst bombarding the island of Cho-do, off the west coast; she went firmly aground on shifting sandbanks and had to be abandoned five days later. After a while it became apparent that a disproportionate amount of naval effort was being applied to shore bombardment as the enemy batteries were continually on the move. Admiral Scott-Moncrieff, who succeeded Admiral Andrewes, therefore granted considerable autonomy to his frigate and destroyer captains in their choice of targets and firing positions. Soon they were penetrating deep into the dangerous channels off the west coast, in order to attack light craft used by the enemy to carry supplies southwards down the coast. For this role the Canadian destroyers were particularly well suited, as they carried radar of more advanced design than any of the other Commonwealth ships.

By the end of 1951 there was continual activity on and around the western islands, many garrisoned by South Korean irregular forces and guerrillas. The North Koreans reacted furiously in December when they realized the extent of allied incursions; it had become 8th Army policy to hold as many offshore islands as possible in order to strengthen the UN bargaining position at the truce talks, but this was easier said than done as it strained naval resources, and senior naval commanders, American as well as Commonwealth, made unavailing representations to UN Command in Tokyo. The island occupation policy was upheld and a number of fierce actions resulted. A strong North Korean attack on two small islands covering the seaward approaches to Sok-to, an island crucial to the UN defence of the area, took place on the night of 15 December 1951 and despite the staunchness of the South Korean garrison the islands fell after two days. Although an attempt to recapture them failed a few days later, the fighting went on. The North Koreans took another nearby island, Sosuap-to, but were then driven off in a bloody counter-attack backed by American carrier aircraft, in which 300 North Korean troops were killed, as were some 700 of the luckless civilian population and several South Korean and American undercover agents working amongst the civilians. These were part of what was known as 'Leopard Force'.

As the major part of the naval forces operating amongst the west coast islands were British and Commonwealth, their command, and that of the island garrisons, was entrusted to Admiral Scott-Moncrieff. His senior staff officers for operations ashore were mostly US Marines who worked extremely well with their allies in the fleet. It was agreed that in view of the heavy casualties incurred at the end of 1951 Leopard Force's highly trained personnel were to be used henceforth for raiding and intelligence-gathering, and large numbers of well-trained Korean marines were inserted on to the most important islands by January 1952. Pack ice in the Yellow Sea affected minesweeping activity, but operations went ahead as it was essential to maintain the initiative and prevent the enemy from wresting islands back from the Korean marines and irregulars. Command of the force afloat was exercised from a cruiser, whose heavier guns could be used to support those of the destroyers and frigates. An aircraft-carrier was kept permanently on station off the west coast to provide immediate close air support for island garrisons when needed. In addition, extremely accurate naval gunnery was required to neutralize a number of enemy guns cleverly sited in the Panmunjon area, from where they sniped at long range against allied ships working the Han estuary.

It had been recognized early in the campaign that if United Nations ships were to operate freely amongst the offshore islands and in the treacherous west coast estuaries, the charts would need drastic revision. Most, dating back some fifty years, had been surveyed by the Imperial Japanese Navy. Apart from the huge tides, reaching over 35 feet at Inchon, there were vicious tide-rips in all the river mouths and the positions of many large mudflats changed almost daily, as the luckless captain of the Thai frigate had already found to his cost. It was therefore decided to devote a major part of the naval effort to hydrographic survey. One of the frigates thus employed was HMS *Amethyst*, whose name had been a household word in 1949 after her dramatic dash to freedom for hundreds of miles down the Yangtse following her illegal arrest by the Chinese communists. Her captain in 1951 was Commander Peter Fanshawe, a naval aviator who, after being shot down in 1943, had been one of the masterminds behind the great escape from Stalag Luft XVII which, a total success initially, ended tragically with the mass execution of escapers on Hitler's orders. Also aboard was the newly promoted and irrepressible Sub-Lieutenant Muschamp, already encountered in HMS *Jamaica* in the earliest days of the war. On first acquaintance he found Fanshawe 'rather austere. But he was very kind to this strange colonial who had been foisted on him and gave me a great deal of responsibility.'

Muschamp was appointed assistant to the ship's navigating officer, whose job was to carry out the hundreds of bearings and soundings required for revision of the charts. *Amethyst* was sent to the Han estuary and work commenced. As the enemy held the north shores, considerable caution was needed. The ship anchored about ten miles from the hostile shore, and the survey party did their work off a Korean patrol boat whose crew, according to Muschamp,

> was presided over by a captain of villainous appearance. His English was non-existent; he looked upon the whole exercise as a chance to line his pockets by selling as much produce as he could get, legally or otherwise, from the galleys and store rooms of His Majesty's Ship *Amethyst*. In this enterprise he was quite quickly foiled by the First Lieutenant, who placed a sentry in the galley, armed with his own 12-bore shotgun. After the Korean had spent most of a day in the sickbay having No. 6 pellets extracted from his nether regions, there was no more attempted filching.

For west coast patrol duties involving contact with the island garrisons as well as American intelligence, radar and air–sea rescue detachments, *Amethyst* carried a Korean naval liaison officer. Fanshawe later recalled what he described as 'a courageous essay into English prose recorded in the log book of my Korean liaison officer':

> Impression of British navy. Still keeping more strict custom of Empire militarism and they pride Royalty, His Majesty's Ship. They keep hard regulation in serious especially put on clothes, salutation and gentlemanship etc. I can see to the military discipline is hard that all crew pious for the officer. I respect their manly brave seamanship. I must recognize Great Britain why, because strong country instead their mainland as big as our country. A people of England like sea and respect seamanship. Their government excited to advancing to abroad by merchant marine with protect by their naval power. It is no wonder that Britain is called the Country of the Navy.

The most important west coast island for the UN forces was Cho–do, possession of which enabled the allies to dominate the estuary leading to Chinnampo, the port of Pyongyang. In addition to its garrison of 4,000 guerrillas it was a principal air–sea rescue centre on which several helicopters were based. Their role was the recovery of allied aircrew shot down on bombing raids against North Korea or in the increasingly fierce fighter battles as the Chinese acquired more Russian-built MiG-15 aircraft. Also on Cho-do were the fighter control and early warning radars which compensated for the US Air Force's numerical deficiency in fighter aircraft, and several covert warfare organizations, each apparently unaware of the other's presence. The communists made every effort to neutralize Cho-do. The mainland was only four and a half miles away but did not appear to be strongly held, although a substantial enemy force was known to be stationed in Chinnampo.

On the morning of 5 October *Amethyst* anchored off the island's principal village in the course of a routine mission. Co-operation with the guerrillas was difficult; apart from the language problem, they frequently forgot to inform the local UN naval commanders of their plans and were given to raiding with inadequate support. On this occasion a boat was sent ashore to contact the resident US naval intelligence officer. He came aboard at once, somewhat agitated, with an American army officer, to tell Fanshawe that a large raiding party had crossed over to the mainland on the previous evening for a quick operation but had run into trouble, was pinned down and in urgent need of fire support. Although neither of the Americans had any responsibility for raiding operations they knew that the defeat of the guerrillas would prejudice a number of their own future covert activities.

As the only reliable link between the ship and the guerrillas, they stayed aboard with their radios as *Amethyst* weighed anchor and steamed to a point some miles up the estuary from where fire could be brought down to protect the guerrillas' flanks as they fought their way back to the beach. The Americans were put ashore with their radios, maps, binoculars and rations and soon established good communications with the frigate. 'Having gone to "Fire for Effect",' wrote Fanshawe, 'we were rewarded with an exultant cry of "You gotten 'em in the guts!" This was splendid and we hoped that it was the enemy who had been thus discomfited. It transpired that this was so. Four shells from our two forward mountings had landed in the main body of the enemy, after which those remaining had dispersed with alacrity.' As the exultant guerrillas began to appear on the beach so did a mass of civilians plus their oxen, which were swum out to the island.

The naval blockade of the west coast gave unlimited opportunity for bold handling of frigates and destroyers in a way that would have delighted Nelson. Prominent in all these operations were the ships of the Royal Australian and New Zealand navies. At times, engagements were fought out at point-blank range. The Australian frigate HMAS *Murchison*, on patrol along the north bank of the Han estuary, came under heavy fire at close range from previously undetected 75mm guns, mortars and machine-guns. Responding over open sights with 4-inch and Bofors guns, *Murchison* silenced the opposition.

Returning to the same area on the following day the ship was met with even heavier fire from the shore. Again, the enemy were taken on with main armament, the gun crews firing 18–20 rounds a minute. The ship was hit several times before the hostile guns were destroyed, and it was then necessary to deal with snipers in the tall grass of the river bank; they too were eliminated. *Murchison* was manoeuvring in a fierce tide race between sandbanks but her captain, Lieutenant-Commander Dolland, handled her superbly; she was soon joined by another ship and both continued their cannonade until the enemy had been wiped out.

Handling of the destroyers was equally spectacular. HMAS *Warramunga*, a former British Tribal class, was bombarding a railway bridge near Chongjin, on the north-east coast and barely 50 miles from the Russian border. Commander Ramsay, her captain, edged the ship up a narrow tidal channel to close the range; he continued the bombardment in waters so confined that in order to return to the open sea it was necessary to stop the engines and allow the tide to turn the ship in its own length; as he began this delicate manoeuvre, five enemy field guns opened up from a concealed position. Ramsay rang the engine room for full astern and made a dramatic exit as his forward guns took on the enemy, silencing three of their guns.

There were numerous examples of similar seamanship on both coasts; the Royal Marines of 41 Commando long remembered the dash with which the American destroyer captains handled their ships inside Wonsan harbour, seemingly heedless of the fire of enemy coastal batteries or of the thickly sown mines; these were swept constantly by the devoted crews of minehunters, many of which were blown up in the process.

If the infantry ashore had to endure harsh conditions in winter, their lot was matched by the deck crews of the United Nations ships; on the British and Commonwealth ships, in the absence of air-conditioning, summer temperatures between decks were well-nigh insupportable. In winter, the endless coast patrols went on despite pack ice and the continual need to remove ice from the ships' superstructures, a task which had to be done manually, often in blizzards and a full gale. Many former crew members would long remember the depressing sight of thick ice forming on the interior bulkhead walls of their messdecks. Theirs was far from being a comfortable war, but the naval contribution was nevertheless decisive. In a highly classified document prepared by Mao Tsetung's staff, signed by Premier Chou En-lai and sent to Moscow in 1953 shortly after Stalin's death, the Chinese High Command freely admitted that their inability to provide naval support for the communist ground forces obliged them to seek victory in Korea by means of renewed frontal land attacks which, without close air support on the scale available to the United Nations, would involve unacceptable casualties. Under such conditions, wrote Chou En-lai, it was time to seek terms for an armistice.

CHAPTER 28

A New Air War

When the Korean War started, the nearest United Nations air power was that of the 5th United States Air Force, part of General Stratemeyer's Far East Air Force. With the primary function of the air defence of Japan, its pilots were not trained in close support of ground operations and their interceptor aircraft were not designed for that role. Little or no air-to-ground attack training had been carried out between 1945 and 1950, and when war broke out, pilots had to rely initially on untrained ground controllers totally unaccustomed to the demands of the land battle. The results of this were tragically apparent in the bombing of the Argylls in September 1950.

The 5th Air Force's day fighters were a mixed bag: some of its squadrons had F-80 Shooting Stars, which were first-generation jets, as were its F-84 Thunderjets. There were also some all-weather fighters, the strange F-82 'Twin Mustang', consisting of two Mustang fuselages connected by a shared wing; the radar operator was in one fuselage, the pilot in the other. Several Shooting Stars had been modified for air photographic reconnaissance, but there were few trained interpretative personnel; this led to the loan of a number of British experts from the RAF whose work was readily acknowledged to have had a decisive effect on the conduct of the air war. 5th Air Force also had some B-26 light bombers and transport aircraft.

Its commander, Major-General Partridge, coped admirably with a host of problems confronting him. The enemy had the initiative; the terrain of South Korea was unfamiliar to his pilots and moreover extremely difficult for low-level navigation and identification of targets; there were strict political constraints on the use of air power; and the airfields in Japan were far from the battlefront, which meant that the jets could spend only minutes above the target. It was to be many weeks before suitable airfields became available on Korean soil. Communications were also a problem; Partridge set up his headquarters in Korea within days of the outbreak of war, whilst Stratemeyer's Far East Air Force HQ remained in Japan. There were huge problems of co-ordination with the ground commanders, and even more with the 7th US Fleet's carriers offshore, whose aircraft were to play a key role in the close support of 8th Army.

Thanks to the skill of the American pilots and their superior aircraft, the North Korean air force was shot out of the skies within weeks, to play no further part in the land battle. Having gained air supremacy over the battlefield, the Americans and their allies could safely operate unarmed light spotter aircraft over the front line; these were used not only for observation and artillery fire control but also as platforms from which airborne controllers could guide fighter-bombers on to their targets. Known as 'Mosquitoes' they were equipped with phosphorus-headed rockets for target marking; the majority were small light aircraft, but T-6 Harvard trainers were also used.

The aircraft of the 5th Air Force were rapidly reinforced from the huge reserves of the US Air Force. Hundreds of F-51 Mustang piston-engined fighters were shipped to Japan for use as fighter-bombers. Designed during the Second World War as an air superiority fighter, the Mustang's performance and range had enabled it to play a decisive role in the air war over north-west Europe. As a ground attack aircraft it carried a good war load, and drop tanks gave it the endurance to orbit over the battlefield awaiting targeting instructions; unfortunately it suffered from having its radiator in an exposed position under the centre section of the fuselage, where even a single hit by a rifle bullet resulted in the loss of its engine coolant glycol and almost immediate seizure of the Packard-Merlin engine. At low level, where the Mustang generally operated in Korea, this usually proved fatal for the pilot.

American Mustangs were soon joined by other United Nations air contingents; the South African government offered to send the personnel of No. 2 'Flying Cheetah' fighter squadron to Korea. Arriving in Japan in November 1950 it was equipped by the Americans; the South Africans agreed to purchase more than 90 Mustangs and had no problems mastering them; many of their pilots had flown them operationally during the Second World War, notably their commanding officer, the redoubtable Commandant van Breda Theron, heavily decorated flying against the Germans and Italians. The skill and dedication of the Flying Cheetahs became legendary and their arrival over a hard-pressed allied unit in the midst of a battle was always greeted with cheers. The South African nationalist government of the day, already veering towards departure from the Commonwealth and the adoption of apartheid policies, ruled that the squadron was to be placed under American and not British command. Whilst a practical move, inasmuch as there was no British air contingent apart from some light aircraft and flying boats, its exceptional pilots were thereby denied the British gallantry awards they undoubtedly earned.

No. 77 Squadron Royal Australian Air Force, also equipped with Mustangs, was the first non-American flying unit in action over Korea.

Despite the early loss of its commanding officer this unit, operating initially from Iwakuni in Japan, then from forward airstrips in Korea, performed with distinction throughout the campaign. During the crucial days of the defence of the Pusan perimeter in the summer of 1950 the Australians flew from Iwakuni early in the morning, carried out a strike mission, then refuelled and rearmed for the rest of the day on an airfield within the sound of the guns near Taegu before returning to Iwakuni at dusk. Later in the campaign the squadron was based on Korean soil. It rapidly gained an extremely high reputation with the Americans. Apart from their contribution in the ground attack role the Australians developed great skill at interdiction – the attack of the enemy's line of communication, particularly the destruction of road transport and the carefully camouflaged dumps on which the NKPA relied for replenishment.

The entry of Chinese forces changed the face of the Korean air war overnight. In mid-October 1950 American aircraft attacking Sinuiju airfield on the banks of the Yalu were fired on by anti-aircraft guns from the Chinese side of the river. Much worse was to come; on the afternoon of 1 November a formation of US Air Force Mustangs flying near the Yalu came under attack from six strange swept-wing fighters. These were identified as Russian-built MiG-15s, at that time the most advanced military aircraft in the world. Its design incorporating a wing derived from German patterns captured in 1945, the MiG was powered by a centrifugal-flow engine derived from the Rolls-Royce Nenes sold commercially to the Russians by the British government as an altruistic if ill-advised gesture in 1946. The MiG immediately showed itself to be far superior to the US Air Force's Shooting Stars, outpacing them by 120 mph. Although the skill of the American pilots enabled them to shoot down a MiG at no cost to themselves in the first all-jet dogfight over the Yalu on 7 November 1950, they knew that without a comparable aircraft, they were outclassed. Fortunately, this was at hand in the shape of the F-86 Sabre which, like the MiG-15, embodied captured German research in its swept-wing design. The first Sabre squadron arrived in Korea in November and in the following month the first MiG-15 was destroyed by a Sabre pilot over Sinuiju.

In the summer of 1951, 77 Squadron RAAF was re-equipped with the British-built Meteor Mk 8; such was the rate of aircraft development at this time that it was already obsolescent, and its arrival was not greeted enthusiastically by pilots who had hoped to fly Sabres. Until August 1951 the Meteors were flown on combat missions up to the Yalu but at the end of that month several engagements took place which confirmed the Australians' doubts over the suitability of the Meteor for combat against aircraft whose speed, rate of climb and agility at altitude gave them the advantage, despite the skill, courage and dash of the Australians and of the RAF pilots attached to 77 Squadron to gain jet combat experience.

By November 1951 aerial reconnaissance had revealed that the enemy were constructing new airfields in North Korea, half way between Pyongyang and the Yalu, from which high-performance fighters could be operated. This posed a grave threat to allied air operations against the enemy ground forces and the decision to bomb the new air bases as soon as possible led to some of the most spectacular air battles yet seen. The Far East Air Force's bombers were first sent in by night, using radar; but as only a few B-29s could be used for this type of mission it was decided to bomb by day. The first such attack took the enemy by surprise and no interceptors were sent up; on the next mission, however, the enemy were ready. Flying with great tactical skill they lured the American fighter escort away from the bombers, which were attacked by swarms of MiGs. By now the Chinese were operating over 450 of these against less than a hundred Sabres. The third bombing attack took place on 23 October against the airfield at Namsi. As the formation approached the target the leading group of 34 Sabres was attacked by over a hundred MiGs whilst another fifty went for the slower F-84 Thunderjets acting as close escort to the B-29s. The airfield was badly damaged, but the bomber crews suffered heavy casualties and shot-up B-29s could be seen limping south, some streaming smoke, others plunging out of control as the crews took to their parachutes.

In all these battles the Australian Meteors were involved as part of the bomber escort; but the writing was on the wall by the middle of November and as the MiGs steadily increased in number it was decided to relegate the Meteor to ground attack and interdiction, for which it was well suited by virtue of its strong construction. By now the Americans had also decided to abandon daylight raids by B-29s over the border area, now known as 'MiG Alley', having lost five of them in the space of one week, with eight more so badly damaged that they were written off. In the last two months of 1951 the MiG sortie rate had risen from just over 2,500 to almost 4,000 a month, and the Far East Air Force had a major problem on its hands.

Meanwhile, although their ability to operate aircraft over the land battle had been eliminated in the first months of the war, the enemy retained the ability to launch nuisance raids against the UN forces. During the summer of 1951 there were numerous daring attacks by night on the allied rear areas, the aircraft used being mainly Russian Yakovlev and Polikarpov trainers. Operating from an airfield in the Sariwon area, flying at low level to evade the American air defence radars, they easily located the brilliantly lit allied rear areas. On several nights in June 1951 airfields as far south as Suwon and Kimpo were attacked by these 'Bedcheck Charlies', and they succeeded in destroying or severely damaging a number of Sabre aircraft on the ground. The Commonwealth Division was not spared their attentions and they could often be heard after dark, flying at low level along the valleys, readily finding targets in the British rear areas where long familiarity with allied air superiority had resulted in extremely lax black-out precautions. The raids were abruptly halted when low-flying American F-94 Starfire night fighters, carrying airborne radar, hunted down the intruders.

British participation in Korean air operations was limited for strategic and economic reasons. The Air Ministry initially considered sending operational flying units to serve under the Americans but various factors militated against this. The RAF was in a state of metamorphosis; it had emerged from the Second World War with a deservedly high reputation, to undergo swingeing cuts as Bomber Command was dismembered and its four-engined bombers consigned to the scrap heap. In 1950 the RAF's jet fighters were the Gloster Meteor and de Havilland Vampire, all needed for home defence or in Germany. A motley array of piston-engined fighters equipped the RAF's Far East Air Force in Singapore, Malaya and Hong Kong, and none could be spared for Korea; the Malayan emergency had placed the RAF in the Far East under enormous strain and the two squadrons assigned to the defence of Hong Kong, though hardly more than a political gesture, were not available for use elsewhere.

The RAF's contribution, though relatively modest, was nonetheless invaluable. Stratemeyer's air command soon found that the US Air Force, still emerging from a difficult birth in 1947, was deficient in several important capabilities, notably ground attack by night and aerial photographic interpretation, at both of which the RAF excelled. Several British experts were therefore despatched from London to join the US Far East Air Force as advisers. One of these was Wing Commander Peter Wykeham-Barnes, heavily decorated for his services as a night intruder pilot over occupied Europe, who became technical consultant on General Partridge's staff at 5th Tactical Air Force, frequently flying operational missions and making a decisive contribution to the success of the air war. Another distinguished RAF fighter pilot, Wing Commander 'Johnny' Johnson, was also attached to HQ 5th Air Force, and a number of RAF pilots were sent out on attachment to American squadrons; in this way the RAF acquired invaluable experience of modern air combat. Others served with the Australians, flying Mustangs, then Meteors.

Throughout the war a detachment of Sunderland flying boats from the RAF's Far East Air Force was maintained at Iwakuni in Japan. Operating alongside American maritime bombers, they rendered sterling service in the coastal surveillance and air-sea rescue roles, frequently flying in appalling weather conditions, notably on anti-submarine patrols off Vladivostok and on the blockade of North Korean ports. Sorties of twelve hours in unheated and draughty aircraft, in temperatures of −20°C, were commonplace, and the return to Iwakuni was equally fraught, often involving blind flying through mountainous terrain in icing conditions. The information provided by such maritime reconnaissance flights was invaluable in the planning of airstrikes against enemy shipping and coastal installations by aircraft of the United Nations fleets.

Away from the battle line, the United Nations air offensive was changing direction; through the autumn of 1951, and until the following summer, the emphasis lay in destroying the North Korean rail system, first by heavy bomber attacks on marshalling yards, then on stretches of track selected for interdiction attacks. The 5th Air Force's fighter-bomber wings were assigned stretches of up to 30 miles as their day's target. Between 30 and 60 aircraft, each carrying two 500-pound bombs, and escorted by Sabres flying high above if within range of 'MiG Alley', dive-bombed the enemy rail system. If opposition was light the pilots, instead of dive-bombing, approached the target in a shallow glide descent to give better accuracy. The earlier attacks on the North Korean road system, or Operation 'Strangle', had not produced the results hoped for; and even the spectacular results of railroad interdiction were to some extent nullified by the enemy's ability to carry out track repair overnight. The ingenuity of the North Koreans and their Chinese allies knew no bounds, as they continually improvised new river crossings and rail ferries where bridges had been destroyed. Photographic reconnaissance revealed movable bridge spans, inserted into gaps during the hours of darkness and removed before first light.

Hundreds of anti-aircraft guns were deployed along the railways under attack and as 1951 drew on, rising aircraft losses began to alarm allied air commanders. In August the 5th Air Force lost 26 fighter-bombers, with 24 badly damaged. In September the figure was 32 and 233, to be more or less repeated in the following two months. But the rail attack campaign was beginning to pay dividends; prisoners told of the dread which they and their comrades had of travelling to the forward areas by train, and it became clear that the Chinese had abandoned any plans they may have had for a further major offensive by the end of October. Attacks by heavy bombers on the enemy railways were only moderately effective owing to the rapidity with which the damage was made good and to the difficulty of hitting pinpoint targets by night. For a short time, B–26 light bombers fitted with 80-million candlepower searchlights were used for night attacks, but although this ensured greater accuracy there were heavy casualties to the bombers, which were highly visible to gunners on the ground once they had switched on their lights.

New strategic targets were assessed early in 1952 and once more the matter of attacks on the hydro-electric industry of North Korea was placed before General Ridgway, who was not in favour, and General Weyland of the Far East Air Force, who was. Ridgway's objections rested on his belief that such strategic bombing could adversely affect progress at Panmunjon, where the truce talks continued fitfully. He also made it clear to Weyland that the full consent of the Joint Chiefs in Washington would have to be obtained before any attack was made. Ridgway held this position until his departure in April 1952. His successor, Mark Clark, was immediately amenable to Weyland's proposals, and ordered planning to go ahead.

There were to be four principal targets: the generating plants at Suiho, Fusen, Choshin and Kyosen. As these would be regarded as key points by the enemy it was essential to deliver the strikes over a two–day period before air defences could be strengthened, and as the resources of Far East Air Force were not up to this, the air power of the 7th US Fleet would be invoked. The Suiho plant was selected as the first target, as it lay only 40 miles from the clutch of enemy airfields around Antung where some 250 MiGs were based, and total surprise was essential if the attack was to succeed without prohibitive casualties. The intricate planning was undertaken by the staffs of Vice-Admiral Clark of the 7th Fleet, and General Barcus, the newly arrived commander of the 5th Tactical Air Force. Whilst Suiho was subjected to an intense fighter-bomber attack there would be simultaneous attacks on the other plants at Choshin, Kyosen and Fusen. After dark the Far East Air Force's heavy bombers would continue to bomb, using radar.

The attack went in late on the afternoon of 23 June 1952 after dense cloud had delayed it for over six hours. Sabres patrolled at altitude in case of interception by the MiGs, naval Panthers attacked the anti-aircraft defences, and Skyraider dive-bombers attacked the generator plant. There was an anxious moment, early in the attack, when huge clouds of dust over the Antung airfields indicated a massed take-off in progress, but the MiGs flew off to safer havens deeper in Manchuria; it seems that the Chinese early-warning radars had interpreted the incoming raid as the long-expected attack on the Manchurian sanctuary airfields, and the precious MiGs had been flown to safety. The attacks went on for four more days and when they had ended, 90 per cent of North Korea's hydro–electric system lay in ruin. The electricity supply all over the north was cut; it was the greatest single airstrike conducted by the United Nations during the war and a triumph of American air staff planning and execution. Only two aircraft were lost, their crews successfully retrieved by rescue helicopters from deep inside enemy territory.

The awesome power of the American military machine was now manifest as the Far East Air Force was reorganized and heavily reinforced in the latter half of 1952. A similar build-up was occurring, however, on the other side of the Manchurian border. By mid–June the Chinese People's Air Force had grown to a strength of 1,800 front-line aircraft, over half of which were modern jets, organized in 22 air divisions. Included in these figures were a hundred jet-engined Ilyushin Il-28 bombers. These would enable the Chinese, should they wish, to launch substantial airstrikes anywhere in South Korea, particularly at the highly vulnerable and unprotected UN lines of communication down the peninsula. The Soviet air strength in the Far East had also increased to some

5,300 aircraft. Photographic evidence revealed that work was in progress on a series of new airfields across the Yalu together with a string of early-warning radars, many well south of the border and capable of detecting allied air movements far to the south of the 38th parallel. The Chinese also installed a number of fighter control radars. All the time, communist anti-aircraft artillery was being poured into the north and some 2,000 guns were in position by the end of 1952. Enemy night fighters, ably controlled from the ground, became active against night raids by American B-29s.

At the same time, there was evidence of growing confidence and proficiency on the part of the MiG pilots, who frequently ventured far south of the Yalu on offensive sweeps, seeking to destroy any piston-engined fighter-bombers they could find. Very early on the morning of 9 August 1952 a patrol of Royal Naval Sea Furies from HMS *Ocean* was attacked by eight MiG-15s whilst escorting a strike by Fireflies from the same ship. Fortunately for the Sea Fury pilots the enemy appeared to be relative novices and handled their attack badly, losing one of their number to the guns of a Sea Fury, the first occasion on which a MiG had been shot down by a piston-engined aircraft and cause for celebration. There was a similar encounter on the following day, when the enemy were clearly much more proficient. As the naval flight commander reported: 'They must have sent the instructors down.' Despite this, the British pilots were credited with two MiGs destroyed and three damaged in these historic encounters.

There was much speculation as to the identity of the best enemy pilots – those who had obviously mastered the essentials of teamwork in air combat and whose gunnery was as precise as their handling of their aircraft. Allied pilots claimed to have had momentary glimpses of their opponents in air-to-air combat and swore that some had distinctly Caucasian features. They could only have been Russians. The radio intercepts of their airborne conversations, however, found that they used Chinese. In his 1951 lecture at the Royal United Services Institute, Wing Commander Wykeham-Barnes commented that as it is possible to fly a fighter aircraft, in or out of combat, on a vocabulary of less than 200 words, Chinese-speaking Russians could have been gaining combat experience over Korea, as indeed were British pilots of the Fleet Air Arm and RAF, attached to American jet fighter squadrons.

Aerial pressure on the communists was kept at a high level until the end of the war. Night attacks by heavy and medium bombers alternated with continual fighter-bomber missions by day against the enemy lines of communication. With the attacks against the hydro-electric plants, the industrial and domestic economy of North Korea was effectively in ruins, but there was a further series of strategic targets worthy of the Far East Air Force's attention. These were the huge dams which conserved North Korea's irrigation water for the production of rice. There were twenty of them, providing three-quarters of North Korea's agricultural water requirement. Their destruction would deprive the communist forces at a stroke of an entire year's rice supplies. There would also be secondary effects from the inundation of military and industrial areas.

Plans were accordingly prepared early in 1953 for a trial attack on a dam across the Potong river, some 20 miles north of Pyongyang. Made of earth and stone, it extended for nearly half a mile across the valley. On 13 May, out of a clear sky, it was attacked by 59 Thunderjets, each carrying a 1,000-pounder bomb. Although spectacular, the attack appeared to have failed, for at the end the dam, though battered, seemed to be holding. During the night, however, the weight of the water behind it collapsed the weakened structure, which burst asunder. The result was comparable to that of the RAF's sensational attack on the Ruhr dams in 1943. A wall of water raced down the Potong valley sweeping aside hundreds of buildings, wiping out great tracts of rice paddy, an airfield, part of the main railway line and two miles of the main north–south trunk road.

Several other dams were attacked with varying success. These attacks then had to stop because of the need to redouble the interdiction campaign against the enemy rear areas, for it was clear from intelligence reports that a final desperate Chinese and North Korean attack, aimed at the US IX and ROK II Corps, was impending. The last confrontations of the war, on land and in the air, were about to take place.

CHAPTER 29

The Last Battles

General Dwight Eisenhower was elected President of the United States on 4 November 1952. Although Winston Churchill welcomed the news he was troubled by the bellicosity of many prominent Republicans and confided to his private secretary that he believed Eisenhower's arrival at the White House would make global war more probable. He was therefore determined to use whatever residual influence he had as an international statesman to bring about some rapport between the Soviet Union and the United States.

Churchill's age and punishing lifestyle had begun to tell; his immediate staff saw a diminution of the old vigour, both mental and physical. Despite frequent references to his resignation in his conversations with the 'kitchen cabinet' at 10 Downing Street, he held on to power – to the evident agitation of Anthony Eden, so long the heir-apparent, but now also in failing health. Even before Eisenhower's inauguration, scheduled for mid-January 1953, Churchill insisted on visiting him. Lord Moran, his medical adviser, forbade him to fly so he went once more aboard the *Queen Mary*, trailing an exhausted staff in his wake. Arriving in New York on 5 January he met Eisenhower privately, but was unable to convince him that an early summit meeting in Moscow would be useful. Shortly afterwards he was to describe the President as 'a real man of limited stature'.

Early in his election campaign, Eisenhower had promised that if elected, he would visit Korea at once to see things for himself. The new British ambassador in Tokyo, Sir Esler Dening, on hearing the election result, wrote to the Foreign Office. Dening had just been to Korea himself and had subsequently talked with General Mark Clark and his British Deputy Chief of Staff, Major-General Shoosmith. Dening believed that when Eisenhower got to Korea he would come under strong pressure from Clark and Van Fleet to do something about the impasse there, probably by opening up the war with a limited offensive. An indefinite stalemate, Dening thought, was unacceptable to the Americans, whilst any attempt to cut losses by evacuating all United Nations troops, even under protection of a truce, would provide a huge propaganda victory for the communists and expose the deserted South Koreans to destruction. Eisenhower, Dening went on, would return to Washington laden with all manner of plans and policies produced by Mark Clark's staff. As many of these were bound to be of an aggressive character, the days between Eisenhower's return to the United States his inauguration on 20 January, when he would take over the Seal of Office, were crucial to British interests and the United Kingdom Liaison Mission in Washington must at all costs ensure a British input to any plans for the ongoing conduct of the war. In Dening's own words:

> I think the Americans here are more under the influence of emotion than practical reason, and I believe that many of the courses that they have in mind, such as the employment of Chinese nationalist troops, the blockade of China, and the bombing of Manchuria, would not really stand up to the test of examination objectively and in detail by military experts . . . I think that the only course for us is to continue with the static war while trying to reduce our casualties. We should go on trying for an armistice and hope that, if the enemy is convinced of our determination to continue indefinitely, he may tire of it before we do and agree to conclude one. Nobody here seems to believe in the possibility of an armistice, least of all the troops in the front line. But General Mark Clark has said he would go a long way to get one and I believe he is sincere. Unfortunately I think he may lean to the belief that opening up the war would bring it about, whereas I personally am afraid it would only involve us in wider commitments and a greater drain on our resources without achieving the desired result.

Dening added that if hostilities were renewed on such a scale, no harm would be done to the Soviet Union, which would stay out of the conflict, cheerfully watching as Britain's economy drained to the lees.

As the world came to terms with Eisenhower's electoral triumph, there was an influential attempt by the Indian government to untangle the prisoners of war issue at Panmunjon. It recommended the setting up of a neutral repatriation commission with delegates from Czechoslovakia, Poland, Sweden and Switzerland to supervise the release of prisoners. No attempt was to be made to coerce prisoners to return (or not) to their home countries, and all were to be released initially from military control to the repatriation commission at exchange points in demilitarized zones. The prisoners were to be classified by nationality and place of domicile, and after this would be free to return to their homeland if they elected to do so. All prisoners were to be fully briefed on their rights, including their freedom to return home. Full access to the prisoners was to be granted to the International Red Cross whilst they were under jurisdiction of the repatriation commission. Finally, if there were still any prisoners who, after 120 days, had not been disposed of, they would become the responsibility of the United Nations. It seemed that this had cleared the way to a truce agreement at Panmunjon; but many snags would arise before this was achieved.

As he had promised, Eisenhower visited Korea in December 1952. During the three days he was in the theatre he was able to visit the 1st Commonwealth Division. Major-General Cassels had left in September 1952 on promotion, to command the 1st British Corps in Germany. He had been an inspired choice for this sensitive post; his previous job in Australia had given him an intuitive understanding of the remarkable Australian soldier and he was approachable by all ranks, a familiar figure as he moved around the divisional area talking informally with anyone he met. His replacement was Major-General Michael Alston-Roberts-West, well proven during the Second World War as a battalion and brigade commander. Cheerfully aware of the misunderstandings that would arise from his use of a triple-barrelled surname he made it clear on his initial visit to the I Corps commander, General Kendall, that he wished to be addressed as Mike West – as he would be known throughout his time in the Commonwealth Division.

During General Cassels' final months the division had strengthened its position along the Kansas line, extending its flanks to the west despite serious manpower deficiencies in some of the Commonwealth battalions (the French-Canadian Royale 22e battalion was some 300 all ranks below its proper establishment). The ongoing requirement to patrol aggressively and take prisoners had already led to friction between Cassels and General Kendall, who persisted with General O'Daniel's policies in this matter. Whilst Cassels never had to invoke his last resort of telling UN Command that his men were being unnecessarily exposed to casualties in these raids, there had been times when he stood out against I Corps headquarters, tacitly supported by the United States Marine Division. Other American divisional commanders, unable to stand up to their corps commander on the patrolling issue, regularly lost men in futile attempts to take live prisoners.

With the approach of autumn 1952, there had been changes as battalions were rotated out of Korea, having served one winter there. They departed with relief, their troopships pulling out from Pusan to the strains of the US Army band that had welcomed them a year earlier, this time playing 'So long, it's been good to know you'. Meanwhile, the Chinese patiently built up their artillery, deploying hundreds of guns newly purchased for hard cash from the Soviet Union. General Van Fleet maintained a defensive posture, pushing outposts forward wherever possible with the aim of blunting the Chinese attacks he expected. These fell initially on the ROK divisions deployed on the central sector north of Chorwon, where the patient restructuring of the South Korean army at the hands of its American advisers at last reaped dividends. The ROK infantry, admirably supported by their own artillery, stood their ground and inflicted heavy casualties on the Chinese when they attacked at the beginning of October.

Rebuffed at Chorwon, the Chinese turned their attention to the I US Corps sector in the west, where the line was held by the US 1st Marine, 1st Commonwealth and 1st ROK Divisions. The initial attack fell on Kowang-san–Hill 355 or Little Gibraltar, now held by the 1st Battalion, Royal Canadian Regiment. The Canadians used their own artillery to great effect and Hill 355 remained in Commonwealth hands until the end of the war.

Following this action, the Chinese turned their attention to the western end of the Commonwealth Division's sector, where the line bent south, embracing a series of ridge features known as the Hook. This was formerly a quiet area for many months where it was customary for newly arrived battalions to be given a spell. In November 1952 the newly arrived 1st Battalion, The Black Watch, was on the Hook. They had been given a rifle company of the Royale 22e to stiffen the defence, and were glad to have the US Marines on their left, just across the divisional boundary, which had been shifted over to the west. They moved into positions vacated by the Marines, badly damaged by Chinese artillery. The outgoing Marine commander's words to Colonel Rose of the Black Watch, 'I give you twenty-four hours', were hardly likely to cheer anyone; but as Rose recorded, 'I bit my lip and let it pass.'

The position had scarcely been taken over when it came under furious attack by the Chinese 399th Regiment. This was fought off, but the defenders had to spend an uncomfortable two weeks under constant fire from snipers, artillery and mortars as they tried to improve their battered fieldworks. These included several outposts given codenames of 'Ronson', 'Warsaw' (the Hook feature itself), 'Seattle', 'Paris', 'Nevada' and 'Omaha'. The importance of the Hook lay in the commanding view it enjoyed over the Samichon valley and that of its tributary the Chogae-dong, across which lay the enemy positions, deeply tunnelled into the hills.

The Chinese launched themselves at the Black Watch again after dark on 16 November; by 9.30 p.m. the battalion area was swamped with artillery and mortar fire and enemy infantry were charging through their own barrage, seemingly indifferent to loss. Colonel Rose shared his command post with the commander of the battalion's supporting artillery battery; they kept their heads, built up a picture of the situation and worked out where their men were still holding out. Since the earlier attack they had been given much help in improving their position by a troop of Royal Engineers who had helped construct deep bunkers and interconnecting tunnels where the defenders sought cover as the Chinese barrage reached its climax. Artillery and mortar fire was brought down on the enemy wherever he appeared in the open.

The Black Watch stayed in their tunnels and bunkers as more guns and mortars were progressively added to the crescendo of fire, including a rocket battery of the US Marines on the left of the position. A Centurion tank was hit and badly damaged as it tried to intervene and had to leave the fight. Colonel Rose threw every spare hand into the mêlée, including his pipers and drummers.

The Royal Engineers who had been working on the defences fought shoulder to shoulder with the infantry. Towards dawn the enemy sullenly withdrew. The battalion had received magnificent support all night from the American Marines as well as from the entire divisional artillery. The Black Watch suffered over a hundred casualties. The enemy, as usual, had dragged as many of their own dead and wounded away as they could, but even so, over a hundred Chinese corpses were found in the battalion area. The young soldiers of the Watch, although new to the division, had fought like veterans under the calm leadership and control of their commanding officer.

In the aftermath of the battle on the Hook General West was determined not to expose his troops to needless casualties by slavish adherence to the corps commander's policy of patrolling merely to take prisoners. The disastrous experience of a patrol of the Royal Fusiliers on the night of 24 November, ambushed inside their own wire and virtually wiped out, losing 14 dead and 20 wounded with a further eight missing, drove West to issue a directive making it clear that whilst it was important to dominate no man's land, 'any form of routine patrolling is dangerous because it invites enemy ambush, it kills initiative, it wearies the men both mentally and physically, and it achieves little'. This instruction was read with satisfaction by commanding officers throughout the division and a copy was pointedly sent to corps headquarters where it was taken to heart; an order was issued that in future, patrols were to be sent out solely for specific tasks.

Whilst this earned West the respect of his battalion commanders, it did little for his personal relationship with General Kendall who, resenting what he regarded as the special treatment he felt he was forced to give to the politically sensitive Commonwealth Division, failed to appreciate the chronic shortage of manpower facing West, none of whose units was remotely up to its war establishment. West's relationship with General Kendall steadily declined to the point where the corps commander publicly criticized the Commonwealth Division and its commander; West eventually felt obliged to exercise his right to report this to the new Commander-in-Chief British Commonwealth Forces in Korea, the Australian Lieutenant-General Wells. He was apparently not the only senior commander who had fallen out with Kendall, for the latter was quietly moved on early in 1953.

After the Chinese raid against the Black Watch every effort was made to strengthen the Hook position. It was recognized in the UN Command that it was dangerous to share a hill feature with the enemy and everywhere except on the Hook this maxim was closely observed. The average distance between the opposing armies varied between one and two thousand yards. On the Hook, however, the nearest Chinese position lay barely 200 yards from the most advanced British platoon. Strengthening the defence involved digging out new bunkers and shelter tunnels, restoring trenches, providing overhead cover for the fighting and observation bunkers, constantly enlarging and repairing barbed wire defences, and laying mines. This work was shared between the Royal Engineers and the assault pioneers of whichever infantry battalion was in the Hook position. These were infantrymen formed into a specialist platoon with additional skills such as minelaying, setting out wire defences and booby traps, and installation of the pre-cast concrete structures made by the Royal Engineers to reinforce command and observation posts.

At the end of January 1953 the Commonwealth Division was taken out of the line for rest and retraining, having been continually at the front since the summer of 1951. General West used the next few weeks wisely; recent operations had revealed dangerous practices, especially when patrolling. The divisional programme worked up from individual skills to exercises for each brigade in turn, enabling West to gauge the mettle of his command. Commanding officers were given considerable latitude in planning their unit training, once the divisional training instruction had been digested. All ranks underwent strenuous physical training and the opportunity was taken to foster the Commonwealth spirit through inter-unit and brigade sports and games. By the time the division went back into the line in March it had acquired a new cutting edge. It reoccupied most of its former positions, held temporarily by the American 2nd Division, which had been given a hard time by the Chinese, particularly in the vulnerable Hook sector, where the defences were once more in ruins. The bunkers, deep communication trenches and shelters, so painstakingly built in the previous autumn, had been almost obliterated.

As it happened, the first unit to reoccupy the Hook was the Black Watch, supported by a troop of 55 Field Engineer Squadron under Captain George Cooper. The position was only 300 yards long and 150 yards wide, straddling the upper contours of the ridge which was crucially important, for if the Chinese gained it they would enjoy an uninterrupted view of the British rear areas. With the approach of the spring thaw Cooper's sappers contended with glutinous mud, and the perils of working in the open so close to the Chinese positions. They first restored the trench linking the fire bunkers and circling the forward contour of the hill. Successive bombardments had reduced this to a shallow, V-shaped depression, unusable by day as it was in full view of the Chinese and any movement drew fire. All work had therefore to be done at night, and as silently as possible.

Enemy mortar fire was incessant but the engineers never gave up. The rifle company deployed on the Hook had two platoons on the forward slope and a third sited a few yards back over the reverse slope. In the forward left-hand post, only 150 yards from the enemy entrenched on the feature known as 'Ronson', the defence was enhanced by a dug-in flame-thrower. The right-hand position faced north-east with good fields of fire over the lunar landscape; but close at hand was a feature known as 'Greenfinger' where patches of dead ground would enable the Chinese to form up for an attack. It was decided therefore to construct a tunnel along the spur running down from the Black Watch position, with a bunker at its end, covering the dead ground. Work on this tunnel continued through April and May, in tandem with improvements to the exposed forward positions, providing robust overhead cover for the defenders. The bunkers were excavated by night in the forward trenches and concrete weapons embrasures inserted before heavy baulks of timber were placed over the top. The pre-cast concrete lintels each weighed over a quarter of a ton and had to be dragged from the engineer field park in the rear by Korean porters who never faltered under fire.

Behind each platoon position was an observation post for the artillery observer and the battalion's own mortar fire controllers. They occupied this by day, retiring for rest at night to the infantry company command post on the reverse slope a hundred yards to the rear. By the middle of May, all these positions were connected by deep trenches reminiscent of the Great War. At night the Hook was on the alert and a hive of activity, this being the time when a Chinese attack was most likely. Daytime, when any movement drew enemy fire, was supposedly a time of rest; but there were many tasks demanding attention: weapons to be inspected and ammunition checked; routine unit administration to be carried out, returns submitted to battalion, rations indented for, reliefs planned, leave rosters updated. Personal cleanliness was all-important and all ranks were required to wash and shave daily, and to keep their clothing clean and serviceable. Only when these tasks were complete could anyone retire to the deep rest bunkers and sleep.

By day and night could be heard the muffled sound of the small petrol generators used for recharging radio batteries (and frequently misused to provide electric lighting for headquarters). Known as 'chore horses' they were a familiar adjunct of soldiering in the British army. Another familiar sound, welcomed as exhausted men came off duty in the trenches, was the muted roar of the cookers or 'hydraburners' on which tea was made in dixies and all food prepared. They were also the only providers of hot water for washing and shaving. None who served in Korea would ever forget the evocative smells as different types of ration fried or boiled on the cookers. That of the prized American canned bacon was perhaps the most desirable, closely followed by the all-in stews and curries prepared by mixing the contents of British 'compo' ration packs. At times, food had to be prepared and eaten in the forward trenches, when the American 'C' or 'Charlie' ration packs were issued on an individual basis and heated up on small, solid-fuel 'Tommy cookers'.

The Chinese persisted with their propaganda campaign. At night their patrols stole up to the wire to pin posters on it, exhorting the 'British stooges' to abandon the Americans. Loudspeakers played what the Chinese imagined was appropriate music; the Black Watch were serenaded on the Hook by pipe tunes and reels. Leaflets were fired over the British lines in canisters, and packets of tea left on the wire with cheerful messages addressed to whichever unit was in the trenches at the time; the troops became keen collectors of the white china peace doves left by the enemy in no man's land. One of these, worn in his head-dress, was a sign that a soldier had been 'at the sharp end'.

West deployed his division with the 28th Commonwealth Brigade on the right, its centre anchored by the Durham Light Infantry on Kowang-san. In the divisional centre was the 25th Canadian Brigade under Brigadier Allard, who had identified and remedied shortcomings such as reluctance to dominate no man's land, poor field sanitation and a tendency to ignore camouflage. Allard was not a man to tolerate sloppy soldiering and his arrival electrified his brigade. On the left of the division was the 29th Brigade reinforced by the 1st Battalion Royal Canadian Regiment, borrowed from Allard to stiffen this vulnerable segment of the line. The United States Marines had been relieved on the Commonwealth Division's left by the US 25th Division, whose right-hand brigade, West noted with satisfaction, was the Turks. As with the Marines, the battalion on the Hook knew that their neighbours would still be there in the morning, no matter how hard-fought the night. This confidence was mutual.

Because of the closeness of the Chinese positions at the Hook, patrolling from there was extremely risky. By 1953 the British, profiting from American experience, were using an unusual aid: a dog troop, run jointly by the Royal Engineers and the Royal Army Veterinary Corps. Some of the animals had been trained to detect mines by sitting where they were laid; it was reported that their performance suffered in winter because they disliked sitting on frozen ground. Others had been trained to look for wounded men; most successful of all were the patrol dogs, trained to detect the presence of the enemy. Some of them, using a combination of scent and sound, were capable of detecting an enemy patrol up to 400 yards away when they stiffened, pricked their ears and 'pointed' silently. Even in the midst of a patrol battle, with the sound of gunfire and the distraction of flares, dogs were able to detect Chinese ambush positions at over 30 yards' range.

With the New Year of 1953 hopes of an armistice began to rise. Through the winter both sides had sought to dominate no man's land whilst avoiding major engagements. On the communist side there had been a cooling of Soviet enthusiasm for Kim Il-sung's bellicosity and in Peking there was consensus among the Chinese rulers, who faced dire domestic problems, that an end had to be reached without loss of face.

In February 1953 General Van Fleet handed over command of 8th Army to Lieutenant-General Maxwell Taylor, a soldier-scholar with an outstanding record as an airborne commander in the Second World War. Unlike his predecessor he had soldiered alongside British and Commonwealth troops and was immediately at ease when paying his first visit to West's division. He came to Korea having been briefed by Secretary of Defense Marshall to avoid casualties by refusing combat whenever possible, in accordance with presidential policy. In London, Churchill and his military advisers were comforted to believe that old friends were once more at the helm in Washington and in Korea.

As a means of restarting the peace talks, General Mark Clark proposed on 20 February that an initial exchange of sick and wounded prisoners of war should take place. The Chinese, seeing a way cleared for an 'honourable' armistice, readily agreed and on 20 April, after tortuous negotiations over the ratio of exchanges between the two sides, Operation 'Little Switch' got under way to the accompaniment of much publicity. Amongst the Chinese and North Korean prisoners returned to the north were many from the special camps near Pusan where they had been receiving advanced treatment for horrific burns caused by napalm. Some of America's leading plastic surgeons had been working here in relays since 1950, with no shortage of guinea pigs on whom to practise their techniques. Visitors to these prison hospitals were treated, if they had the stomach for it, to a pageant of grotesques; men with their entire faces burnt or shot away, lacking ears, eyes, mouths and noses in many cases. At the hands of some of the world's finest surgeons they had been patiently reconstructed and given therapy and basic skills which, it was hoped, would afford them a chance in life on their return home. Many of these horrors were to be seen, led by their sighted but maimed comrades, as they passed across the demarcation line at Panmunjon during Little Switch.

Six days after the start of the prisoner exchange, full armistice talks began again. There was now a detectable air of urgency, as though the North Korean and Chinese delegates were conscious of the need to conclude the war on the most advantageous terms; as these included the settlement of a demilitarized zone or DMZ on the best tactical terms that could be attained, the United Nations forces braced themselves to repel any imminent assault. They did not have long to wait; a number of savage local attacks were launched against allied lines right across the peninsula in the next three months.

On the extreme right of the I Corps sector a dominant mountain feature known as Old Baldy had been the scene of bloody fighting in 1952, changing hands several times. In March 1953 it was held by a Colombian battalion which was driven off after a brief fight. Maxwell Taylor gave orders that it was to be left in enemy hands rather than incur more United Nations casualties. The Chinese immediately turned Old Baldy into a citadel, from whose summit they commanded a matchless view of the American positions. The allied front line had an outpost, in the shadow of Old Baldy, nicknamed Porkchop Hill, standing high above the valley floor overlooked by the Chinese firmly established on a ridge of Old Baldy named Hassakol. This lay only 600 yards from Pork Chop, which by April 1953 had little real tactical significance but was retained because of its psychological value and as a useful patrol base and listening post. The American main line of resistance (MLR) lay a further mile to the south on commanding ground, facing Old Baldy.

Pork Chop was held by units of the US 7th Division; on 16 April it was garrisoned by Company 'E' of the 31st Infantry, under Lieutenant Thomas Harrold, one of whose platoons was held back in the MLR as a reserve. Counting his attached artillery observation party and some engineers he could dispose of nearly a hundred men. Harrold expected to be attacked; throughout the day he and his men could hear the muffled sound of singing from the depths of Hassakol, where the Chinese were gathering in their tunnels. After dark, Harrold put out his usual standing patrols, charged with giving early warning of hostile movements in the valley. He also sent out a ten-man fighting patrol with the aim of grabbing a prisoner, reducing the garrison of Pork Chop to 66 men.

At 10.30 p.m., without a preliminary barrage, the Chinese poured out of their tunnels and rushed towards Pork Chop, overwhelming the fighting patrol and listening posts, only a few of whom got back to Harrold's position. At 11 p.m., a devastating artillery and mortar barrage hit Pork Chop. Harrold fired an SOS rocket to summon immediate artillery defensive fire in front of his position, which ran along the uppermost contour of the hill, linking a series of bunkers. The supporting battery illuminated the scene with starshell, then engaged with high explosive which the Chinese seemed to ignore, charging on up the slope and into Harrold's trenches, showering them with grenades which killed or wounded most of their occupants. Harrold called for all the artillery support which could be brought to bear. Despite this, by 1 a.m. the only parts of Pork Chop still in American hands were Harrold's command post bunker and some outlying weapon slits.

In the command post Harrold assembled his artillery observer, whose radio was still working, one of the platoon commanders and some NCOs. One of them stood in the entrance, shooting down anyone who tried to get in, stacking the corpses to block the door. The company clerk helped him, punctiliously asking his superior NCO for permission to fire whenever another Chinese appeared. Harrold reported on the radio to his battalion commander who, as was the American custom, referred the situation to the regimental commander, Colonel Kern. At this point both battalion and regimental commanders appeared to think that Harrold was still in possession of the entire Pork Chop feature and all that was needed were reinforcements.

At 2 a.m. Kern ordered two platoons forward from the main position with orders to report to Harrold. One platoon got lost, the other almost reached Harrold's position to be scattered by a Chinese machine-gunner on the roof of the command bunker. The platoon fell back in confusion under heavy artillery fire. Its youthful commander, Second Lieutenant Denton, however, rallied the dozen or so survivors, addressed them forcibly on their duty to their comrades on Pork Chop, and returned with them towards the fight; owing to a misunderstanding they were picked up at this point by a tank and carried back to the battalion's main position, much to the fury of the ardent platoon commander. He reported the situation to his commanding officer who decided to launch a counter-attack with two companies at first light.

In Harrold's command post the situation was critical. The enemy threw a grenade through the weapon slit, wounding Harrold and several of his party and destroying the radio. Somehow a telephone line had remained intact and Harrold was able to speak to his remaining platoon, still back in the MLR. He called for continuous illumination of the hill by artillery and mortars; in the light of the flares hundreds of Chinese could be seen swarming over Pork Chop, trying to winkle out the remaining defenders. Harrold called for fire on his own position, which he sealed in with sandbags as the shells came down. At 4 a.m. he received the discouraging news from divisional headquarters that the next move of the Chinese would be to blow in the roof of the bunker; Harrold calmly stated that he intended to stick it out, and advised his commanding officer that any relief party would need flame-throwers and rocket launchers to dislodge the Chinese. He and his men sat in the dark, listening to the Chinese digging away at the roof. Then the artillery fire could be heard switching to the northern slope of the hill and they knew that the counter-attack was coming in.

It was now 4.40 a.m. The company commanders of the counter-attacking force had been told that there were no longer any Americans alive on Pork Chop. One of them, Lieutenant Clemons, thought his commanding officer's plan was hideously flawed as it involved the two companies attacking simultaneously from opposite sides of the hill, with every risk of colliding in the half light at the top. Clemons decided to rush directly from the MLR to the top of Pork Chop, which saved him and his men from the Chinese artillery whose fire fell ineffectually behind them as the breathless troops, burdened with heavy weapons including flame-throwers, arrived at the summit to clear the Chinese from the bunkers.

The enemy were skilled and courageous, dodging the flames by running back over the reverse slope, throwing dozens of grenades as they returned to extinguish the fires and re-enter the bunkers, from which they fought on until a 3.5-inch rocket launcher was fired into the weapons slit of each in turn. Fighting their way up to the hilltop, Clemons and his men reached the command bunker, freeing Harrold and the other survivors. The advance could go no further, for every time one of Clemons' men showed himself he was fired at, as Clemons had predicted, by the other counter-attacking company from the opposite side of the hill. Harrold and the walking wounded started to make their way back to the MLR but disaster overtook the second counter-attack company as Chinese artillery fire caught them in the open.

Dawn broke on Pork Chop, reduced to a shell-torn shambles of bodies, broken wire and collapsed trenches and bunkers, amidst which those still alive vainly sought cover. Clemons counted heads and found that his garrison consisted of 35 of his own company and about 20 from Harrold's, who were dazedly digging themselves out of their bunkers, and a few from the right flank company. A further company, commanded by Clemons' brother-in-law Lieutenant Russell, now joined the battered garrison on Pork Chop. The Chinese were massing for a counter-attack which materialized almost at once. The hilltop was accurately ranged by the artillery of both sides, who kept up a furious fire as the opposing infantry fought hand-to-hand with bombs, fists and bayonets.

At midday, Clemons received orders to thin out preparatory to giving up the hill. He told the runner who brought the message to go back to battalion headquarters and tell the colonel that he was holding out but hard pressed, and that any weakening of his force would result in its being overwhelmed. He realized that his predicament was still perceived only dimly, if at all, by higher levels of command. This was confirmed when, at 2.45 p.m., a public relations team, complete with photographers, arrived on the hill, in search of material for a feature article in the *Stars and Stripes* on 'a successful battle'. He sent them packing with the message that he had to have more troops; nevertheless, Russell's company of nearly 60 relatively fresh men was taken away. Clemons was left with 25 men, whom he deployed in two groups, both under savage fire as they attempted to strengthen their position; by now there were few who believed they would leave the hill alive.

Somewhat belatedly Colonel Kern realized the predicament of the men on Pork Chop. He sought advice from his divisional commander, Major-General Trudeau, a standard US Army procedure which baffled the British and Commonwealth staffs, who had been trained to delegate downwards, trusting the commander on the spot to fight his battle and backing him to the hilt. Trudeau passed the matter back to I Corps and 8th Army and at once flew forward by helicopter to see for himself. At the battalion command post he found that the commanding officer had indeed displayed initiative and had reinserted the company taken out of the fight, placing it under the energetic command of Second Lieutenant Denton, the officer who had already rallied his shaken men after their initial flight from the hill. Gathering his own men and stragglers from other rifle companies he led them back to the cooks' bunker on Pork Chop without attracting the enemy's attention.

Clemons called up his battalion headquarters as General Trudeau arrived there, reporting that only 20 of his men were still alive and that the end was near unless reinforcements reached him soon. Trudeau, greatly impressed with the fighting spirit on Pork Chop, flew back to Kern's regimental command post where the corps commander, Major-General Clarke, had just arrived. Just as at the Imjin battle, where four levels of command were standing on one spot issuing orders, there was a risk of similar over-control now. It was agreed on the spot that although Pork Chop was of little tactical significance, the Chinese, who had now committed a whole division, were attacking it in such strength to test the Americans' resolve, and that any weakness at this juncture would increase the power of the communist negotiators' demands at Panmunjon. Trudeau asked Clarke to state categorically that once the hill had been recaptured and consolidated, it would not be abandoned again 'in the foreseeable future', implying that in the last resort it was expendable, but also that Trudeau did not want to see lives squandered unnecessarily.

Whilst the generals laid their plans the irrepressible Denton had arrived at Clemons' command post on top of Pork Chop; he personally sited each of his men in weapon slits, all the time under heavy fire, telling them that although they had made a shaky start, they were going to see it through now. At this their spirits rose.

Towards the end of the day, two hitherto uncommitted companies of the 2nd/17th Infantry were ordered to relieve Clemons; having been fascinated spectators of the day's battle they were under no illusions as to what could befall them and moved hesitantly. The first platoon of this force eventually arrived on Pork Chop at 9.30 p.m., as masses of Chinese started to pour across the valley floor in another attack. The Chinese guns caught the new arrivals in the open as they reached Clemons on top of the hill and before they could take up defensive positions, causing heavy casualties and scattering the rest all over Pork Chop; it was hours before they could be rallied and sorted out. Their company commander, unfamiliar with the terrain, asked Denton to remain with him and he gallantly obliged as his weary men made their way to the rear.

The enemy resumed their assault on the command bunker, placing a machine-gun on its roof, from which it played over the entire American position as attempts were made to throw grenades at it through the bunker's weapon slits. Several brave men charged out to kill their tormentors; in one of these sorties, Denton was wounded but one of his men killed the intruders. Three large shells then landed on the bunker roof, partially caving it in; some of the wounded began to scream but Denton silenced them. He was in radio contact with two self-propelled multi-barrelled anti-aircraft guns parked at the rear of the hill, undetected as yet by the Chinese. These weapons had a devastating effect against the Chinese on the bunker roof. Denton indicated his position to them by means of a phosphorus grenade tied to a flare. The enemy, assuming it to be a distress signal, closed in for the kill. In the bunker the entombed men waited for the end; one began to pray aloud. There was a sudden silence. One of the men found a hole and looked out, to see the Chinese fleeing in confusion; a full company of the 2nd/17th had arrived in the nick of time and dug in on top of the hill. There were several attacks next day but the

Chinese had lost their enthusiasm, retiring into the depths of their tunnels under Hassakol. Denton insisted on staying on Pork Chop until he had personally defuzed the booby traps set by his men.

This was not to be the last fight for Pork Chop, but it remained an inspiring example of what the American fighting man could achieve given good leadership; it was certainly a performance of a very different order from that of the luckless 24th Division at Taejon in the terrible summer of 1950 or of the 2nd at Kunu-ri. General Clarke was true to his word; Pork Chop was honourably abandoned on Maxwell Taylor's orders shortly before the signing of the armistice three months later; the Chinese never set foot on it again and it remains to this day a silent memorial, in the middle of the demilitarized zone, to a gallant defence.

The Chinese attacked the Hook fiercely on 7 May, probably to test the defences; a few days later the Black Watch handed their battered positions over to the 1st Battalion, The Duke of Wellington's Regiment. A unit which enjoyed a reputation for rugby football, its ranks included many players of distinction, among them a future England captain. The 'Dukes' (as they were, and still are, known) were recruited from the Halifax area in West Yorkshire, home of their depot since the 1880s, and where the regiment, the old 33rd Foot of which the Great Duke himself had once been the commanding officer, was regarded as very much part of the town's history. The battalion had arrived in Korea in the previous November and was already familiar with the Hook area and the valley of the Samichon. They were short of soldiers, their strength on arrival in Korea having been barely 600. Occupying the Hook on 13 May, they immediately set about its ruined defences; the recent attack on the Black Watch had given notice of an impending Chinese offensive. The Assault Pioneer platoon, commanded by Second Lieutenant Stacpoole, recently commissioned from Sandhurst, had been trained in wiring, minelaying, booby-trapping and the construction of bunkers when the division was out of the line; they had to practise these newly acquired skills within a few hundred yards of an alert and aggressive enemy.

An uneasy calm reigned over the Dukes' front for the first ten days but on the night of 17 May, increased patrol activity was detected on the enemy side. A Chinese deserter who came across a day later spoke freely; a major attack was imminent and the Chinese patrolling had been for reconnaissance purposes. The deserter gave a remarkably detailed description of the Chinese plan, to be carried out by eight companies drawn from two regiments of the 133rd Division. He added that the officers and NCOs who would lead the attack had been studying the Dukes from concealed observation posts. Stacpoole and his pioneers, ably assisted by the Royal Engineers, redoubled their efforts. On the night of 20 May some 4,000 shells and mortar bombs fell on the Hook in two and a half hours as probing attacks were launched against the forward positions. This was assumed to be a dress rehearsal, to pinpoint the Dukes and chart their defensive fire plan. On the following night there was another bombardment and the battalion braced itself for the inevitable.

For three days, there was almost no patrol activity, but the Chinese kept up steady artillery and mortar fire on the Dukes' wire and forward positions. The divisional artillery was continually in action against Chinese working parties digging communication trenches and covered ways leading towards the Hook. All night, activity could be heard from the enemy trenches. Throughout this period Auster aircraft of the division's Air OP and Light Liaison flights were observing from a safe height and the information they gleaned, together with air photographic missions, confirmed what could be seen on the ground. On the evening of the 28th, the routine Auster patrol was heavily engaged by anti-aircraft guns; all day, Chinese medium and heavy artillery had pounded the Hook, methodically seeking to destroy observation and command posts, wire, and fire trenches. The Dukes' commanding officer, Lieutenant-Colonel Bunbury, realizing that the attack was imminent, ordered reserve platoons forward. The move was barely complete when, at 7.53 p.m., five minutes after sunset, a tremendous concentration of enemy fire was brought down on the Hook. Within minutes, out of the smoke rushed the Chinese infantry, hurling grenades and explosive charges into the defenders' trenches. Hand-to-hand fighting broke out. The surviving defenders sought cover in the bunkers and tunnels, from which they continued to fight until the Chinese blew in the entrances with satchel charges, entombing the occupants.

As the platoons on the forward edge of the Hook fought for their lives, further waves of Chinese could be seen in the gathering darkness making their way forward; they were engaged by every weapon within range, including artillery and tank guns. In preparation for such an emergency, the entire artillery resources of I US Corps had been registered on the area and an awesome concentration of fire was brought to bear on the Hook. The whole area, only a few hundred yards square, resembled the surface of the moon; in the preceding week over 20,000 shells and mortar bombs – half within the last twenty-four hours – had landed on the Dukes' position. The enemy artillery was skilfully handled; just over half an hour into the attack its fire was expertly switched from the forward positions to the reverse slopes to catch reinforcements moving up.

By 8.30 p.m. Chinese infantry were to be seen on top of the Hook but were prevented from moving further forward by Stacpoole's wire, in which they became entangled, suffering heavily as defensive fire came down on them. The full weight of the Commonwealth divisional artillery – three field regiments, a medium battery of 5.5-inch guns and a light regiment of 4.2-inch mortars – was augmented by that of I US Corps – three battalions and two batteries of

155mm field guns and howitzers, and a battery apiece of 8-inch and 240mm howitzers. A rocket battery added its noisy and spectacular contribution.

A second attack came in at 8.45 p.m., directed at a platoon on the north-eastern side of the position, where it was supported by a Centurion of the 1st Royal Tank Regiment; dug in near the crest, its 20-pounder canister rounds and machine-gun caught the attackers in the open as they tried to cross the defensive wire. All over the Hook feature, lethal close-quarter battles were taking place; control was impossible and all depended on the individual soldier. Nearly two-thirds of the Dukes were national servicemen with little more than their basic training behind them. Their pay was less than £2 a week, and none would have the right to vote in any sort of election until his twenty-first birthday. Few were more than 19 years old, and their platoon officers little older; yet they fought the Chinese to a standstill. A third Chinese attack came shortly after midnight; the enemy, clearly illuminated by starshell and mortar flares, were once more unable to breach the wire and were shot down on it in dozens. Over 30 bodies were found here the next morning, which the Chinese had been unable to drag away.

Colonel Bunbury sensed that the Chinese had shot their bolt with this last assault, and ordered an immediate counter-attack to clear the Hook. The enemy were still much in evidence on the summit and an artillery strike was ordered, using variable timing (VT) shells with radar fuzes, bursting precisely low above the heads of the enemy to clear them off the top before the trench clearance began. Every man who could carry a weapon was sent into action as the Dukes swept across the top of the Hook, finally reaching the position formerly held by the first platoon to receive the force of the Chinese attack. It was unrecognizable as such, so great was the destruction wrought by the Chinese artillery and demolition charges. One of the engineers described what he saw:

> I went to the forward positions and never saw such a mess. The six-foot trenches, even those which had overhead cover, were shallow hollows . . . Several Chinese dead were there and unfortunately some of ours; no one seemed to have survived from the Gunner OP bunker, which was almost flattened. It was really World War I stuff. [Immediately, the sappers got to work to repair the defences.] It was a question of digging out the collapsed trenches, throwing the spoil downhill on the enemy side, and shoring up with timbers . . . This produced intermittent but reasonably accurate mortar fire, especially on one bunker which was ranged accurately by the Chinese. Corporal Garrett did a very steady job there . . . American planes carried out strike after strike on the other side of the valley, keeping the Chinese heads down whilst they were in circuit . . . Our lads shovelled the earth over the top for all they were worth . . . until another strike came. We were full of admiration for the Yankee planes.

Repairs went on despite continuous enemy fire, as frantic efforts were made to disinter the men buried alive in their tunnels and bunkers by the enemy bombardment. One section of nine men emerged unscathed after over nine hours' entombment. Enemy were still present on and around the Hook and these had to be dealt with. The deep field of defensive wire laid with such difficulty by the assault pioneers was damaged by enemy shellfire but held up the Chinese attack at its most critical stage, preventing the entire position from being overrun. Such was the efficiency of the British and American artillery support throughout the battle that actual contact with enemy soldiers was limited to the rifle company on the Hook feature itself, although the entire battalion position had received heavy artillery, mortar and machine-gun fire throughout the night.

The enemy left much equipment on the Hook, indicating meticulous preparation of the attack, which had set out to destroy the Dukes and permanently secure the Hook feature. Over fifty satchel charges, containing up to ten pounds of explosive for bunker attacks, were picked up. The Chinese had aimed to breach the wire using crude Bangalore torpedoes – lengths of iron piping filled with explosive and thrust into the entanglement. Hundreds of grenades were left by the enemy together with many so-called 'Burp guns', the crude but highly effective version of a Russian sub-machine-gun with a circular 75-round magazine and an extremely high rate of fire – hence its name. It was ideal for close-quarter fighting in trench systems and far more effective than the shoddy and unreliable Sten gun used by the British. Against masses of Chinese attacking by night, the British No. 4 rifle was cumbrous and unable to give the close-range volume of fire needed.

Apart from the resolution of the Dukes, the decisive element in the repulse of this, the greatest attack endured by any single battalion in the Commonwealth Division, was the artillery. It was a resounding endorsement of the British system of having gunner officers right forward, sharing the life of the infantry they supported. It was also an occasion for celebration by the Royal Engineers who, like the gunners, faced the dangers of the front line to give responsive support and advice.

Documents taken from the body of a Chinese officer on the Hook confirmed that the initial attack against the Dukes' forward platoons had been made by a specially trained assault engineer company supported by infantry. The second and third waves had consisted of one and two infantry companies respectively, followed by an entire battalion whose task was to roll the Dukes off the hill. In the event this phase was frustrated by the stand of the company on the Hook itself and the tremendous weight and accuracy of the defensive artillery. A further Chinese battalion, held back in reserve to clear the battlefield, succeeded in removing most of the enemy dead and wounded. However, nearly a hundred mangled bodies were counted on the wire, around 'Green Finger' and its tunnel, on 'Ronson' and actually on the Hook. A further 70 dead Chinese were to be seen within a few hundred yards after daylight next morning. A conservative estimate of enemy casualties was 250 killed and 800 wounded, or about 65 per cent of the forces committed.

The full intentions of the Chinese were further revealed when the documents taken from the officer's body were translated. Headed 'A Plan to annihilate the enemy and to establish merit', the following points were listed:

1. Carry out orders firmly. Attack wherever it is ordered. Guarantee to occupy Hill 161 [The Hook].
2. In this combat mission, I guarantee to lead all comrades of the platoon to the front line without incident.
3. Lead the troops while I am in command. Thinking must be clear. Organize combat mission carefully. Know the usage of the combat power. Be front of the troops when the circumstance is in the developing stage.
4. Love the lives of the comrades during the combat and to fight skilfully. Not to be evacuated while suffering minor injury.
5. Only need spirit to fight to the end.
6. Guarantee to carry out the policies and regulations in treating prisoners of war and to capture more living ones.

Platoon Leader Huang Kui
26 May 1953

Despite the enormous damage done to their positions, the Dukes' casualties were moderate: 20 dead, 86 wounded and 20 posted as missing, most of whom were taken prisoner in the first enemy onslaught or dug out by the Chinese. It had been an outstanding display of grit by a very young battalion, against some of the best troops in the Chinese People's Army.

Frustrated at Pork Chop and now on the Hook, the Chinese looked elsewhere for a resounding success which would give them a tactical advantage in what they knew were the dying weeks of the war. Time was running out; only two days before the battle on the Hook, the UN team at Panmunjon had hardened their line and demanded a reply, by 1 June, to their proposals for the composition of the Neutral Nations' Repatriation Commission which, as originally proposed by the Indians, would be responsible for all prisoners not wishing to be returned to their own countries after the end of hostilities.

On 2 June the coronation of Queen Elizabeth II was marked by an eccentric but spectacular display of smoke shells, fired by the Commonwealth divisional artillery over the Chinese positions. As the canisters burst hundreds of feet above the ground, falling in graceful arcs to build up a red, white and blue smoke screen, soldiers on both sides stood up in their trenches to watch. The Durhams took advantage of the diversion to send a patrol which laid out a quantity of air recognition panels prominently on a hillside on the Chinese side of no man's land in the form of the Royal Cipher, before returning unscathed to their own lines.

The target for the next, and last, Chinese attack was the Korean-held Kumsong sector where six ROK divisions were assailed on 13 July by the best part of five Chinese armies. An attack on this scale had not been seen for two years and it took the defenders by surprise. There can be little doubt that it was made in response to recent bellicose pronouncements by Syngman Rhee who, alarmed by the evident determination of the Americans and their allies to end the fighting as honourably (for them) as possible, had announced his intention of ignoring any armistice signed at Panmunjon and carrying on the war alone if necessary. For good measure, and without reference to Mark Clark, he released thousands of North Korean prisoners of war who, he claimed, had refused repatriation.

The ROK army was no longer the derisory force it had been in the opening months of the war; its men were well equipped, and patient training had reaped its dividends. Although the Koreans fell back before the first shock, they fought hard, inflicting heavy losses on the Chinese. American reinforcements were rushed to their aid and the line stabilized. Although the enemy had gained a few miles and changed the line on which the cease-fire would be operative, they had not achieved the final decisive victory they needed, and had suffered over 28,000 casualties in the process.

With the signing of the armistice only a matter of days away, the Chinese did not give up. On 24 July they attacked the US Marines, recently returned to their former positions to the left of the Commonwealth Division. The attack was directed at a series of hills on the boundary between the two divisions, and the 2nd Royal Australian Regiment on the Hook became involved. As if to repay the support given by the Americans in the Dukes' fight two months earlier, the full weight of the Commonwealth divisional artillery was brought to bear, firing 13,000 shells in a few hours. The Australians had to watch impotently; athirst to join the battle, they were tied to their positions by the wall of shellfire between them and the enemy. The Chinese tried again on the following night, to be met by another barrage as a full corps target was fired, every gun firing ten rounds. Brigadier Wilton of 28 Commonwealth Brigade estimated that between two and three thousand Chinese bodies, caught in this, were to be seen lying on the western slopes of the Hook. Only 43 marines and two Australians were killed in two nights of bombardment. At no time did the enemy get into the American or Australian trenches.

There were one or two more half-hearted attacks on the marines, easily thrown off; the Commonwealth sector remained quiet as the last hours passed. On 27 July, allied and communist delegates met at Panmunjon to sign the truce agreement, which was to be effective at 10 p.m. that night. During the day, there were short outbursts of firing along the line, but at the appointed hour the gunners received the welcome order to 'empty guns and cease firing'.

On both sides of the firing lines, soldiers emerged from their bunkers and slit trenches; at some points where the lines lay close to each other, men approached their late enemies, at first cautiously, then with confidence. Cigarettes were exchanged and there was even a limited amount of fraternization. But there were urgent matters to attend to. The armistice agreement laid down a strict timetable which left little time for rejoicing. Both sides had to pull back their forces, supplies and equipment at least two kilometres within seventy-two hours, to create the four-kilometre demilitarized zone or DMZ. This called for a major logistic operation, which continued as the next requirement of the armistice was met, stipulating a forty-day period in which all minefields, wire entanglements and defence works were to be made safe and the demarcation fences constructed. It demanded a major effort from the sappers, who had created what they now had to destroy, gloomily watched as their explosives blew up the bunkers and emplacements built with such enormous effort. The DMZ was closed to all on 13 September and has remained since then an empty and haunted tract. From the fence marking its southern edge can still be clearly seen the hills for which so many men on both sides died.

Once the battlefield had been demilitarized, the United Nations forces reestablished the Kansas defence line. For the Commonwealth Division this involved constructing positions immediately south of the Imjin, on ground familiar to anyone who had fought there in 1951. With the approach of winter only months away, it was decided to provide as much hutted accommodation as possible and building materials were arriving at Pusan before long. The Commonwealth divisional headquarters was moved to a site within hailing distance of Castle Hill on which Major Angier's 'A' Company of the Glosters had fought their last battle. To the dismay of quartermasters, there was a speedy return to peacetime accounting.

Now came the turn of the prisoners. The Panmunjon agreement provided for the exchange within sixty days of all who had opted for repatriation and for those who declined repatriation to be put into the care of the Neutral Nations Commission. Operation 'Big Switch' saw 12,773 United Nations personnel and about 75,000 Chinese and North Koreans exchanged. As the first allied prisoners passed across to freedom, they had many harrowing tales to tell.

CHAPTER 30

The Waters of Babylon

In the middle of 1951 the War Office published a pamphlet giving instructions for British personnel in the event of capture. They were to limit the information given under interrogation to their surname, Christian names, rank, date of birth and service number. No other questions were to be answered, and it was stressed that threats were not permitted in any case under the terms of the Geneva Convention. Once captured, the reader was reminded that the only man he could be sure was a friend was the man he knew well before capture. All were warned to beware of hidden microphones during questioning. There was to be no discussion of 'shop' between prisoners. The enemy would certainly imply that other prisoners had already talked freely, that the captive's unit had been identified and that further reticence was a waste of time as it would delay the onset of friendly treatment and the passage of information to next of kin. The leaflet concluded with a stern warning against the giving of parole, or of broadcasting on the enemy's radio.

The author of this document, promulgated before anything was known of conditions in the Yalu camps and in any case months after the great majority of British prisoners had been taken, was evidently under the impression that the rules of the game were unchanged since the Second World War. In Korea, however, captives were to undergo treatment very different from that in the German *Kriegsgefangenlager*.

The United States, communist China and the North Korean People's Republic had not signed the Geneva Convention of 1949 laying down instructions for the conduct of prisoners and captors alike and emphasizing the importance of neutral inspection of prison camps. As far as the Chinese and North Koreans were concerned, all who were taken prisoner whilst fighting communism were war criminals and thus not entitled to protection. There were, however, marked differences between the Chinese and North Korean methods of handling enemy prisoners. The North Koreans regarded prisoners primarily as a source of forced labour, intelligence information, and finally as subjects for political indoctrination. Chinese policy was based from the outset on the so-called 'Lenient Policy' evolved over the years of civil war as a means of absorbing captured Kuomintang soldiers into the People's Army. Compared to that of the North Koreans it appeared relatively humane: the prisoner was offered political education as a means of redemption, but if he showed lack of responsiveness – or worse, active resistance – he was liable to beatings, starvation, deprivation of medical treatment and prolonged solitary confinement under barbaric conditions.

In the first weeks of the war a mixed bag of captives fell into North Korean hands. Thousands of ROK soldiers who were taken in the opening battles were absorbed into the NKPA, preferring this option to that of summary execution. Great numbers of these would be recaptured by UN forces later in the campaign, to become useful political pawns in Syngman Rhee's armoury. As American troops arrived piecemeal from Japan, hundreds fell into North Korean hands. The able-bodied were herded away, the sick and wounded left to die at the roadside or murdered on the spot. The North Koreans lavished no medical care on their prisoners and as they were force-marched north hundreds of men simply lay down by the road and died.

Near Pyongyang a transit centre was situated in a disused mine. Known to hundreds of UN prisoners as 'the Caves', it was presided over by sadistic guards revelling in the misery inflicted on the inmates who lay in dank tunnels through which ran a stream of icy water. Food supplies were minimal and barely edible, there was no sanitation and men soon began to die from sickness and malnutrition. It was to this terrible place that a group of sick and wounded survivors of the Glosters were brought early in May 1951 following the Imjin battle. They had already marched for many nights, hiding by day to avoid attack by allied aircraft, often beaten by their guards and losing several of their number *en route*. A junior officer in the party, Lieutenant Terry Waters of the West Yorkshire Regiment, had been sent as a reinforcement to the Glosters sometime before the battle, in which he had been seriously wounded in the head and arm. During the march north he disregarded his own injuries to encourage his men. On arrival at the Caves the group were thrown into the insanitary tunnel with hundreds of South Koreans and Americans, many near death. A North Korean political commissar invited the British prisoners to join a 'Peace Fighters' organization, promising good food and medical treatment if they did. The offer was unanimously rejected; but Waters saw that few of his men would survive long under such conditions and ordered them to accept the offer. He refused to go with them, having assumed responsibility for upholding the honour of his country and adoptive regiment, even though he realized he was dying. Gangrene had set in and he knew his time was short. The North Koreans applied every pressure on him to join the others, including the offer of surgical treatment, which he declined; he remained steadfast, dying a few days later.

At first, in contravention of the Geneva Convention, the Chinese and North Koreans accommodated officers, non-commissioned officers and soldiers in the same camps, and a measure of organized resistance to indoctrination could be sustained. The Chinese, realizing that the presence of the officers was sabotaging their 'Lenient Policy', then put corporals and below in two principal camps, at Pyoktong and Choksong, up near the Yalu. Until early in 1951 these had been run by the North Koreans, but as the death rate was getting out of hand the Chinese took control of all the major camps. The first batch of British prisoners to arrive at Pyoktong had been taken north of Seoul in January 1951, most of them from the Royal Ulster Rifles. They found a camp full of Americans taken in the battles of the previous summer and in the retreat following China's entry into the war. Leaderless and demoralized, many had lost all interest in survival; twenty or more were dying every day and several British prisoners later claimed to have witnessed a series of mass burials of up to 1,500 in pits near the camp. It was many weeks before the new arrivals, working under Chinese supervision, were able to make the place habitable. After this, there was no more forced labour and the Chinese began to implement the 'Lenient Policy'.

The first step was the completion of a lengthy questionnaire. It began innocuously with personal and family details, then a potted autobiography, leading more subtly to questions on political affiliations, sentiments on arrival in Korea, opinions on the Chinese People's Volunteers, and on the current British Labour government. Failure to complete the form as directed carried the penalty of indefinite solitary confinement; from what the prisoners had already seen by the time they reached their appointed camp, they had every reason to believe that this was no idle threat. This did not stifle ribald humour. One soldier gave his address as 'No. 1234567 Private Stalin, Joe, Red Army, 1 Kremlin Terrace, Moscow'. An officer, answering the question 'Have you ever committed a serious crime?' responded, 'Yes – travelling 1st class on a 3rd class ticket from Woking to Waterloo.' Because the Chinese had limited interpretation facilities at this stage, these and other facetious replies continued to mystify and infuriate them.

The camps where most British captives found themselves bore no resemblance to those of the Second World War. They were actually large Korean villages in part of which the normal population still resided. The prisoners, their guards and indoctrinators were billeted in compounds around the village. There was little or no barbed wire or watch towers as there was virtually no chance of an inmate making a successful escape and returning to friendly lines. There were accordingly no mass escape plans, as had been common during the war, although a number of individuals made repeated attempts to get away. The pugnacious adjutant of the Glosters, Captain Farrar-Hockley, was one of these; he had been one of the last on top of Hill 235 when Colonel Carne gave the order for the survivors to break out, but was forced to surrender when surrounded shortly after. He had been a prisoner for only a few hours when he made the first of his many escape bids whilst crossing the ford over the Imjin near where the Glosters' listening patrol had wrought such execution only a few nights earlier. He was recaptured here as on subsequent occasions, but never gave up and endured frequent savage punishment as a hard-core 'reactionary'.

During the prisoners' march north Farrar-Hockley came across another determined escaper and resister. Fusilier Kinne of the Royal Northumberland Fusiliers was captured on the last day of the Imjin battle as his battalion fought its way to safety. Like Farrar-Hockley he was well endowed with the aggression and bloody-mindedness which, combined with regimental pride, patriotism and frequently a deep religious faith, form the weapons of those who resist imprisonment. Both men were subject to barbaric treatment in an attempt to break their spirits and discourage others from attempting to escape. Kinne was to be a superb example to his fellow men; utterly rejecting any attempts by his captors to turn him with the 'Lenient Policy', he felt the full weight of their wrath as a result. He was repeatedly beaten, tortured, starved and subjected to long terms of solitary confinement; right to the end of the war he fought on, suffering his final bout of solitary after flaunting a rosette in his head-dress on the day of the Queen's Coronation in June 1953. One of the punishments he endured was confinement in a wooden box in which he had to sit at attention while poked with bayonets, beaten and urinated on by his guards. He regarded 29 August 1952 as a high point of his imprisonment, for on that day the Chinese guard who was beating him with the butt of his sub-machine-gun was killed when it went off. Kinne roared with laughter, so was clubbed insensible and thrown into a hole where he remained in solitary confinement for almost a month, being taken out for frequent beatings. After his session in the hole Kinne was sentenced by a Chinese military court to a year's solitary, and given a further six months when he asked for medical treatment for the double hernia he had suffered in an earlier escape attempt. His inspirational conduct earned him the George Cross.

A total of 977 British officers and men fell into the hands of the enemy in Korea; of these the largest proportion came from the Glosters, their attached personnel and supporting gunners. They had fought until exhausted, and had it not been for officers like Farrar-Hockley, reluctantly ordering his men to lay down their arms when further resistance would have been suicidal, the death toll would have been appalling. Many of those marching north under the guns of their escorts had known earlier captivities; Mr Hobbs, the Regimental Sergeant-Major, captured in Belgium in 1940 serving with the regiment's 2nd Battalion; Major Guy Ward of the gunners, taken in Crete in 1941. Captain Farrar-Hockley's batman had been captured at Arnhem in 1944. Some had been prisoners of the Japanese and one of these, Lance-Corporal Aylward – known throughout the battalion as 'Jungle Jim' – had been confined by them for a time at the Munsan-ni staging camp in North Korea (known from the inmates' diet as the Bean Camp) where, to his dismay, he presently found himself once more.

After many long night marches in which the relatively fit took it in turns to carry the sick and wounded, the survivors of the Glosters reached the Yalu camps in mid-June. Here at least were some friendly faces – the men of the Royal Ulster Rifles and the 8th Hussars captured earlier in the year.

The British, however, formed only a small part of the prison population in North Korea. Well over 5,000 Americans were captured during the war, most of them in the first six months, of whom only 3,746 survived to be repatriated in 1953. In addition to these were over 200 Turks, who proved to be the most difficult for the Chinese to cope with. The Turks were adamant that none of their personnel would co-operate. Whenever a man had to go to the medical centre for treatment, or to the camp office for an interview, he was escorted by two fellow Turks. The penalty for collaboration with the camp staff was death and several waverers were thus disposed of. The death sentence was also presumably extended to a luckless Armenian introduced by the Chinese to the Turkish compound as an 'interpreter', who disappeared without trace. There were also small groups from most of the other United Nations contingents. In all, 13,444 UN prisoners were returned from the camps in Operations 'Big and Little Switch'. Of these, 359 UN prisoners were to refuse repatriation: one of them was British, 23 were American and 335 ROKs, most of whom had been northerners forcibly conscripted into the ROK army.

Once the prisoners had been settled into their camps they found that they were in for a concentrated education course. They were reminded yet again that they were war criminals; but a crumb of comfort was extended. If they proved good and attentive pupils and accepted their mentors' line of reasoning, they would enjoy all the benefits of the 'Lenient Policy'. Living conditions, even in the Chinese-run camps, were extremely bad until the end of 1951 when they improved somewhat, but to no higher standard than that of the local population. Medical officers such as Captain Hickey of the Glosters were constantly frustrated in their efforts to minister to the sick. Although rudimentary medical and surgical treatment was given, including an inoculation programme to avert the risk of epidemics, the Chinese attitude was inconsistent; in some camps the sick were grossly neglected. However, many returning prisoners in 1953 spoke warmly of a Chinese woman doctor who had confided that her life's ambition was to go to Edinburgh for a post-graduate course.

In Camp 5, at Pyoktong, which was set up as early as January 1951, over 1,600 prisoners, mostly Americans, died in the first eight months from starvation, sickness, loss of morale, neglect of battle wounds and sheer brutality. Despite these disgraceful conditions there was no lack of communist propaganda material showing that the prisoners were being well treated. Whether from coercion, the promise of rapid passage of mail to and from home, or of extra medical treatment for collaborators, many prisoners readily signed documents describing their agreeable life as guests of the Chinese People's Republic, admitting that they had realized the error of 'fighting for the rotten cause of American capitalism'. By the start of the truce talks in mid-1951 hundreds of UN prisoners had made such public statements praising the Chinese 'Volunteers' for their kindness and openly sympathizing with the enemy.

As their imprisonment dragged on, seemingly with little hope of early release, many of the British prisoners, especially the reservists, saw their demobilization date approach and pass; by the end of 1951 most should have been back in the United Kingdom as their units returned home; the effect on morale inevitably brought a significant fall in the level of resistance to indoctrination, which continued unabated even after classes had ceased to be compulsory. Those who attended voluntarily after this were assured of privileges denied to those who absented themselves; the Chinese correctly assumed that this policy would foster divisiveness and mistrust in the camps, and it was not long before informers were at work; 'reactionaries' were identified and reported and the slightest hint of an escape attempt nipped in the bud. After release from captivity, collaborators who had thus compromised themselves were ostracized by their fellow prisoners and were later the victims of physical assault on the troopships bearing them back to England.

From late in 1951 there was a discernible improvement in conditions in the camps, which were seen as no worse than those in the Chinese army or among the local population; but the quality of life, whether in terms of accommodation, granting of privileges or quality of rations, depended on the degree of co-operation given by the prisoners to their 'teachers'. The full joys of the Lenient Policy were available only to those who agreed unconditionally to accept the indoctrination thrust at them remorselessly for hours every day. As long as attendance was compulsory, the prisoners were subjected to interminable dissertations on Marxism and the advantages of communism over the capitalistic world. The British soldier is not the best of listeners to this sort of lecture and the 'teachers' were frequently reduced to incoherence by the barracking of their audiences.

The same spirit of resistance surfaced again when the prisoners were allowed to put on a concert party to celebrate Labour Day in 1952. Before the show they were told to parade through the village brandishing red hammer-and-sickle flags; they refused and the assembled Chinese press photographers had to be content with a flag-carrying party of prison guards followed at some distance by a laggardly parade of prisoners. The stage show was an example of what in the British army would be described as 'dumb insolence', into which any number of subtle gags were introduced. The compère was Sergeant Sykes of the Glosters, an accomplished stand-up comic, assisted by a noted 'reactionary' planted in the audience, whose heckling, carefully scripted beforehand and hugely appreciated by the audience, was far beyond the translating ability of the Chinese in the hall. Sykes was arrested on stage by the enraged camp staff following a recitation:

> They seek him here, they seek him there,
> They seek the bugger everywhere –
> Should he be shot, or should he be hung,
> That damned elusive Mao Tse-tung?

As the guards closed in on Sykes, the audience rioted; the outcome was a climb-down, with resultant loss of face, by the camp authorities. With Sykes freed, the prisoners dispersed quietly to their quarters.

The re-education curriculum covered every aspect of camp life. Any extra-curricular activity such as sing-songs, amateur dramatics, language classes or hobbies groups had to include a 'political' element; if it failed in this respect it was classified as illegal and the participants branded as 'reactionaries' liable to incur assorted punishments. All letters home were carefully examined, and if they did not contain passages gratefully extolling the Chinese communist regime they were destroyed. As a result, hundreds of prisoners who were otherwise totally unmoved by the 'education', duly included exaggerated praise for their captors in their letters, in the hope that these would reach their loved ones. What the Chinese failed to appreciate was that there were some former prisoners of the Germans in the Yalu camps, privy to a simple code used during the Second World War for passing information to intelligence agencies at home. Certain expressions, punctuation marks and other nuances were recognized by recipients of letters from the camps, who passed them on to the appropriate authorities.

One method of ensuring that letters reached home was to entrust them to British communists who were allowed to visit the camps. One of these, Monica Felton, was prominent in several communist front organizations, such as the Women's International Democratic Federation and its British affiliate the British National Assembly of Women. She returned home from her first visit to North Korea in 1951 with dozens of letters from British soldiers which she forwarded to their families, on whose front doorsteps she was liable to arrive unannounced to give glowing accounts of life in the North Korean socialist paradise and in the prison camps. Mrs Felton's reward was the Stalin Peace Prize for 1952. Her clients in the camps were those marked out as 'progressives', already held in contempt by the 'reactionaries'. A small number had declared, on capture, that they were card-holding members of the Communist Party of Great Britain, thus gaining immediate privileges and a posting to Camp 12, the 'Peace Fighters' camp. Camp 12 was luxurious in comparison with the Bean Camp and far removed from the deadly squalor of the Caves; converts from Camp 12 were sent to other camps as missionaries, recruiting 'progressive' prisoners who would then spread the word in their compounds.

Although the International Red Cross were not allowed to visit any of the camps for many months, and were excluded permanently from some, there were other visits from communists and fellow-travellers in the west. Alan Winnington of the *Daily Worker*, and an Australian, Wilfred Burchett, who was the correspondent for two French communist newspapers, lectured audiences in several camps (where they were met with cries of 'traitors' by some of their audiences), spoke to many individual prisoners, and like Mrs Felton, offered to take personal mail back to England. A British communist solicitor, Jack Gaster, went to North Korea on behalf of the International Association of Democratic Lawyers in 1952 and, interviewed by the *Daily Worker* on his return, claimed that the prisoners in Korea were getting better rations than their families at home, were not being indoctrinated, and were administering their own democratic disciplinary codes which provided for the punishment of escapers and persistent resisters by allotting them 'extra sanitary fatigues'. Fusilier Kinne knew all about these.

As the Chinese began to realize that they were confronted by a hard core of rebellious customers like Farrar-Hockley and Kinne, they changed their policy. The education classes ceased to be compulsory at the end of 1951. Officers and senior ranks were segregated into smaller camps graded according to the intransigence of the inmates; some, like Camp 3, acquired notoriety as punishment camps. In the Pyoktong camp one exasperated Chinese political officer, who had failed to convince his audience that the communist party alone had the monopoly of truth, harangued them in menacing terms, summing up with the words: 'We shall keep you here ten, twenty, thirty or even forty years if necessary until you learn the truth, and if you will not learn it, we will bury you so deep that you won't even stink.' Even so, a hard core of 'reactionaries' remained unmoved. Those of junior rank were transferred to other camps, and Pyoktong became the favoured residence of malleable prisoners who were granted privileged status and visited by selected foreign guests.

After the officers had been moved to Camp 2 at Pinchong-ni the Chinese arraigned Colonel Carne of the Glosters on a trumped-up charge, placing him in solitary confinement early in 1952, where he remained for virtually the rest of the war. He was already recognized by all the inmates not only as the senior officer but as the moral leader of the UN officer captives. Even after this, his influence was felt by all, and just as his calmness on Gloster Hill had inspired those around him, his example, even when held incommunicado, heartened his fellow prisoners. While still amongst the other captives towards the end of 1951 he embarked on a project which was to be a tangible symbol of his spirit. Using a hammer and some nails as his tools he fashioned a small stone Celtic cross. It was presented when finished to the Glosters' Anglican chaplain Sam Davies who placed it on a makeshift altar for the Eucharist on Christmas morning, celebrated in an unheated classroom from the walls of which posters of Marx, Lenin, Stalin and Chairman Mao stared bleakly down. Davies' chalice was a Chinese army-issue mug, his paten a mess-tin. Until then it had been possible to conduct a few religious services in the camp, but the Chinese observers of that memorable communion service soon placed constraints on all religious activity. In defiance of the gaolers it flourished, albeit secretly, as in the early persecuted church.

The well-loved collects and devotions of Cranmer's Book of Common Prayer had been committed to memory and a *samizdat* camp prayer book was compiled under the noses of the guards. It was lettered and illuminated on paper issued to the prisoners for use in rolling home-made cigarettes and hand-bound within the stiff cover of a communist tract. It took months to produce and was completed shortly before the prisoners were released in August 1953. Major Ryan of the Ulsters carved a wooden paten for the celebration of Holy Communion at Easter 1952. The identity of the carver was discovered and Ryan's devotion earned him extended solitary confinement. The Chinese, imbued with Marxist dialectic, could not stomach the thought of Christianity in their midst, although their inconsistency was revealed by the granting of permission for five celebrations of Holy Communion during the period of captivity, with an official issue of bread and wine for sacramental use.

Against the witness of the professed Christians in the camps was the conduct of those who had been members of the communist party, or who were 'turned' once in communist hands. Of the British, the most notable was Marine Andrew Condron of 41 Commando. He was one of the prisoners taken at Koto-ri in November 1950 and sent to Kyongg-ji on the Manchurian border for intensive indoctrination with the aim of forming a prisoners' 'peace group'. It was the party's policy for members in the armed forces to comport themselves as exemplary soldiers, and Condron was no exception. He is remembered as having fought courageously prior to capture and, once in the camps, for his solicitude towards his fellow prisoners, as an industrious member of prisoners' welfare committees and well to the fore in supporting the interminable lectures which formed a large part of the curriculum. He was a principal recruiter of 'intermediaries' – prisoners who voluntarily took up posts in the camps in return for privileges denied to 'reactionaries'. Condron was the only British prisoner who opted against repatriation; he spent many years exiled in Peking writing propaganda in association with some Americans who had adopted the same course.

Absurd as the propaganda might have been it did make an impression on some; when Operation 'Big Switch' took place in the summer of 1953 every British prisoner was carefully interviewed as soon as possible after release. The ostensible purpose of these interviews was to obtain 'hot' information on conditions in the camps and to glean anything of value which might add to existing intelligence on the communist forces. The covert purpose, however, was to assess the degree to which the Chinese had managed to put across their propaganda in the camps. The returned prisoners were therefore graded, following their debriefing, into three categories; those graded as 'Black' – perhaps no more than 40 – were identified as convinced communist fellow-travellers, some speaking candidly of their 'conversion', and warmly praising the way in which Condron and others had relieved the rigour of imprisonment. Others, who merited a 'Grey' grading, admitted that they had accepted the offer of good treatment conditional on acceptance of the rules of camp life and of the communist message. The majority, however, were graded 'White', having either actively resisted or, through lack of intelligence or interest, failed to absorb the tortuous dialectic. During the course of the interviews many soldiers complained of the conduct of fellow prisoners both before and after capture, and it was possible for the interrogators, by taking cross-references, to build up a comprehensive picture of the overall conduct of the British prisoners.

It was clear that even after the officers and senior ranks had been segregated from the men, a number of natural resistance leaders like Kinne had emerged and also that the many junior NCOs – corporals, bombardiers and even lance corporals – had retained a degree of authority over their fellow prisoners. The reason for this maintenance of a form of corporate discipline was immediately identified as regimental pride. One reservist NCO of the 8th Hussars who had been a card-carrying communist before going to Korea was taken prisoner in January 1951; at once he was used by the enemy to interrogate captured American airmen and was still doing this when, after the Imjin battle, another NCO from his regiment was sent to the same camp. The first NCO attempted at once to 'turn' the new batch of prisoners, but the newly arrived NCO succeeded in holding his group together. The collaborator, having chosen repatriation in 1953, probably regretted having done so, for his former fellow prisoners had many scores to settle with him once they were freed.

Perhaps because of the absence of a close regimental system, American prisoners did not take happily to conditions in the Chinese camps. Many found it impossible to adapt their diet to that of the Asian peasant which formed the staple; as was the case with many European prisoners of the Japanese in the Second World War, they were unable to eat unpolished rice or sorghum, whose high content of Vitamin B could have prevented many of the ailments which beset them. In Washington, the Joint Intelligence Committee, alarmed at statistics showing that a third of American prisoners had actively collaborated with their captors in varying degrees, launched a major interrogation exercise to try and identify the cause. A further problem arose from a Pentagon claim of November 1951 that some 5,500 Americans had been massacred after surrendering since July 1950. This was almost certainly an inflated figure, resulting from the listing of many as 'missing' when most probably they had been killed in action. Even so, to this day there are veterans of the Korean War in America who contend that somewhere in North Korea or Manchuria there are still American captives who have never been declared as such by the North Korean and Chinese authorities.

CHAPTER 31

The Great Prison Mutinies

Responsibility for the custody and administration of enemy prisoners of war in Korea was assumed by the United States on behalf of the United Nations. The logistical task alone was beyond the capacity of the South Koreans and there were doubts at UN Command that the prisoners would be fairly treated. By the end of August 1950 there were no more than a thousand NKPA captives in the US Army stockades near Pusan, but MacArthur's subsequent destruction of the NKPA led to the construction of huge prison compounds on Koje-do, an island off the south coast some 25 miles from Pusan. Koje is mainly hilly, with little flat ground; at the time it was the home of a large fishing and subsistence farming community numbering some 118,000. As General Ridgway remarked, it was 'hardly the ground a sane man would have chosen to erect camp sites'.

By the spring of 1951 the camps, built to hold 38,400, held more than 150,000 NKPA and CCF prisoners as well as 100,000 assorted internees and refugees, and an overflow camp was built on the larger island of Cheju-do off the southwest coast. The prisoners on Koje were guarded by a mixture of low-grade ROK and American line-of-communication troops who had no experience of prison camp duty and whose main preoccupation was to get away from the place as soon as possible. By the middle of 1952 there had been no less than ten changes of commandant in eighteen months. Many of the ROK guards, aware that the prisoners were receiving better rations from US Army sources than theirs from the ROK army, became involved in the black market flourishing in the squalid villages adjoining the compounds. Brothels abounded, adding to the distractions available for the malcontents. Most dangerously, the ROKs were not subject to the disciplinary powers of the American commandant, who was powerless to insist that they turn up for duty. The Koje camp consisted of four main enclosures, divided into eight compounds, each containing hutted accommodation built for 1,200. From the start each held up to three times that number. Further extensions of the compounds merged them into one huge conglomerate.

United Nations Command Intelligence discovered before the end of 1951 that selected North Koreans allowed themselves to be captured, in order to exercise control over their compatriots in the Koje camps. The head of these, Pak Sang-hyon, had served in the Soviet-trained team who had supervised the setting up of the North Korean People's Republic in 1945. He quickly established his authority as unquestioned political leader of the North Koreans on Koje. Under his guidance, cells of approved party members were established in each compound; one of their tasks was to identify prisoners hostile to Kim Il-sung's regime, who were marked down for elimination as and when the occasion arose.

So great was the overcrowding in the compounds, and so few the guards (about one to every fifty prisoners) that the commandant and his staff rapidly lost control. They ran the camps from outside the wire, relying on the prisoners' committees, supposedly under democratically elected leaders, to conduct routine administrative duties.

It was only a matter of time before the tensions behind the wire at Koje erupted; the first attack on UN guards came in June 1951 after three men in a fatigue party were beaten to death by other prisoners. Another flare-up in August resulted in more deaths; by now the hard-line NKPA prisoners were in full control of at least half the compounds, which guards no longer dared enter. Dissident prisoners were being tried and sentenced to death by kangaroo courts presided over by hard-liners and 15 executions took place within the wire during September. When it appeared that a group of anti-communists were in danger of their lives, 200 troops stormed the threatened compound to rescue them.

The Chief of Staff of the US 2nd Logistical Command, which supervised all UN prison camps from its headquarters at Pusan, wrote to General Van Fleet at 8th Army on 18 September urgently requesting reinforcements and pointing out that an explosive situation had developed because of communist infiltration, overcrowding and general uncertainty over the outcome of the Panmunjon talks. Van Fleet immediately visited Koje and was horrified by what he saw. He ordered a complete overhaul of the island's security system and the formation of the 8137th Military Police Group, consisting of three police battalions and four guard companies. This was followed by the attachment of an infantry battalion, so that by Christmas 1951 over 4,000 American and ROK troops were based on the island. Even so this was barely half of what 2nd Logistical Command had asked for.

The reinforcements had come too late to arrest a rapidly worsening situation, for an attempt in December to screen the thousands of civilian internees amongst the military captives was met with riots and mass demonstrations in the compounds. In a few days 14 prisoners and internees had been killed and many wounded, often by their fellow inmates. The situation had slithered out of control, aided by a lax camp regime which had allowed the prisoners to set up unsupervised metal-working shops in the compounds, ostensibly to develop vocational and technical skills which would help them after release, where all manner of lethal weapons – hatchets, spears, knives and flails tipped with barbed wire – were being mass-produced. A generous ration of petrol, issued to fuel the prisoners' stoves, went to manufacture Molotov cocktails. Gates and sally ports in the compounds were habitually left open to allow the entry and exit of prisoners' working parties without the need for guards to supervise them; as a result there was virtually unrestricted movement within the camp complex.

By now, none of the guards dared enter the compounds even by day unless heavily escorted; at night they were strictly a no-go area despite evidence of nightly beatings and murders of dissenting non-communists. It was only a matter of time before a pitched battle took place and the screening of internees provided the excuse. The inmates of Compound 62 fought the 3rd Battalion of the 27th US (Wolfhounds) Infantry Regiment who were sent in to restore order in February 1952. This battle-hardened unit set about the prisoners with such gusto that 55 of them were killed outright and 22 fatally injured; another 140 lay wounded as the troops backed out of the body-strewn compound. One American soldier had been speared to death and 38 wounded. This was clearly a case of overkill resulting from unrestricted automatic fire by troops untrained in riot control duties, and it provided the communist world with a news scoop it needed. Within days the Chinese and North Korean delegations at Panmunjon were raging against this 'sanguinary incident of barbarously massacring our personnel' and news of the incident was blazoned abroad by the world's left-wing press.

Worse was to follow. On 13 March 1952, a non-communist working party was stoned as it marched past the wire of a hard-liners' compound. A passing ROK army detachment promptly opened fire with automatic weapons, killing ten prisoners. Once more the American delegates at Panmunjon were subjected to a tirade from the communists over the 'barbarous massacre'.

If the screening of civilian internees and refugees had caused trouble it was as nothing to the reaction of the hard-liners when, in accordance with United Nations directives, the Koje commandant, Brigadier-General Dodd, commenced the screening of military prisoners to identify those who refused repatriation to communist China or North Korea once an armistice had been signed. The compounds seethed with rebellion, and 'intimidation' of waverers developed into summary executions. When medical teams attempted to enter one compound to succour a badly beaten prisoner they were set upon by a howling mob and taken prisoner. Incredibly, General Dodd ordered an unarmed party of ROKs and Americans to rescue them. They vanished into a seething crowd and one of the ROKs was literally torn apart. The others were extricated under covering fire from outside the wire.

Despite this incident the screening went ahead. Ten out of 17 compounds had been processed by the end of April 1952, revealing large numbers of prisoners wishing to remain in UN hands rather than be repatriated. The remaining seven compounds held the hard-liners, who threatened to resist screening by every means at their disposal. After asking Ridgway for more combat troops for Koje, Van Fleet announced to UN Command on 28 April that he would send the troops in on May Day but warned that this was bound to set off a general mutiny. Ridgway, scenting danger, signalled the Joint Chiefs in Washington, recommending cancellation of the screening and that the entire population of the seven hard-line compounds be counted as opting for repatriation. The chiefs, anxious for an easy let-out, readily agreed.

On 6 May, a complaint was received by Lieutenant-Colonel Raven, commanding the 94th Military Police Battalion in charge of Compound 76. Some of its inmates alleged that they had been beaten by guards. Raven was asked to get hold of General Dodd, as the prisoners wished to lay their complaints before him. In return, if he agreed to speak to them, they would co-operate and be registered and fingerprinted. This drew Raven and Dodd to the compound next day, where, as they were talking, a snatch party rushed out and seized the two Americans. Raven managed to escape but Dodd was carried into the compound and into a tent. A sign was then hoisted in the compound: 'We Capture Dodd. As long as our demand will be solved his safety is secured. If there happen brutal act such as shooting his life is in danger.' This was followed by a reassuring message from Dodd; he was being correctly treated, believed he could sort things out, and no troops were to be deployed against the compound until after 5 p.m. It was now shortly after 3.15. Panic signals were sent to 2nd Logistical Command whose commander, Brigadier-General Yount, was told by 8th Army not to use force unless sanctioned by Van Fleet.

Yount then despatched his Chief of Staff, Colonel Craig, to take command on Koje. Craig ordered extra machine-gunners, gas masks and stun grenades. The prisoners laid their demands before Dodd; they wanted jeeps for inter-compound travel, telephones and office equipment. These seemed modest enough and Dodd agreed to provide them. But Seoul was not having any of this. A battalion of infantry was sent on a tank landing ship from Pusan, followed by further infantry and a company of medium tanks. ROK naval craft surrounded the island in case of a breakout and combat aircraft of the US Navy, Marines and Air Force stood by. Brigadier-General Colson, Chief of Staff I Corps, was ordered to Koje to take command; meanwhile the temporary commander, Colonel Craig, was ordered to send a written demand to the prisoners for Dodd's immediate release, as he was no longer in command and had no authority to make concessions of any sort. A time limit was to be set; if the deadline passed, the compound would be stormed.

General Colson arrived on Koje that evening after a fraught day. Early on 9 May he sent the written warning to the prisoners, as ordered by Van Fleet.

Whilst they digested this, he strengthened the guards on all compounds, deploying machine-guns conspicuously around the camp. He then gave orders to the commander of the 38th Infantry to prepare for the storming of Compound 76 at 10 a.m. the following day; he was to use his entire inventory of weapons if need be – tanks, heavy machine-guns, flame-throwers and tear gas. The prisoners were also told that there was to be no more movement between compounds. Their reaction was to put Dodd on the telephone, asking that this restriction be lifted, as he had been promised his freedom if the scheduled general meeting of prisoners' delegates went well.

Colson, anxious to spare Dodd, agreed. He felt that he was arguing from a position of great strength; and in any case, his assault force would not be ready until the morning of the 10th, when the tanks would have arrived. His complaisancy came near to causing catastrophe, for the communists, after assembling, convened a 'court martial' on Dodd, arraigning him for the deaths of 19 prisoners which they alleged had taken place under his command. Replying to a further demand to release Dodd, the senior military prisoner, Colonel Lee Hak-ku of the NKPA, refused to release his captive who, he said, had signed a confession admitting his 'inhuman massacre and murderous barbarity'. Colson, now recognized by the prisoners as commandant, prudently declined Lee's invitation to join Dodd inside the wire.

Dodd's 'trial' went ahead; he was allowed to telephone Colson, asking for an extension of the deadline from 10 a.m. to midday on the 10th so that the trial could be completed. Colson passed the request on to Van Fleet, who turned it down. Meanwhile the relief force assembled outside the wire; judge and jury, having received Colson's message, looked out of the tent where the trial was being conducted, to find that they were confronted by 11,000 fully armed troops, joined as darkness fell by 20 M-46 Patton tanks, some of which were fitted with flame-throwers. Visibly moved, the communists returned to the courtroom to pass a message that they would endeavour to complete their proceedings by 10 a.m. on the morrow.

The next morning the prisoners sent a series of aggressive counter-demands. Colson was informed that all 16 compounds were believed to be standing by for a mass breakout if the attack on Compound 76 went ahead. Ominously, the villages clustered against the outer wire of the camp were suddenly emptied of their population. The 10 a.m. deadline slipped by as Colson sent in a placatory message assuring the prisoners, in answer to their demands, that there would be no more compulsory screening, that he had no authority to discuss repatriation which remained a matter for Panmunjon, and that there were no objections to the formation of prisoners' committees, a matter which could be discussed following the release of General Dodd. A new deadline for this was set for midday. Colson took it upon himself to allow the extension even though it was in direct contravention of Van Fleet's orders.

Midday came and went; then there was a further call from Dodd; the prisoners had rejected Colson's reply, but would submit a redraft, drawn up by themselves and Dodd, which would satisfy their honour. Colson tried another written approach; this too was turned down. Eventually, a formula acceptable to the communists was agreed between Colson, Dodd and the prisoners; in it, the generals admitted guilt for many of the killings in the compound, promised humane treatment in future, the abandonment of forced screening and, finally, approval of a prisoners' representative group. At 9.30 on the evening of 10 May, Dodd was allowed to walk to freedom; the communists had wanted to keep him in for the night and release him ceremonially, garlanded with flowers, on the following morning; but Colson had had enough. The armed host outside the wire retired without firing a shot and calm descended on the camp.

On 11 May, a hugely relieved Ridgway handed over the United Nations Command to Mark Clark and flew home. The communists had scored a public relations triumph by achieving a moral ascendancy over the armed might of the US Army and humiliating the UN high command. In Clark's eyes, Dodd and Colson had seriously compromised the position of the UN delegation at Panmunjon in the ongoing discussion over repatriation, now the main bone of contention. They had given the communists the excuse to break off the talks altogether and it was only Admiral Joy's patience and diplomacy which kept them going. Mark Clark, faced with the Koje crisis as he assumed command, was merely told by Ridgway on arrival in Tokyo that 'we've got a little situation over in Korea where some prisoners have taken in one of the camp commanders and are holding him hostage'. Clark had no idea where Koje was, or what went on there. His reported reaction on realizing the import of Dodd's capture was 'to let them keep that dumb son of a bitch, then go in and level the place'.

A Board of Inquiry which assembled immediately at 2nd Logistical Command came to a finding, promulgated on 15 May, that infuriated both Van Fleet and Clark; Dodd and Colson were not to blame. Regardless of this, and because he felt humiliated in the first week of his new command, Clark ordained that both officers be demoted to colonel. The verdict on the two officers was upheld all the way to the top and endorsed by Truman as Commander-in-Chief. History should be kinder to Dodd and Colson. As the men on the spot they faced an incandescent situation. Colson's innate humanity would not permit him to condemn the naïve Dodd to what appeared to be imminent execution; there was a distinct threat of mass breakout on a terrifying scale, and had the situation exploded, large numbers of innocent prisoners would certainly have been killed.

Brigadier-General 'Bull' Boatner from the 2nd Infantry Division was now given command of Koje. His first step was to subdivide the compounds in order to make them more manageable; work began at once despite the furious objections of the inmates. As the result of a change of policy, troops from other UN contingents were posted to Koje for short tours of guard duty. The Netherlands battalion was joined by a detachment from the Greek battalion, a rifle company of the King's Shropshire Light Infantry and another of the Royal Canadian Regiment, and the formidable 187th Airborne Combat Team was brought across from Japan.

'B' Company of the Shropshires was detailed to represent the United Kingdom in what was known as Peter Force, the British Commonwealth element of the Koje guard. It was commanded by a seasoned soldier, Major Dawney Bancroft, who briefed his men thoroughly on the train journey down to Pusan. The battalion had been in Korea for a year and seen plenty of action; all ranks were fit and well trained; above all, many had received training when in Hong Kong in what was known in the British army as 'aid to the civil power'. This included drills for riot control, governed by the application of minimum force. Bancroft and his men were greeted at the wire by well-informed prisoners brandishing a variety of lethal-looking home-made weapons and banners bearing the legend 'Welcome B Company KSLI'.

General Boatner welcomed the new arrivals, telling them that he had asked specifically for a British detachment, having acquired a high opinion of their army in Burma. Bancroft was told that his detachment was to maintain control from *outside* the compounds; he questioned this, holding that if he were to fulfil his mission he and his men would need to get in amongst the prisoners and establish their authority by personal contact. He asked if his company could be given sole responsibility for one compound, and when General Cassels visited the camp a few days later he backed Bancroft. Boatner decided to take a chance and handed the hard-liners' Compound 66 over to the Shropshires. At once they set out to establish their moral supremacy. Bancroft insisted on the highest standards of turnout; his men moved at a brisk pace to the Light Infantry drill book, fascinating the prisoners who lined the wire every morning to watch the Union flag hoisted on a high pole, and lowered at sunset, whilst the guard presented arms and a bugler sounded the appropriate calls on a captured Chinese instrument. After the first day, the ceremony was warmly applauded by the prisoners.

On 29 May an attempt by the inmates to cut the inner wire fence gave Bancroft the chance he needed and he readily complied with the deputy commandant's order to enter the compound and destroy buildings being used by the prisoners as a command post and medical centre. The Shropshires, expecting trouble, went in firmly to the accompaniment of hysterical barracking by the inmates, who did not however offer resistance. A search of the buildings revealed a huge armoury of illegal weapons, maps, money and reserves of medical supplies stolen from the camp dispensary, all obviously hoarded with a view to supporting a mass escape. Much of the money was traced back to the

ROK guards, who had been intimidated into stealing it. Next morning, two ter-rified prisoners begged the Shropshires to take them out of the compound; their senior officer, they said, had lost much face as a result of the search and had ordered all prisoners to fight to the death when the British next tried to enter the compound.

By 3 June the Shropshires had taken over Compound 66 completely, finding out many disturbing things in the process; for weeks, the prisoners had been fashioning war clubs from baulks of firewood studded with ten-inch nails and had been hoarding petrol for their fire bombs. Each compound boasted a black-smiths' shop where spears, knives, machetes, wire cutters and gas masks were being made. On the same day there was an occurrence which did much to secure the Shropshires' position in the camp. The senior North Korean officer called for an American army ambulance to remove a sick NKPA officer from the compound; when it arrived, the casualty was marched to the compound gate and the Korean driver, after tearing off the sick man's hat and ripping off his badges of rank, literally pitched him into the ambulance. Bancroft, who was standing by, immediately ordered the driver to pick up the hat and restore it, and the rank badges, to the Korean officer. It was the first of many infringe-ments of the Geneva Convention witnessed by the Shropshires at the camp. That night a prisoner threw a message over the wire to the effect that hence-forth the inmates 'would comply with the orders of the English gentlemen'.

Three days later, all civilians had been evacuated from the villages adjoining the outer wire and the full measure of a year's neglect was apparent. There were tunnels linking them with the compounds, more dumps of weapons, and evi-dence of a well-developed black market in which prison rations were bartered for materials which could be used for escape purposes.

When the announcement of the Shropshires' arrival on Koje was made in London, Mr Attlee, now Opposition leader, had commented in the House of Commons that 'had the British been running the camps the present trouble would have been avoided'; this was flattering but indiscreet, for a small but anglophobic element of the American press now waited eagerly for some new disaster on Koje which would give the lie to Attlee's statement. One of their correspondents there was heard to say that 'The Brits will get no press cover until they make a nonsense; then they'll hit our headlines.' Despite reinforce-ment of the guards, there was a strong feeling that a further crisis was impend-ing, and it came after 7 June when General Boatner was instructed to rehouse the prisoners. The Koje population was to be cut down to 50,000 and orders were given for the rearrangement of the compounds, limiting the occupants of each to 500 instead of between 3,500 and 7,000. Information was reaching Bancroft from insiders, and tunnelling within Compound 66 was suspected. When the Shropshires went in with mechanical diggers there was uproar, the hostile American press men gleefully gathering round to watch as the prisoners acted up for their benefit, brandishing inflammatory posters. To Bancroft's relief, they took down their banners when told to do so.

On 10 June Boatner issued orders for the 7,000 inmates of Compound 76 to be moved and rehoused. At dawn the well-disciplined American airborne troops went in, ready for the worst. No shots were fired, although the prisoners, many wearing gas masks, fought viciously from prepared trenches. The paratroops used hundreds of gas and stun grenades and soon the compound was littered with over a hundred dead and wounded. A large crowd of prisoners, seeking to give themselves up to the authorities, tried to get to the main gate but were rushed by a horde of screaming hard-liners who dragged them back and slaughtered them. It was some hours before the compound was subdued; a search revealed evidence of another imminent mass breakout. The next compound for rearrangement was number 66, guarded by the Shropshires. During the night following the battle in Compound 76, ladders discovered against the fence were removed on Bancroft's orders. When his batch of prisoners was moved two days later there was no trouble, although a murdered dissident was found in one of the huts and three more tunnels were located.

By 17 June the moves were complete and Boatner issued new instructions for the handling of prisoners. Bancroft was still not satisfied and in response to his representations he was allowed to get on with the job in his own way. He was given charge, shared with the Canadian unit, of the new Enclosure 3, consisting of four compounds each holding 500 prisoners. He supervised a secret democratic ballot by the prisoners for the election of their representatives, then explained to them his plan for the building of recreational facilities, accommodation, drainage and an athletics field. Mail, hitherto issued only fitfully if at all, was handed out to his prisoners for the first time in months. They were told that henceforth they were expected to observe the same disciplinary standards as the Shropshires. This produced remarkable results as the prisoners felt that if they fell short of British army standards they would lose face; within days all British officers were being saluted when inside the compounds and prisoners stood to attention when addressed by even a junior British NCO. Senior NCOs as well as officers were addressed as 'sir'. A large audience turned out every day to watch and applaud the colours ceremony, and every single prisoner stood to attention in the compound when Bancroft entered. There was a notable atmosphere of good humour in Enclosure 3; very soon, a sergeant was left in charge for much of the time, enjoying the full co-operation of the inmates. Within a few days, all the Shropshires were moving freely and unarmed amongst the prisoners.

On 6 July a sports day was held in one of the compounds, at which the organization and discipline, entirely in the prisoners' hands, was excellent. Bancroft, who had received a formal invitation from the senior Korean officer, was loudly cheered when he took his place after the prisoners had been called to attention by their own leaders. Several sports and games new to the Koreans had been taught by the British troops, notably tug-of-war, which was taken up with enthusiasm. A few days earlier the UN guard troops had put on a sort of tattoo for the benefit of everyone on Koje. The Shropshires gave a demonstration of Light Infantry drill, and the 187th displayed their intricate Honor Guard drill, which even Bancroft had to admit was 'excellent – one could never hope to see better'. There was a boxing match between the Shropshire light-weights and the well-fed heavies of the Netherlands battalion, which the latter won convincingly.

Bancroft was determined from the start to keep the profile of the British army high and in this he succeeded; when he wanted to build a soccer pitch for his prisoners he asked the US army engineers for the loan of a bulldozer. When their officer demurred with the excuse 'Hell, Major, Rome wasn't built in a day', Bancroft replied, 'Well, it bloody well would have been if I'd been there.' He got his machinery and the enthusiastic help of the American sappers. His hold over the North Koreans, previously so fanatical in their hatred of the UN troops, was uncanny. A war wound had left him with a characteristic limp, which was imitated by the prisoners, much to his amusement. When it was announced that the Shropshires were returning to the Commonwealth Division, a deputation of senior prisoners appealed to Boatner asking for them to stay on the island: the prisoners were, they said, prepared to behave for the British troops, who treated them as humans in accordance with the Geneva Convention, but would not guarantee their conduct for anyone else.

The Shropshires left with mixed feelings; in their short stay they had greatly enhanced the reputation of their regiment and of the British army, but had been profoundly disturbed by what they saw on arrival; the low-grade troops who were in charge had appalled them by their cavalier attitude to Asian personnel. Afterwards, Bancroft committed his observations to paper; he noted the improvement wrought by General Boatner, who sacked all the staff he took over and replaced them within two weeks because of their sheer inefficiency. When the Shropshires got to Koje they frequently saw American and ROK sentries asleep at their posts. Civilians living right up against the wire were conversing with the prisoners and presumably passing intelligence to them. Nearly all the Americans were offensive towards the prisoners, treating them like cattle, using the pretext that 'they're savages, and anyway, Congress never ratified the Geneva Convention'. All this changed with the arrival of Boatner and the 187th Airborne, whom Bancroft and his men recognized as fellow professionals.

Many years later, Bancroft, now a Brigadier, was back in Korea as British Defence Attaché in Seoul. In that capacity he was required to attend the Panmunjon talks from time to time. One day he realized that the senior North

Korean negotiator on duty, now a general, was none other than the former senior NKPA officer from Enclosure 3 on Koje. Their eyes met briefly across the table and there was a bare flicker of recognition from the Korean. Bancroft asked to see him privately after the formal meeting; but the Korean was not prepared to admit, even in the privacy of an interview room, that he was the man for whom Bancroft had developed a grudging respect fifteen years earlier. They parted without even shaking hands, though Bancroft sensed that the other man would have dearly wished to greet him; but to have admitted in front of the other delegates that he had once been a prisoner of war would have brought much loss of face. They never met again.

There was an interesting political side effect following General Cassels' selection of the KSLI and the Royal Canadian Regiment for duty on Koje. Whilst the temporary posting of the Shropshires was seen in Whitehall as no more than a routine deployment, the Canadian government took violent exception to the work, despite their earlier insistence that the Canadian contingent was to be seen as part of a United Nations force for policing duties. They sacked the unfortunate head of the Canadian Military Mission in Tokyo on grounds that he had not informed his home government of the move, and even tried to censure the Australian General Bridgeford, commanding British Commonwealth Forces, for allowing Cassels to deploy Canadian troops on such a politically sensitive task.

The anti-communist prisoners were presently transferred to new camps on the Korean mainland (from which they were released *en masse* by Syngman Rhee in 1953 before the armistice was signed) and after their departure life became quieter on Koje, although the hard-core leaders maintained their antagonism towards their captors until the armistice had been concluded in July 1953. Some of the sick and wounded were returned under the terms of 'Little Switch' and the rest who had opted for repatriation were sent home in 'Big Switch', a performance which led to extraordinary demonstrations on the part of the communists as they were loaded on to the trucks which were to carry them over into North Korea; on the orders of their own leaders they divested themselves of the American kit with which they had been issued, hurling jackets, boots, even trousers at the bemused representatives of the world's press who were on hand to film and report on this last act of defiance. Needless to say, the media of the communist bloc made much of it.

Postscript

In the words of John Foster Dulles, 'A potential aggressor miscalculated.' The Soviet Union had reluctantly given Kim Il-sung the green light for invasion on the assumption that he could match his boast of quickly reaching Pusan before the United States could hurry to the rescue. The sacrifice of the first ill-prepared Americans to arrive in Korea just – but only just – managed to impose delay on the North Koreans, enabling the full might of the United States to rush to the help of the aggrieved party. It was a supreme test for Washington; it could so nearly have become an earlier Vietnam, but Dean Acheson's initiatives managed to mobilize United Nations support for what became the first of a new sort of coalition war: the first UN war, fought with a very real threat of the use of nuclear weapons, it was also the last great Commonwealth military venture and a turning point in Anglo-American relations. After Korea there was no dodging the fact that Britain was now a tributary power of its former colony.

The Korean War would affect Britain's economy to an extent unforeseen when Clement Attlee's government took the only course open and agreed to furnish ground forces to serve the United Nations cause. Apart from the moral imperative to meet 'the distant obligation' recognized by Attlee, Britain needed to prove to Washington that it remained its staunch ally and was prepared to shoulder its responsibilities for the defence of western Europe by rearming at whatever cost. Had it not done so it seemed to Attlee, Bevin and Shinwell that the Americans would have turned away from their commitment to Europe. Even so, Treasury officials blenched at the effects on Britain's balance of payments once the costly nuclear programme and its concomitant, the V-bomber force, got under way. Within a year of the outbreak of the Korean War Britain's modest surplus of £307 million in 1950 had plunged to a deficit of £369 million and thereafter continued downwards. The need to divert meagre industrial resources, already vitiated by the recent war, to military production led to a disastrous collapse in the export trade – which had been picking up following the devaluation of sterling in 1949. As one historian has written: 'There are power-ful reasons for supposing our best hope for the kind of economic miracle enjoyed by so many western European countries was scattered in fragments in the committee rooms of Whitehall, on the hills above the Imjin in Korea and along the Rhine in Germany as British occupation forces were rearmed in readiness for a Stalinist assault.'

When the Korean War began, Britain was still recognizably a wartime society; austerity, rationing, drabness, hoardings in the streets bearing the Orwellian slogan 'Work or Want' – all remain part of the folk memory of these years. Yet recovery had been in sight; the optimism of the time was reflected in the Festival of Britain, planning for which was far advanced when North Korea invaded the south. The dream of a New Jerusalem proffered by the victorious Labour Party in its election campaign of 1945 evaporated in the light of harsh economic reality and the Conservatives who came to power in 1951 found they could do little to arrest the descent into a permanent state of debt.

As far as Peking was concerned there can have been only relief at the signing, without undue loss of face, of the armistice in July 1953. It now seems prob-able that China had been given encouragement to join the conflict by Stalin, whose euphoria at Mao's victory over Chiang seems to have overcome his habit-ual caution. MacArthur's apparent intention to advance to the Yalu, and even beyond, was the additional spur which drove Mao to order the 'Volunteers' into North Korea. It is doubtful, however, that the Chinese wished to do more than warn off MacArthur, which they hoped to do by inflicting the reverse at Unsan on the 1st Cavalry Division and then breaking contact. It was MacArthur's resumption of the drive north after Thanksgiving in late November 1950 which tripped the massive Chinese response and the precipitate retreat of the UN forces from North Korea.

China, racked by thirty years of civil war and, from 1937 to 1945, the strug-gle with Japan, wanted nothing more than a period for readjustment. Famine, disease and huge natural calamities were part of their history and these contin-ued; it was no time for a prolonged war. What persisted after the armistice was an abiding fear of America's Far Eastern intentions and a deep paranoia in Peking over the loyalties of China's teeming population.

America's experience in Korea was not a happy one; yet again they had elected to back 'their man' – in this case Syngman Rhee – who, like Chiang Kai-shek, turned out to be a liability. In subsequent engagements in Indo-China Washington's experiences with its clients proved no more successful. But in Korea they displayed again their readiness, once committed, to expend American money and lives in defence of democratic principles, even if this meant bolstering a dubious regime.

A bleak future lay ahead for North Korea. For a while there was lavish aid from the communist bloc for the rebuilding of shattered cities and their infrastructure; but with the collapse of support from both the old Soviet Union and China, the Democratic Republic can now only struggle on, begging bowl in one hand and cudgel in the other as it continues to pursue its vendetta with the South. In many ways the struggle between the two has reverted to that obtaining prior to the 1950 invasion, for border skirmishes continue, and in the past three years there have been attempts to land saboteurs in South Korea from submarines. A substantial American garrison remains below the Demilitarized Zone, and the size of its army headquarters in Seoul betrays the existence of contingency plans for rapid reinforcement in the event of any North Korean incursion.

The two states are separated physically by the DMZ and their own elaborate fortifications, stretching back for miles on each side of the wire. In the south, the army is at continuous readiness. It bears no resemblance to the lightly armed gendarmerie which faced the North Koreans in 1950, and is a highly motivated, well-equipped force. The visitor driving north from Seoul passes huge tank barriers and fieldworks, and the concentration of military might steadily increases as the DMZ is approached. There is no attempt to conceal the presence of a very large army in the border area; it is pointed out to visitors to the front line that the North Koreans have hundreds of guns and missiles in place for an immediate bombardment of the South, and that Seoul is well within range of most of them.

The presence of the DMZ and these fortifications remind one that despite the sacrifices of 1950–3, the aim of unifying Korea failed, in the teeth of five centuries of history in which the Yi dynasty held the peninsula under one rule. Neither North nor South can claim to have been liberal democracies since 1953; Syngman Rhee clung to power until forced into exile in Hawaii in 1960 and his governance hardly prepared the country for parliamentary democracy. In 1961 an army-led coup under General Park Chung-hee appeared to stabilize the situation, and a series of army-sponsored leaders began to bring the economy into shape; but Park was assassinated in 1979, having already survived an attempt on his life by North Korean special forces.

Whilst Park's regime, and that of his protégés, was hardly democratic, it laid the foundations of South Korea's miraculous economic revival. He was instrumental in fostering a rapport with Japan which ensured massive investment, the development of strategic industries, generous American subsidies and the continuing presence of American forces. Despite this renaissance, South Korea's recent history has been punctuated with crises; visitors in Seoul soon grow accustomed to the whiff of tear gas in the underground stations and the menacing presence of riot police. Although 1988 saw the triumphal staging of the XXIVth Olympics in Seoul, the fragility of the export-based economy was revealed by the international recession which burst on the Far East in 1998. This will test the resilience of the Korean people as the next millennium dawns.

The Korean War was fought almost entirely with the weapons and technology used in the Second World War, but as it developed, certain new elements were introduced. The helicopter began to show its versatility – not yet as an instrument of battlefield mobility delivering firepower, weapons and combat units but as a flying cargo truck in rough country, an invaluable rescue and ambulance vehicle, and as a personal transport enabling commanders to move rapidly around the combat zone. The introduction of the modern main battle tank in the form of the Centurion – then superior to anything in the American or North Korean armoury – was hardly spectacular; but even as a sophisticated mobile pill-box it proved indispensable once the static phase of operations set in.

This was the first war in which high performance jet aircraft met in combat and many air fighting lessons were taught and learned. The value of the large aircraft-carrier as a means of projecting air power well beyond the range of land-based aircraft was evident; the Americans have never forgotten this, whilst successive British governments have yielded to other temptations and even now are considering abandoning the plans to build two big carriers announced in the 1998 Defence White Paper. Korea saw the end of the massed parachute assault, though powerful lobbying has resulted in Britain's retention of a parachute capability more than forty years after the last combat descent, at Port Said in 1956. The alarming experiences of British and Commonwealth infantry in Korea, facing enemy attacks at close range and generally by night, revealed the shortcomings of the bolt-operated magazine rifle, and by the mid-1950s the semi-automatic FN rifle was replacing the faithful Lee-Enfield. The use of active infra-red light for use at night was just beginning to make itself felt in Korea in 1953, since when vast advances have been made in the use of night fighting aids for the combat arms.

The British army began to change after Korea. Within ten years the last conscripts had left and the all-regular army became a reality. Whereas in 1950, Staff College doctrine laid down that the infantry existed to march and fight, the demands of nuclear warfare and the resultant needs for protection and battlefield mobility put them into armoured personnel carriers.

The proximity of the 1953 cease-fire line to the 38th parallel stands as a reproach to any who thought that the unity of North and South could be attained by mere force of arms. Since 1953 the two Koreas have glared across the wire at each other, frequently indulging in aggressive local actions which, though for the most part undetected by the world press, still bear witness to the deep animosity between the two regimes. United Nations veterans returning to the South, however, are confronted with an almost unbelievable transformation; the desperate poverty and chaos of 1950–1 have been swept away. Magnificent motorways link the teeming cities and the railroad system compares more than favourably with what passes for one in the United Kingdom.

Universities turn out thousands of well-educated technocrats; the arts and sciences thrive side by side. There is huge national pride in a historic culture which was somehow kept alive even through the darkest days of Japanese occupation and the ravages of 1950–3. Any foreigner identified in the streets of Seoul or any other town by his war veteran's lapel badge is greeted warmly by people of all ages, many with tears in their eyes as they express their thanks for what the United Nations forces did to help them in their extremity fifty years ago. In Pusan, at the United Nations cemetery, bus loads of beautifully turned out children arrive daily to pay tribute to the men of many nations who lie there, laying flowers on each grave and praying, in what is an almost unbearably moving spectacle.

All this, however blurred the final military outcome, is abundant proof that it was worth the effort. World communism, heartened by earlier successes, was firmly confronted and rebuffed, and its leaders henceforth knew that if they were to emerge on top, they would have to resort to methods of far greater subtlety than those essayed by Kim Il-sung and his backers. In the end, their cause withered and died.

Glossary

Whilst the author has been at pains to avoid littering the text with the abbreviations and acronyms beloved of Staff College instructors, the following list may be found of use, especially when studying the appendices to this book.

A&SH, Argylls	Argyll and Sutherland Highlanders
BCFK	British Commonwealth Forces Korea (HQ: Kure, Japan)
BCOF	British Commonwealth Occupation Force (Japan)
Bde	Brigade. Two or more make up a British Division. Also Brigade Group – an infantry brigade augmented by the addition of armoured and artillery units, enabling it to operate independently for limited periods
Bn	Battalion
Bty	Battery (of artillery; US equivalent = Company)
CCF	Chinese Communist Forces
CIGS	Chief of the Imperial General Staff
CNS	Chief of Naval Staff (UK equivalent = First Sea Lord)
Comwel	Commonwealth; as in 1 Comwel Div
COS	Chief(s) of Staff
Coy	Company; normally a major's command
CP	Command Post
CRA	Commander Royal Artillery. The senior gunner officer in a British division, holding the rank of Brigadier, and the commander's artillery adviser
CRE	Commander Royal Engineers. A Lieutenant-Colonel, fulfilling for the engineers a similar function to that of the CRA
Div	Division. A balanced military formation, usually commanded by a Major-General, and capable of sustained operations with the help of its integral supporting arms and services. Two or more divisions comprise an Army Corps
DLI	Durham Light Infantry
DMZ	Demilitarized Zone

EUSAK	8th United States Army, Korea; the UN field command
Fd Regt	Field regiment (UK/Commonwealth artillery; US equivalent = Field Artillery Battalion)
FEC	Far East Command (HQ: Tokyo). The UN's supreme command agency for the Korean War
FOO	Forward Observation Officer. A gunner officer and his signals party, situated in the forward infantry positions to control artillery fire support
Glosters	The Gloucestershire Regiment
GSO	General Staff Officer. Member of the staff branch responsible for operations, intelligence and field security
Inniskilling DG	The 5th Royal Inniskilling Dragoon Guards
Int	Intelligence
JCS	Joint Chiefs of Staff
kia	Killed in action
KMAG	Korean Military Advisory Group, US Army
KOSB	King's Own Scottish Borderers (usually referred to as 'The Borderers', *never* as 'Kosbies')
KRIH or 8H	8th King's Royal Irish Hussars
KSC	Korean Service Corps
KSLI	King's Shropshire Light Infantry
LAD	Light Aid Detachment. The smallest element of the REME (see below), attached to major units for immediate repair and recovery of vehicles, weapons and equipment in the field
LO	Liaison Officer
L of C	Line(s) of Communication
LST	Landing Ship, Tank
MASH	Mobile Army Surgical Hospital (US; also Norwegian in Korea)
MOD	Ministry of Defence
Mx	The Middlesex Regiment
NAAFI/EFI	Navy, Army and Air Force Institutes/Expeditionary Force Institutes. The organization for provision of canteen and other retail services to British and Commonwealth field forces; its personnel wore the uniform of the RASC (see below) to satisfy the requirements of the Geneva and other Conventions
NKPA	North Korean People's Army
OC	Officer commanding. Normally applicable to a major in a company/squadron size sub-unit
OP	Observation Post
Ord	Ordnance
Pl	Platoon. The smallest sub-unit of a battalion-size unit, commanded by an officer (or frequently by a sergeant), comprising three rifle sections and a platoon HQ including a light (2-inch) mortar detachment known as 'the platoon commander's artillery'
PLA	People's Liberation Army (communist China)

PPCLI	Princess Patricia's Canadian Light Infantry
PW	Prisoner(s) of war
RAMC	Royal Army Medical Corps
RAOC	Royal Army Ordnance Corps. Responsible for the provision, storage and issue of all warlike stores, clothing and ammunition (since absorbed into Royal Logistic Corps)
RAP	Regimental Aid Post. In a combat unit, the location of the RMO and his staff, and the point to which all battle casualties are taken for immediate treatment and assessment
RAR	Royal Australian Regiment
RASC	Royal Army Service Corps. Responsible for the provision of land (and some sea) transport in the British army, also the movement and issue of rations, fuel and ammunition in the combat zone (since absorbed into Royal Logistic Corps)
RCHA	Royal Canadian Horse Artillery
RCR	Royal Canadian Regiment
RCT	Regimental Combat Team. US Army. A self-contained formation containing elements of infantry, armour and artillery and capable of conducting independent operations
Regt	Regiment
REME	Royal Electrical and Mechanical Engineers. Responsible for the repair and recovery of all army equipment, weapons and vehicles in the combat zone and rear areas
RF	Royal Fusiliers
RHQ	Regimental Headquarters
RM	Royal Marines
RMO	Regimental Medical Officer (see RAP above)
RNF	Royal Northumberland Fusiliers
ROK	Republic of (South) Korea
ROKA	Republic of Korea Army
RUR	Royal Ulster Rifles
R 22e R	Royale 22e Régiment (Vingt-deuxième, or 'VanDoos')
Sqn	Squadron. Either an air force unit, or, in the British and Commonwealth forces, a sub-unit of an armoured regiment commanded by a major
Tp	Troop. The smallest sub-unit of an artillery, armoured, signals or engineer regiment
USMC	United States Marine Corps
WO	War Office, London/Warrant Officer

Casualty Figures

The United States bore by far the greatest burden of the UN forces in the war. In 37 months of fighting it despatched over 5.7 million men to the theatre, of whom 33,629 were killed in action and over 20,000 in non-combat accidents; 103,284 Americans were wounded in action and over 5,000 posted as missing or prisoners. The US Navy was engaged throughout in blockade, bombardment, mine warfare and the air support of ground forces. Its carrier aircraft flew a total of 275,912 sorties. The US Air Force flew over 700,000 strategic and 625,000 tactical sorties and lost 1,200 aircrew in the process; 1,500 enemy aircraft were claimed destroyed, including 808 MiGs, and a further 925 claimed as damaged. The USAF stated that over half the enemy troop casualties were caused by airstrikes; it is hard, however, to accept the clinical precision of their claim that 145,416 enemy troops were killed, 74,589 vehicles and 9,417 pieces of railway rolling stock destroyed.

The ROK army suffered appallingly: over 46,000 killed in action, 101,300 wounded, and over 12,000 missing. Other UN casualties amounted to 14,103 of which the UK share was 1,078 killed in action, 2,674 wounded and 1,060 missing or prisoners.

Enemy casualties are far harder to quantify. The American Joint Chiefs of Staff summary of 27 July 1953 gives the following estimates. Chinese: 401,401 killed,* 486,995 wounded, and 21,211 captured. North Koreans: 214,899 killed, 303,685 wounded, and 101,680 missing or captured. It was calculated that 2 million civilians perished in North Korea – or 20 per cent of the total population.

*Amongst these was Mao Tse-tung's eldest son.

APPENDIX II

Outline Order of Battle

8th US Army Korea (EUSAK) Established in Korea 13 July 1950

From the few hundred unprepared men of Task Force Smith in July 1950 the US Army effort expanded to three army corps comprising seven divisions (six army, one marine). Various UN contingents were subsumed within EUSAK; apart from the 1st Commonwealth Division, all these were at no more than brigade level and most were of battalion size.

Commanders, EUSAK

13 July–23 December 1950	Lt-General Walton H. Walker (killed in traffic accident)
26 December 1950–14 April 1951	Lt-General Matthew B. Ridgway
14 April 1951–10 February 1953	General James Van Fleet (promoted General August 1951)
11 February 1953–31 March 1955	General Maxwell D. Taylor

Commanding Generals, I US Corps

2 August–10 September 1950	Major-General John B. Coulter
11 September 1950–18 July 1951	Lt-General Frank W. Milburn
19 July 1951–28 June 1952	Lt-General John W. O'Daniel
29 June 1952–10 April 1953	Lt-General Paul W. Kendall
11 April–13 October 1953	Lt-General Bruce C. Clarke

Commanding Generals, IX US Corps

12 September 1950–31 January 1951	Major-General John B. Coulter
31 January–24 February 1951	Major-General Bryan Moore (killed in helicopter crash)
5 March–23 December 1951	Lt-General William B. Hoge
24 December 1951–30 July 1952	Major-General Willard G. Wyman
9 August 1952–9 August 1953	Lt-General Reuben E. Jenkins

Commanding Generals, X US Corps

September 1950–14 July 1951	Major-General Edward M. Almond
15 July–5 December 1951	Major-General Clovis E. Byers
5 December 1951–9 July 1952	Lt-General Williston B. Palmer
July 1952–	Lt-General Isaac D. White

US Divisions

US Army divisions in Korea normally consisted of three infantry regiments (= brigades) apiece, with an artillery regiment of three field artillery battalions with 105mm guns and a medium battalion with 155mm guns. Each division had a combat engineer battalion, anti-tank company, reconnaissance company and supporting service units. The 1st Cavalry Division fought and was organized as an infantry division. 'Regimental Combat Teams' (RCTs) could be formed by augmenting an infantry regiment with an artillery battalion, additional support troops, and sometimes a tank battalion.

1st US Cavalry Division

Commanders

18 July 1950–4 February 1951	Major-General Hobart R. Gay
5 February–16 July 1951	Major-General Charles D. Palmer
17 July–22 December 1951	Major-General Thomas L. Harrold

The division was pulled out of Korea early in 1952 and returned to Japan.

Composition
5th, 7th and 8th Cavalry Regts
61st, 77th, 82nd* and 99th Artillery Bns
70th Tank Bn
8th Combat Engineer Bn
92nd AA Bn
16th Reconnaissance Coy

2nd US Infantry Division

Commanders

8 July–6 December 1950	Major-General Laurence B. Keiser
7 December 1950–14 January 1951	Major-General Robert B. McLure
14 January–1 September 1951	Major-General Clark L. Ruffner
21 September 1951–4 May 1953	Major-General James C. Fry
5 May 1953–March 1954	Major-General William J. Barriger

The asterisk denotes a unit equipped with 155mm medium guns.

Composition
9th, 23rd and 38th Inf Regts
12th*, 15th, 37th and 38th Artillery Bns
72nd Tank Bn
2nd Combat Engineer Bn
82nd AA Bn
2nd Reconnaissance Coy

3rd US Infantry Division

One regiment arrived in Korea in August 1950; the main body landed at Wonsan in November.

Commanders

10 November 1950–19 October 1951	Major-General Robert H. Soule
20 October 1951–28 April 1952	Brigadier-General Thomas J. Cross
29 April–8 October 1952	Major-General Robert L. Dulaney
9 October 1952–9 May 1953	Major-General George W. Smythe
10 May–16 October 1953	Major-General Eugene W. Ridgings

Composition
7th, 15th, 65th (Puerto Rican) Infantry Regts
9th*, 10th, 39th and 58th Artillery Bns
64th Tank Bn
10th Combat Engineer Bn
3rd AA Bn
3rd Reconnaissance Coy

7th US Infantry Division

Commanders

15 September 1950–11 February 1951	Major-General David G. Barr
12 February–4 December 1951	Major-General Claude B. Ferenbough
5 December 1951–3 July 1952	Major-General Lyman L. Lemnitzer
4 July 1952–21 March 1953	Major-General Wayne C. Smith
22 March–13 October 1953	Major-General Arthur G. Trudeau

Composition
17th, 31st and 32nd Infantry Regts
31st*, 48th and 57th Artillery Bns
73rd Tank Bn
13th Combat Engineer Bn
15th AA Bn
7th Reconnaissance Coy

After a period as Command reserve and reinforcement training formation in Japan the division took part in the Inchon landings as part of the newly assembled X Corps, its ranks swelled by over 8,000 Katusas, or locally enlisted ROK soldiers. It later took part in the campaign in the north-east around the Chosin reservoir, and from 1951–3 in the central sector.

24th US Infantry Division

Commanders

To 21 July 1950	Major-General William F. Dean (captured)
22 July 1950–24 January 1951	Major-General John B. Church
25 January–20 December 1951	Major-General Blacksheet N. Bryan

Composition
19th, 21st and 34th Infantry Regts
11th*, 13th, 52nd and 63rd Artillery Bns
70th Tank Bn
3rd Combat Engineer Bn
26th AA Bn
24th Reconnaissance Coy

24th Division was replaced by 40th Division in January 1952; it returned to Korea in July 1953.

25th US Infantry Division

The division served in Korea from July 1950 and remained there throughout the war.

Commanders

10 July 1950–24 February 1951	Major-General William B. Kean
25 February–13 July 1951	Major-General S. Sladen Bradley
14 July 1951–17 July 1952	Major-General Ira P. Swift
18 July 1952–26 June 1953	Major-General Samuel T. Williams
27 June–2 August 1953	Brigadier-General Louis T. Heath

Composition
24th (all-black, later disbanded), 14th, 27th and 35th Infantry Regts
8th, 64th, 69th and 90th* Artillery Bns (the all-black 159th Artillery Bn was disbanded in October 1951 at the same time as the 24th Infantry Regt)
89th Tank Bn
65th Combat Engineer Bn
21st AA Bn

40th US Infantry Division (California National Guard)

The division arrived in Korea early in 1952 to replace the 24th Infantry Division.

Commanders

To 2 June 1952	Major-General Daniel H. Hudelson
3 June 1952–29 April 1953	Major-General Joseph P. Cleland
30 April 1953–January 1954	Major-General Ridgley Gaither

Composition
160th, 223rd and 224th Infantry Regts
143rd, 980th and 981st Artillery Bns
578th Combat Engineer Bn
40th Reconnaissance Coy

The division left Korea on release from federal service and returned to the USA in 1954.

45th US Infantry Division (Oklahoma National Guard)

The division arrived in Korea in December 1951 to replace the US 1st Cavalry Division. It was released from federal service and returned to the USA in April 1954.

Composition
179th, 180th and 279th Infantry Regts
158th, 160th, 171st and 189th* Artillery Bns
120th Combat Engineer Bn
14th AA Bn
45th Reconnaissance Coy

British and Commonwealth Forces in Korea

Australia

Initially one infantry battalion, later two
Base facilities in Japan
One aircraft carrier, two destroyers, one frigate, RAN
One fighter squadron and a transport flight, RAAF

Canada

One brigade group
Three destroyers, RCN

One squadron of transport aircraft, RCAF
Cargo shipping

India

One parachute field ambulance unit

New Zealand

One field artillery regt
One transport coy, RNZASC
Two frigates, RNZN

South Africa

One fighter squadron, SAAF

United Kingdom

Initially, an infantry brigade headquarters and two battalions from Hong Kong, followed by a brigade group from the UK with supporting services and provision of staff, combat and support units to make up the 1st Commonwealth Division from midsummer 1951. A Royal Marines Commando 1950–1. Elements of the Far East Fleet including aircraft and support carriers, two cruisers, eight destroyers and frigates. Fleet replenishment ships, one survey vessel, one hospital ship, one headquarters ship. A flying boat detachment and two light aircraft flights, RAF.

In December 1950 BCOF, the British Commonwealth Occupation Force in Japan, hitherto an Australian responsibility, became British Commonwealth Forces Korea, with outstations in Korea at Pusan and along the lines of communication to EUSAK and the Commonwealth units in the field. Until July 1951 the three component brigades of what became the 1st Commonwealth Division served under command of various US divisions in I and IX Corps: 1st Cavalry and 2nd, 3rd, 24th and 25th US Infantry Divisions.

In order of their arrival in Korea the orders of battle of the Commonwealth brigades were as follows (the * denotes the initial component units; relieving battalions are shown in their order of arrival in Korea).

27 (later 28) Commonwealth Brigade

1st Bn Middlesex*; 1st Bn Argyll & Sutherland Highlanders* (August 1950)
3rd Bn Royal Australian Regt (September 1950)

1st Bn King's Shropshire Light Infantry, 1st Bn King's Own Scottish Borderers (April 1951); 2nd Bn Princess Patricia's Canadian Light Infantry (February–May 1951)
1st Bn Durham Light Infantry; 1st Bn Royal Fusiliers; 1st Bn Royal Australian Regiment; 2nd Bn Royal Australian Regiment; 16 Fd Regt RNZA (from January 1951)

29 Brigade Group

1st Bn Royal Northumberland Fusiliers*; 1st Bn Glosters*; 1st Bn Royal Ulster Rifles*; 1st Bn Royal Leicesters; 1st Bn Welch Regt; 1st Bn Royal Norfolk; 1st Bn Black Watch; 1st Bn Duke of Wellington's; 1st Bn King's (Liverpool)
8th King's Royal Irish Hussars*; 5th Royal Inniskilling Dragoon Guards; 1st Royal Tank Regt; 'C' Sqn, 7th Royal Tank Regt*
14th, 45th* and 20th Fd Regts RA; 170* and 120 Mortar Btys RA (combined to form 61 Light Regt RA); 11th* and 42nd Lt AA Btys RA
55* and 12 Fd Sqns RE; 64 Field Park Sqn RE (all combined to form 28 Fd Regt RE on formation of 1st Comwel Div)

25 Canadian Infantry Brigade Group

2nd*, 1st, 3rd Bns Royal Canadian Regt
2nd*, 1st and 3rd Bns Royale 22e Regt
2nd*, 1st and 3rd Bns Princess Patricia's Canadian Light Infantry
C*, B and A Sqns, Lord Strathcona's Horse
2nd* and 1st Regts Royal Canadian Horse Artillery
23rd* Fd Sqn RCE

After the formation of 1st Commonwealth Division, the artillery regiments were placed under control of a gunner brigadier (Commander Royal Artillery) at divisional HQ. A divisional signals regiment and a divisional transport and supplies column were also formed from the brigades' former signals and RASC, RNZASC and RCASC resources. Commanded by Lieutenant-Colonels, these contained elements from the UK, Canada, Australia and New Zealand. Two RAF light aircraft units – one an Air Observation Post, the other Light Liaison – were added to the Commonwealth Division in 1951. The aircraft were flown respectively by Royal Artillery officers and by officers and NCOs of the Glider Pilot Regiment.

Commanders of 1st Commonwealth Division

July 1951–September 1952	Major-General A.J.H. Cassels
September 1952–October 1953	Major-General M.M. Alston-Roberts-West

Other UN Assistance in Korea

Belgium	One infantry battalion. Arrived January 1951, served in US 3rd Inf Div (with British 29th Bde at Battle of Imjin). 103 kia. Air transport detachment.
Colombia	One infantry battalion. Arrived June 1951, served in US 24th and 7th Divs. 131 kia. One frigate.
Denmark	Hospital ship *Jutlandia*.
Ethiopia	Augmented 'Kagnew' ('Conquerors') infantry battalion, drawn from Imperial Guard. Casualties n/k.
France	One infantry battalion, 'Bataillon Français'. Arrived November 1950. Served with US 2nd Div. 261 kia. Naval elements included a destroyer.
Greece	Reinforced infantry battalion. Casualties n/k. Air transport squadron.
Italy	Hospital unit.*
Luxembourg	One rifle company.†
Netherlands	One infantry battalion, raised from the Van Heutz Regt. Arrived November 1950. Served in US 2nd Div. 120 kia. One destroyer on station in Korean waters from July 1950.
Norway	Mobile Army Surgical Hospital (NORMASH).
Philippines	One battalion combat team.
Sweden	One general hospital.‡
Thailand	One battalion combat team ('Royal Thai Forces Korea'). Arrived October 1950. Served with 187 RCT, 29 British Bde, US 1st Cav Div, US 2nd Div. 125 kia. Two frigates (one abandoned after grounding).
Turkey	One brigade group.

The UN Command declined some offers of military assistance – conspicuously those of Chiang Kai-shek from Formosa, and smaller detachments which did not meet the criteria of size or military value laid down by MacArthur's staff.

*A General Hospital which ministered to the Korean population in the Seoul area. (Italy did not achieve UN membership till 1955.)
†Formed part of the Belgian battalion.
‡Based in Pusan, ministering to the civil population as well as UN personnel.

APPENDIX III

The Republic of Korea Army (ROKA)

At the outbreak of war in 1950 the ROKA had some 115,000 men organized into eight weak divisions: Capital, 1st, 2nd, 3rd, 5th, 6th, 7th and 8th. (There was no 4th Division, this being an inauspicious number for Koreans.) By mid-1953 huge expansion had taken place, as had a total retraining and re-equipment of the army, which now stood at a strength of nearly 600,000. Sixteen divisions were in the field and more were forming.

Once incompetents like General Chae Pyong-duk, Chief of Staff in 1950, had been weeded out, a new generation of highly motivated Korean officers assumed higher command. The ROK Marine Corps, created in 1949, became an élite force of three battalions and an independent unit for special operations.

By late 1951, a ROK infantry division contained the following elements: headquarters, three infantry regiments each of three battalions, a combat engineer battalion, an anti-tank company, ordnance, signals, medical and quartermaster companies, and an artillery battalion of three companies. All equipment was of American origin.

APPENDIX IV

The North Korean People's Army (NKPA)

The development of the NKPA is described in the main text. The aim of these notes is to enlarge upon the salient differences between the NKPA and the ROK army at the outset of the war; these were considerable and go a long way to explain the poor initial showing of the South Koreans.

A typical NKPA rifle division in June 1950 contained around 12,000 officers and men. It was organized as follows: headquarters (including a political company headed by the divisional political commissar, with representation at all HQ levels down to battalion); a reconnaissance company; machine-gun battalion; three infantry regiments each of three battalions, a mortar battery and a field artillery company; an artillery regiment of two field, one medium and one self-propelled battalion; a mortar battalion, an armoured infantry battalion in personnel carriers; a signal battalion and a transport battalion.

The following divisions took part in the opening offensive against the south (those marked * had been partly formed from Korean-manned formations in the Chinese People's Liberation Army):

1st*, 2nd, 3rd Guards, 4th*, 5th* (ex PLA 164th Division), 6th* (ex PLA 166th Division), 7th*, and the recently raised 19th, 13th and 15th. In addition there was the 105th Armoured Brigade of three battalions equipped with Soviet T-34/85 tanks and the 206th Mechanized Infantry Regiment. Both 3rd Guards and 4th Rifle Divisions were awarded the honour title 'Seoul' for their performance in capturing the city.

The invasion force was organized on Soviet principles as a 'Front' under command of General Kim Chaek; this was divided into two 'armies' – actually army corps. The 1st Army comprised the 1st Rifle, 3rd Guards, 4th and 6th Rifle Divisions and 105th Armoured Brigade; the 2nd Army consisted of the 2nd, 5th and 7th Divisions. The newer formations were held back in reserve.

Additional forces available to General Kim Chaek included a heavy artillery regiment with 122mm guns, anti-aircraft units, a motor-cycle reconnaissance unit, an engineer brigade, extra signals units, guerrillas, seaborne commandos, internal security units and the border constabulary. Given the preponderance of manpower and weaponry it is hardly surprising that the North Koreans met with such success in the opening weeks, and all the more creditable that the inexperienced Americans, initially outnumbered and outgunned, together with their South Korean allies, managed to rally and hold the NKPA on the Naktong.

Bibliography

Books and articles

Ambrose, S.E. *Rise to Globalism: American Foreign Policy 1938–76*, New York, 1971.

Anon. Articles in *The Globe and Laurel* (Royal Marines' Journal), Vols LVIII and LIX, describing the activities of 41 Commando.

Anon. *History of 29 Brigade Group*, prepared under instructions of Brigadier R.N.H.C. Bray, Korea, May 1954. IWM.

Anon. *The Korean Journal. 1st Royal Tank Regiment in Korea*, published by the regiment, 1953.

Anon. *The Diehards in Korea*, published by the Middlesex Regiment, 1983.

Argent, A. 'A Battalion Prepares for War', (Australian) *Infantry Journal*, Vol. XVIII, No. 2, May–June 1972. The battalion's intelligence officer describes the methods used by Lt-Colonel Green to transform an under-strength occupation battalion into a formidable fighting unit in a matter of weeks.

Bailey, J.B.A. *Field Artillery and Firepower*, Oxford, 1989.

Barnett, C. *The Lost Victory: British Dreams, British Realities 1945–50*, London, 1995. Correlli Barnett's masterly analysis of the state of the nation leading up to the Korean War.

Breen, Bob. *The Battle of Kapyong*, Georges Heights, NSW, 1992.

——(ed.). *The Battle of Maryang-san*, Georges Heights, NSW, 1994. Two excellent short studies, designed to teach basic principles of infantry fighting to young officers; sharply critical of certain British units and commanders at times, not always with justification.

Breuber, W.B. *Shadow Warriors: The Covert War in Korea*, New York, 1996.

Cleaver, Lt C.A. *Study of US Army Personnel Problems* (especially the performance of black soldiers and their integration), Office of the Chief of Military History, US Army, Washington DC, undated. IWM.

Coad, Major-Gen. B.A., CBE, DSO. 'The Land Campaign in Korea'. Lecture at Royal United Services Institute, London, 29 October 1951. *RUSI Journal*, Vol. XCVII, No. 585, February 1952. A 'sanitized' version of what is to be found in his papers at the Imperial War Museum (see below).

Cole, H.N. *NAAFI in Uniform: Expeditionary Force Institutes in Korea*, Aldershot, 1982.

Condron, A.N. (ed.). *Thinking Soldiers*, Peking, 1955. A collection of memoirs gathered by the sole British prisoner who opted to stay with the Chinese.

Cotterell, A. *East Asia: From Chinese Predominance to the Rise of the Pacific Rim*, London, 1993. Presenting the Korean War as one of many factors contributing to the current balance of power in the Far East.

Cumings, Bruce. *The Origins of the Korean War. Vol. II: The Roarings of the Cataract*, Princeton, 1992. An absorbing and scholarly account of the machinations of Korean politics leading up to 1950.

Cumings, Bruce and Halliday, J. *The Unknown War: Korea*, New York, 1988.

Cunningham-Booth, A. and Farrar, P. (eds.). *British Forces in the Korean War*, published by the British Korean Veterans' Association, 1988.

Davies, The Revd S.J. *In Spite of Dungeons*, London, 1954. Inspirational account by the chaplain of the Glosters of how the faith was kept by Christian prisoners of the Chinese in Korea.

Evanhoe, E. *Dark Moon*, US Naval Institute, 1996. Special Forces operations in Korea.

Farrar-Hockley, A. *The Edge of the Sword*, London, 1955. The classic account of what happened to the Glosters during and after the Imjin battle, recounted by their adjutant, a notable escaper and resister.

Gaston, P. *Thirty-Eighth Parallel: The British in Korea*, Glasgow, 1976.

George, A.L. *The Chinese Army in Action: The Korean War and its Aftermath*, New York, 1967.

Godfrey, Major F.A. *History of the Royal Norfolk Regiment*, Norwich, 1993.

Green, Olwyn. *The Name's still Charlie*, University of Queensland, 1993. Affectionate biographical study of the outstanding commander of 3 RAR (killed in action in Korea) by his widow.

Grey, Jeffrey. *The Commonwealth Armies and the Korean War*, Manchester, 1988. Extremely useful as a comparative study of the various reactions to the war within the 'old' Commonwealth.

Grist, Lt-Col. D. *Remembered with Advantage*, Gloucester, 1976. Vivid and affectionate memoir of a devoted regimental officer in the Glosters.

Gugeler, Russell A. (ed.). *Combat Actions in Korea*, Office of the Chief of Military History, US Army, Washington DC, 1970. Detailed, and astonishingly frank, accounts of small unit actions.

Harding, Col. E.D. *The Imjin Roll*, Gloucester, 1981. Details of all who took part in the celebrated stand of the Glosters, with casualty lists.

Harris, R. 'Chinese Armed Forces', article in *Brassey's Annual*, 1951.

Hastings, M. *The Korean War*, London, 1987.

Heren, Louis. 'A Reporter in Korea', article in *Brassey's Annual*, 1951.

Hoare, J.E. 'Centenary of Korean–British Diplomatic Relations', *Journal of the Royal Asiatic Society*, 58: 1–34, 1983.

Hua, Qingzao. *From Yalta to Panmunjon: Truman's Diplomacy and the Four Powers, 1945–1953*, New York, 1993. A Chinese academic's perspective.

Jackson, R. *Air War over Korea*, London, 1973.

Jackson, W.G.F. and Bramall, E.N.W. *The Chiefs*, London, 1995.

Kahn, E.J. Jr. 'No One But the Glosters', *New Yorker*, 26 May 1951.

Kim Chae-dong. *Foreign Intervention in Korea*, Aldershot, 1993. A Korean academic's perspective on the war which virtually destroyed his country.

Kissinger, Henry. *Diplomacy*, London, 1994.

Lansdown, J. *With the Carriers in Korea, 1950–53*, Worcester, 1992. Graphic descriptions of the role of the Fleet Air Arm.

Lee, D. *Eastward: A History of the RAF in the Far East, 1945–1972*, London, 1984.

Linklater, E. *Our Men in Korea*, HMSO, 1951. A semi-official and thus carefully selective account by an outstanding journalist, covering the first few months of the war.

Malcolm of Poltalloch, Lt-Col. G. *The Argylls in Korea*, London, 1952.

Manchester, W. *American Caesar: Douglas MacArthur, 1880–1964*, New York, 1978. One of the best biographies of the great commander; whilst giving MacArthur due credit, this is no hagiography and clearly illuminates the flaws in his character that led to his downfall in 1951.

McCormack, G. and Gittings, J. (eds.). *Crisis in Korea*, London and Amsterdam, 1977. Academic essays of a decidedly Marxist hue, dealing with events in Korea since the start of the war in 1950.

Millett, Allan. 'A Reader's Guide to the Korean War', *Joint Forces Quarterly*, Washington DC, Spring 1995. A bibliography with an invaluable concise commentary by one of America's leading academic experts on the Korean War.

——*Understanding is Better than Remembering: The Korean War 1945–1954*, Kansas State University, 1997. Text of the Dwight D. Eisenhower Lecture in War and Peace, 1997.

Moore, D. and Bagshawe, P. *South Africa's Flying Cheetahs in Korea*, Johannesburg, 1991.

Nalder, Major-Gen. R.F.H. *The Royal Corps of Signals: A History of its Antecedents and Development, 1800–1955*, London, 1958.

O'Ballance, E. *Korea 1950–53*, London, 1969.

Park Il-sung. *The Role of the Replacement Training and School System in Developing the Republic of Korea Army 1945–53*. Master's thesis presented at Ohio State University, 1992.

Pedersen, The Revd L.U. *Norge I Korea*, Oslo, 1991. Lorentz Pedersen was the chaplain of the Norwegian MASH (NORMASH) and has written a perceptive and compassionate account of the war as seen by a non-combatant who spent much of his time in the forward area.

Perrett, B. *Against all Odds*, London, 1995. A rousing account of the fight for Pork Chop Hill.

Rees, D. *Korea: The Limited War*, London, 1964.

Ridgway, General Matthew B. *The Korean War*, New York, 1967. Personal account by the general who changed the direction of the war; curiously ambivalent in its judgements, particularly on MacArthur and Van Fleet.

Rose, D. *Off the Record: The Life and Letters of a Black Watch Officer*, Staplehurst, 1996.

An excellent account of life on the Hook by the officer commanding the Black Watch during its battles there.

Roshey, W. *Koje Island: The 1952 Korean Hostage Crisis*, Institute of Land Warfare, Association of the US Army, 1994. IWM.

Sawyer, R. *Military Advisors in Korea: KMAG in Peace and War*, Washington DC, 1962.

Stone, I. *The Hidden History of the Korean War*, London, 1952. A political attack on Truman's Asian policy, hinting that he was under the influence of Chiang Kai-shek as well as the 'easterners' in Washington, led by J.F. Dulles.

Stueck, W. *The Korean War: An International History*, Princeton, 1995. Magisterial academic work, raising many interesting points, such as the influence of the American far right in frustrating the efforts of Acheson and Sir Oliver Franks to persuade Truman to recognize communist China. It also argues that Truman pursued policies regarding the repatriation of communist prisoners of war which led to the events of 1952 on Koje Island and stalled the Panmunjon talks.

Summers, H.G. *Korean War Almanack*, New York, 1990.

Sutton, D.J. (ed.). *The Story of the Royal Army Service Corps and the Royal Corps of Transport, 1945–82*, London, 1983.

Thomas, Lt-Col. P., RM. *41 Independent Commando RM, Korea, 1950–52*, Royal Marines Historical Society Proceedings, 1990.

Thompson, Reginald. *Cry Korea*, London, 1951. A journalist's 'hot' memoir of a tour in Korea at the height of the war.

Walker, A. (ed.). *A Barren Place: National Servicemen in Korea, 1950–54*, London, 1994. A collection of personal narratives.

Warner, P. *The Vital Link: The Story of Royal Signals, 1945–85*, London, 1989.

Westover, Capt. J. *US Army: Combat Support in Korea*, Department of the Army, Washington DC, 1955. A series of interviews with US officers and soldiers concerned with operations other than infantry, armour or artillery. Essential to students of engineer support and logistics in the Korean War.

Whatmore, D. *One Road to Imjin*, Cheltenham, 1997. A National Service subaltern with the Glosters vividly describes his experiences.

Whitney, Major-Gen. C. *MacArthur: His Rendezvous with History*, New York, 1956. An adulatory biography by MacArthur's personal staff officer.

Wykeham-Barnes, P.G. 'The War in Korea, with special reference to the difficulties of using our air power.' Lecture at Royal United Services Institute, London, 5 December 1951. *RUSI Journal*, Vol. XCVII, No. 586, May 1952.

Official Histories

Australia

O'Neill, R. *Australia in the Korean War. Vol. I: Strategy and Diplomacy. Vol. II: Combat Operations*. Canberra, 1981 and 1985. As to be expected from an author who saw action in the infantry during the Vietnam War and is currently Chichele Professor of Military History at Oxford, this meets the standards of Australian military history set for the First World War by C.E. Bean and his colleagues and for the Second World War by Gavin Long.

Canada

Wood, Herbert F. *Strange Battleground: Official History of the Canadian Army in Korea*, Ottawa, 1966.

New Zealand

McGibbon, I. *New Zealand and the Korean War. Vol. II: Combat Operations*, Auckland, 1996.

Republic of Korea

Suk Lee-hyung (general editor). *History of the United Nations Forces in the Korean War*, 5 vols, Seoul, 1972–7. Published under the auspices of the South Korean Ministry of National Defense; covers all activities of every UN participant by land, sea and air. As the entries have been mainly drafted by the nations concerned, they are not necessarily totally objective and tend to gloss over less creditable episodes. However, as an overall guide to the huge UN effort it stands alone and is a remarkable publishing achievement.

United Kingdom

Farrar-Hockley, General Sir A. *The British Part in the Korean War. Vol. I: A Distant Obligation. Vol. II: An Honourable Discharge*, London, 1990 and 1995. The official, and comprehensive, British account.

United States

United States Army in the Korean War. Various volumes, including:
  Appleman, R. *South to the Naktong, North to the Yalu*, Washington, 1961.
  Mossman, B. *Ebb and Flow: November 1950–July 1951*, Washington, 1990.
Anon. Historical Branch US Marine Corps. *US Marine Operations in Korea 1950–53*, Washington DC, 1962.
(see also above under Gugeler)

British Government Publications

Cmd 7631, February 1949: Statement on Defence.

Cmd 7633, February 1949: Memorandum of Secretary of State for War on Army Estimates, 1949–50.

Cmd 7895, March 1950: Statement on Defence.

Cmd 8078, March 1950: Summary of Events leading to Korea.

Cmd 8475, February 1952: Summary of Events (first of new Conservative government)

Cmd 8477, February 1952: Memorandum of Secretary of State for War on Defence Estimates 1952/3.

Cmd 8716, December 1952: Summary of the Indian proposals for resolution of the prisoners-of-war problem.

Cmd 8768, February 1953: Statement on Defence 1953.

Cmd 9072, February 1954: Memorandum of Secretary of State on Defence Estimates 1954/5 (containing casualty summary for Commonwealth Forces in Korea).

Documents

Public Record Office, Kew

CAB 21:	1987	14/45/5. Military Situation reports.
	1988	14/45/6 Pt I. UK and Commonwealth Forces.
	1991	14/45/9. Implications of UK participation in UN police action.
	3057	9/102. Churchill's visit to Washington, January 1952.
	3318	14/45/1 Pt III. Situation in Korea.
	3320	14/45/6 Pt II. UK and Commonwealth Forces in Korea.
WO 216:	728	40/4586. Morale of British troops in Korea.
	345	38/4065/7. Letter from Lt-General Robertson on Imjin battle.
	741	41/4835. Brigadier Taylor and 28 Commonwealth Brigade.

CAB series: Minutes of Cabinet Meetings, 1950–3.

WO 281: War Diary, 27 Commonwealth Brigade, September–December 1950.

Joint Planning Staff: JP[50] 82 (Final) 1 July 1950. Report on the situation in Korea.

Liddell Hart Archive, King's College, London

President Harry Truman's Office Files (microfiche)

Reels MF 427–423. Korean War files: Wake Island talks; Koje Island situation; Armistice talks; State of the ROK army; Instructions to General MacArthur on occupation of North Korea, October 1950; Record of the actions taken by the Joint Chiefs of Staff Committee relative to United Nations operations in Korea, 25 June 1950–30 April 1951.

Joint Chiefs of Staff Papers (microfiche)

JCS Series: Microfiches 68, 76, 79. Part of the collection of papers, running to many thousands of pages, of the JCS 1776 group of files containing vast amounts of information on every conceivable aspect of the Korean War, ranging from instructions given to successive commanders of 8th Army to procedures for adoption by the unified UN Command, plans for the evacuation of Korea, General Ridgway's periodic reports to the Joint Chiefs in Washington, the debate over bombing the Yalu power complex, and the reinforcement of UN forces in Korea. The researcher can easily be engulfed in this morass; but it affords the British student of the war the best possible source of information short of crossing the Atlantic.

S–XA: Military History in Korea: events in South Korea 25 June–1 July 1950. A key document outlining the day-to-day military situation, North Korean preparations for invasion, international agreements, organization of the NKPA.

S–XB: The history of the first year of the war, covering all aspects of operations: political and military preparations, efforts towards a peace settlement, impact on Korean population, economic and social factors, and statistics.

MFF 8: Armed Forces oral histories: interviews with senior US Army officers, conducted in 1970–2 by students at US War College, including Generals Almond, Mark Clark, Ridgway and many others.

MFF 9: Korean War studies: Report of State Department research mission to North Korea: Office of Intelligence Research Report No. 5500, 2 April 1951. An invaluable document for study of the way in which the People's Democratic Republic had been run since 1945 – in many ways far more effectively than had the South under the American military administration and Syngman Rhee's governance.

Australian War Memorial Archives, Canberra ACT

AWM 85: War Diaries Japan/Korea 1950–4.

AWM 89: O'Neill papers (used by Professor O'Neill in preparation of the Australian Official History).

AWM 114: 665/7/10. Royal Australian Navy in Korean waters.

    665/7/33. Collection of CCF combat reports.

    665/7/33. Notes on enemy tactics. Compiled by HQ 1 Commonwealth Division after Operation Commando in 1951.

Unpublished documents, mostly in Imperial War Museum, London

Angier, Major P. Letters to his wife from Korea. IWM 91/8/1.

Coad, Major-General B.A. Miscellaneous papers including text of address to Royal United Services Institute (see above, p. 378). IWM.

Fanshawe, Captain P.E. Captain of HMS *Amethyst* in 1951. Miscellaneous papers relating to the west coast survey. IWM 67/353/2.

Man, Colonel A. Miscellaneous letters and documents referring to his command of the 1st Battalion Middlesex Regiment in Korea. IWM 82/19/1.

Muschamp, M. Midshipman's log 1950. Personal account, 'How we sank the North Korean Navy'. Privately held.

Stacpoole, The Revd Dom A.J. Documents relating to the Duke of Wellington's regiment on the Hook, where Stacpoole served as platoon commander of the assault Pioneers and gained the Military Cross. IWM 94/26/1.

Stowe, Gunner E. Letters describing his experiences as a recalled reservist and service in Korea 1950–1. IWM 86/85/1.

Taylor, Brigadier G. Various items of correspondence relating to his command of 28 Commonwealth Brigade and supersession. IWM 96/12/1.

West, General M.A.R. Notes on CCF tactics, 1953. Paper by Brigadier P. Gregson, Commander Royal Artillery 1st Commonwealth Division, 1953. Summary of operations. Infantry Liaison letters Nos 1 and 2, July and October 1953. Letter from General Dwight D. Eisenhower to West, 7 December 1953. IWM.

Whatmore, Colonel D. Memoir, later used in his book *One Road to Imjin*. IWM 93/29/1.

Index

Ranks and titles are generally the highest mentioned in the text